# INSIGHT GUIDE

# Israel

**Discovery**
CHANNEL

**APA** PUBLICATIONS

Part of the Langenscheidt Publishing Group

L

# ABOUT THIS BOOK

## Editorial

*Project Editor*
**Pam Barrett**
*Managing Editor*
**Dorothy Stannard**
*Editorial Director*
**Brian Bell**

## Distribution

*UK & Ireland*
**GeoCenter International Ltd**
The Viables Centre
Harrow Way
Basingstoke
Hants RG22 4BJ
Fax: (44) 1256-817988

*United States*
**Langenscheidt Publishers, Inc.**
46–35 54th Road
Maspeth, NY 11378
Fax: (718) 784-0640

*Worldwide*
**APA Publications GmbH & Co.**
**Verlag KG (Singapore branch)**
38 Joo Koon Road
Singapore 628990
Tel: (65) 865-1600
Fax: (65) 861-6438

## Printing

**Insight Print Services (Pte) Ltd**
38 Joo Koon Road
Singapore 628990
Tel: (65) 865-1600
Fax: (65) 861-6438

©1999  APA Publications GmbH & Co.
Verlag KG (Singapore branch)
*All Rights Reserved*
*First Edition 1992*
*Fourth Edition 1999*

**CONTACTING THE EDITORS**
Although every effort is made to provide accurate information in this publication, we live in a fast-changing world and would appreciate it if readers would call our attention to any errors or outdated information that may occur by writing to us at: **Insight Guides, P.O. Box 7910, London SE1 8ZB, England. Fax: (44 171) 620-1074. e-mail: insight@apaguide.demon.co.uk**

This guidebook combines the interests and enthusiasms of two of the world's best known information providers: Insight Guides, whose titles have set the standard for visual travel guides since 1970, and Discovery Channel, the world's premier source of nonfiction television programming.

The editors of Insight Guides provide both practical advice and general understanding about a destination's history, culture, institutions and people. Discovery Channel and its Web site, www.discovery. com, help millions of viewers ex-plore their world from the comfort of their home and encourage them to explore it firsthand.

## How to use this book

The book is carefully structured both to convey an understanding of the State of Israel and its culture, and to guide readers through its diverse sights and activities:

◆ To understand modern **Israel** you need to know something of its past. The **Features** section explores the history of the dynamic young state, and the complex cirumstances

EXPLORE YOUR WORLD

that brought it about, after the years of exile.

♦ The main **Places** section provides details of the sights most worth seeing. The main places of interest are coordinated by number with full-colour maps.

♦ The Travel Tips section provides a convenient point of reference for practical information on accommodation, restaurants, holidays and religious festivals, travel, and specialist tour operators. Information may be located quickly by using the index printed on the back cover flap.

♦ The **photographs** are chosen not only to illustrate the out-

standing religious and historical sites, and the beauty of the landscape, but also to convey an impression of the everyday lives of the Israeli people.

## The contributors

This new edition was edited by **Pam Barrett** and builds on several earlier editions by **George Melrod** and **Simon Griver**. This edition was comprehensively updated by Griver, a long-time resident of Israel who also compiled the **Travel Tips** and wrote the text for the Insight picture features, which focus on topics of particular interest, from religious shrines to Israel's four seas.

The editors chose writers with in-depth knowledge of their subject and a close affinity with Israel. **Geoffrey Wigoder**, **Walter Jacob** and **William Recant** wrote the history chapters, which provide a foundation for the rest. **Helen Davis**, **Mordechai Beck**, **Barbara Gingold**, **Asher Weill**, and **Nancy Miller** contributed to the Features section, writing on people, religion, crafts, culture and language, and archaeology. **Matthew Nevisky** wrote about the Old City of Jerusalem, **Michal Yudelman** was our Tel Aviv correspondent, and **Daniel Gavron**, **Muriel Moulton**, **Leora Frucht**, **Bill Clark**, and **Amy Kaslow** all brought their detailed knowledge to bear in writing other chapters for the Places section.

Most of the stunning photography is by **Richard Nowitz** and **Gary-John Norman**, but there are also valuable contributions by **Werner Braun**, **Sammy Avnisan**, **Eddie Gerald** and others.

## Map Legend

| | |
|---|---|
| —— ·· — | International Boundary |
| — — | Disputed Boundary |
| ▬▬ | Palestinian Autonomy |
| ⊖ | Border Crossing |
| —·—·— | National Park/Reserve |
| — — — | Ferry Crossing |
| Ⓜ | Subway |
| ✈ ✈ | Airport: International/ Regional |
| 🚌 | Bus Station |
| 🅿 | Parking |
| ⓘ | Tourist Information |
| ✉ | Post Office |
| † ✝ | Church/Ruins |
| ✝ | Monastery |
| ☾ | Mosque |
| ✡ | Synagogue |
| ⌂ ⌂ | Castle/Ruins |
| ∴ | Archaeological Site |
| ∩ | Cave |
| ⚱ | Statue/Monument |
| ★ | Place of Interest |

The main places of interest in the Places section are coordinated by number with a full-colour map (e.g. ❶), and a symbol at the top of every right-hand page tells you where to find the map.

# CONTENTS

View over
the Negev

# THE PROMISED LAND

*Israel defies indifference. Its long history draws visitors*

*but the real attraction is its great diversity of people*

Israel is intense. Few locations offer as much per square kilometre to sustain the spirit, feed the intellect and stimulate the senses. It is a place where three continents – Africa, Asia and Europe – meet, and the landscape and the people are a fusion of these three continents, a sometimes infuriating mixture of conflict and harmony. After all, this is the Promised Land to which, it is said, Moses led the Children of Israel. It is where Abraham forged his covenant with God, Christ preached his sermons, and Mohammed ascended to heaven on a horse.

You don't have to be a believer to savour all this. The miracles may be a matter of personal faith, but what can't be historically disputed is that this is the land of the Bible, the cradle of monotheism, a geography familiar from childhood religious instruction. The names resonate in our minds and stimulate our curiosity: Jerusalem, the Galilee, Bethlehem, Nazareth, Yafo, Jericho and the River Jordan.

At the site of the Temple you can pray at the one remaining wall the Romans left intact. You can walk along the Via Dolorosa to the Church of the Holy Sepulchre. You can visit the El-Aqsa Mosque on the Temple Mount where the Prophet Mohammed came to pray during his lifetime. Around the River Jordan you can drink in the atmosphere of a place where so much history has been made in the past two millennia, most recently the emergence of modern Israel, "the Jewish State", as a complex dynamic entity.

The empty stretches and open blue skies of the Arava and Negev deserts aside, this is one of the world's most densely packed pieces of real estate. Israel's population is approaching 6 million, while 2 million Palestinians live in the Gaza Strip and West Bank. For many visitors the enduring attraction of Israel is its people – the inheritors of the rich tapestry of invading cultures which have woven their history into the region.

Contrary to perceived stereotypes, most Israelis are neither right-wing religious zealots nor left-wing Peace Now activists. Most are middle of the road, looking for peace with security. Most Palestinians, too, realise that violence is counter-productive. They want a state of their own, however small, and a decent standard of living.

Ultimately peace seems likely to prevail, not because Israelis and Palestinians will ever fall in love with each other but because the alternative is too unpleasant to endure. ❑

**PRECEDING PAGES:** praying at the Western (Wailing) Wall; a Passover meal; apple harvest on a kibbutz; a Bedouin family near Bethlehem.
**LEFT:** an Orthodox Jew with a *shofar* (ram's horn) at the Western Wall.

# TERRA SANCTA.

*A Petro Laicstain perlustrata, et ab eius ore
et schedis a Christiano Schrot in tabulam redacta.*

**MARE MORTVVM**, olim Salinarum
vallis, prædicatæ foecunditatis, et amœnitatis: quam Iordanis
mediam irrigabat: adeo vt ob fœcunditatem paradiso Dei
conferebatur. Post autem Sodoma euersa, et vicina
opida, mutata est in illam sterilitatem, quæ hodie
adhuc conspicitur. Diuinæ ultionis admiranda
vestigia.

Athona
non torrens
Hic multa tuguria et collap sunt
uetusta et sed sine
nominibus
Dibon
Iazer
Bethonim
Limas
Beelmeon
Salabim
Terra Macces
Naballa
Nemra Medh
Elon
Diblathaim
Amor
Sabama
Bethsemes
PERAEA
Bethiessimoth
rhæi
Esthomaitin
Nephaath
Aroen
Bamoth uallis
Abarim mons
Areopolis castrum
Abila Li sany
Nain
Enon
Nebo
Mons Psga
Sabaruc
Mons Nebo
Galaroch
Machepunta
TENAE RCH
Alexandria Siittin
Bethabara
Engadi mons
Massada
Vallis benedictionis
Betha bara
Desertum Maon
Galgala
Quarentana mons
Herodiu
S.Saba
Hetæi
Adonim
Gophna toparchia
TRIBVS
IVDAEA.
Desertum Adomin
Coena
BENIAMIN
Terra regia
Desertum Sinæi
Ephrem
Bethel
Rama
Bethlehem
Maon
Samaria
Sichem
TRIBVS IVDA.
Iebusaei
HIERVSALEM
Enachim
Gazer
Iuda Montana Iu
Hebron
TRIBVS SIMEON
Thamnatica regio
Lidda vel Diospolis
TRIBVS DAN
IDVMAEA
Azotus siue Ascol
thijm
Philis
Ioppe Iaffa
Castrum Beroldi

DENS.

# Decisive Dates

**10,000BC–6000BC:** Some of the world's first human settlements are established in the Jordan Valley, Judean Desert and Mediterranean coast.
**3,000BC:** Canaanite city kingdoms develop, based on trade between Mesopotamia and Egypt.

## THE BIBLICAL PERIOD

**c.2000BC:** Abraham settles in Be'er Sheva.
**c.1280BC:** Moses leads Israelites out of Egypt.
**c.1225BC:** Joshua captures Jericho.

**c.1000BC:** King David declares that Jerusalem will be his capital.
**c.950BC:** King Solomon builds the First Temple.
**722BC:** Assyrians destroy the kingdom of Israel.
**586BC:** The First Temple is destroyed after the Babylonians conquer Jerusalem and send the Jews into exile.
**546BC:** The Jews return to Jerusalem after the Persians defeat the Babylonians.
**520BC:** The Second Temple is built.
**444BC:** Jerusalem's walls are rebuilt.
**333BC:** Alexander the Great conquers Jerusalem but allows the Jews freedom of worship.
**164BC:** Successful Jewish uprising led by Maccabees after Seleucid Greeks defile the Temple.

**63BC:** The Romans conquer Judea; it is subject to Roman decree but remains autonomous.
**37BC:** King Herod assumes the throne, founds Caesarea and rebuilds the Second Temple.

## THE CHRISTIAN ERA

**c.AD30:** The crucifixion of Christ.
**66:** The Jews revolt against Rome.
**70:** The Romans recapture Jerusalem after a long siege and destroy the Temple.
**73:** Jewish zealots in Masada commit mass suicide rather than be taken by the Romans.
**132:** Bar Kochba's revolt against the Romans fails, and most of the Jews go into exile.
**325:** Constantine, the Byzantine emperor, converts to Christianity. Palestine is recognised as the Holy Land, and Constantine's mother Helena arrives a year later to identify the sacred sites.

## THE MUSLIM CONQUEST

**638:** Fired by the new religion of Islam, Muslim armies conquer Jerusalem.
**691:** The Dome of the Rock is built on the Temple Mount.
**705:** The El-Aqsa Mosque is built.
**750:** Abassid caliphs succeed the Umayyads.
**969:** Fatimid rule begins.
**1009:** Fatimids destroy the Church of the Holy Sepulchre.

## CRUSADERS, MAMELUKES AND OTTOMANS

**1099:** Crusaders establish the kingdom of Jerusalem.
**1149:** The current Church of the Holy Sepulchre is consecrated.
**1187:** Saladin defeats the Crusaders.
**1260:** Mamelukes take control of the Holy Land.
**1267:** Nahmanides re-establishes Jerusalem's Jewish community.
**1291:** The last Crusader stronghold in Akko falls to the Mamelukes.
**1492:** Many Jews return to the Holy Land after expulsion from Spain.
**1516:** The Ottomans capture Palestine.
**1541:** Suleiman the Magnificent completes the construction of Jerusalem's walls.
**1799:** Napoleon occupies parts of the Holy Land.
**1832:** The Egyptian Mohammed Ali captures Palestine and holds it for eight years.

## THE BIRTH OF ZIONISM

**1878:** The first Zionist settlements are established in Rosh Pina, Rishon Le-Tsiyon and Petakh Tikvah.

**1881:** Anti-Semitism in Russia, after the assassination of Tsar Alexander II, forces millions of Jews to emigrate. Many go to the United States and Western Europe; some come to Palestine.

**1897:** Theodor Herzl convenes the first-ever Zionist Congress in Switzerland.

**1901:** The Jewish National Fund is established to acquire land in Palestine.

**1917–18:** The British capture Palestine and publish the Balfour Declaration favouring "the establishment in Palestine of a national home for the Jewish people".

**1920:** Arab riots make the British rethink their policy.

**1923:** The British cede the eastern part of Palestine to the Jordanian Hashemite dynasty.

**1925:** Large-scale Jewish immigration from Central and Eastern Europe.

**1933:** Hitler assumes power in Germany, increasing Jewish emigration.

**1945:** World War II ends, and the full horrors of the Holocaust become known. Survivors emigrate to Palestine but are imprisoned by the British in Cyprus.

**1947:** The UN votes for the partition of Palestine into Jewish and Arab states, and the British prepare to withdraw.

## THE ESTABLISHMENT OF ISRAEL

**1948:** David Ben Gurion proclaims the State of Israel and becomes the first prime minister.

**1949:** An armistice agreement is concluded after the War of Independence.

**1950:** The Law of Return guarantees the free immigration of world Jewry. The Jordanians formally annex East Jerusalem and the West Bank, and Egypt takes the Gaza Strip.

**1956:** Israel captures and then returns the Sinai following the Suez campaign.

**1963:** Levi Eshkol becomes prime minister.

**1964:** The PLO is formed.

**1967:** Israel captures East Jerusalem, the West Bank, Gaza, the Sinai and the Golan Heights during the Six Day War. Golda Meir becomes prime minister on the death of Levi Eshkol.

**1973:** The Yom Kippur War.

**1977:** The Likud leader Menachem Begin

becomes prime minister, ending 29 years of Labour government.

**1978:** Egyptian President Anwar Sadat visits Jerusalem, and an Israel–Egypt peace treaty is signed the following year.

**1982:** Israel invades Lebanon, and the PLO is expelled to Tunisia.

**1987:** The Intifada (Palestinian uprisings in the West Bank territories) begins.

**1991:** Scuds fall on Israel during the Gulf War.

**1992:** Yitzhak Rabin becomes prime minister.

**1993:** Israel and the PLO conclude a secret deal in Oslo. Rabin and Arafat later shake hands at the White House, Washington DC.

**1994:** Peace agreement signed with Jordan.

**1995:** Yitzhak Rabin is assassinated, and Shimon Peres, architect of the Oslo Agreements, takes over as prime minister.

**1996:** Binyamin Netanyahu becomes Israel's first directly elected prime minister. Yasser Arafat is elected leader of the Palestinians.

**1997:** Israel pulls out of most of Hebron, having previously withdrawn from all the major cities in the West Bank and Gaza.

**1998:** Israel celebrates the 50th anniversary of independence and statehood. Peace negotiations falter, then resume with Israel agreeing to further withdrawals from the West Bank. Gaza International Aiport opens. ❑

**LEFT:** mosaic depicting an ancient Hanukkah Menorah. **RIGHT:** Binyamin Netanyahu, elected Israel's prime minister in 1996.

# THE DAWN OF CIVILISATION

*The early history of Israel, familiar to many through biblical stories, laid the foundations of Jewish faith and sowed the seeds of future conflict*

The dusty desert sign on the highway down from Jerusalem points northwards to "Jericho – The World's Oldest Known City". At the northern tip of the town is a rather unimpressive series of wooden fortifications. Remarkably, however, scientists estimate that these fortifications were built 9,000–10,000 years ago. Evidence suggests that mankind first established farming communities, and the other trappings of civilisation as we know it, several thousand years before that. Caves in the Mount Carmel range near Haifa on the Mediterranean Coast have yielded jewellery and agricultural implements from 12,000 years ago.

But as the remains at Jericho indicate, 7,000 BC was an important era in the evolution of Neolithic man. In the 1980s Israeli archaeologists discovered a treasure trove of artefacts dating from this period in a cave in the Judean Desert 48 km (30 miles) south of Jerusalem. The find, which includes woven fabrics, agricultural tools, decorated human skulls, carved figurines and painted masks, is on display in the Israel Museum. From these objects anthropologists have concluded that late Stone Age man was far more advanced than had been believed.

## According to Genesis

Such archaeological evidence is anathema to ultra-Orthodox Jewry, which has always insisted that the Creation took place nearly 6,000 years ago. By then, both ancient Egypt to the southwest and Mesopotamia to the northeast had been established as powerful and sophisticated civilisations. Canaanite tribes emerged about 5,000 years ago, founding city-kingdoms based on trade.

About 4,000 years ago, the book of Genesis relates, Abraham, the son of a wealthy Mesopotamian merchant family in the city of Ur (today in Iraq), became the first man to

recognise a single deity. Rejecting the idolatry of his father, he travelled westwards and pitched his tent near Be'er Sheva.

Abraham is today revered as the father of monotheism. Although he believed in one God, he did not keep to just one woman, and the world might have become a less complicated

place had he done so. The Arab and Islamic heritage traces its roots to Abraham through his first son, Ishmael, born to his concubine Hagar, while the Judeo-Christian lineage can be traced back to Isaac, Abraham's second son, born to his wife, Sarah.

Sibling rivalry, Genesis tells us, compelled Abraham to cast out Hagar and Ishmael, whose descendants would forever bear enmity to the offspring of Sarah's son Isaac. Even a complete atheist would have to admit that the Bible got that right. The precise location of Abraham's tent is not known, which is probably just as well, for his burial site, the Tomb of the Patriarchs in Hebron, has seen far too many corpses.

---

**PRECEDING PAGES:** a map of Israel from 1584.
**LEFT:** Moses receives the stone tablets from God.
**RIGHT:** early shekels show fruits of the earth.

Jews and Arabs have massacred each other in Hebron throughout history.

Sibling rivalry, beginning with Cain and Abel, is an ever-present theme in Genesis. Isaac's own twin sons quarrelled when Jacob, egged on by his mother Rebecca, cheated Esau out of his birthright by tricking his blind father. And Jacob saw the pattern recur when his own sons sold Joseph, his favourite child, into slavery in Egypt.

## The Children of Israel

Jacob was also known as Israel (Hebrew for "he struggles"). The name was given to him the wilderness. During the Children of Israel's 40 years wandering in the wilderness Moses was given the Torah, including the Ten Commandments, on Mount Sinai. His successor, Joshua, took the Children of Israel back to the Promised Land, scoring his first success in the Battle of Jericho in 1225 BC.

Though the Israelites defeated the indigenous Canaanites and settled on the inland hills, making Hebron their capital, they were unable to conquer the coastal plain where the Philistines in the south and the Phoenicians in the north reigned supreme. The historical importance of these peoples, especially the Phoenicians, who

after a dream in which he fought with an angel descending from a ladder leading up to heaven. All told Jacob had 12 sons and one daughter whose descendants are known to us as the Children of Israel.

Joseph prospered in Egypt, where he became a senior advisor to the Pharaoh. He was reunited with his family after a drought compelled them to look for food and shelter in the Land of the Nile. The Book of Exodus relates how successive generations of Pharaohs subsequently enslaved the Children of Israel.

In one of the most enduring of all biblical narratives, Moses, the Israelite, led his people out of bondage, across the Red Sea and through

### LAYING THE FOUNDATIONS

It was during Joshua's era that many of the tenets of Judaism were established. The festival of Passover (Pesach), held in the spring, recalls the Exodus from Egypt, and the miracles which preceded it, while Pentecost (Shavuot) marks the giving of the Torah to Moses on Mount Sinai.

Religious Jews today congregate at the Western (Wailing) Wall for dawn prayers at Pentecost, after spending the night studying the holy book. The Feast of Tabernacles (Succot), which is also known as the Festival of Rejoicing, recalls the 40 years spent in the wilderness and celebrates the joy of returning to the Promised Land.

had migrated from Greece, is often overlooked.

The Phoenicians, who settled in the cities of Akko and Tyre in Northern Israel and Southern Lebanon, are believed to have devised the first alphabet and invented glassmaking. And the Philistines in Ashdod and Ashkelon in the south were skilful metalworkers who were able to manufacture sophisticated weaponry.

The Israelites coexisted with their coastal neighbours, sometimes trading, sometimes fighting. Led at first by warrior-judges such as Gideon and Samuel, they felt the need for a king, who would strengthen the people by uniting the tribes. Saul was selected, and he set the

though he did win access to the Mediterranean.

Most importantly, in historical retrospect, David conquered a Jebusite hilltop enclave. He decided that the fortress settlement, perched near commanding mountain peaks, with a plentiful supply of fresh underground spring water, would make an excellent new capital. So he moved his court and administration there from Hebron and called his new capital Jerusalem. The city also helped unite the 12 tribes because it was located on neutral territory.

David's son Solomon became renowned for his wisdom. He consolidated his father's achievements and extended the Israelite

scene for the golden age that his successor David was to bring about.

## The establishment of Jerusalem

David ascended the throne a little over 3,000 years ago. A scholar, poet and notorious womaniser, he secured his place in history through military prowess and leadership, extending the Israelites' borders to the Red Sea in the south and Syria in the north. But despite his early victory over the mighty Goliath, with a slingshot, he was unable to vanquish the Philistines,

**LEFT:** Joshua's men hang enemy kings.
**ABOVE:** a medieval view of Solomon and Sheba.

empire down to the Arabian peninsula and northeastwards to the Euphrates. He inherited his father's taste for beautiful women, and sealed strategic alliances by marrying princesses. His exact relationship with the Queen of Sheba remains unclear.

Most significantly, Solomon constructed the resplendent Temple to house the Ark of the Covenant, the focus of Jewish faith that was believed to contain the actual tablets of the Ten Commandments that were given to Moses on Mount Sinai. A stroll around the Temple Mount in Jerusalem today conveys what a vast building it must have been.

Despite his reputed wisdom Solomon left no

strong successor. Soon after his death tribal jealousies resulted in civil war and the secession of the 10 northern tribes who set up their own state, known as Israel in Samaria. The southern state of Judah, based on the tribes of Judah and Benjamin, remained faithful to Solomon's descendants. For two centuries an uneasy coexistence prevailed.

This was the age of the prophets. Isaiah attacked corruption, and Elijah denounced the idolatrous cult of Baal introduced by Israel's King Ahab and his wife

### YEARNING FOR HOME

In Psalm 137, an exiled poet wrote the oft-quoted lines: "By the waters of Babylon we sat down and wept when we remembered Zion."

Jezebel. In 722 BC Israel fell to the Assyrians, and the people were dispersed. The fate of the "Ten Lost Tribes" is still unknown, and people in every corner of the globe occasionally claim descent from them.

The southern state of Judah survived by accepting Assyrian hegemony. This status quo endured for 150 years. Its end was foretold by the prophet Jeremiah, who preached gloom and doom and the destruction of Jerusalem.

## By the waters of Babylon

Jeremiah's prophecies came true in 586 BC. The Babylonians, led by Nebuchadnezzar, superseded the Assyrians, sacked Jerusalem, destroyed the Temple, and transported the élite of Judah to Babylon.

In fact, this exile only lasted 40 years, until the Babylonians were defeated by the Persians, whose leader Cyrus the Great allowed all exiled peoples to return. The Temple was rebuilt, but the glorious age of Solomon was not recaptured. Judah remained an obscure Persian province for the following two centuries.

The balance of world power moved west to Europe, away from Egypt, Assyria and Persia. In 333 BC Alexander the Great conquered the region, and Greek rule began. For several centuries the Jews were allowed freedom of worship, but policies gradually became more obtrusive, culminating in the 2nd century BC with the sacrificing of a pig in the Temple and the prohibition of Jewish rituals such as circumcision and the observation of the Sabbath.

Armed resistance led by the Hasmonean family known as the Maccabees saw the Greeks defeated and Jewish control over Jerusalem restored. In 164 BC the Temple was rededicated, a victory celebrated to this day during the festival of Hanukkah.

## The Roman Empire

The subsequent century of Jewish sovereignty saw prosperity, as past glories and lands were recaptured. But this taste of freedom was then lost for 2,000 years. In 63 BC the Romans conquered Judah, which, as Judea, was subject to the decree of the Roman governor of Syria but remained an autonomous province with its own kings. The best known was Herod the Great, who reigned from 37–4 BC, and was given extra territory, expanding his kingdom to include all of Israel and much of today's Jordan. He rebuilt the Temple and constructed grand new cities, such as Caesarea on the coast, which he dedicated to Rome. But Herod and his successors were ruthless despots who even killed their own children in their paranoia over potential conspiracies. Oppressed by Rome and its merciless vassal kings, the Judeans were ripe to be influenced by messianic preachers. ❏

**LEFT:** a romantic depiction of Noah's Ark.
**RIGHT:** Marc Chagall depiction of David with his harp.

# EMPIRES AND EXILE

*Successive empires conquered, flourished, then disappeared, while the Jews
were scattered across the globe without a land of their own*

The son of a Galilean carpenter, Christ had a limited impact in his own lifetime, at least in Jerusalem. Few historical accounts even mention him and the best-known contemporary historian, Josephus, only devotes some sentences to an obscure Galilee preacher. The Romans felt threatened enough to execute him, although in those days of massacres and constant bloodshed that was no great distinction.

But a devoted band of Christ's followers were convinced that their leader was the messianic saviour the Jews craved. In the following decades the determination of these disciples was to change history. Christianity spread north and east to Armenia and Byzantium, and southwards, taking root in Africa, especially in Egypt and Ethiopia, and subsequently took hold in Rome and the rest of Europe.

The Jews themselves were unimpressed. For them Christ remains just one of a string of false messiahs, distinguished only by the fact that so many Gentiles accepted his teachings and interpreted them as good reason to persecute the Jews themselves, who were branded as Christ-killers. There is no historical evidence that the Jews conspired in the crucifixion of Christ, but when Rome subsequently embraced Christianity a convenient scapegoat was needed to draw attention away from its own culpability. The claim that the Jews were Christ-killers became the basis for anti-Semitism down the centuries.

Not that the Jewish establishment of the time would have shed a tear at Christ's execution. The aristocratic Sadducees, who controlled the priesthood, and the scholarly Pharisees, who interpreted the law, would have regarded Christ – those who were aware of his existence – as an undesirable subversive element.

The Essenes might have been more impressed. This ascetic cult was in all likelihood a major influence on Christ's philosophy. As a result, the Essenes' culture and writings in the Dead Sea Scrolls (which are displayed in the Israel

Museum and include the oldest known version of the Old Testament) are of major interest to Western society.

## Zealotry and defeat

The Zealots would have been too wrapped up in the nationalist struggle against Roman occu-

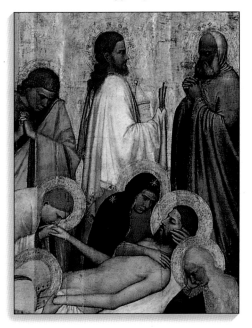

**LEFT:** the Madonna and Child. **RIGHT:** an illuminated manuscript depicts Christ's death.

pation to pay much attention to a Galilean preacher. Increased Roman oppression, most notably the decision by the Roman emperor Caligula to have his image installed in the Temple, strengthened the Zealots' popularity.

In AD 66 the Jews rebelled. The Romans imported major reinforcements, and the revolt was slowly crushed. By 69 only Jerusalem and several fortress outposts were holding out. After a year-long siege, Jerusalem was captured. The Romans sacked it, burning the Temple and carrying its sacred contents back to Rome. The city was renamed Aelia Capitolina, and all vestiges of Jewish culture were destroyed, except one wall of the Temple – the Western

Wall – which was left standing to remind the Jews of Roman sovereignty.

Masada was the most famous of the fortresses which held out, but resistance was futile; the soldiers of the Roman 10th Legion finally conquered the hilltop stronghold in AD 73. But they were denied the satisfaction of capturing its inhabitants: the Zealots – nearly 1,000 of them – committed mass suicide.

Another failed Jewish uprising against the Romans in 132, led by Simon Bar Kochba, saw most Jews executed, sold into slavery or exiled, and this date is often considered as the start of two millennia of exile.

## From Christianity to Islam

It is one of the great ironies that in the Holy Land, where Christ was born, preached and died, Christians have remained a small minority. By the 5th century they did form a majority, but the Roman Empire was already crumbling. The Persians temporarily conquered the region in the 7th century (before the Byzantines reasserted control), and in 640 the Arab followers of Mohammed swept through the region converting many to Islam. Mohammed's emphasis on the Oneness of God and the need to revive Jewish rituals such as circumcision and dietary laws struck a popular chord.

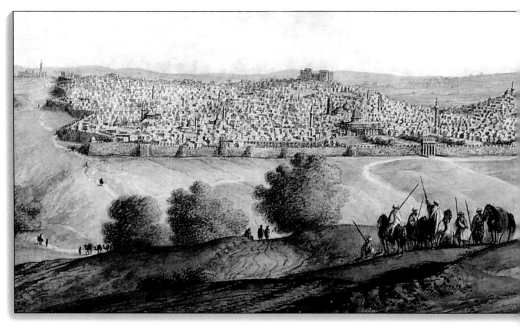

Jewish culture continued to flourish, especially in the Galilee. The Mishna, the Talmudic commentary on the Old Testament, was written by sages in Tiberias in the 2nd and 3rd centuries, while rabbinical scholars in the Mount Meron region near Safed penned the mystical texts that comprise the Kabbalah. But as Christianity took root in the region, after being embraced by the emperor Constantine the Great and the Eastern Roman Empire early in the 4th century, the Jewish presence in the Holy Land dwindled into insignificance. From that point until modern times, the glory of Jewish culture was to be accomplished in what became known as the Diaspora.

### EMPRESS HELENA'S ROLE

After Emperor Constantine the Great embraced Christianity in the 4th century, his mother, Empress Helena, became an enthusiastic convert to the new religion, and played a key role in its dissemination. It is believed that she made a pilgrimage from Byzantium in the 4th century in order to identify the principal sites of Christendom, and to initiate the construction of shrines in these places. These holy sites include the Church of the Nativity in Bethlehem, the Church of the Holy Sepulchre in Jerusalem and the Church of the Annunciation in Nazareth, all sites which are revered by most branches of Christianity to this day.

Islam and the Arab world have coveted the Holy Land ever since. Abraham, the father of the Arab people, is buried in Hebron, while Mohammed is believed to have made a journey on horseback, after his death, to the Temple Mount in Jerusalem from where he ascended to heaven. In 691 Caliph Abd Al-Malik, horrified by the neglect of the Temple Mount, built the Dome of the Rock over the supposed site of Mohammed's ascension. Several decades later the El-Aqsa Mosque was built on the southern section of the Temple Mount. Jerusalem was now sacred to three major religions – Judaism, Christianity and Islam – attracting pilgrims

Templars, while the El-Aqsa Mosque was transformed into a church. The Kingdom of Jerusalem, ruled by King Baldwin I, who was installed in 1100, held sway over several subservient principalities.

The ostensible aim of the Crusades was to fight the infidel, but in reality the Crusaders slaughtered far more Christians than nonbelievers. En route, especially in the Balkans, they laid waste entire Orthodox Christian communities. In the Holy Land itself, Christian villagers turned out to greet their supposed liberators, only to be put to the sword. Although the Crusaders were sponsored by the Church,

from all three. But if individuals were content to visit, others wanted not only to come and see but also to conquer.

## Crusaders and infidels

Islamic control of the Holy Land especially irked the Christians of Europe. As a result, during the 11th century the Pope inaugurated a series of crusades which saw Christianity in possession of virtually the entire Holy Land by the end of the century. The Dome of the Rock was commandeered as the headquarters of the

**ABOVE:** Jerusalem from the Mount of Olives, painted by Luigi Meyer in the late 18th century.

many of their number were motivated by imperialist ambitions.

The Crusaders built a network of hilltop fortresses, from Nimrod in the north to Jerusalem in the south, and ruled until 1187, when the Egyptian leader Saladin was victorious at the Horns of Hittim in the Galilee. Slowly the Europeans lost their foothold in the Holy Land. Even Richard the Lionheart, who led the Third Crusade in 1188, could not turn the tide. Four more Crusades delayed the inevitable, but in 1291 Europe lost St Jean d'Acre (Akko), its last stronghold in the region, to the Mamelukes, who in their turn had defeated Saladin.

## Mamelukes and Ottomans

The Mamelukes are the least remembered of the Holy Land's conquerors. For nearly 250 years these slave warriors to the sultans of Egypt, who had been brought from Asia to be trained as élite soldiers, ruled over the region from Egypt to Syria. Despite their ornate architecture, this was an era of decline from which the Middle East has never fully recovered. As Europe flourished and America was discovered, the balance of world power slipped further away from the Eastern Mediterranean.

The rise of the Ottoman Turks stopped the rot, at least for a while. The Holy Land, too,

regained some lustre after the Ottoman conquest in 1517. Suleiman the Magnificent, who ruled from 1520 to 1566, revived the economy of the region and built the impressive walls around the Old City of Jerusalem.

But from the 17th century the Ottoman Empire went into a decline that was to last for 300 years. The Holy Land gradually became a semi-desert, and Jerusalem degenerated into a crumbling village. The Ottomans, like the Mamelukes before them, ruled Palestine as a province of Syria, further belittling the status of the region in general and Jerusalem in particular. Voltaire, in his philosophical dictionary compiled in the mid-18th century, described the

city as a barren wilderness of rocks and dust.

Napoleon's brief conquest of parts of Palestine in 1799 spelled a revival of interest in the Holy Land by the European powers. As the Ottomans weakened, the British and the French vied for hegemony. Offended by the fact that the Christian sites in the Holy Land were dominated by Greeks, Armenians and Ethiopians, the Catholic, Protestant and Russian Orthodox churches were encouraged by their governments to build their own institutions.

In the event, it was the British who wrested control of Palestine from the Ottomans in 1917 during World War I. However, the League of Nations mandate stipulated that the British were to be temporary custodians. Even though significant numbers of Jews had begun returning to their ancestral homeland from the late 19th century onwards, nobody could have predicted that in just three more decades possession of much of Palestine would return to its ancient owners.

## In exile

In nearly 2,000 years of exile the Jewish people never forgot Israel. They faced Jerusalem when they prayed and took to heart the sentence from Psalm 137: "If I forget thee, O Jerusalem, let my right hand forget her cunning." But while the Jews never forgot Jerusalem, for many years they showed no great inclination to return. Many individuals made pilgrimages to the Holy Land, but there was no significant mass movement to return to Zion.

Over time, the conventional Orthodox belief took root that the return would occur only with the coming of the Messiah. Eventually it was a combination of European enlightenment, nationalism and anti-Semitism that shook this conviction and promoted the belief that a return to Zion was necessary, both for the physical survival of Jews threatened by extermination and for the perpetuation of Jewish culture corroded by assimilation.

For the most part, the first millennium of exile was unremarkable. Most Jews lived in the Middle East and the Mediterranean basin, where they suffered what was to become a familiar mixture of intolerance and persecution while being patronised for their skills, crafts and merchant abilities. But if Islam and Orthodox Christianity, centred in Constantinople, had occasional outbursts of anti-Jewish sentiment, these paled into insignificance compared with the experiences the Jews were to have in Europe in their second millennium of exile.

## Inquisitions and pogroms

By the 11th century large Jewish communities had established themselves in France and Germany. They arrived just in time for the Crusades, and a familiar pattern of massacres was begun which was to haunt the Jews all the way to Auschwitz. The Church institutionalised the belief that the Jews were satanic Christ-killers, who craved money above all else.

Nevertheless, in the 11th, 12th and 13th cen-

into Africa in the 14th and 15th centuries, it turned its attention to the non-Spanish, non-Christian infidels in its midst. For a century, under the Inquisition, Jews were either massacred or forced at sword point to convert. Finally, in the 1490s – just as Columbus was discovering America where the Jews would enjoy a new golden age – they were expelled from Spain. Many stayed, worshipping secretly; others returned to North Africa or settled in the newly emerging Ottoman Empire. Several thousand returned to the Holy Land, settling in Jerusalem and in Safed, which became a centre of Jewish scholarship. Some found their way to Holland

turies the Jews entered a golden age, especially in Spain, where Jewish aristocrats formed a bridge between the Christian north and Moorish Arab Muslim south. Communal life and autonomous religious institutions flourished in both Spain and Germany, and the Jews even developed their own languages – Ladino and Yiddish – medieval Spanish and German respectively, mixed with Hebrew and written with Hebrew characters.

But as Spain drove the Moorish infidels back

**LEFT:** an idealised view of 18th-century Jerusalem.
**ABOVE:** delegates to the Sixth Zionist Conference in Basle, 1903.

### PERNICIOUS RUMOURS

The image of Jews as Christ-killers was a pernicious one which was very hard to dispel. Along with it went a number of other superstitions, fomented or at least encouraged by the clerical authorities. One particularly unpleasant myth that persisted into the 20th century was that Jews killed Christian children so that they could use their blood for Passover rituals. The Jews were also blamed for the Black Death which swept Europe in 1348, and it was widely believed that they poisoned wells to spread the epidemic. Additionally, the fact that Jews were the only money-lenders, when the church forbade Christians to engage in usury, gave them a reputation for avarice.

and subsequently to England, when Oliver Cromwell legalised the community "expelled" in the 13th century.

Germany's Jews fared no better. Hounded by the Church, communities moved to Poland and Russia, establishing *shtetls*, small self-sufficient communities. The Pale of Settlement defined where they could live, excluding them from Russia itself, while pogroms kept them in constant fear. Ironically, the Pale of Settlement in Eastern Europe became a kind of homogenous Jewish state where Yiddish-speaking Jews evolved their distinct ethnic culture.

### Emancipation and nationalism

The Industrial Revolution and the forces of the Enlightenment transforming Europe also affected Jews. Some turned to messianic cults such as Hassidism, but with nationalism sweeping across Europe many became secularised.

At the same time Europeans started investigating Jewish culture. The discovery that Hebrew was a Semitic language related to Arabic, outside Indo-European linguistic evolution, contributed to the rise of anti-Semitism. Previously the Jews had suffered religious persecution but were at least accepted into the Church, albeit often through forced conversions; now they were set apart racially.

Some Jews were assimilated into middle-class European society. In England, Benjamin Disraeli's father had the country's future prime minister baptised rather than bar mitzvahed when he was 13. But baptism did not make many Jews of mainland Europe seem European enough. Ultimately, they were still persecuted. The Enlightenment, with its anti-religious liberal emphasis, often worked against the Jews, who were viewed as religious fundamentalists. Voltaire railed against them, and his anti-religious rationalist writings were developed in the 19th century by a young German Jew named Karl Marx, who rejected his heritage and spoke of a war against capitalists and clerics.

In this era of great change some Jews remembered Jerusalem. British philanthropists like Moses Montefiore and the Rothschilds set up Jewish communities in Jerusalem and new agricultural villages like Rishon Le-Tsiyon, Zikhron Ya'akov and Rosh Pina.

Meanwhile, the assassination of Tsar Alexander II in Russia in 1881 was blamed on the Jews and unleashed awesome pogroms. Jews emigrated in their millions to Western Europe and especially to the United States, which from the outset had guaranteed religious freedom in its constitution. But some Jews, eager to return to Palestine, were persuaded by the philanthropists to settle in the Holy Land.

### The birth of Zionism

But it was in France that modern political Zionism was conceived. In the 1890s a young Viennese-Jewish journalist, Theodor Herzl, was sent to Paris to cover the trial of Captain Alfred Dreyfus, the French Jewish officer who was

---

### LOOKING FOR A PEACEFUL LIFE

The *shtetls* of Eastern Europe were small self-sufficient village communities in which Jewish people retained their own culture and way of life. They were portrayed romantically in the musical *Fiddler on the Roof*, based on the Yiddish stories by Sholom Aleichem about Tevya the Milkman, whose faith in God helps him to overcome all the trials and tribulations of life under the Tsars.

The rabbi's blessing in *Fiddler on the Roof* – "God bless the Tsar and keep him far away from us" – reflected the antagonism that the Russian rulers had developed towards the Jews, and the Jewish desire to be left undisturbed.

framed as a spy and blamed for his country's defeat in the Franco–Prussian war of 1870. As the trial unravelled, Herzl despaired of the fate of European Jewry. Though an assimilated Jew who knew virtually nothing of his cultural roots, Herzl wrote a book, *Altneuland (Old-new Land)*, describing the re-establishment of a Jewish commonwealth in ancient Israel. He was written off as a dreamer, to which he responded, "If you will it, then it will be."

In 1897 Herzl convened the First Zionist Congress in Basle, establishing the World Zionist Organisation, the forerunner of the Israeli government. He lobbied political leaders and

British support for a Jewish homeland. This lent the Zionist movement the international legitimacy it desperately needed.

If the likes of Herzl and Weizmann gave the Zionist movement diplomatic access, the foot soldiers in the field were the Jews of Eastern Europe. As Tsarist Russia hurtled towards the revolution, increasing numbers of ideologically motivated Zionist socialists found their way to Palestine. Between 1904 and 1917, some 100,000 came, though less than half stayed.

Among them was a young lawyer's son named David Ben Gurion who was to assume the leadership of the *yishuv*, the pre-state Jewish

courted European royalty, making his only trip to Palestine in 1898 to meet Kaiser Wilhelm II of Germany when the latter visited Jerusalem.

After Herzl's premature death in 1904, the unofficial leadership of the Zionist movement fell to Chaim Weizmann, a Russian-born professor of chemistry at Manchester University. Weizmann won the confidence of the British ruling élite, and after the conquest of Palestine in 1917 that meant everything. Most importantly, he persuaded the British Foreign Secretary, Arthur Balfour, to issue a declaration promising

**LEFT:** Zionist visionary Theodor Herzl.
**ABOVE:** Turkish cavalry officers in Palestine, 1917.

entity. These men, products of pre-revolutionary Russia, were essentially Bolsheviks with a more liberal, humane streak. They set up trade unions, rejected the capitalist villages of the Rothschilds, and established their own agricultural collectives, called kibbutzim.

At first the indigenous Palestinians welcomed the Jewish settlers. Their numbers were small, they brought wealth and development, and, while most Palestinians lived on the inland hills, the newcomers were prepared to settle the humid, sparsely populated coastal plain. But the Balfour Declaration took the Arabs by surprise and indicated that they had greatly underestimated the Zionist potential. ❏

# PERFIDIOUS ALBION

*The Balfour Declaration promised British support for a Jewish homeland,
but Israel soon became embroiled in international realpolitik*

Even today the question is often asked in the Middle East: did the British favour the Arabs or the Jews during the Mandatory period? The answer is probably that they favoured neither and that, as elsewhere, they pursued their own interests.

In the aftermath of World War I, Arthur Balfour and David Lloyd George were strong supporters of the Zionist cause because they perceived a Jewish homeland as a potentially friendly outpost of Empire. The notion also appealed to the religious sentiment of British Protestants. But Balfour had underestimated the strength of Arab nationalism that would emerge from the ashes of the Ottoman Empire, as well as the emerging economic and strategic importance of Middle East oil.

The British government's most hostile opponent of the Balfour Declaration was Edwin Montagu, Secretary of State for India, and the only Jew in the cabinet. Like a large section of secular world Jewry, he fiercely opposed Zionism because it called into question his national loyalties. He insisted that Judaism was a religion, not a nationality.

## Arab riots

Britain's miscalculation in making the Balfour Declaration soon became apparent. In March 1920 a bloody riot in Jerusalem left more than 200 Jews dead. Widespread Arab violence soon made the British regret the Declaration, and in 1921 Winston Churchill, the Colonial Secretary, previously a fervent Zionist sympathiser, told Chaim Weizmann that 90 percent of the British government was opposed to a Jewish homeland in Palestine.

But the Zionists were better organised than the Arabs and more determined than the British. The Histadrut trade union organisation was founded in 1920, while the Haganah, an underground paramilitary organisation, effectively

**LEFT:** a Henschel portrait of a Palestinian Arab.
**RIGHT:** Zionist Dov Ber Borochov and friends in Plonsk, Poland, 1920.

defended Jewish settlements and became the forerunner of the Israel Defence Forces. Tel Aviv developed as the flourishing economic capital of the emerging Jewish entity, and kibbutz agricultural settlements made the local Jewish population self-sufficient in food.

Most vitally, large numbers of Jews began

emigrating to Palestine. In the 1920s the Jewish population of Palestine doubled from 85,000 to 170,000. The Arab population numbered about 850,000. These Jewish newcomers included socialists disillusioned by the results of the Russian Revolution, as well as numerous middle-class merchants and professionals from Poland. While David Ben Gurion and his socialist followers became the establishment through the Jewish Agency, a kind of government in waiting, the right-wing nationalist revisionist movement of Vladimir Jabotinsky also enjoyed strong support.

In particular, Jabotinsky and his supporters vehemently opposed Churchill's unilateral decision in 1923 to cede all of Palestine east of the River Jordan, nearly two-thirds of the land mass of Palestine, to Britain's Arabian Hashemite ally Emir Abdullah.

## The rise of Nazism

Hitler's 1933 assumption of power in Germany, together with the rapid economic development of Palestine, attracted even larger numbers of Jewish immigrants. While the majority of Jews saw Palestine as a safe haven from anti-Semitism, many were now being drawn there for other reasons. Palestine's coastal plain, where most Jewish towns were established, was no

In an attempt to win Arab support for the impending war with Germany, the British passed a White Paper limiting Jewish immigration to 20,000 a year. So, as the Nazi stranglehold tightened around Europe, there was nowhere for Jewish refugees to flee. In effect, the British U-turn meant that, by refusing entry visas to Palestine for Jewish refugees trying to escape persecution, they were assisting Adolf Hitler in his Final Solution. Even after the full horror of the concentration camps was known, the British did not relent, detaining some 73,000 refugees, many of them concentration camp survivors, in detention camps in Cyprus.

longer dominated by sand dunes and swamps. There were bourgeois boulevards lined with large houses, shops and banks, schools, universities and hospitals. An immigrant with means could live well here, while a poorer man could earn a reasonable working wage.

By 1939, on the eve of World War II, the Jewish population of Palestine had doubled again to 350,000. Bitter hostility to Zionism was led by Haj Amin Husseini, the Grand Mufti of Jerusalem, who consolidated his position as local Arab leader and formed an understanding with Hitler. The region might have been more peaceful had the more moderate King Abdullah of Jordan gained the upper hand.

### POLITICAL MACHINATIONS

Shortly after World War II, Emanuel Shinwell, a Jewish member of Clement Attlee's Labour cabinet in Britain, was proud to identify with the Zionist cause and the establishment of the State of Israel. However, he pointed out that, as Secretary for Energy in His Majesty's Government, he was duty-bound to protect British interests, and that involved sympathising with Arab states, whatever his personal feelings. Other British politicians were less candid about where their sympathies lay and also about the often unscrupulous choices involved in realpolitik. But of course, the making and breaking of promises often seems to be an integral part of political life.

All the same, Ben Gurion and the Jewish Agency insisted that there was no alternative but for Jews to support the British war effort. The revisionists were not so certain. Irgun Zvi Leumi, led by Menachem Begin, agreed to a ceasefire with the British for the duration of the war, but an extremist fringe, Lehi, led by Yitzhak Shamir, continued to attack British targets throughout World War II. Many Jews, however, enlisted in the British Army, which even formed a Jewish brigade; this provided invaluable experience for subsequent battles.

The revelation of the Nazi atrocities made the Jews of Palestine all the more determined to achieve independence. The horrors of the Holocaust were no surprise to the Zionists, who had always feared something of the sort but had expected it to be Russian rather than German-inspired. The prevailing belief was that, had Israel existed at the time, 6 million Jews could have been saved.

## Stalin to the rescue

Ben Gurion, grasping post-war realities, switched the focus of his lobbying from London to Washington. An intense diplomatic offensive was launched at the newly formed United Nations in New York, and quiet channels were opened to the Soviet Union. The support of Joseph Stalin in the establishment of Israel was to prove crucial. The United States, which voted against the UN-sponsored partition of Palestine in 1946, supported the same resolution a year later. Britain abstained both times. But Stalin, though undoubtedly anti-Semitic, saw a potentially socialist Israel as a Marxist bulwark against the puppet Arab administrations being set up by Britain and France. Consequently he threw his full weight, as well as that of his European satellites, behind the Zionists. He voted for the UN partition plan in November 1948 and even sent arms to help Israel during the War of Independence.

The right-wing Irgun and Lehi denounced Ben Gurion's diplomacy as futile. Their strategy was simple – to bomb the British out of Palestine. British soldiers were killed, Irgun and Lehi members were hanged, and more British soldiers were killed in retaliation. Following the bombing in 1947 of the British administra-

tive HQ at the King David Hotel, which killed 91 people, British public opinion clamoured for a withdrawal. After much government deliberation, the pullout was fixed for 15 May 1948.

Although the socialists and revisionists had a violent mutual hatred, it was probably their joint efforts that brought about the establishment of Israel. Ben Gurion's diplomatic success at the United Nations and in gaining the support of both Stalin and the US president, Harry Truman, gave the Jewish state international legitimacy. The revisionists' all-out war against the British forced their withdrawal.

And so modern Israel arose from the ashes

of the Holocaust. Yet it is one of the myths of our time that this is why Israel came into existence, a romantic idea that appeals to a poetic sense of justice: the Jewish people suffered but were compensated with their own state.

This is not the way Israelis see it. They argue that Israel came into being despite the Holocaust, and that had just 1 million of the 6 million who perished reached Israel, the birth of the state would have been easier. They recall that while Israel enjoyed much international sympathy after the Holocaust, little was done to help. Israel had to work hard to swing the UN vote, and when the British withdrew it was left completely alone to face the Arab world. ❏

**LEFT:** British soldiers in Jerusalem, 1917.
**RIGHT:** young David Ben Gurion in Turkish fez.

# THE SECOND EXODUS

*The birth of the new state was a difficult one, and in subsequent years political and economic vision were vital for survival*

As Israelis danced in the streets following the Declaration of Independence in May 1948, they knew that there would be little to celebrate in the ensuing months. Though vastly outnumbered by the surrounding Arab armies, better organisation saw the Israel Defence Forces not only defend Jewish territory but also conquer large areas of the Negev and Western Galilee that had been allocated to Palestine under the UN partition plan.

However, if subsequent Israeli military victories were relatively swift, this first war ground on for nearly a year, costing the new country 6,000 lives, about 1 percent of the Jewish population. Jerusalem saw especially fierce fighting. Under the UN plan the city was meant to enjoy international status, but Jordanian Legionnaires overran the Old City, including the Jewish quarter, while the western, Jewish half of the city was besieged for months, relieved only when a new road was built through the hills. Eventually the city was divided into two, with the Israelis controlling the western half and the Jordanians annexing the eastern section, including the holy sites, as well as the entire West Bank. Egypt helped itself to the Gaza Strip, and Arab Palestine never came into existence.

## The fate of the Palestinians

The Israelis have always officially claimed that the Palestinians ran away from their homes in 1948 to escape the fighting, expecting to return after an Arab victory. The Palestinians claim that they were forcibly expelled. Research shows that there is some truth in both versions. About a third of the 500,000 Palestinians living in the region that was to become Israel were coerced into leaving, becoming refugees in surrounding countries; about a third voluntarily fled, and the final third stayed put and eventually became citizens of Israel, which today has an Arab minority of some 20 percent.

**LEFT:** British troopships become a temporary home.
**RIGHT:** the first glimpse of the Promised Land.

Meanwhile, David Ben Gurion set about building his new nation. The architect of such institutions as the Histadrut trade-union movement and the Haganah, now renamed the Israel Defence Forces, Ben Gurion was easily able to outflank the world Jewish leader Chaim Weizmann, who also aspired to lead the new nation.

Ben Gurion offered Weizmann the post of president, the titular head of state.

At the same time, while allowing the revisionists led by Menachem Begin to participate in Knesset elections, Ben Gurion acted tough, outlawing their paramilitary organisations and blowing up a ship, the *Atalena*, bringing arms for Irgun in June 1948. Menachem Begin and his Herut Party, which won 14 out of 120 seats in the 1948 elections, were to remain in the political wilderness for nearly 20 years until, in the run-up to the Six Day War in 1967, Begin was invited by prime minister Levi Eshkol to join a national unity government. In elections a decade later, he won outright power.

Although harsh with his opponents, Ben Gurion knew how to delegate responsibility. After his socialist Mapai Party won 46 seats in the 1949 Knesset elections, he formed a coalition with the Stalinist Mapam Party to the left and religious and liberal groups to the right. Ben Gurion became prime minister and defence minister. Moshe Sharett, as foreign minister, became his heir apparent and eventually the second prime minister.

Within the army, Ben Gurion advanced the promotion of the daring one-eyed Moshe Dayan, a notorious womaniser who had sustained his injury while fighting for the British in Syria.

Another man who caught Ben Gurion's attention was the dashing young Yitzhak Rabin, commander of the Harel brigade, who was given a leading role in the armistice agreements negotiated after the War of Independence.

## The Law of Return

The most significant new legislation introduced by the Knesset was the Law of Return of 1950, guaranteeing free immigration of world Jewry to Israel. The religious parties wanted to restrict immigration to candidates whose mothers were Jewish, but in the wake of the Holocaust and of the Nuremberg Laws, which had defined any-

### DEVELOPING FOR DEFENCE

Ben Gurion had a good eye for young talent, both inside and outside the army. In particular, he spotted the creative organisational abilities of a young Polish immigrant called Shimon Peres (who would become prime minister in 1984) and charged him with the task of developing a defence manufacturing infrastructure. Peres's accomplishments were remarkable, giving Israel a nuclear capability and enabling the country to produce its own tanks and fighter aircraft. Many Israeli weapons, such as the versatile Uzi sub-machine gun, became sought-after export items, and the existence of this successful industry no doubt boosted Israel's confidence during decades of war.

body with one Jewish grandparent as Jewish, this same yardstick was adopted.

In the years following the establishment of Israel, waves of immigrants flooded in. Nearly 700,000 arrived between 1948 and 1951, doubling the population. By 1964 another 500,000 had arrived and the population passed 2 million. But the European-born founding fathers were surprised to find that large numbers were arriving not only from Eastern Europe but also from Morocco, Egypt, Yemen, Iraq and other Arab countries, where entire Jewish communities were expelled in an anti-Zionist backlash.

By the 1960s Israel's Jewish population was split 50–50 between Ashkenazi European Jews and Sephardi Oriental Jews. This cultural divide, accentuated by socio-economic gaps, would generate major tensions in the 1970s.

## International orientation

Ben Gurion had planned to pursue a neutral policy in the Cold War. During the War of Independence the USSR was the only country to send arms, though the USA had turned a blind eye to the military aid given to Israel by American Jewry. But although a Stalinist party shared power in Israel's first government, the country was a parliamentary democracy with more in common with the West.

Moreover, Israel needed financial aid, and only the USA could supply that. So in 1949, when Israel took a loan of $100,000 from the USA, a pattern of economic dependence was begun. In parallel, Israel's relations with the Soviet Union were strained as Stalin refused to allow free emigration of Soviet Jewry.

However, Israel, in partnership with Britain and France, antagonised both the USA and the Soviet Union in 1956 when it launched the Suez campaign. Following the nationalisation of the Suez Canal by Egypt's president, Gamal Abdel Nasser, British and French paratroopers seized the canal, and in less than a week Israeli troops had occupied all Sinai. But the Americans sided with the Egyptians, forcing the British and French to relinquish control of the canal and compelling the Israelis to withdraw from Sinai. Instead of being humiliated, Nasser became a hero.

## Economic development

Despite Israel taking in so many impoverished immigrants and illiterate newcomers, plus the cost of remaining on a constant war footing, the economy developed steadily during the 1950s and 1960s. Major national projects were undertaken, including the draining of the Hula Swamp in the Upper Galilee and the building of the national carrier bringing water from the north to the Negev. The desert literally turned green. Forests were planted on the barren hillsides, and the arid land was transformed.

Even with its burgeoning population, the country was self-sufficient in food, and a major export industry, especially in citrus fruit, devel-

oped. Highways were built, and a health, education and energy infrastructure was put in place. In this formative stage, the Arab boycott and the unwillingness of overseas investors to put money into a country that might soon be driven into the sea turned out to be an asset, for Israel developed a home-owned industrial infrastructure. The economy was heavily centralised and socialist, but there was scope for entrepreneurs with the patience to unravel bureaucratic red tape.

In this stage of the country's development, donations from overseas Jewry, especially from North America, were a vital source of capital.

In addition, a reparations agreement was concluded with the West German government which compensated hundreds of thousands of survivors, or relatives of victims, for the loss of life, the suffering, and the property lost during the Holocaust. Menachem Begin bitterly opposed this agreement, insisting that no amount of money could atone for the devastation caused by the Nazis.

In 1963, when Levi Eshkol became the third prime minister, Israel was not a wealthy country, nor a full member of the industrialised world, but fortunately it did not suffer from the food shortages, disease and illiteracy which characterised most of the developing world. ❏

**LEFT:** illegal immigrants gaze out from a British ship.
**RIGHT:** a waxwork model of Chaim Weizmann.

# COMING OF AGE

*Through wars and internal strife Israel has struggled to maturity while*
*world opinion has fluctuated between praise and blame*

The Arabs have always maintained that Israel instigated the Six Day War in 1967 in order to seize more Palestinian territory. This interpretation of history overlooks the blockade of the Straits of Tiran by the Egyptian president, Gamal Abdel Nasser, which cut off the shipping route to Israel's Red Sea port of Eilat, as well as his boast that he would drive the Jews into the sea.

With hindsight, Nasser's threat was probably bluff, but Israel was not to know. As the Yom Kippur War revealed six years later, Israeli intelligence was poor at the time, and a first strike was crucial for such a tiny country with no strategic depth. So Israel took Nasser's threats at face value and attacked, and the Egyptian air force was destroyed on the ground minutes after the war started. The Golan Heights, from which Syria had been bombarding northern Israel, were captured. Israel also won the Sinai peninsula and Gaza Strip from Egypt, and the West Bank from Jordan. Jerusalem was reunited. Defence Minister Moshe Dayan and Chief of the Army Yitzhak Rabin were hailed as heroes.

## Permanently on the map

Israel was never the same after the Six Day War. It wasn't only that the borders had changed and more than a million Palestinians had fallen under Israeli occupation. Perceived worldwide as the underdog in the Middle East conflict, Israel was now viewed as the oppressor. But the West, especially the United States, now saw Israel as a potentially strong and reliable ally in the Cold War confrontation with the USSR. Military collaboration strengthened between Israel and the USA, while Britain and France maintained the arms embargo imposed at the start of the Six Day War.

Israel itself was intoxicated by its own success. Prime Minister Levi Eshkol died and was replaced by Golda Meir, who had grown up in

the United States and was able to consolidate the US–Israeli romance. The country's new euphoria was not even tempered by a war of attrition between 1967 and 1970, in which Egypt shelled Israeli forces across the Suez Canal, nor by the emergence of the Palestine Liberation Organization (PLO), which carried out bloody

terrorist attacks against Israeli targets, including the killing of 11 Israeli athletes during the Munich Olympic Games in 1972.

When Jordan and Egypt annexed the West Bank and Gaza Strip, the PLO had been suppressed and its leader, Yasser Arafat, imprisoned. But after 1967 the PLO was encouraged to spearhead the Arab nations' campaign to regain "the Zionist entity". By 1970 the PLO was so strong that Arafat attempted, with Syrian backing, to take over Jordan. In a 10-day bloody war in "Black September", King Hussein quelled the attempted Palestinian coup. Syrian troops massed on the border turned back when Israel indicated it would intervene to support the

**LEFT:** celebrating Independence Day in Jerusalem.
**RIGHT:** soldiers reach the Western Wall, 1967.

Hashemite Kingdom. Arafat and his fighters were expelled to Lebanon.

## War and peace

The PLO was popularly viewed as a terrorist organisation that would eventually go away, and Israel considered itself invincible. In 1973 the Yom Kippur War stunned the nation. With a surprise assault the Egyptians, under President Anwar Sadat, conquered much of Sinai while the Syrians nearly broke through to the Galilee. Israel recovered, counter-attacked, re-took the Golan Heights and even managed to cross the Suez Canal before the Americans, who for the

terised by bitter divisions over the direction of Israeli society. After 29 years in power, Labour lost office because of its failures in the Yom Kippur War. Moreover, Begin's populism appealed both to young Oriental Jews, alienated by the Ashkenazi socialist establishment, and to Orthodox Jewry, attached to the biblical sites in the West Bank, which now became known as Judea and Samaria.

Yitzhak Rabin had first allowed right-wing Jews to settle Hebron and other West Bank towns in 1975, and in so doing opened a floodgate. Under Begin and his successor, Yitzhak Shamir, tens of thousands of Jews settled the

first time became committed allies of Israel by airlifting emergency military supplies to the Middle East, forced a ceasefire.

But the war restored Egyptian pride and was portrayed by Sadat as a great victory. He signed a peace treaty with Israel in 1979 in exchange for the return of the Sinai peninsula. Remarkably, he did not shake hands with Golda Meir, or her successor Yitzhak Rabin, but with Menachem Begin, the right-wing nationalist who won the 1977 election.

## The birth of two-party politics

Begin's success changed the face of Israeli politics which became a two-party affair, charac-

### SUPPORT FROM THE USA

By the late 1970s the United States had come to view Israel as a significant player in its Cold War global strategy, and also a vital support to NATO's vulnerable south-eastern flank, which comprised the two bitter enemies Greece and Turkey. This meant that large sums of money – about $1.5 billion a year – were ploughed into Israel to pay for arms and to improve the country's military capabilities. Another $1.5 billion was given annually to help repay the loans taken out for previous acquisitions and, subsequently, for the expensive redeployment needed after the Sinai withdrawal in 1982. Such close ties with the USA naturally deepened the USSR's hostility towards Israel.

West Bank and the Gaza Strip, and the Palestinians saw the little that was left of their homeland slipping away from them.

All the same, the right-wing Likud, though nationalist in character and reluctant to relinquish land, tended to make pragmatic concessions when pressured by the USA. Begin gave up Sinai after American arm-twisting, and received the Nobel Peace Prize for his pains.

## Anti-Zionism

Israel's close identification with the USA made it a target for Soviet Union hostility. The communist bloc, Arab and Muslim nations and the developing world combined to isolate Israel as a pariah nation. The country was depicted as a racist state; Zionism was denounced by a UN resolution as an intrinsically fascist ideology.

The tactic was extremely effective, and even many of Israel's friends in the liberal West distanced themselves from Zionism. And this was before Likud came to power and when there was barely a settler in the West Bank. For Israelis, anti-Zionism was the flip side of anti-Semitism. Persecuted in Europe as Semites, they were now being denounced by the Semitic Arabs as European colonialists.

Ironically, while the Soviet Union was hounding Israel diplomatically and arming Syria, it eased restrictions on Jewish emigration. More than 180,000 Jews reached Israel from the USSR in the 1970s, and an even greater number emigrated to the USA.

Begin won a second election victory in 1981 and the following year turned his attentions on Lebanon. Israel's northern neighbour had been a model of democracy and affluence despite its divisions between Maronite Christians, Druze, Sunni and Shi'ite Muslims and Palestinian refugees. But the arrival of the PLO and its fighters in 1970 had disturbed the delicate balance, and the country plunged into civil war in 1975. The PLO used Lebanon as a base for attacks on Israel from sea and land.

Ariel Sharon, the Minister of Defence, convinced Begin that a military incursion into Southern Lebanon was required to clear out PLO bases. An invasion was launched in June 1982. Begin, like the rest of the nation, was surprised to learn a short while later that Israeli

tanks were rolling through the streets of Beirut. The Americans intervened to prevent the Israel Defence Forces from finishing off Arafat, who was given safe passage to Tunisia.

In the aftermath of the war Begin lost his previous vigour. The great orator fell silent and resigned the following year. He felt betrayed, not only by Sharon but also by his Finance Minister, Yoram Aridor, whose economic policies led to three-digit annual inflation.

## The years of power sharing

The 1984 election result was inconclusive, and a rotation pact was agreed, with Labour's Shi-

mon Peres serving as prime minister until 1986, followed by Likud's Yitzhak Shamir for the subsequent two years. Peres withdrew Israeli troops from Lebanon, with the exception of a security belt closest to the Israeli border, and stabilised the economy, reducing the annual rate of inflation from 425 percent to 16 percent.

During the two decades that Israel had occupied the West Bank and Gaza, relations between the Israelis and Palestinians had deteriorated. Immediately after 1967 the Palestinians were infatuated with Israeli liberalism and the economic opportunities that occupation brought. A free press flourished, municipal elections were held, and employment in Israel,

**LEFT:** President Sadat is greeted by Begin in 1977.
**RIGHT:** checking Palestinian work permits.

mainly in menial jobs, saw improvements in the Palestinians' standard of living.

But things turned sour, especially after the Likud triumph in the 1970s, as it became clear that Israel was integrating the Palestinian territories into a Greater Israel. Right-wing settlers were becoming more powerful, and the Israeli government was talking of annexing the biblical Land of Israel.

Palestinian frustration exploded in 1987 with the outbreak of the Intifada, which was characterised by the throwing of rocks and Molotov cocktails at Israeli troops, and by strikes preventing Arab workers from coming to Israel.

World opinion strongly sympathised with the Palestinians, and the demographic debate was renewed in Israeli politics, with Labour speaking of territorial concessions. The elections of 1988 saw Likud win the upper hand in a closely fought contest. Shamir continued to lead a national unity government, which broke down in 1990; he then formed a right-wing coalition.

## The collapse of the Soviet Union

The unexpected disintegration of the USSR meant that, from 1990 onwards, Russian-speaking Jewry flooded into Israel. Over 800,000 immigrants had arrived by 1998. The demise of the Soviet Union saw Israel renew diplomatic relations with the states of Central and Eastern Europe and the former republics of the USSR. In addition, the supply of Russian-made arms to Syria and the PLO dried up.

Before the post-Cold War situation could be digested, Iraq invaded Kuwait, and the Gulf War ensued in 1991. Scud missiles fell on Israel but, under American pressure, the right-wing government did not retaliate in order not to disrupt the allied coalition, which included Syria.

By November 1991 Israel was sitting round the table with the Palestinians and Syrians at the Madrid Peace Conference. In the wake of these preliminary peace talks, China, India and much of Asia established full diplomatic relations with Israel for the first time. African countries such as Nigeria renewed ties, and the UN resolution equating Zionism with racism was repealed. But Shamir stalled on progress in the peace talks, continuing to expand settlements in the West Bank. A confrontation with the United States was averted by Yitzhak Rabin's election victory in 1992.

## Peace accords and assassination

Though Rabin had been elected on a dovish platform, Israelis and the wider world were surprised by the secret agreements concluded with the PLO in Oslo. In September 1993 Prime Minister Rabin and PLO Chairman Yasser Arafat shook hands on the White House lawn, and by 1994 Israel had withdrawn from most of the Gaza Strip and all the towns on the West Bank save for Hebron. A peace agreement was signed with Jordan, and Morocco and Tunisia opened low-level diplomatic offices in Tel Aviv.

The peace process, combined with the end of the Arab economic boycott, ongoing immigration and a penchant for developing innovative high-tech products, saw the economy boom. Average annual growth of 6 percent in the early 1990s enabled the standard of living to rise rapidly to Western European levels.

But Rabin's right-wing religious and nationalist opponents were unimpressed by the economic benefits of peace. The opposition to territorial compromise strengthened following a terrorist bombing campaign by the extremist Palestinian Hamas movement. Vociferous anti-government demonstrations took place as the right took to the streets.

A young law student, Yigal Amir, decided to take matters into his own hands. He stalked

Rabin for several months, with a pistol in his pocket. His opportunity came following a peace rally in Tel Aviv in November 1995, when he took advantage of a lapse in security to pump three bullets into Rabin's back from point-blank range.

In the shocked aftermath of the assassination of a widely respected leader, the premiership was assumed by Foreign Minister Shimon Peres. As architect of the Oslo Accords, he had won the Nobel Peace Prize, along with Rabin and

### MINOR INCONVENIENCES

The Intifada had one trivial but inconvenient aspect for some Israelis: no more popping over to dine in their favourite West Bank restaurant in Ramalla, or to buy cheap groceries in Gaza.

## Netanyahu puts on the brakes

Binyamin Netanyahu became the first prime minister to be chosen directly by the electorate. He would have won more handsomely under the old system, by which the Knesset faction with the best chance of forming a government received a mandate from the president. He won because of a late, pragmatic move to the centre: in contravention of traditional Likud policy, he agreed to abide by the Oslo Agreements, even to meet Yasser Arafat.

Arafat, and he now pushed ahead vigorously with the peace process. However, Syria's President Hafez El-Assad refused to meet him, even though Peres had agreed in principle to return the Golan Heights.

Persuaded by a large lead in the polls, Peres brought forward elections by six months to May 1996. But a lacklustre campaign, combined with further terrorist attacks by Hamas and Hizbullah missiles raining down on the Galilee, saw Peres defeated by the narrowest of margins.

**LEFT:** Yitzhak Rabin, assassinated in 1995.
**ABOVE:** Binyamin Netanyahu meets Yasser Arafat.

Ideally Netanyahu wanted, as a permanent settlement, the status quo of the first stage of Israel's withdrawal from the population centres of the West Bank and Gaza. For their part, the Palestinians demanded the full status of statehood in most of the West Bank and Gaza, including some arrangement on East Jerusalem, a sticking point even for liberal Israelis.

After the Israeli withdrawal from half of Hebron in 1997, negotiations became bogged down over percentage points for Israeli redeployment. In late 1998 Israel agreed to further troop withdrawals, linked to Palestinian commitment to suppress Islamic extremists. As ever, the outcome was impossible to predict. ❑

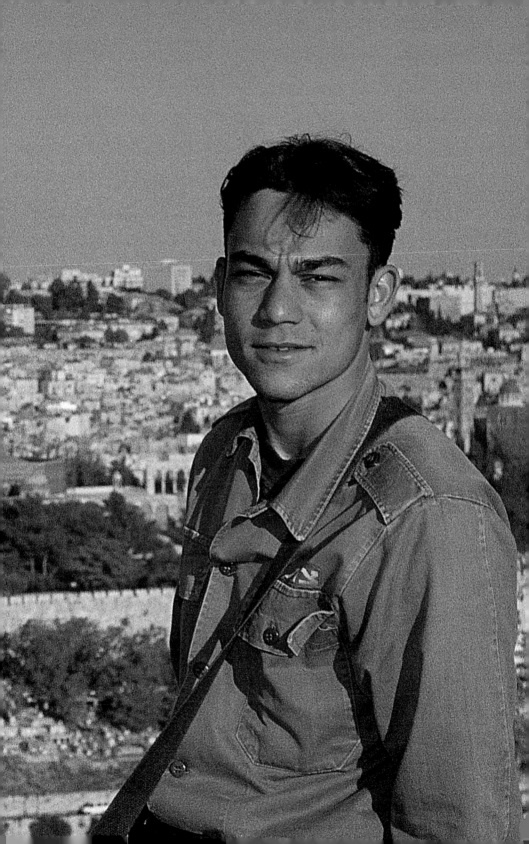

# ISRAEL TODAY

*Amid much rejoicing, Israel celebrated its 50th anniversary in 1998.*
*But, while the economy now flourishes, the quest for peace goes on*

Israel confounds expectations. It is a nation rooted in religion, yet the majority of the people are brazenly secular, turning to religion only for births, barmitzvahs, weddings and funerals. There are picturesque bastions of orthodoxy in Jerusalem, in Bnei Brak near Tel Aviv, and elsewhere a quaint mixture of medieval Poland and the Middle East, but for the most part long rabbinical beards are rare, many restaurants serve forbidden un-kosher foods, the Sabbath is barely observed, and women dress anything but modestly.

It is the army generals rather than the rabbis who have forged the nation's values. Modern Israel is a nation whose military has a peerless reputation for executing the swift, the precise and the dramatically unexpected. Yet the ubiquitous Israeli soldier, rifle slung casually over his shoulder, appears slovenly and unregimented. This informality extends even to the Israel Defence Forces (IDF), but it was these long-haired paratroopers, unshaven officers and pot-bellied reservists who undertook the Entebbe rescue, bombed the Iraqi nuclear reactor and triumphed in the Six Day War.

## Vigorous democracy

Israel's greatest achievements, however, have not been on the battlefield. A nation has been created out of immigrants from more than 80 countries, who shared a religious heritage and a desire to return to their ancestral homeland, but little else – not even a language. In the street you will hear an astonishing Babel of languages: Russian, English, Arabic, Amharic, Hungarian, French, Persian, Spanish, Yiddish. But Hebrew, the language of the Bible, has been resurrected and adapted to everyday life.

Even more surprisingly, parliamentary democracy has flourished – despite the fact that most Israelis originate in countries with no experience of such democracy; despite the frictions between religious and secular, right and left, Arab and Jew; and despite the centrality and power of the army. Even when Prime Minister Yitzhak Rabin was gunned down in 1995, there was no danger of the Knesset's sovereignty being overthrown.

If a general seeks political power he does not

plan a coup d'état but resigns his commission and enters the political fray. The late Yitzhak Rabin was a former chief of staff of the IDF, and half a dozen other former generals served in Binyamin Netanyahu's first government, including Defence Minister Yitzhak Mordechai, Agriculture Minister Rafael Eitan and Infrastructure Minister Ariel Sharon. The leader of the Labour opposition, ex-Foreign Minister Ehud Barak, is a former army chief. Another political safety-valve is the system of proportional representation, which allows all interest groups to be represented in parliament, enabling small parties to hold the balance of power between the major blocs, often granting

**PRECEDING PAGES:** soldiers on the Mount of Olives.
**LEFT:** young kibbutznikim.
**RIGHT:** shoppers on Ben Yehuda, Jerusalem.

them disproportionate powers. Civil rights, freedom of the press and an independent judiciary further reinforce democratic values in a country that takes an exuberant pride in flouting authority and disobeying regulations.

## Organised chaos

The eye may initially see Levantine chaos and Mediterranean madness, but beneath the surface is a society that functions effectively. The wars have been won, the desert has bloomed, high-tech industries compete on world markets. From a socialist base, a dynamic capitalist economy has been built with sustained economic growth, enabling Israel, with considerable military aid from the United States, to enjoy living standards comparable to those of Spain or Italy.

The diverse landscape and climate complement the heterogeneous nature of the people. The heat of the summer leaves the country parched and brown except for the ripening grape vines, cotton fields and well watered lawns. But, come November, the rains begin, driving forcefully down throughout the winter, and occasional snowfalls can cover inland hills. Flash floods in the desert destroy all in their path, uprooting trees and shifting boulders. By spring the countryside is ablaze with flowers

and fields are as emerald as Ireland. But then the rains cease and gradually the land becomes thirsty and faded. The land, like its people, is in a state of constant flux and renewal.

## In-gathering of the exiles

The essence of this ongoing change is *aliyah*, Hebrew for immigration. Since 1989 more than 900,000 immigrants have poured into Israel, principally from the former Soviet Union, though some 25,000 were from Ethiopia. This represents 15 percent of Israel's population, the equivalent of Britain taking in 8 million immigrants, or the USA 40 million.

The process has been tackled with relish,

### GAINS AND LOSSES

The role of Israeli women, like that of their counterparts in the West, has changed over the past few decades. They have cut the umbilical cord tying them to their homes but have not escaped entirely from their traditional roles. They are expected both to pursue a career and to raise a family, which many do most successfully, but they have lost ground in other areas. On the kibbutzim, women once undertook the same jobs as men, however tough; today they tend to be found in the kitchen and the kindergarten. In the army, many women fought as front-line troops for Israel's independence, but today they do not occupy combat positions, although some are now training as pilots.

though inevitably problems abound. Housing shortages resulted in the setting up of caravan sites (especially for the more acquiescent Ethiopians) which many fear will become ghettoes for the weaker sectors of society. And unemployment plagues the newcomers, most of them highly educated professionals who must often accept a drop in status. Many fall a long distance. Physicians sweep the streets with clinical meticulousness, and former members of prestigious orchestras in Moscow and Minsk serenade passers-by in pedestrian malls with the best-quality busking in the world.

Rebuffing the attempts of both the right-wing

ica and Turkey fleeing military juntas; from Iran escaping the ayatollahs, and most recently from the Soviet Union and Ethiopia.

There has also always been a steady flow of immigrants from North America, Northern Europe, South Africa and Australasia – immigrants prepared to forgo comfortable lives to rebuild Zion. Golda Meir, prime minister 1969–74, grew up in America, while former President Chaim Herzog was born in Belfast. There are prejudices against newcomers, but immigrants can eventually reach the top despite their heavily accented and awkward Hebrew.

Nurtured by government attempts towards

Likud administration and the subsequent Labour government to absorb them, the new immigrants set up their own party for the 1996 elections, winning 7 out of 120 Knesset seats.

But Israel is good at blending waves of newcomers into its society. Jews came from Russia before the revolution; from Germany and Austria fleeing the Nazis; from Poland, Hungary and Romania out of the ashes of the Holocaust; from Iraq, Syria, the Yemen and North Africa escaping Arab anti-Zionism; from Latin Amer-

**LEFT:** a post office employee shows one of the thousands of letters addressed to God and Jesus.
**ABOVE:** a Russian concert violinist turns to busking.

social integration, the cultural mosaic becomes a melting pot. Contemporary Israeli music attests to the fusion between East and West. Food, too, produces interesting combinations: *felafel* and chips, goulash and couscous, chicken soup and *kubbe*.

## A stable economy

Ben Gurion built Israel's economy around the extremely powerful Histadrut trade-union movement. Onto this socialist base – which encompasses agricultural production through the kibbutz collectives and moshav cooperatives, much of the health service, and industrial conglomerates that include the country's largest bank – a dynamic capitalist system has been grafted. In the 1980s, three-digit inflation caused chaos, but since 1986 economic order has largely been restored, with manageable inflation and economic growth averaging 6 percent annually during most of the 1990s.

Meanwhile, the Histadrut is in decline, and many of its unprofitable assets have been sold off. Even so, union membership today is remarkably universal, from the blue-collar industrial workforce to senior management and

> **MIXES AND MUDDLES**
>
> In the 1980s, when three-digit inflation raged, Israelis spoke of their "muddled" economy as opposed to the "mixed" economies of Western Europe.

seas. By 1997 the figure had exceeded $20 billion. This has been accomplished with almost no natural resources except the potash, bromine and other minerals extracted from the Dead Sea. Through efficient automated and computerised mining techniques, the Dead Sea Works export $600 million-worth of goods a year.

Israel's prosperity is epitomised most tangibly in the glistening glass high-rises of the Diamond Exchange in Ramat Gan, adjacent to Tel Aviv, the nerve-centre of a

members of the professions. The high-status composition of its membership has seen the Histadrut retain much of its influence when union movements elsewhere in the world are diminished. But while the Histadrut is still capable of calling a general strike – visitors may be surprised to find that all the banks are on strike, or doctors are seeing only emergency cases – its power has been diluted by a combination of Likud rule and the kind of competitive-edged capitalism needed to sell commodities overseas.

For the fact is that Israel must export to survive. The early 1990s saw the country selling about $12 billion worth of goods a year over-

$5 billion-a-year export industry in polished diamonds, precious stones and jewellery.

Other exports include high-tech machinery, computer software and electronic goods, agricultural produce and petrochemicals, with some 40 percent of goods sold to Western Europe, a further 30 percent to North America and 20 percent to the Far East. As an associate member of the European Union, and with a free trade pact with the US, Israel has tariff-free access to the world's two largest markets.

Israel also enjoys an income approaching $3 billion a year from tourism, and a similar sum from donations by the country's supporters, channelled through organisations such as the

Jewish Agency, responsible for bringing immigrants to Israel, and the Jewish National Fund, which takes care of afforestation.

In addition, US aid amounts to over $3 billion a year. This began in the 1970s when Israel was perceived as an important ally against the USSR, but in the post-Cold War era such help can't be taken for granted. US aid is viewed ambivalently by Israelis: it has allowed them to build an affluent society, but it also makes them more dependent on the United States.

### A SENSE OF PROPORTION

Israelis respect their leaders but don't venerate them. Netanyahu is popularly known as "Bibi"; his private life receives wide coverage, and he is satirised in a TV programme called *Hartzufim*.

negotiations between Yitzhak Rabin and Yasser Arafat begun in 1993. Setting up a Palestine council to administer and legislate for all the territories occupied by Israel since 1967 (except for East Jerusalem) proved a daunting test of diplomatic skills. On the right, the West Bank settlers – one of whose maverick sympathisers killed Rabin – do not wish to yield an inch. On the left, the doves of Peace Now want to cede the territories unilaterally.

The pragmatic Netanyahu has been caught

### The quest for peace

The main anxiety caused by dependence on the USA concerns peace and territorial compromise. Many Israelis fear that USA pressure to hand back more land to the Arabs will leave Israel vulnerable to future attack. The return of the Golan, for example, which the USA has pressed for, is strongly opposed. Giving up Sinai for peace with Egypt was one thing; it is now a vast, demilitarised desert providing an effective trip-wire should Egypt ever want to attack. More fraught with difficulties were the

**LEFT:** a female instructor teaches a new recruit.
**ABOVE:** children at the exuberant festival of Purim.

between the intransigent right-wing elements in his government and the more dovish centrists whom he needs if he is to retain power. Consequently, progress in the peace process has been slow. But what of the silent majority, whose opinions are seldom heard, despite a flurry of international attention during Israel's 50th anniversary? Many of them switched their allegiance from Shimon Peres to Netanyahu in the 1996 election, fearing Peres was giving away too much too quickly. Yet opinion polls show that 70 percent of Israelis support the peace process and territorial compromise, and this should ensure the survival of the process despite Netanyahu's brinkmanship. ❑

# THE PEOPLE OF ISRAEL

*This tiny country comprises an exotic mixture of people, many born elsewhere but all regarding Israel as home*

The only valid generalisation to make about Israelis is that there is no such thing as a typical Israeli. The in-gathering of the exiles has brought Jews to Israel from 80 countries, and, beneath their sometimes surly surface, they can behave with Latin American panache, European civility or overwhelming Middle Eastern hospitality.

Israeli society itself has distinctly different sectors, including black-hatted ultra-Orthodox Jews and more modern Orthodox Jewry, as well as secular European (Ashkenazi) Jews and more traditional Oriental (Sephardi) Jews. New immigrants from the former Soviet Union now comprise 15 percent of Israeli society, while Ethiopian Jews add diversity to the social landscape. Slick Tel Aviv city people are increasingly prevalent, but the pioneering spirit lives on and rugged, bronzed kibbutznikim can still be found.

Kibbutz dwellers aside, Israelis are predominantly urban and suburban creatures. More than half the population lives in the country's three largest cities. Jerusalem has a population of 600,000, over 2 million people live in the Greater Tel Aviv area, and an additional 500,000 in the Haifa Bay conurbation.

The Arabs are more rural. About one-fifth of Israel's population of over 6 million belongs to the Arab minority, which is mainly Muslim but also includes Christians and Druze. Many Arabs are still loyal to their nomadic Bedouin tribes even though they have moved to permanent accommodation. Discussion of Israeli Arabs doesn't include the 2 million Palestinians of the West Bank and Gaza.

Israel's other minorities include several thousand Circassians, Turkic Muslims from the Southern Russian Caucasian mountains brought to the region in the 1800s to protect Ottoman interests. The Samaritans are an ancient Samarian sect, and the Bahá'í religion has its world headquarters in Haifa. The Negev town of Dimona is home to several hundred Black Hebrews, and in the 1970s the country took in over 100 Vietnamese boat people. Israel also has an estimated 200,000 guest workers.

Educational institutions and the army have been powerful influences for social assimila-

tion. The Hebrew language enhances social cohesion, and, although communities may jealously guard their distinct Jewish traditions, inter-marriage between European and Oriental Jewry is common. Some figures put it as high as 25 percent.

The native-born Israeli is often known as a sabra, after the prickly pear, a cactus fruit which has a spiky outside but a sweet and succulent heart. This is an appropriate description of young Israelis who are brash, self-confident and always in a hurry. Yet they can also be surprisingly considerate, and their openness and curiosity delight the gregarious as much as they intimidate the reticent.

---

**PRECEDING PAGES:** Orthodox Jews in Me'a Shea'rim.
**LEFT:** everyone's idea of a sabra.
**RIGHT:** a confident young Ashkenazi woman.

## Secular Jewry

For many non-Jews the term "secular Jewry" would seem to be a contradiction in terms. Many Jews, too, argue that Judaism is a religion and not a nationality and, therefore, Jews can be Orthodox or not Orthodox but never secular. Such semantic discussions overlook the realities of everyday Israeli life. The fact is that most Israeli Jews define themselves as both secular and Jewish.

It is difficult to ascertain who is a secular Jew. By and large European Jews clearly identify themselves as secular, Orthodox or ultra-Orthodox and tend to be more extreme in their

allegiances. It was secular Ashkenazi Jews from Europe who were the architects of the state in the early 1900s. Oriental Jews, who mostly came later, in the 1940s and 1950s, are more traditional. Many non-religious Oriental Jews have assimilated the European contempt for Orthodoxy, but most remain more respectful and even deferential.

The divide between Ashkenazi and Oriental Jewry remains today, although inter-marriage is common. But virtually all of the most impoverished Jewish Israelis are Oriental, and it is this deprived sector that is antagonistic to Ashkenazi Jewry. This sector of society also tends to have strong religious leanings and is

hostile to the secularism of Ashkenazi Jewry. However, most Oriental Jews have made it out of the poor apartment buildings constructed for them when they arrived, and many have prospered. Take, for example, some of the most senior men in recent governments: Foreign Minister David Levy was born in Morocco, while Defence Minister Yitzhak Mordechai came originally from Iraq and Deputy Prime Minister Moshe Katzav hailed from Iran.

## Politics and religion

Israel's secular Jews share the liberal, universalist views of their North American and Western European counterparts. Democracy, freedom of expression and minority rights are the sacred values. Most would not mind if their daughter wanted to marry a non-Jew but might well be more bothered if she brought home a black-hatted ultra-Orthodox Jew. Though secular Jews firmly hold the reins of political power, there is an almost paranoid belief that they are slipping out of their hands.

Secular Jewry, especially in Jerusalem, feels it is a besieged community, threatened demographically by both the Arab minority and ultra-Orthodox Jewry, both of which have much higher birth rates.

Secular Jewry often complains about the existence of Orthodox religious parties, but the fact is that it is impossible in Israel to separate politics from religion. The left-wing Meretz faction, which together with allies on the left of the Labour Party probably commands the support of a third of Israelis, spearheads the political fight against Orthodox attempts to legislate over the definition of a Jew, over social

### BENDING THE RULES

Where religious rules are concerned it is sometimes hard for outsiders to know where lines are drawn between the acceptable and the unacceptable. Take dietary laws, for example. McDonald's, the multinational hamburger chain, undertook detailed market research before moving into Israel. The result was that bacon McMuffins were non-starters, because pork of any kind is forbidden, but cheeseburgers were introduced successfully, even though kosher laws prohibit the mixing of meat and milk products. But bread is not permissible during Passover, so McDonald's gets round this by serving cheeseburgers in buns made of potato flour instead of wheat.

issues like abortion, or the import of un-kosher meat and pig rearing, or practical matters such as the closing of roads on the Sabbath.

But it would be a mistake to assume by reading the political map from left to right that secular Jewry only commands minority support. There is often a great deal of support on the right for secular causes. Prime Minister Binyamin Netanyahu himself, like most of the Likud leaders, is a staunchly secular figure. His personal lifestyle has never endeared him to his religious bedfellows in his coalition government. He is currently married to his third wife, and his second wife was not Jewish.

Indeed the Tzomet bloc within Likud, led by Rafael Eitan, is known for its anti-clerical leanings, but political expediency has led to an alliance between the essentially anti-religious Likud and religious elements. Likud is reluctant to relinquish the West Bank and Gaza for security and nationalistic reasons, while the religious cherish the biblical concept of the Land of Israel. Moreover, Likud has traditionally relied on support from the Oriental communities, who incline towards tradition.

## Family values

Although many people are surprised by the extent to which Israel's secular majority disregards religious practice, it would be misleading to think that Israelis have no regard at all for religion.

On substantive issues such as marriage and burial, opinion polls consistently show that the majority of Israelis support the Orthodox monopoly of these rites. This has greatly anguished the Reform and Conservative movements, imported to Israel from America, which attempt to adapt Judaism to the modern age, and in particular to integrate women into the synagogue service.

The fact is that secular Israelis have Zionism, which remains an ideology capable of attracting a high level of commitment to the building of the state and is closely linked to conservative family values. And even the most outwardly secular of Jews still tends to have an inner belief in the essential Jewish values – belief in God and a divine plan. This fills the

spiritual vacuum. In the wake of Yitzhak Rabin's assassination young Israelis found these values helped them to cope with their grief over the death of an admired leader.

Like the post-Christian West, post-Jewish Israel suffers from rising crime, violence, drug addiction and inner-city poverty. But, despite a growing divorce rate, family ties remain strong; there is a deep respect for symbols of state, and, on the whole, young people are highly motivated to serve in the army.

Secular Israel is at once both radical and conservative. The long-haired teenager with an earring through his nose, for example, doesn't

usually complain about having a short back and sides and submitting to army discipline at the age of 18. The divisions in Israeli society, though real, are misleading. The assassination of Yitzhak Rabin, a left-of-centre secular Ashkenazi, by Yigal Amir, a right-wing religious Jew from a Yemen-born family, seems to epitomise enmities. But this violent deed was an astounding, exceptional event. When the chips are down Israelis have a surprising capacity for joining ranks.

## Orthodox & Ultra-Orthodox

To a secular Jew the Orthodox and ultra-Orthodox groups have much in common. Both strictly

**LEFT:** a kibbutznik looking at ease with himself.
**RIGHT:** enjoying a beer at a pavement café in Tel Aviv's Sheinkin district.

observe the all-encompassing world of Halacha – Jewish Orthodox practice. This means that the men keep their heads covered and pray at least three times a day. Kosher dietary laws are strictly followed, and the Sabbath is a day for absolute abstention from work, including "lighting a spark": thus making travelling, cooking, switching on a light and even smoking prohibited activities.

The diverse head coverings of the men often indicate degrees of Orthodoxy. Generally, the larger the *kippa* (skull cap) the more Orthodox the wearer. The *kippot* range from the small knitted variety, worn by the modern

Orthodox, to the big black knitted ones of the mainstream Orthodox, and the large black skull caps worn beneath even larger black hats by the ultra-Orthodox.

A woman's clothes are a good indication of the Orthodox Jew's lifestyle. A man with a small knitted *kippa* is likely to be accompanied by a woman wearing "immodest" jeans or other contemporary Western clothing. Women in the large mainstream community will wear long dresses and keep their arms covered, but many no longer wear wigs or head scarves.

Women in the ultra-Orthodox communities are literally kept under wraps. Not a square inch of flesh is seen other than the face and hands. The ultra-Orthodox woman cannot be in an enclosed room with men other than her immediate relatives. At weddings and parties women will sit in a separate area.

Ultra-Orthodox Jewish society comprises a collection of sects as much medieval Eastern European as biblical in their origins. This is why, on Saturdays (Sabbaths) and festivals, the men wear fur hats more suitable for a Russian winter than a Middle Eastern summer.

## Anti-Zionism to ultra-Zionism

Historically all Jews were by definition Orthodox, and three or four centuries ago all of Eastern European Jewry would have followed a moral code similar to that of Me'a Shea'rim today. Growing secularism in 19th-century Christian Europe compelled Jews to find other outlets of cultural expression, and Zionism emerged as a secular movement. Therefore all Orthodox Jews were anti-Zionist to begin with, opposed to the use of Hebrew, the holy tongue, for everyday use and to the notion that a Jewish state could contemplate any degree of separation between synagogue and state.

However, in the 1920s a strong national religious movement emerged, combining the nationalistic values of Zionism with the tenets of Orthodoxy. With its own kibbutzim and workers' movements, it was bolstered by the mass immigration of Oriental Jewry which had deeper ties with Jewish tradition.

Commanding the political support of about 10 percent of the population, the national religious movement, which historically contained strong elements of liberalism, veered sharply to the right after 1967 when the Gush Emunim settlers' movement sprang from it. Holding the

### UNDERCOVER ASSIGNMENT

Female visitors to the ultra-Orthodox quarters of Me'a Shea'rim in Jerusalem and Bnei Brak near Tel Aviv should take seriously the warnings not to wear immodest dress. It isn't just friendly advice, and the dress code is not simply a rather quaint custom; those in violation of the edict may be sworn and spat at and even stoned.

It's one of those occasions when it's wise to put aside one's own feelings about personal choice and resist the desire to cock a snook at a repressive male-dominated community. Respect the rules and cover up as much as you can while you are in these areas. You will also feel more anonymous and find it easier to explore.

Land of Israel to be sacred, the movement has come to be perceived as the fiercest opponent of territorial compromise. The national religious movement runs its own schools, distinct from their secular counterparts.

Ultra-Orthodox Jewry, known in Hebrew as *Haredim*, also has its own education system. These black-clad communities are at best critical of Zionism, at worst still opposed to the Jewish state. Each sect has its own rabbinical leaders, and most of them are based in New York rather than Jerusalem.

The largest and best known *Haredi* sect is the Lubavitchers. Under the late Rabbi Schneerson, who was revered by his followers as a messianic figure, the Lubavitchers took a pro-Israel hawkish stand supporting continuation of Jewish control of the West Bank. The Satmar, on the other hand, which also has its headquarters in New York, refuses to recognise the government of Israel as the legitimate representative of the Jewish people.

An extreme Jerusalem-based sect called Netorei Karta even supported the PLO when its charter called for the destruction of the Jewish state. This sect holds that the Zionists are worse than the Nazis, for while the latter sought to destroy the Jews physically, the former are destroying the Jewish people spiritually.

## Prayer power

All these sects, even those with pro-Zionist leanings, tend to have contempt for the institutions of modern Israel – the flag, the army, the Supreme Court, etc. Few ultra-Orthodox Jews serve in the army, and those who do will often end up in the Rabbinical Corps, checking that kitchens are kosher. Even the right-wing Lubavitchers argue that praying for the strength of Israel is as important as fighting for it.

As a result secular Jewry dislikes ultra-Orthodox Jewry's lack of patriotism, while the ultra-Orthodox hold secular Jews in contempt for their non-religious lifestyle. Orthodox Jewry is often caught in the middle, justifying and condemning both sides.

Despite this lack of common ground, secular Israel exercises a certain degree of tolerance, mainly because the ultra-Orthodox parties hold the balance of power between left and right.

**LEFT:** at Jerusalem's Western (Wailing) Wall.
**RIGHT:** an Orthodox Jew at prayer.

Moreover, many Jews believe that to harass the ultra-Orthodox communities could leave them open to charges of anti-Semitism.

## Oriental Jewry

Religious Jews from Asian and African countries have never fitted neatly into the European pattern of sects, though Israel's European religious establishment did succeed in imposing black hats and suits on many Jews from Yemen and North Africa. But ultimately Sephardi religious leaders like the charismatic former Chief Rabbi Ovadia Yosef, who retains his oriental robes, have prevailed. His Shas political party

controls nearly 10 percent of Knesset seats. Much of Shas's support comes from traditional rather than Orthodox Oriental Jews, indicating that the divide between observant and non-observant Sephardis is narrower than that between their European counterparts.

About 20 percent of Israeli Jews are Orthodox. This number has remained constant over the past decade for, though Orthodox Jewry has a higher birth rate, the overwhelming majority of Jewish immigrants from Russia are secular.

## Russian Jews

"Let My People Go" was the slogan used by campaign activists pushing for the right of

Soviet Jewry to emigrate freely. Nobody believed it would actually happen even in the 1970s, the era of détente, when nearly 400,000 Soviet Jews were allowed out, about half of them reaching Israel, the rest heading for the United States.

But as glasnost gained momentum in the late 1980s, the right to emigrate was suddenly granted to Soviet Jewry during the final months of the decade. For Israel the event was as momentous as the breaching of the Berlin Wall. It was like a dam bursting. During the course of 1990 more than 200,000 Jews reached Israel, while in 1991 the figure was over 170,000.

group. By 1998 more than 800,000 had arrived in the latest wave of immigration, making more than a million Soviet-born Israelis when combined with the émigrés from the 1970s and Soviet veterans from earlier in the century.

The full political and economic potential of Russian-speaking Jewry is yet to be realised. True, it was these new immigrants who, despite their hawkish tendencies, voted in the more dovish Labour Party in 1992 as a protest against Likud neglect of their economic needs. Then, disillusioned by both Labour and Likud, the renowned refusenik Natan Scharansky, who had spent years in Soviet prisons fighting for

After the break-up of the Soviet Union the pace slackened, but still some 60,000 Jews arrived each year from the former Soviet republics.

Not every Russian-speaking Jew wanted to go to Israel. The USA has allowed in about 40,000 annually, while Germany, Canada and other Western countries have taken in tens of thousands more. More than a million Jews remain by choice in the former Soviet Union, keeping their options open and maintaining an anxious eye on political developments.

## Transforming Israel

During the 1990s, Russian-speaking Jews surpassed Moroccans as Israel's largest immigrant

### LANGUAGE OF CHANGE

As a result of the huge waves of Russian immigration since 1990, Israel's urban landscape has taken on a decidedly Slavic feel. Cyrillic shop signs abound, vying for space with Hebrew, English and Arabic lettering. Newsstands are bursting with Russian-language publications, and in some suburbs of Tel Aviv and Haifa, Russian is the lingua franca. Russian-speakers have their own state-run radio station, and cable TV brings them all the major television channels from Russia.

The newcomers are learning Hebrew as they become assimilated, but in the meantime it is interesting to see the impact of yet another language in this polyglot nation.

the right to emigrate, set up his own immigrant party, Yisrael Ve'Aliyah, and gained an impressive seven seats (6 percent of the vote) in the 1996 Knesset elections. Scharansky joined Prime Minister Binyamin Netanyahu's right-wing government, where he haggled over the negotiations, in his own language, with Yvette Liberman, the Russian-born director of Netanyahu's office.

Initially there were fears that the newcomers would cause crowding in the professions, because, generally speaking, the latest wave of Russian immigrants has a high educational profile. Many are scientists and engineers, musicians and teachers. Even before this latest wave of immigration started, Israel had the world's highest per capita proportion of doctors. With 15,000 more doctors among the newcomers, many could not at first qualify for medical licences or find work in their professions, but they have proved to be very flexible and willing to undergo re-training where necessary.

Understandably it took a little while for some of the Russian-speaking newcomers to master Hebrew and became accustomed to the more assertive behaviour of Western society, but most have adjusted well. There is usually a period of about a year spent sweeping the streets, washing dishes or doing some other kind of menial work before an immigrant manages to find a job in his or her own profession.

These new immigrants have changed the demographic balance of Israel. Before their arrival, Israel had a small Oriental Jewish majority. Russian Jewry has tipped the scales back in favour of Ashkenazi Jewry, although some 10 percent of these newcomers are Oriental Jews from the ancient Persian-speaking communities in Georgia, Azerbaijan and the Russian Caucasus as well as Uzbekistan.

## Kosher and un-kosher

In the main, Russian-speaking newcomers are Ashkenazi and secular, but between 30 and 50 percent of newcomers are not Halachically Jewish. This means that they qualify for Jewish citizenship by virtue of having one Jewish grandparent (as stipulated in the Law of Return

**LEFT:** Russian immigrants arrive at Lod Airport in the early 1960s.
**RIGHT:** Russian-language newspapers are now widely available in Israel.

of 1950) but do not meet the Orthodox Jewish requirement of having a Jewish mother.

Even those who do have often had little opportunity to learn about their Jewish heritage while growing up under the Soviet regime. Israel was already a highly secular society before the newcomers arrived, and once they have been assimilated, the Russian immigrants may push for more secular legislation, disturbing the already delicate religious–secular status quo. At present a large number of Russian- speaking newcomers cannot be buried in Jewish cemeteries or have Jewish marriage ceremonies.

Most of these newcomers are not Zionists. The immigrants of the 1970s risked imprisonment in order to leave for Israel. The majority of those who came in 1990 and 1991 had a profound sense of Jewish identity; they put out their wings and migrated at the first opportunity. But recent arrivals have a less clear agenda, although many are seeking a more secure economic life amid the greater opportunities of Israel.

The latest wave of immigrants represents over 20 percent of the Jewish population. Undoubtedly they and their children will assimilate Zionist norms of allegiance to the state, service in the army, and fluency in Hebrew. In parallel, they will contribute some of their old culture to their new home, and the influence of their secularism is likely to move Israel even further away from traditional Judaism.

## Ethiopians

The dramatic airlifts of Ethiopian Jews from the heart of Africa to the Promised Land in 1984 and 1991 captured the world's imagination. For centuries Ethiopian Jews had cherished the dream that one day they would return to Jerusalem. The dream finally came true, but the reality has been somewhat different from their expectations.

## Alienation

The sense of alienation felt by many Ethiopians has been exacerbated by the reluctance of Israel's rabbinical authorities to recognise the unequivocal Jewishness of the Ethiopians. Thus they are required to undergo symbolic conversion to Judaism by being immersed in a ritual bath. In addition the *kessim* are not permitted to officiate at marriages.

The younger generation (half the community is under 18) have been adept at assimilating Israeli values. The vigour with which they have protested their grievances through demonstrations, the media and political lobbying bodes

Before arriving in Israel, most Ethiopian Jews had been semi-literate subsistence farmers living in simple villages, usually without electricity or any modern conveniences. Being thrust into a fast-moving, high-tech society has been traumatic, especially for those people who were over 30 when they arrived. For the young, change is always easier.

Some of Israel's 70,000-strong Ethiopian Jewish community have done well. Adisu Massala, for example, was elected to the Knesset in 1996 as a Labour Party delegate, and Belaynesh Zevadiah became Israel's vice-consul in Chicago. Both men were children of the *kessim*, the community's religious leaders.

well for the future. For its part, the Israeli establishment has allocated major resources for the education of the young generation and has introduced positive discrimination measures, such as more generous mortgages than those available to other new immigrants.

While racism against the Ethiopians is rare (the most anti-Ethiopian racist sector in Israeli society is probably found among the new immigrants from Russia), the community sometimes suffers in rather odd ways. For example, the Health Ministry decided that Ethiopians were not suitable blood donors because of a higher incidence of Aids, tuberculosis and other diseases. Instead of the decision being announced publicly, a secret memo was sent to donation staff asking them to accept Ethiopian blood and then throw it away. The discovery of the policy provoked a storm of protest. An enquiry found that the policy was justified on health and safety grounds but that its underhand method of implementation was inappropriate.

## Dramatic rescue

The Ethiopians began reaching Israel via Sudan in the early 1980s, and Operation Moses in 1984 saw 7,000 people airlifted to Israel. Most of them had trekked hundreds of miles across the desert to the Sudanese border, and many

of Africa. Those who reached Israel in the early 1980s came primarily from Tigre, while the subsequent wave originated principally from Gondar. Although the two groups use the same Amharic alphabet they speak different Ethiopic languages.

After initially refusing to bring to Israel the Falash Mura, Ethiopian Christians who had converted from Judaism in the 19th century, the government airlifted some 5,000 to Israel during 1996–97. In addition, several thousand Ethiopian Jews who remain in the remote northern province of Qara are likely to emigrate to Israel in the coming years.    ❑

others had died en route. Even more dramatically, during a single 24-hour period in 1991 14,000 Ethiopians were flown to Israel as part of Operation Solomon. These people had been gathering in Addis Ababa over the course of a year but had been prevented from leaving by the Marxist regime. The Israeli Air Force succeeded in rescuing them just as the regime was toppled by rebels.

The history and geographical dispersion of Ethiopian Jewry is somewhat unclear, but in modern times most were located in two regions

**LEFT:** an Ethiopian soldier guards a tomb at Hebron.
**ABOVE:** Ethiopian women selling their crafts.

### THE LOST TRIBES RETURN

The origins of the Ethiopian Jews are shrouded in mystery. Known in Ethiopia as *falashas* (invaders), they are believed by some scholars to be remnants of Dan, one of the Ten Lost Tribes. Some claim they are descendants of King Solomon and the Queen of Sheba. Cut off from world Jewry for two millennia, the community has sustained remarkably similar traditions. There are distinctions, though; for example, the Ethiopians took with them into exile the Five Books of Moses and the stories of the Prophets, but have no knowledge of the Oral Law, which was codified only after the fall of the Second Temple in AD 70.

# ISRAELI ARABS

*Israel's Arabs occupy an anomalous position, yet most live harmoniously with their Jewish neighbours while retaining cultural ties to the Arab world*

**N**ot all the Arab inhabitants of Palestine heeded the call of the surrounding states (and "promptings" from the nascent Israeli army) to flee their homes when the State of Israel was established, despite the promise that they would be able to return within weeks once the Jewish state had been snuffed out by the invading armies.

About 150,000 remained, and numbers have since grown to their present 1 million. Half of Israel's Arab population is urbanised in the towns and villages of the Galilee. There are large Arab communities in Nazareth, Haifa, Ramla, Yafo and Jerusalem.

Israeli Arabs – 77 percent are Muslim, 13 percent Christian and 10 percent Druze and Bedouin – are faced with the paradox of being at once Arab, with linguistic, historic, cultural, religious and familial ties to the Arab world, and also citizens of a state which, since its inception, has been in conflict with that world. And yet Israel's Arabs have managed to walk the tightrope.

The only legal discrimination against the Arab population is that they are not liable to military conscription – although they may volunteer – because it is thought to be unreasonable to ask them to fight against their co-religionists and kinsmen. Only the small Druze community is subject to the draft – and that is at its own request.

But exemption from military service has proved to be a double-edged sword. The army is the great equaliser, the shared national experience, the common thread that unites Israelis from wildly differing backgrounds. Exclusion from it inevitably involves social handicaps. In a more tangible form, it renders Israeli Arabs ineligible for certain jobs and state benefits.

In spite of this and other disabilities, the Arabs of Israel have flourished, making great strides in health, education, and generally improved living standards.

**LEFT:** a dignified Druze village elder.
**RIGHT:** waiting for customers by the Jaffa Gate.

One indicator of the process of change is education. Arab illiteracy has plunged from 95 percent in 1948 to just 5 percent today. While in 1948 only 32.5 percent attended grade school, now all have five to eight years of education, and more than 50 percent nine to 12 years, reflecting the growing numbers of Arabs

enrolling in Israeli institutes of higher learning.

Most Israeli Arab parents choose to send their children to Arabic-language schools, which combine instruction in Arab history and culture with that of the Jews.

Today around 8,000 Arabs are studying at Israeli universities. Others travel abroad to study; but, unlike the Arabs from the West Bank and Gaza, they cannot go to the Arab world because they carry Israeli passports.

The impact of education and of involvement with Israel's vigorously open and democratic society have been profound. These days most young Arabs live with their own Western-style nuclear families and are economically independent of their elders. There is still, to be sure, strong attachment to traditional values and customs, but these are tinged with a clear preference for the comforts of the affluent West.

Israeli laws granting women equal rights have helped to liberalise attitudes towards women in Arab society. The changing aspirations of women (and of their husbands) are reflected in the birthrate – down from an average of 8.5 children per family in 1968 to 4.8 in the late 1990s, although it is not expected to fall to the Jewish average, which is 3.2 children per family.

For all that, there is a strong trend towards present there are eight Arab members of the Knesset out of a total of 120, representing a broad spectrum of opinion.

## The Druze community

Although some of the first clashes between the Jewish pioneers in the l880s and the local residents were with Druze villagers in Metula and other parts of the Galilee, Israel's Druze community has traditionally been loyal to the Israeli state. Young Druze are conscripted into the Israel Defence Forces (at the community's own request), and many serve in the regular army in the paratroops, armoured corps and recon-

the polarisation of Jewish and Arab Israelis, despite the programmes to foster understanding among youngsters which are arranged by Israel's Education Ministry.

A spiral of radicalism is not inevitable. A new breed of young Arab mayors and leaders – educated in Israel and at ease with the Israeli system – is emerging at a grass-roots level. They are demanding that facilities in their areas be brought up to the standard of those of their Jewish neighbours, and their style demonstrates a self-confidence that is at once proudly Arab and unequivocally Israeli.

The increasing Arab clout in the political arena is another significant development. At

### TRADITIONAL CRAFTS

Traditionally the Druze were successful hill farmers, but with the development of modern agriculture this activity has declined. However, their traditional weaving, carpet-making, basketwork and other crafts are still flourishing. There are a number of Druze villages with interesting markets selling handicrafts. Daliyat el-Karmel, south of Haifa, is an attractive village, a popular spot for tourists; and the Golan Heights villages of Majdal e-Shams and Mas'ada also specialise in local craftwork. But handicrafts don't keep an entire community employed, and most young Druze these days find work in either industry or the flourishing service sector.

naisance units, and border police. Traditionally a warlike people, always ready to defend their interests, they have proved to be first-class soldiers, and large numbers of Druze have been decorated for bravery.

In the Lebanon War of 1982–84, Israel's Druze found themselves in a delicate position when the IDF was aligned with Christian forces in Lebanon fighting the Lebanese Druze. It is a tribute to the strength of the friendship between the Jews and the Druze that their alliance survived this period.

The Druze have been a persecuted minority in the Middle East since they broke away from mainstream Islam in the 11th century, accepting the claims to divinity of the Egyptian Caliph El-Hakim Abu Ali el-Mansur. For this reason they have always tended to inhabit inaccessible mountain ranges, where they could defend themselves against their enemies. Most Druze today live in the Mount Lebanon region of Lebanon and in Jebel Druze in Syria; some 70,000 of them are in the hills of the Galilee and on the Carmel Range in Israel, with a further 15,000 in the Golan Heights. There are records of Druze communities in the Galilee as early as the 13th century, but the first Mount Carmel settlement was established in 1590 when Syrian Druze fled their homes after an abortive revolt against the Turkish sultan.

Druze villages are not very different from Arab villages in the Galilee and the coastal plain, although the elders do not wear black headbands with their *keffiye* head-dresses. The older Druze tend to cultivate impressive moustaches. The women dress in modern clothes, the younger ones in jeans and short-sleeved blouses. The young men are indistinguishable from Israeli Jews, and indeed many of them affect Hebrew names, such as Rafi or Ilan.

There are conflicting tendencies to assimilate into the Jewish society, or to convert to Islam and assimilate into the local Arab community, but these are definitely minority movements, and most Druze are proud of their own identity and culture and do not inter-marry with other communities.

Some Israeli Druze live in mixed villages, notably Pekiin in Galilee, where they coexist with their Christian Arab neighbours and some Jewish families, who have lived there since Second Temple times.

The Druze were recognised as a separate religious community with their own courts in 1957. Their religion is said to be similar to that of the Isma'ili Muslims. The sheikhs, the religious leaders of the community, guard its secrets, and the ordinary Druze are simply required to observe the basic moral laws prohibiting murder, adultery, and theft.

They have their own interpretations of Jewish, Muslim and Christian prophets, believing that their missions were revealed to a select group, the first of whom was Jethro, the father-in-law

of Moses. One of the Druze religious festivals is an annual pilgrimage to what is believed to be the grave of Jethro, near the Horns of Hittim in Galilee.

Serving alongside the Druze in the minorities unit of the IDF are the Circassians – about 3,000 of whom live in Israel. They are a Caucasian mountain people, originating in Russia; most of them are blond, and have blue or green eyes. Although many of the Russian Circassians are professing Christians, the Middle East branch of this people are Muslims. Almost all the Israeli Circassians live in the village of Kfar Kama, overlooking Lake Kinneret in Galilee, and in Rehaniya, just north of Safed.

**LEFT:** a Druze funeral procession.
**RIGHT:** a shopkeeper in a Galilean village.

## The Bedouin

The Bedouin is the quintessential Arab, the nomad herdsman, dressed in flowing robes, riding his camel across the sands, pitching his tent under the palms before riding on to his next camping site. Like many romantic images, this one, which was fostered by old Hollywood films, is false – or at least somewhat out of date.

Some 20 percent of Israel's 70,000 Bedouin people live in the Galilee and the coastal plain, in settled villages which are

### USING DESERT SKILLS

Bedouin are not conscripted into the Israel Defence Forces, but many of them serve in the army as scouts and trackers, utilising their traditional skills, and several have reached senior rank.

dams which they have built themselves, as well as former Nabatean structures, which they have carefully restored. They also utilise ancient water cisterns which they have excavated and, of course, make use of existing wells.

Scores of Bedouin fled from the Negev from 1947 to 1949, around the time of Israel's War of Independence, but later returned. The situation was stabilised in 1953 when a census was conducted, with all those present at the time being accepted as citizens of Israel.

Formerly wandering freely between Transjordan, the Judean Desert, the Negev and Sinai, the Bedouin were forced to recognise the new international realities in the early 1950s. Israel's Bedouin are now confined to an area east of Be'er Sheva extending north as far as the former border with Jordan, and south as far as Dimona. This is only around 10 percent of the area over which they once wandered, but includes some excellent farming land. Today, there is no tribe that does not farm as well as herd its flocks.

The traditional life of the Bedouin shepherds which involved moving the herds from pasture to pasture, is a thing of the past, and their camps have long been permanent in the Negev. Their nomadic tradition, and their tendency to live with their dwellings spread out all over the desert, have made it difficult to plan modern villages for them.

Today most of the major tribal centres have their own elementary schools, and there is now a modern high school at Kuseifa near Arad. Bedouin take education seriously, walking more than 16 km (10 miles) to school where necessary. It is a common sight, when driving from Be'er Sheva to Arad or Dimona, to see a Bedouin boy walking through the desert, his nose buried in the pages of a book, or sitting on a rock, writing in a notebook.

Bedouin arts and crafts still exist, with a flourishing home industry, based on weaving, sewing and embroidery. These wares are on sale in many places, notably in the Be'er Sheva market which is held every Thursday, and is a popular tourist attraction. ❏

virtually indistinguishable, to an outsider's eye, from other Arab villages. Traditions are stronger in the Negev, and you may still be invited for coffee, reclining on cushions and rugs of black goat's hair, but few Bedouin still live in the traditional manner. Some do still live in tents, and quite a few possess camels and herd sheep and goats, but increasing numbers are moving into permanent housing and finding work in construction, industry, the service sector and transportation.

The Bedouin farm the loess soil extensively, growing mostly barley and wheat but also cucumbers, tomatoes, peppers, watermelons, almonds, figs and vines. For irrigation they use

**LEFT:** a Bedouin stall in Be'er Sheva market.
**RIGHT:** tending the fire in a traditional tent.

# THE CHRISTIANS

*A plethora of denominations flourishes among Israel's Christians,*
*the majority of whom are Arabs*

Nowhere in the world is the observant traveller more aware of the rich and fascinating diversity of Christianity than in the Holy Land. On a morning's stroll through the Old City of Jerusalem you might encounter Greek Orthodox or Syrian Orthodox monks, Ethiopian and Coptic clergymen, Armenian priests, Catholic priests and, without knowing it, clerics and scholars from virtually every Protestant church in Christendom.

There is no mystery to the extraordinary variety of Christian congregations in the Holy Land. From the time of the Byzantines (324–636) through the era of the Crusader kingdoms (1099–1291) and 400 years of Ottoman rule (1517–1917) until today, churches sought to establish – then struggled to retain – a presence in the land where their faith was born.

The result is a plethora of denominations served by some 2,500 clergy from almost every nation on earth. The Greek Orthodox, Roman Catholics, Syrian Catholics, Russian Orthodox, Maronites, Chaldean Catholics, Armenian Catholics, Greek Catholics, Armenian Orthodox, Syrian Orthodox (Jacobites), Copts and Ethiopian Orthodox have all secured claims, sometimes competing ones, to holy sites.

The "younger" churches – such as the Anglicans, the Church of Scotland, the Pentecostals, the Church of Christ, the Baptists, the Brethren and the Mennonites – also maintain institutions and congregations, as do the Seventh Day Adventists and the Jehovah's Witnesses.

## Guaranteed freedoms

The founding of Israel provoked unease among Christians, who were uncertain what to expect from the new state and were deeply suspicious of Jewish intentions (the Vatican only recognised Israel in 1994). But Israel's Declaration of Independence spelt out the state's attitude to the diverse faiths within its borders, pledging to "guarantee the freedom of religion, conscience,

education and culture [and] safeguard the holy places of all religions".

The Six Day War of 1967, which left Israeli forces in control of the old city of Jerusalem, revived religious misgivings. Yet the Israeli government has been scrupulous in its attitude towards the rights and prerogatives of the

churches, adhering to the intricate balance created by the Ottoman rulers and British Mandatory authority in apportioning responsibility for the holy places. As a result, relations have been good – or at least correct – between the Jewish state and the churches. Indeed at times the Israeli government has found itself a reluctant referee of intra-Christian rivalries.

A recent phenomenon that is having an impact on the face of the Holy Land and Christian–Jewish relations is the world-wide growth of Christian Zionism, which regards the birth of the State of Israel as a fulfilment of biblical prophecy. Over the past decades, theological and ecumenical institutions have mushroomed

**LEFT:** Russian Orthodox Easter service.
**RIGHT:** a Greek Orthodox priest in Bethlehem.

to cater to this movement and enable young Christians to study in Israel.

The "Christian Embassy" in Jerusalem – the focus of much Christian-Zionist activity – has intrigued many Israelis. But it has dismayed others, who fear that the intention of its proclamations of friendship is the conversion of Jews. This suspicion was given expression in vociferous opposition to a Mormon project on 1.6 hectares (4 acres) of land overlooking the Old City. Permission was eventually granted, although many

### CROSSING THE DIVIDE

The chairman of the Philosophy Department at the Hebrew University is a much-respected Catholic: Father Marcel Dubois, a Dominican monk.

feared it would open the door to various other groups, including the Apostolic Church of Switzerland, and the Hope of Israel Church in California, who are keen to establish bases in the Holy Land.

But the work of Christian–Jewish reconciliation is not the sole preserve of the new churches. The Roman Catholic order of the Sisters of Zion, established in Jerusalem in 1855 by French Jewish converts, has been working towards such understanding for many years.

Every year, some 250,000 pilgrims visit the order's Ecce Homo Convent next to the Second Station of the Cross on the Via Dolorosa, and many stay to hear the sisters speak of Jesus the Jew and of Judaism as the wellspring of their faith. The sisters hold language classes for Jews and Arabs, and have set up a department of adult education at the Hebrew University. The German Mary Sisters also have a presence in Jerusalem and are in the forefront of the reconciliation movement.

### Arabic language

The grassroots language of Christianity in Israel is Arabic. The great majority of Israel's 100,000 Christians (including the 13,700 Christians of East Jerusalem) are Arabs, and their clergy are either Arabs or Arabic-speaking.

The allegiances of Christian Arabs in Israel clearly favour the established Patriarchates: there are 35,000 Greek Catholics, 32,000 Greek Orthodox, and 20,000 Roman Catholics. There are small communities of Anglicans and Lutherans (both churches are stronger on the West Bank than in Israel itself), and despite over 100 years of missionary work by more than 50 organisations, there are less than 1,000 local Arab adherents of Evangelical churches. There are also about 2,000 Messianic Jews, mostly immigrants from Eastern Europe.

The Roman Catholic Church has established indigenous orders, including the Rosary Sisters and the Sisters of St Joseph, and at its seminary trains Arab priests from both Israel and Jordan.

Arab Christians, while growing in numbers and flourishing economically – particularly those living in areas that attract Christian tourism – have been hesitant about asserting themselves politically to press issues of specifically Christian concern. As a group, the Christian community displays many of the characteristics of a marginal minority: trying to maintain a balance between its Christian identity, Arab nationalism and delicate relations with Muslim neighbours – all within the context of a Jewish society.

Nonetheless, an Anglican Arab clergyman is prominent in the Arab-Jewish Progressive List for Peace, a political party which supports the establishment of a Palestinian state on the West Bank. Israel's Greek Orthodox community, on the other hand, traditionally supports the oddest political bedfellow: the Communist Party. ❑

**LEFT:** the Church of All Nations.

# Guest workers

Israel attracts several million tourists each year. But above and beyond the short-term visitors, whether they are pilgrims drawn by the holy sites, or sun-worshippers attracted to the country's beaches, Israel also has a large number of longer-term guests.

These include youngsters from around the world wishing to experience Israel in a more profound way on a longer stay, either as a kibbutz volunteer or on an archaeological dig, or perhaps studying in a religious institution. Back-packers travelling around the world often stay longer than planned, attracted by the informality and vitality of Israel and the fact that casual work is easy to find and there is no shortage of cheap, youth-hostel-type accommodation.

In fact, the availability of unskilled employment in Israel has attracted workers from around the world. There are an estimated 200,000 foreign workers in the country, about half of whom are on legal contracts. This category includes Romanian construction workers, Thai agricultural labourers and Filipino domestic servants. (Somewhat ironically, there are more than 200,000 unemployed Israelis.) In addition there are around 100,000 illegal workers, mainly from Nigeria and Ghana, the majority of whom live in Tel Aviv where they work as house cleaners and factory hands.

These overseas workers took the place of the many Palestinians who worked in Israel until the outbreak of the Intifada. Frequent strikes by the Palestinians, and Israeli army border closures due to terrorist attacks, meant that employers could no longer rely on their Palestinian workforce and had to seek alternative sources of labour from overseas. But although increasing numbers of Palestinians have returned to work since 1996, the number of guest workers remains constant.

The abundance of foreign workers in Israel contradicts the Zionist tenet of a Jewish state based on Jewish labour. Many Israelis decry the situation from an intellectual standpoint, but nonetheless are happy for someone else to do the menial work. Like most middle-class parents in the Western world, they would rather their own children became managers and professionals than blue-collar or manual workers.

**RIGHT:** the thriving construction industry depends upon guest workers.

While legal Romanian and Thai workers tend to be males on contract, sending money home to their families, the West Africans are often in Israel en famille, creating a guest-worker-style situation similar to that in parts of Western Europe. There are so many West African workers in the area around the old bus station in Tel Aviv that it is sometimes known as "Little Lagos". These workers tend to maintain a low profile, fearing expulsion, but their children are a lot less passive. Some local authorities accept the children into schools, others don't.

Israel's newspapers regularly carry articles on the subject, some urging mass expulsions of the guest workers, others promoting the granting of

legal residency status to those who apply. Some denounce the dilution of the state's Jewish character, others applaud an enriching cosmopolitan element. Despite these conflicting opinions, the fact remains that while the foreign workers continue to comprise an important cog in the Israeli economic wheel, the status quo is likely to prevail.

Ultimately, politics as much as economics will dictate the outcome. If Arab terrorism is quelled, then the Israeli government will once again give preference to Palestinians seeking employment in Israel. In such an instance Israel's guest workers, whether legal or illegal, may suddenly find themselves out of a job and unwelcome in a land that many have come to look on as home. ❑

# RELIGIOUS VARIETY

*Israel is the Holy Land to followers of three major religions.*

*But it is also a focus for members of many alternative sects*

The sheer intensity of the religious ardour in this small country is overwhelming: in Jerusalem's Old City, Jews at the Western Wall, Muslims at the Dome of the Rock and Christians at the Church of the Holy Sepulchre may well be saying their prayers simultaneously, to say nothing of the myriad other synagogues, churches and mosques in the Old City alone. Similarly, the diversity of religious experience here is in a category all its own. Hassidim wearing 18th-century *kapotas* and *shteimels* (coats and hats) rub shoulders with robed monks and nuns from every Christian denomination, East and West, while Muslim *imams* in *tarboosh* and *galabiyah* mingle with secular Israelis and pilgrims to the Holy Land.

Many of the holiest biblical sites have acquired synagogues, churches and mosques over the centuries, and even today visitors of one faith may well find themselves paying respects to a chapter of their own history in the house of worship of another.

## The Jewish presence

Jewish spiritual life revolves around the home, house of study (*cheder* for youngsters, *yeshiva* for adolescents and adults) and synagogue – of which the latter is the most accessible to the visitor. Jerusalem's 500 synagogues range from the humblest *shtible* and Sephardi community synagogue to the gargantuan Belzer Center (which seats 3,500) and the Great Synagogue in King George Street. Other large synagogues include the Central, Yeshurun and Italian.

The Orthodox pray three times a day, but it is at weekends and festivals that the liturgy is at its most elaborate. The modest Hassidic premises are compensated for by the fervour of the prayers. Such groups exist in Safed and Bnei Brak, and in Jerusalem's Me'a Shea'rim and Ge'ula districts. Among the warmest and most approachable of the Hassidic groups is

**LEFT:** a Torah scroll and its keeper.
**RIGHT:** a rabbi officiates at a bar mitzvah at the Western Wall.

the Bratslav, whose Me'a Shea'rim premises contain the renovated chair of their first and only *rebbe* Rabbi Nahman. He was famous for his stories and sayings. "The world is a narrow bridge; the main thing is not to be afraid at all" is one that Israelis have taken to heart.

At the other end of Me'a Shea'rim is Karlin,

whose devotees screech their prayers – unlike their Ge'ula neighbours, Ger, whose tightly-knit organisation is reflected in their operatic music and self-discipline: "A true Ger Hassid," says one believer, "never looks at his wife." A similar outlook is espoused by Toledot Aharon, whose purity of purpose is matched by its animosity towards political Zionism, which it views as usurping the divine process of redemption. In this it follows the line of Neturei Karta (Guardians of the City), which has its own government-in-exile and campaigns for political autonomy. Both groups oppose the Conservative and Reform Movements, which have their own centres and desegregated houses of prayer in Jerusalem (on Agron and King David streets, respectively).

## The cycle of the Jewish year

The framework of Jewish piety is determined by the lunar cycle beginning around September and October with Rosh Hashana (the New Year) and Yom Kippur, the Day of Atonement – a rigorous 25-hour fast. Synagogues are packed; services are long but moving. If you're Jewish, and whether you hail from Minsk, Marrakesh or Manhattan, you're sure to find at least one service meeting your liturgical needs. An unusual and controversial custom precedes

December, when nine-branched candelabra shine in most homes in celebration of the Maccabean victory over the Greeks some 2,300 years ago. The fate of Haman, who tried to kill the Jews during the Babylonian captivity, is recorded in the Scroll of Esther and read on Purim (a cheerful, noisy festival held in March). In spring, everyone spring-cleans for Passover, the annual feast celebrating the Exodus from Egypt. Seven weeks later comes Shavuot, the Feast of Weeks, when thousands congregate at the Western Wall for dawn prayers, having spent the night studying the holy book, the Torah. Between Passover and

Yom Kippur: Kaparot, which entails swinging a white chicken above the head of the penitent, after which the slaughtered fowl is sold or given to charity. This ceremony can be witnessed in most open market places.

Succot, the Festival of Rejoicing, combines harvest gathering and prayers for winter rains and is celebrated on secular kibbutzim as well as by the Orthodox. Celebrants live in temporary huts for seven days. During the evenings, the pious let down their sidelocks to dance, somersault and juggle to intoxicating music. Some Hassidic sects cap off the ceremonies with a children's candlelit procession.

More lights burn during Hanukkah, in

### CONTEMPORARY ORTHODOXY

Orthodoxy has become fashionable, and in the past two decades, waves of "returnees" have passed through special *yeshivot* ceremonies for the uninitiated, and have eventually been able to weave themselves into the fabric of local religious life. Their devotion takes expression in a variety of ways: there are those Jews who integrate their Western careers or professions with a pious daily routine, and at the other end of the scale there are such phenomena as the popular Selah Torah Rock Band, which is now located at the Israel Center on Jerusalem's Strauss Street, and which blends Jewish and Western musical styles with consummate ease.

Shavuot the Orthodox invest Independence Day and Jerusalem Unity Day with spiritual significance, creating new festivals. The cycle reaches full circle in summer with the three-week period of mourning for the Temples, culminating in a day-long fast on Tisha B'Av.

## New Messiahs

There is a growing presence in Israel of Evangelicals, whose belief in the redemption has made them enthusiastic supporters of Zionism. In the mid-1990s Jerusalem's Christian Embassy on Brenner Street attracted over 5,000 people from 40 countries to participate in its Christian version of the Feast of the Tabernacles. Another sort of backing comes from Nes Ammim, a semi-collective village near Akko where Christians of various denominations work the land.

Most of the traditional Christian communities in Israel, numbering roughly 120,000 people, devote themselves to lives of prayer and meditation, preserving the presence of their church in the Holy Land and watching over traditional New Testament shrines. With the West Bank in its control, Israel holds practically all the "Holy Land", and the devoted visitor can follow in the footsteps of Jesus from his birth in Bethlehem and his early life at Nazareth, to his Crucifixion at Golgotha, in Jerusalem.

Christian groups celebrate some 240 feasts and holy days a year, using two separate calendars, the Julian and the Gregorian. This provides three dates for Christmas: 25 December for Western Christians, 7 January for Greek and Russian Orthodox, Syrians and Copts, and 19 January for the Armenians, and two sets of Holy Weeks. Only genuine pilgrims are allowed into Bethlehem for Christmas, where the main events take place at the Church of the Nativity.

This also applies to Easter Week, when there is a re-enactment of Jesus's last days: walks from the Mount of Olives, complete with palm branches, and along the Via Dolorosa to the Church of the Holy Sepulchre. Here, two ceremonies take place: the Washing of the Feet on Maundy Thursday, and the Kindling of the Holy Fire by the Orthodox and Eastern Churches on Holy Saturday. The carrying of the cross on Good Friday between the Praetorium and Calvary (Golgotha), along the Via Dolorosa, is repeated weekly by the oldest resident group of priests, the Franciscans. One of the most revered Christian sites is Yardenit, the place of Jesus's baptism on the River Jordan. There is also a rival "Site of the Baptism" further south near Jericho.

## Dialogue of hope

The existence of modern Israel has brought together Christian, Muslim and Jew in a rare opportunity for inter-faith dialogue. Such encounters provide a means of transcending the most intransigent problems. As Dr Abu Ghosh

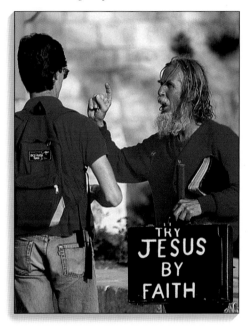

of Israel's Sharya Muslim Court says: "Islam is extraneous to the present political strife. Islam, Christianity and Judaism can live peacefully side by side, as is the case in Israel."

The French Dominican priest Marcel Dubois, chairman of the Hebrew University's Philosophy Department, believes "we are witnessing a Christian rediscovery of the continuity in the design of God". Posted to East Jerusalem in 1962, Dubois became an Israeli citizen on Christmas Day, 1974. In his position, he is perfectly aware of the many tensions that exist around him, but speaks for more than just himself when he observes that "Jerusalem is the capital of contradictions". ❑

**LEFT:** Bethlehem's Milk Grotto. **RIGHT:** a latter-day prophet hammers home his message.

# THE PALESTINIANS

*Nobody pretends that the Israelis and the Palestinians will ever be best friends,*
*but on both sides there is a genuine desire to end the conflict*

The birth of the Palestinian national movement was a reaction to Zionism. As Jews began buying up Arab land at the turn of the century, so the indigenous Arab population was compelled to question its own identity. Historically that identity had revolved around the extended family, the village, the Arab people and Islam. But in the modern world of emerging nations such an identity was either too parochial or too broad.

Just as many people – Jews and non-Jews – originally opposed the notion that the Jewish people constituted a nation, so the Palestinians found their legitimacy under fire from both friends and foes. Arabs within Palestine and outside it spoke of pan-Arabism and of one Arab nation encompassing North Africa and Asia Minor. Often such talk cloaked the expansionist ambitions of Syria, Jordan and Egypt.

## Irreconcilable aims

For the Jews, of course, the Palestinian national movement which denied the right of a Jewish state to exist could never be reconciled with Zionist aspirations. Moderate Palestinian leaders, as well as the Hashemite kings (King Abdullah and his grandson, King Hussein), who were amenable to coexistence with the Jews were unable to counter the militant rejectionism of Syria and Egypt and of local leaders such as Sheikh Haj Amin Husseini.

The tragedy of the Palestinian people was the inability of its leadership to accept the fait accompli of a Jewish state. Arab anger is understandable, because European anti-Semitism, which drove Jews back to the Middle East, resulted in the loss of Palestinian land. But attempts to "drive the Jews into the sea" in 1948 and 1967 and the expulsion of over a million Jews from Arab countries saw Israel strengthened territorially and demographically.

The founding of the PLO in 1964 proved to be a crucial stage in the evolution of the Palestin-

ian national entity. Even so, Yasser Arafat, its leader since 1965, found himself imprisoned in Damascus. The fact is that since the Muslim conquest Palestine had been ruled from Damascus, and the region had become known as Lower Syria. Thus the modern Syrians saw Palestine – and for that matter Lebanon and

Jordan – as an integral part of the modern Syrian nation.

The Six Day War of 1967, and the further expansion of Israel, saw the PLO come into its own. It was now in Syria's interest to encourage Arafat to regain Arab lands. Before 1967 the West Bank was in Jordanian hands, while Gaza was under Egyptian rule. But if the PLO and its many factions, each owing allegiance to a different Arab leader, were puppets designed to restore Arab sovereignty over as much of Israel as possible, Arafat – and most especially the Palestinians of the West Bank and Gaza – proved to be more independently minded than either Israel or the Arab world had anticipated.

**LEFT:** a proud Palestinian profile.
**RIGHT:** deep in conversation.

## Occupation and acrimony

Israel, after its occupation of the West Bank and Gaza in 1967, enjoyed good relations with its newly-conquered Palestinian subjects. Many of the Arabs of the West Bank and Gaza, for their part, were initially beguiled by Israeli liberalism and other Western ways. A free press was set up, universities were established, elections were held for the local municipalities, and the economy flourished. It must be said that one reason it flourished was through the menial work done cheaply by Palestinians in Israel.

Israel presumed that the Arabs of the West Bank and Gaza would prove as malleable as

Palestinian notables in the West Bank and Gaza also felt alienated from the PLO leadership. Arafat, who built his own organisational hierarchy first in Jordan, then in Lebanon and finally in Tunis, was often viewed as a wealthy Diaspora leader who represented the millions of Palestinians living in Jordan, Syria, Lebanon, Egypt, the Gulf and elsewhere in the world, but was out of touch with the Palestinians on the front line of Israeli occupation.

## The effects of the Intifada

PLO tactics in the 1970s and 1980s were a mixture of terrorism and diplomacy. Terrorist

those who had stayed behind in 1948 and taken up Israeli citizenship. But Israeli Arabs were mainly village people, while those of Gaza and the West Bank had a large urban intelligentsia who identified strongly with the Palestinian nationalism espoused by Arafat and the PLO.

When given the right to assume Israeli citizenship, the 150,000 Arabs of East Jerusalem refused the offer to a man. It took the Israelis, even those on the left, many years to appreciate that Palestinian nationalism was not going to go away, just as many progressive Palestinians continued for many years to think that Zionism was a passing phenomenon.

But while rejecting Israeli hegemony, the

attacks against civilians in Israel and around the world forced the Palestinian question onto the international agenda. Moreover, Arafat forged powerful alliances with the Soviet bloc and the Third World, which unswervingly supported the Palestinian cause. But while the PLO succeeded in causing Israel untold political and economic damage and creating a climate of national insecurity, it was unable to achieve its goal of an independent Palestinian state.

The momentum for change came from within the West Bank and Gaza. The Intifada began in December 1987 in the Gaza Strip as a spontaneous uprising spawned by resentment against Israeli occupation. Within days it had become an orchestrated campaign against Israeli troops, characterised by the throwing of rocks and occasional Molotov cocktails. The rebellion spread to the West Bank.

A new young Palestinian leadership was emerging in the West Bank and Gaza at this time. While it didn't discourage the throwing of stones at the Zionist enemy, it was also prepared to enter into dialogue with Israel. Faisal Husseini, nephew of the arch anti-Zionist Sheikh Haj Amin Husseini, learned fluent Hebrew as a gesture of goodwill towards Israel.

Arafat jumped on the Intifada bandwagon. But it was the local Palestinian leadership that

Arafat's stock fell even further after he threw his support behind Iraq's Saddam Hussein after the 1990 invasion of Kuwait. This isolated him from many of his Arab allies and caused the mass expulsion of the affluent Palestinian communities of the Gulf. The collapse of the Soviet Union, the PLO's superpower patron, saw Arafat down and, many assumed, out.

## Gaza via Madrid and Oslo

But Yasser Arafat proved more resilient and compromising than many gave him credit for. He was allowed to attend the Madrid Peace Conference in 1991 as part of the Jordanian

was calling the tune, while Arafat and his entourage in Tunis looked increasingly remote from the Palestinians in the front line. Arafat put out diplomatic feelers, letting it be known that he was prepared to recognise Israel and discontinue terrorist tactics. But a brief flirtation with American diplomats in the late 1980s ended when Arafat was unable to prevent his own people from launching terrorist attacks against Israel. Nor was the right-wing government in Israel prepared even to contemplate an indirect dialogue with Arafat.

**LEFT:** group portrait in an Old City Café.
**ABOVE:** a Palestinian policeman on duty.

### DAVID AND GOLIATH

From the start, the Intifada was designed to make both Israeli liberals and the country's Western allies uncomfortable – and it succeeded. The objective was to get the international media to show pictures of Palestinian women and children defenceless against the might of the Israeli army. The fact that the "defenceless" Palestinians were throwing rocks and stones only heightened the biblical comparison with David taking on the mighty Goliath.

The Palestinians appeared to have hit on a winning formula and believed that it was only a matter of time before the Israeli Goliath would be felled.

delegation. Furthermore, no Palestinian leader of any stature in the occupied territories had emerged to challenge his primacy during the period of the Intifada.

After the election of the Labour government in Israel in 1992, Arafat seized the olive branch held out by Rabin's dovish advisors, and in less than a year he was shaking hands with the Israeli prime minister on the lawn of the White House in Washington. In 1994 he arrived in triumph in Gaza as Israel withdrew its troops from most of the Gaza Strip.

By 1995 the Palestinian Authority's jurisdiction comprised the major West Bank towns,

## Arafat consolidates his position

Since the election of Binyamin Netanyahu in 1996, Arafat has pursued an ambiguous policy of cooperation and conflict. In the first two years of Netanyahu's administration the Palestinian leader was unable to wring territorial concessions from the Israelis, apart from a withdrawal from half of Hebron. Clearly the status quo remains unacceptable to the Palestinians, and yet Arafat has taken advantage of the stalemate to consolidate his position.

Hamas remains a popular opposition movement, combining Islamic fundamentalism, militant Palestinian nationalism and fervent

excluding Hebron, and Arafat's rule over more than 2 million Palestinians living in the West Bank and Gaza was confirmed through democratically held elections.

The assumption of power may have brought Arafat international legitimacy, but it also brought problems in its wake. The Islamic fundamentalists of Hamas stepped into the rejectionist vacuum left by the PLO's acceptance of Israel and carried out a viciously successful bombing campaign inside Israel that came dangerously close to derailing the peace process. Under Israeli pressure, Arafat was compelled to crack down on Hamas in order to save the Oslo Accords.

rejection of Israel's very existence. The release of the Hamas leader Sheikh Ahmed Yassin from an Israeli prison in 1997 (in exchange for captured Mossad agents who bungled an operation in Jordan) and his return to Gaza should have given the movement an enormous boost. And yet Arafat has successfully restrained Hamas. In part the Islamic opposition has been muted by repressive tactics by the Palestinian police and security agents. But for the most part the Hamas leadership – caught in a dilemma – has restrained itself.

In theory Hamas would like to unleash a terror campaign of suicide bombers as it has done so effectively in the past. Yet the repercussions of Hamas terrorism have been only negative for the Palestinians. Arafat remained committed to the Oslo Accords even after Likud came to power, and he has clearly demonstrated that he is prepared to bow to Israeli pressure, even to outlaw Hamas if necessary. Of course this also conveniently allows the Palestinian leader to restrain his most potent opposition.

## Restrained by economic realities

It is the economic needs of the Palestinians which have enabled Arafat to gag Hamas. Blowing up Israelis is still an immensely popular concept for many Palestinians, but its economic

their own stamps and currency, and compete in the Olympics and the World Cup, they will not be truly independent until they control their own borders, and until they are able to develop their own economic infrastructure.

The future won't be easy: passions run too high for that. Peace negotiations in 1998 reached an impasse when Netanyahu balked at the US suggestion of Israeli withdrawal from 13 percent of the West Bank, and Arafat repeated his commitment to independence by May 1999. But there is a will for peace on both sides and the process, however slow, appears to be irreversible.                                    ❏

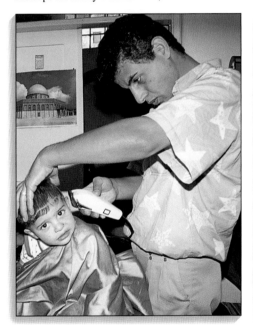

consequences are disastrous because the Palestinians remain economically dependent on Israel. The autonomous Palestinian zones are plagued by the problems which characterise the developing world – inefficiency and lack of organisation, exacerbated by corruption. Promises of aid from the industrialised countries have not always materialised because the Palestinians have not presented sufficiently viable infrastructure projects.

So while the Palestinians have their own flag,

**LEFT:** showing off the fruit harvest.
**ABOVE:** a boy submits to the barber's scissors.
**RIGHT:** souvenirs with a stamp of approval.

## A WORKING ARRANGEMENT

Some 70,000 Palestinians have permits to work in Israel, and several hundred thousand work illegally. A series of industrial parks on the border with Israel is planned – one already exists at Erez on the northern tip of the Gaza Strip – where Palestinian workers will be employed in Israeli-owned factories. It has been a difficult truth to swallow, but Arafat and the Palestinian people realise that they need the Israelis if they are to survive. The closures which follow Hamas bombings prevent Palestinians from working in Israel and form an economic blockade which precludes movement between the West Bank and Gaza, and trade with the rest of the Arab world.

# WHERE TO FIND THE BEST BARGAINS

*Shopping malls offer air-conditioned comfort, but it's the traditional markets which give the true taste and aroma of the Middle East*

Markets around Israel display a diverse range of goods, from the tempting fresh fruit and vegetables in Jerusalem's Makhane Yehuda and Tel Aviv's Carmel Market to the antique trinkets in Yafo's Flea Market.

The market that should on no account be missed is in the Muslim Quarter of Jerusalem's Old City. It is not so much that there is anything on sale which is particularly worth buying, but simply that the "souk" offers Western visitors the ultimate oriental experience.

This is a bazaar in the classic sense of the word. The narrow alleyways are bustling with raw energy, chaotic noise and the smells of exotic spices. Straight down from the Jaffa Gate along David Street are all the kitsch stalls selling T-shirts, religious icons and a variety of Holy Land paraphernalia. Store owners will invariably ask well above the value of an item, so visitors should be prepared to bargain. But the real heart of the "souk" is the spice market – turn left into Shuk Ha-Basamim just before the end of David Street. This dark narrow labyrinth is no place for those who suffer from claustrophobia, but it is heaven for anyone who loves the pungent aromas of coffee and spices.

Gastronomes will also enjoy the huge array of pickles, spices, dried fruits and nuts on offer in Jerusalem's Makhane Yehuda, while the best bargains in the country in clothes as well as food are to be found in Tel Aviv's Carmel Market. Other markets of interest include the one in Akko's Old City and the Druze market in Daliyat el-Karmel, just south of Haifa.

◁ **NUTS ABOUT NUTS**
Israelis love dried fruit and nuts, but much of the produce is imported from as far afield as California.

△ **FIELD-FRESH FOOD**
As the seasons change, so does the fresh home-grown produce on the stalls of Makhane Yehuda market.

## BE'ER SHEVA'S BEDOUIN MARKET

Thursday is the day to be in Be'er Sheva. Neither the recent removal of the Bedouin market to a location just south of the Central Bus Station, nor the increasing profusion of tourist trinkets, has entirely dulled the ethnic authenticity of the market, where Negev nomads come to trade their wares. Although it's open all day, it's best to get here shortly after dawn to enjoy the full essence of the market as the Bedouin trade camels, goats, and agricultural produce. Carpets, clothes, jewellery and other arts and crafts are also available.

The highway to the south is strewn with traditional encampments but with government land appropriations and financial inducements, most Bedouin are moving to fixed villages, a change increasingly reflected in the character of the market.

▽ **BUSINESS, OLD & NEW**
Contrasting lifestyles in Tel Aviv's Nakhalat Binyamin arts and crafts market, held every Tuesday and Friday.

▽ **ANTIQUE ATTRACTIONS**
Yafo's flea market offers bargain-hunters a selection of antique goods from Europe and the Middle East.

△ **OLD CITY VENDORS**
The shopkeepers in the Muslim Quarter of Jerusalem's Old City reflect the essence of the Orient.

◁ **BARGAIN TIME**
Towards the end of the day fresh market produce is often sold at throw-away prices.

▷ **THE TRENDY END OF THE MARKET**
A sax player in Florentin, a ramshackle but trendy neighbourhood in south Tel Aviv.

# EVOLUTION OF THE KIBBUTZ

*Israel's kibbutzim are no longer socialist settlements,*

*but they remain successful economic units and pleasant places in which to live*

The kibbutz, the Israeli version of a socialist collective commune, has been regarded as proof that Marxist economic theories can be put into practice. But is this true? Ironically, the latest challenge to the functioning of the kibbutz is economic success. This crisis stems from both the wealth of individual kibbutzim (the plural of kibbutz) and the general affluence of Israeli society. Yet it is the inherent liberalism, social tolerance and pragmatic compromise of Marxist orthodoxy that enables the kibbutz to survive.

Beneath the ostensibly egalitarian economic surface of contemporary kibbutz society there are vast differences in the amount of money each member may have. Today's kibbutznikim are likely to have their own private bank accounts and credit cards, dabble on the Stock Exchange and even own property outside the kibbutz.

## Flourishing economy

Yet the kibbutz movement is still flourishing despite, or perhaps because of, the gradual breakdown of traditional socialist ideology. Today there are about 130,000 people living on 270 kibbutzim in Israel. They represent 2.5 percent of the country's population. The kibbutzim produce 33 percent of Israel's agricultural output and 6.3 percent of its manufactured goods.

Kibbutz lifestyles have changed out of all recognition since 1909 when the first Russian-born pioneers established the original kibbutz at Dganya, where the River Jordan flows out of the Sea of Galilee. Within a decade there were 40 more kibbutzim. Moreover, these settlements enjoyed greater prosperity and social cohesion than the capitalist farms founded by the Rothschilds and other philanthropists in places like Rishon Le-Tsiyon, Petakh Tikva and Zikhron Ya'akov.

By the time the State of Israel was established in 1948 the kibbutz formed the backbone

of Israeli society. Kibbutz members, while always a small percentage of Israeli society, were looked up to as the social and moral ideal of what a person should be, not least because the kibbutzim had transformed large tracts of arid land into fertile fields. But even more importantly the kibbutzim, which had been

strategically located as pioneering outposts, were created in order to define the borders of the Jewish state.

Most of the Palmach, the élite fighting force of pre-state Israel, were kibbutz members, because by definition the kibbutzim attracted people who were eager to defend the country's borders from the battlefront. The combative traditions of the kibbutz have been maintained today, and most young members are still eager to volunteer for élite combat units.

## From austerity to affluence

The kibbutz initially succeeded because members were motivated to work together, pool very

**LEFT:** spring in full flower at Kibbutz Brenner.
**RIGHT:** life was tough for the pioneers.

limited resources and prevail against the odds in overcoming both a hostile environment and the Arab enemy.

It was in a climate of austerity that the kibbutzim laid the foundations for future prosperity. By the harnessing of agriculture and technology, the finest fruit and vegetables were grown, bringing premium prices on European markets. Varieties of cows were bred to produce the highest milk yields, and chickens that laid large numbers of eggs.

But perhaps the greatest kibbutz invention was drip irrigation, developed by members of Kibbutz Netafim in the 1960s. This system uses

Thousands of members left the kibbutzim, lured by the more individualistic lifestyle of the city. Many kibbutz children would choose not to return home after serving in the army. But there was always an equal number of veteran Israelis or new immigrants eager to take their place as the new pioneers.

## Tarnished image

It is difficult to know when the kibbutz stopped being universally admired as a place for selfless pioneers. One important date was 1977, when the Labour Party lost the reins of power. The right-wing prime minister Menachem Begin

networks of pipes that drip water onto crops or trees, thus penetrating deeply into the soil and utilising minimal amounts of water. Drip irrigation works on a time clock and can be very simple, but in recent times sophisticated options have been added, such as computer control and fertilisers in the pipes.

The kibbutzim also diversified into industrial and tourist enterprises. In the 1960s and 1970s austerity was gradually replaced by a more middle-class lifestyle. But a kibbutz member's home remained a modest place, and money was channelled into communal projects such as dining halls, swimming pools, sports and educational facilities and cultural amenities.

poured scorn on the kibbutzim, not least because they had traditionally given their support to Labour governments.

Begin described kibbutz members as "millionaires who sit around their swimming pools all day". It was an unfair label, but it stuck. In particular Begin was politically exploiting the fact that kibbutzim were almost exclusively Ashkenazi, and even at its most austere their lifestyle was, nevertheless, considerably more desirable than the poverty suffered by the Oriental Jews in the nearby development towns of the Negev and the Galilee.

Somewhat unfairly, in view of their prominent role in both the Palmach and the contemporary army, the kibbutznikim were now portrayed as traitors rather than patriots, because they were generally opposed to the war in Lebanon in 1982 and espoused territorial compromise over the West Bank and Gaza.

It was also during this period that the kibbutzim got themselves into an economic mess. They borrowed large sums of money from Israeli banks in the early 1980s when annual inflation was triple-digit and the banks charged high interest rates. The economy stabilised in 1986, but the interest rates remained locked at exorbitantly high percentages. Many kibbutzim staved off bankruptcy through loan repayment

to nearby towns by opening up to the general public the enterprises that were already functioning for kibbutz members – catering, laundering, kindergartens and garages. Tourism also brings in substantial amounts of revenue on many kibbutzim as a lot of visitors are interested in a taste of Israel's best-known lifestyle. (See page 94 if you are interested in spending time on a kibbutz.) And these days you don't even have to be a kibbutz member to live on one more permanently: some settlements will rent out spare houses to tenants.

The founding fathers of the movement would heartily disapprove of today's developments.

arrangements with bank and government help. However, this bailing out succeeded only in further tarnishing the kibbutz image.

## Economic evolution

The 1990s have seen the kibbutzim go from economic strength to strength, though some communal settlements still totter on the brink of bankruptcy. In particular, kibbutzim near urban centres have profited by selling off land for the construction of housing or industry. These settlements have also provided profitable services

**LEFT:** youngsters hitch a tractor ride.
**ABOVE:** the swimming pool at Ein Gedi kibbutz.

### THREE DIFFERENT PATHS

There are three kibbutz movements in Israel today: the national religious kibbutz movement combines a communal way of life with Jewish Orthodoxy, while the other two – Meuhad and Artzi – are secular in outlook. The latter two movements split from each other back in 1951, when Meuhad members denounced Stalin as an anti-Semitic dictator while adherents of Artzi remained faithful to the USSR and the party line. The Artzi movement realised that the Soviet experiment was going wrong long before the collapse of the Soviet Union in 1991, but it still leans more towards orthodox socialism than does the Meuhad.

Sixty years ago a kibbutz member who received a gift of money from wealthy relatives overseas had to hand it over to the communal kitty. Today a typical kibbutz member would certainly not contemplate handing over an inheritance or a win on the national lottery, let alone a gift, to the commune.

Nevertheless, egalitarianism remains the essence of the kibbutz. All houses are the same size, even though the amount of electronic gadgetry inside may vary enormously, and no kibbutz member is allowed to own a car. Income is distributed evenly, although more progressive kibbutzim may offer bonus incentives for working overtime.

The nuclear family has replaced the Marxist belief in alternative social structures. Kibbutz children were once brought up in communal baby houses by educational professionals, seeing their parents only at certain times of the day, as it was believed that they should be part of the community first and foremost. But these days a child's place in the modern kibbutz is once more with his or her parents.

From the point of view of socialist ideology the kibbutz may not be what it used to be or aspired to become, but it is still a very attractive place to live for a variety of other reasons. It offers a rural life-style, guaranteed work in a number of different professions, and comfortable living standards, including a house and garden. So when a well-established kibbutz advertises for new members, the number of applicants usually far exceeds the number of places available.

### KIBBUTZ CUISINE

Kibbutz Dan takes advantage of its position, surrounded by tributaries of the River Jordan, to run a restaurant, the Dag on the Dan, where it serves delicious freshly-caught trout.

### FINDING OUT FOR YOURSELF

Visitors wishing to sample life on a kibbutz or moshav can either stay at one of the many kibbutz and moshav guesthouses dotted around the country, or volunteer to work for a period of not less than a month. Guesthouses are often in isolated rural areas in the northern Galilee, but a few are within easy reach of Jerusalem and Tel Aviv. They usually offer all the facilities of a comfortable hotel.

You can make bookings through the Kibbutz Hotels Chain, 90 Rehov Ben Yehuda, Tel Aviv 60131, tel: (03) 524-3358. Prospective volunteer workers should contact Ikhud Hakvutzot Vehakibbutzim, Hayarkon 124, Tel Aviv, tel: (03) 524-6154.

## The moshav movement

For the Jewish pioneers who wanted a less socialistic form of communal living when the earliest settlements were founded, the moshav offered a more individualistic alternative. Nahalal in the Galilee, the first moshav, was set up in 1921 by a breakaway group of settlers who were disillusioned by the socialist constraints of Dganya, the very first kibbutz. One member of this breakaway group was Shmuel Dayan, the father of Moshe Dayan, who was to become defence minister and hero of the Six Day War in 1967.

In the moshav each family runs its own household and farms its individual plot of land, but machinery is shared and marketing is done jointly. There are about 400 moshavim in Israel, but most members now work in regular jobs, renting out their land to private farmers. The co-operative moshav (shitufi), on the other hand, is much closer to a kibbutz in that farming and industry are performed jointly. Income is shared equally between members, and households then spend their money as they wish. ❑

**LEFT:** harvesting tomatoes.

# The Army

The Israeli army is like no other army in the world. During basic training soldiers learn to salute their superiors, accept orders without question and stick to clearly defined dress codes. Thereafter, rules are made to be broken. Officers are never saluted, orders can be negotiated, and a pink T-shirt worn as a vest keeps the soldier warm in winter. The Israel Defence Forces are highly effective, as has been proved on many occasions. Maybe a soldier's right to question an officer's orders is a strength rather than a weakness. In the heat of battle orders are usually obeyed, and dramatic victories have been won.

Even as the peace process gains momentum, Israel is still a nation at war. The ubiquity of soldiers in Israel clearly shows this. Toting sub-machine-guns, they are everywhere: travelling on buses, hitchhiking at roadside stations, sitting at pavement cafés and strolling through city streets.

Israeli male soldiers fall into several categories. There are young conscripts aged 18 to 21 doing their three years' national service, and a small number of professional soldiers, usually officers, who carry on afterwards. Then there are the reservists. *Miluim*, Hebrew for reserve duty, involves men being plucked away from their families for a month or six weeks a year (more during times of military tension) to serve on the Lebanese border or the West Bank. There are, of course, rugged types who enjoy the lifestyle, but most Israelis see *miluim* as a burden they would rather evade. The unpopularity of *miluim* does have a dovish effect, however, putting pressure on the government to find a solution to the border problems which make reserve duty necessary.

However, military service isn't as compulsory as many believe. About a third of Israeli Jewish men do not enrol for the army when they are 18. Ultra-Orthodox Jews can request a deferment to study, and youngsters deemed unsuitable because of delinquent behaviour are not called up. Also, any 18-year-old who insists that he does not want to serve will not be drafted. The number of teenage applicants for combat units is still higher than the places available, so regiments can pick and choose. National service is officially compulsory for Jews, but Muslims and Christians are exempt. Bedouins, who are renowned for their tracking abilities, serve as volunteers. Druze and Circassians are conscripted, at their own request.

Women often fought as front-line soldiers in the struggle for independence, but the IDF has confined them to non-combat roles since 1948, although they are conscripted for two years. The Supreme Court ruled in 1995 that the army must accept women for pilots' courses; several dozen have enrolled, but none has yet qualified. Women's rights groups are now requesting that the paratroopers take female soldiers. Sexism aside, the army is not a bastion of conservatism in Israel as it is in other countries. Homosexuals, for example, have always been accepted.

Although scruffy in appearance, the military places great value on smart technology. It is the Israeli Air Force more than any other branch of the services that has ensured the country's military edge over its Arab neighbours. In an era of satellite surveillance there can be no more Yom Kippur-style surprise attacks, and anti-missile systems being developed, like the Arrow, will reduce the threat of long-range attacks.

As the Israeli army prepares itself for the 21st century the principal threat to the country is perceived to be terrorism, and enemies further afield, in particular Iran and Iraq. But even during an era of peace Israel is likely to be a nation in uniform for some time to come. ❑

**RIGHT:** tug-of-war for new recruits.

# LANGUAGE AND CULTURE

*In just over a century a language has been reborn and a new culture*
*forged from the talents of Israel's diverse population*

Had one to name the single most fundamental contribution made by Israel and the Jewish people to mankind, obviously the immediate answer is the Old Testament which, together with the New Testament writings, forms the philosophical and moral web underlying most of our civilisation's values. And that book, for all its five millennia or so, remains the most important source and inspiration for much of Israel's cultural creativity.

It is, of course, only one of the strands, but it is the most pervasive. Other distinct strands are the great literary creations of the Jewish exile – the Mishna and the Talmud – the accumulated wisdom of 2,000 years of Jewish thought. No less important is the cumulative experience of modern statehood in a society whose population has multiplied more than sixfold since independence and, through force of circumstances, has developed a siege mentality which has produced a siege culture.

Israel, like the United States before it, has often been described as a "melting pot" as it has struggled with the absorption of 1.5 million immigrants from 100 nations, speaking 70 languages. But a better image would be a *bouillabaisse*, the classic Mediterranean fish stew in which all the elements form a homogeneous whole, while each retains its own character, distinct identity, and flavour.

## Hebrew: a language reborn

One of the most remarkable facets of the rebirth of the Hebrew nation was the revival of the Hebrew language. Through the 2,000 years of dispersion it had become almost solely a language of worship and expression of the yearnings for Zion. Some small communities of Sephardic Jews in Jerusalem used Hebrew for everyday speech, but the *lingua franca* of the Jews in exile became either the language of the country in which they found refuge, or Yiddish,

**PRECEDING PAGES:** a concert at Jerusalem's Sultan's Pool. **LEFT:** studying hard on the Hebrew University campus. **RIGHT:** a Torah scribe.

a combination of Hebrew and medieval German; Ladino, which was Hebrew mixed with Spanish; or Mughrabi, a North African blend of Hebrew, Arabic and French. The first pioneers who arrived in 19th-century Palestine brought with them their own languages, usually Yiddish or Russian, but they insisted on using

Hebrew in conversation in the early agricultural communities, and its re-creation became a cornerstone of Zionist ideology.

The rebirth of Hebrew was virtually the work of one man, the Zionist thinker and leader Eliezer Ben Yehuda. Born in Lithuania in 1858, he emigrated to Palestine in 1881 and saw the revival of the language as an indispensable aspect of the political and cultural rebirth of the Jewish people. With single-minded, almost fanatical, determination he embarked on a lone campaign to restore the Hebrew tongue as a vibrant, living vehicle for everyday expression. When he and his new wife Dvora arrived in Yafo he informed her that they would converse only in Hebrew, and their son Itamar became the first modern child with Hebrew as his mother tongue. Ben Yehuda's efforts horrified the Orthodox population of Jerusalem who, when they realised he proposed using the holy tongue to further secular, nationalist and political causes, pronounced a *herem* (excommunication) against him. To this day, the Ashkenazi ultra-Orthodox Jewish community condemn the secular use of Hebrew and the defilement of the holy language, and confine themselves to Yiddish for everyday speech.

The introduction of Hebrew for everyday use was not greeted with universal acclamation

media he coined thousands of new words relating to every aspect of life and every discipline. Not all of them took root; modern Hebrew, the all-purpose language of the country in every field, still borrows words from other languages which sound familiar to non-Hebrew speakers. Ben Yehuda's *sah rahok* ("long-distance speech"), for instance, never displaced "telephone", nor did *makushit* ("something that is tapped upon") take the place of "piano".

## The question of slang

No one has yet successfully coined Hebrew words to replace the ubiquitous "automati",

even by the non-Orthodox, or the supporting Zionist bodies and organisations abroad. Bitter battles were fought over the language of instruction at the Betsal'el School of Art in Jerusalem (founded in 1906) and the Technion (founded in 1913). German was the official language of the latter, and it took a strike by faculty and students to compel the supporting institution, the Hilfsverein, to give way. A few years later the language of instruction in all schools in the country (except for those of the ultra-Orthodox) was established as Hebrew.

Ben Yehuda compiled a dictionary of Hebrew, established an academy, and founded and edited several periodicals. Through these

### CROWNING ACHIEVEMENT

The crowning achievement of Ben Yehuda's life was his *Dictionary of Ancient and Modern Hebrew*, completed after his death by his son Ehud and his second wife, Hemda (Dvora's younger sister). This dictionary, and the Academy of the Hebrew Language, which he established in 1890, were the main vehicles through which a new, modern vocabulary was disseminated. Ben Yehuda wrote in the introduction to his dictionary: "In those days it was as if the heavens had suddenly opened, and a clear, incandescent light flashed before my eyes, and a mighty inner voice sounded in my ears: the renascence of Israel on its ancestral soil."

"mekhani", "democratia", etc., although the existence of such words in the language seriously disturbs Hebrew purists. Some slang neologisms would undoubtedly make Ben Yehuda turn in his grave: "Tremp" (clearly from "tramp") is the Hebrew for "hitchhiking", a sweat-shirt is a "svetcher", over which you might pull a "sveder" if it gets cold. When your "breks" fail, the garage might find something wrong with your "beck-ex" or even, God forbid, with your "front-beck-ex". Most of these words have Hebrew equivalents, but they have usually been pushed aside in common usage.

Despite these contemporary dilutions, there's no denying that Hebrew is once more a thriving, and still-evolving, vehicle of daily discourse employed in great works of literature and the backs of postcards alike.

## The written word

If the heartbeat of a nation's culture lies in the written word, then Israel has a problem because, despite the revival of Hebrew, there are no more than 4 or 5 million people worldwide who can speak and understand it, and certainly no more than 3 million who can comfortably read it. Hebrew can be considered an arcane, rather exotic language, one where those who choose to write in it must inevitably be faced with the frustrations of writing for a minuscule audience. But a lively, articulate and robust body of literature has evolved nevertheless. While the giants of modern Hebrew – Bialik, Tchernikhovsky, Brenner, Agnon (who won the Nobel Prize for Literature in 1966), and others – are still required reading in schools, they are supplemented by indigenous, increasingly Israeli-born writers whose work can stand comparison with the best of the world's contemporary authors.

One of Israel's best writers (and certainly the best-known abroad) is Amos Oz. A former member of Kibbutz Hulda who now lives in Arad, Oz is heavily influenced by the "return to the soil" labour-Zionist mores espoused by the founding fathers of the kibbutz movement. Many writers who maintain a prolific literary output belong to the "Palmach Generation" (the Palmach was the pre-state élite fighting force drawn from the kibbutzim). Among them are

Haim Guri, Moshe Shamir, S. Yizhar, Benjamin Tammuz and Hanoch Bar Tov. An important phenomenon of the last 15 years or so has been the maturing of a group of writers of Sephardic origin for whom Arabic, rather than Yiddish, was a formative influence. Such writers include A.B. Yehoshua, Samy Michael and Amnon Shamosh, whose *Esra Safra and Sons* became a popular television series.

A literary phenomenon is Ephraim Kishon, Israel's best-known humorist, a prophet somewhat without honour in his own country; his books have sold millions of copies overseas, especially in Scandinavia and Germany.

Literature has been deeply influenced by the deaths of millions of Jews in the Holocaust. It is that theme which is the all-pervasive *leitmotiv* in the writings of Aharon Appelfeld, whose books have been widely translated, and in those of Abba Kovner, "Ka-Tsetnik" (the pseudonym of Benzion Dinur) and many others, all of whom experienced that period themselves. A younger generation of writers is exploring more universal literary themes. The Lebanon war, increased political polarisation, the appearance of anti-democratic trends in Israeli society, and the spectre of racism are rightly the concern of these intellectuals.

The centre ground in Israeli writing is held

**LEFT:** the language in secular use.
**RIGHT:** Israeli novelist Amos Oz.

today by those who came to literary maturity after the Palmach days and whose vision was tempered through the fires of austerity, of absorption of immigrants, and four wars of survival. Such writers include Yitzhak Ben Ner, Shulamit Hareven, the late Ya'akov Shabtai, Yoram Kaniuk, and others.

Poetry holds a special place in Israel's literary life. According to a calculation based on books and the literary magazines, 10,000 new poems are published in the country every year. The publication of works by Yehuda Amichai, Dan Pagis, Natan Zach, or T. Carmi are awaited as avidly as a novel by a best-selling author.

## Music – from classical to jazz

The musical life of Israel is a good example of the country's bipolarity. There is a constant inflow of immigrant musicians, and an outflow of performers who have reached the highest international peaks. Yitzhak Perlman, Pinchas Zuckerman, Shlomo Mintz, Daniel Barenboim: all received their training in Israel and went on to glittering careers on the world's concert platforms. Israel's orchestras, including the Israel Philharmonic, the Jerusalem Symphony, the Be'er Sheva Sinfonietta and many chamber groups, have provided homes for hundreds of players. Their rehearsals are a babel of Russian, German, Romanian, French and English –

united by a lot of music and a little Hebrew.

Israelis are a concert-going people: subscription series to the major orchestras are sold out, and a subscription to the IPO is jealously handed down from parents to children. Zubin Mehta, born in Bombay in 1936, and one of the world's foremost conductors, has led the IPO since 1991, and has done much to involve himself with Israel's struggle for survival. Music-loving tourists have many opportunity to hear well-loved pieces performed by some of the world's greatest talents. Plácido Domingo, incidentally, got his first job at the (late-lamented) Israel Opera, where he spent a year. The standard of choral singing is also very high, especially among the United Kibbutz Choir, the Rinat National Choir and the Camaran Singers.

Israel hosts a series of international musical events, including the Artur Rubinstein piano competition, the Pablo Casals cello competition, a triennial international harp contest, the Zimriya choirs festival, and annual music festivals in Jerusalem, Kibbutz Ein Hashofet and, notably, at Kibbutz Ein Gev on the shores of the Sea of Galilee.

But it is not only lovers of classical music who are catered for. In Tel Aviv, particularly, there is a great deal of popular music around. While jazz aficionados will do better elsewhere, rockers, pop singers and balladeers are out in force. Moshe Wilensky, Yoram Taharlev, Nurit Hirsch, Sasha Argov and, above all, Naomi Shemer write music that is played on radio and television from Metula to Eilat. Pop superstars include Ofra Haza, Ilanit, Yehoram Gaon, Arik Einstein, Shalom Hanoch, and the sensational Dana International.

### DANA ROCKS THE BOAT

Victory in the 1998 Eurovision Song Contest, which reckons to have about 100 million viewers around the world, focused widespread media attention on Dana International, the glamorous pop singer who is as famous for her sex change operation (she was born Yaron Cohen) as for her numerous platinum-disc releases. The ultra-Orthodox community is not amused, particularly as Dana cannot easily be dismissed as a passing phenomenon, appealing only to teenage audiences. Gaining followers in unexpected quarters, she has become a symbol of secular resistance to ultra-Orthodox attempts to impose restrictions on Israel's cultural life and media output.

A new generation of ethnic singers has given a sense of ethnic pride to young Israelis of Sephardic background. And members of the Iranian Jewish community have formed a band, the Nash Didan (meaning "Our People"), writing and singing songs in Aramaic, in an attempt to keep the fast-dying biblical language alive.

## Dance greats

Israel owes its place in the world of dance to four women. The first was a Russian-trained ballerina, Rina Nikova, who came to Palestine in the 1920s determined to create a local art form incorporating themes from the Bible, Middle East tradition, folk dance and Russian classical ballet. The second, Sarah Levi-Tanai, harnessed the Yemenite dance tradition, one of the richest and most exotic of the Middle East, into a modern framework, creating the Inbal Dance Theatre, the forerunner of several other successful ethnic groups. The third, Baroness Bethsabée de Rothschild, founded the Batsheva and Bat Dor dance companies, which remain leading exponents of modern dance in Israel. In recent years the two companies have been joined by the Kibbutz Dance Company and the Israel Ballet, the country's only classical ballet company. The fourth woman was Martha Graham, who was undoubtedly the formative influence on modern dance in Israel.

A company rare in concept and achievement is Kol Demama ("Voice of Silence"), a group composed of deaf and hearing-impaired dancers, whose performances are electrifying. The training method developed by director Moshe Efrati is based on vibrations through the floor transmitted by the dancer's feet.

Folk-dance groups abound, and there is no kibbutz or town that doesn't have its own troupe. Outstanding among them is Hora Yerushalayim, a Jerusalem-based group, whose four companies perform at home and overseas. Israelis love to dance, and many festive occasions end up with exuberant *horas, krakoviaks, debkas*, Hassidic dances and other European and Arab dances, now part of the heritage.

## Theatrical roots

Israeli theatre owes its origins to the melodramatic tradition exemplified in the first Hebrew theatre in the world, Ha-Bimah, founded in Moscow in 1917 (and moved to Palestine in 1931). Since then theatre has come a long way in style, presentation, method, and especially content. Of all the arts in Israel, theatre is perhaps the most socially involved, with a new generation of playwrights breaking taboos, tackling controversial topics, and attempting to act as the mirror and conscience of society.

Concerns of the past, the Jewish experience in pre-war Europe, the Holocaust, all these still manifest themselves on the Israeli stage, but, increasingly, dramatists are addressing themselves to contemporary issues, problems of daily

life in Israel, the Arab–Jewish conflict, alienation between ethnic, religious and other social groups. A new play by Hanoch Levin, Yehoshua Sobol or Hillel Mittelpunkt is a major event which will be dissected, analysed and discussed as energetically as the Camp David Accords. Hanoch Levin, especially, is a defiant, iconoclastic writer whose works inevitably cause controversy and attract attempted censorship. But his irreverent, nihilistic, often obscene satire makes him Israel's most interesting and original theatrical talent.

The major repertory theatres, most of which enjoy substantial official support, such as the Ha-Bimah, Cameri, Ohel, Haifa Municipal

**LEFT:** Zubin Mehta takes a bow.
**RIGHT:** ballet flourishes in Israel.

Theatre, Be'er Sheva Municipal Theatre and Jerusalem Khan have subscription series which are usually fully attended. The language barrier prevents visitors from sharing in the rich offerings, but efforts are being made to bridge the gap. Several theatres are experimenting with earphone translations, and others are staging productions in English.

Great popular success has attended a recent annual theatrical innovation: the festival of Alternative Theatre in Akko, a lively occasion of theatrical dynamics, innovative performances and indoor and open-air attractions.

A programme enjoying substantial support is

Omanut La'am ("Arts for the People"), a state-run enterprise bringing theatre to settlements and development towns in outlying areas which don't generally get a chance to see live performances. For thousands of new immigrants and youngsters, Omanut La'am performances are their first introduction to the world of theatre.

## Cinema blossoms

Film as an art form in Israel still has a long way to go. Many of its productions are strictly for local consumption and are based on sitcoms, sexcoms, and in-joke situations such as teenage affairs, marital conflicts and army life. Such products are known as "Burekas" (named after a popular kind of flaky pastry pie).

However, the Israeli film industry is taking off, and the Jerusalem Film Festival, held annually in July since 1983, is its showcase. The opening gala takes place at Sultan's Pool and subsequent showings are at the Jerusalem Cinemathèque. Israeli cinema-goers have been ill served in the past by cinema owners, but this situation has changed in a radical way with the opening of the Cinemathèque, which not only shows the best films in town but is also the place where the capital's beautiful people go to see and be seen. And Tel Aviv now has a sybaritic cinema complex, the Rav Chen, which incorporates five movie theatres.

The one international superstar in Israel's cinematographic life is the movie mogul Menahem Golan, who became one of the movers and shakers in Hollywood, together with his cousin, Yoram Globus.

## Painters and sculptors

Israeli art owes its fundamental quality to a combination of two factors: a classical European tradition brought here by the country's early painters and art teachers, and the influences of the special quality of the light and the natural attributes of the country.

Israeli visual art, possessing its own individual character, has been created in a comparatively short space of time, since the establishment of the Betsal'el School of Art in Jerusalem in 1906. Israeli artists have experimented with all the movements and trends of the contemporary art world from expressionism to cubism, from Russian social realism to environment and performance art, but few have managed to make the quantum leap from local to universal recog-

### MOVIES WITH A MESSAGE

Serious film-making in Israel began in the early 1920s and 1930s. Most of the output consisted of documentaries, whose main purpose was as a fundraising device aimed at demonstrating the Zionist effort to audiences abroad. These early films, with their images of muscle-rippling pioneers making the desert bloom, against a background of stirring music and an exhortatory sound track, became known as "Keren Kayemet" films after the Hebrew name of the Jewish National Fund which sponsored them. Today they seem amateurish, but, like the propaganda films made in post-revolutionary Russia, they are interesting social documents.

nition. Among contemporary artists who have are Ya'akov Agam (his kinetic room at the Pompidou Centre in Paris is a seminal work), Menashe Kadishman, Avigdor Arikha, Mordechai Ardon and Joseph Zaritsky.

Dany Karavan and Ygael Tumarkin are two sculptors well known abroad whose work can be seen all over Israel. Marcel Janco (1895–1984), founder of the Dadaist Movement, Reuven Rubin (1893–1974), painter of lyrical large-scale canvases, and Anna Ticho (1894–1980), with her exquisite line drawings of her beloved Jerusalem hills, have also gained a considerable following.

Tel Aviv, and Old Yafo. There are others in Jerusalem, Haifa, Ein Hod (an artists' village to the south of Haifa which staged the Sculpture Biennale in 1990), and Safed, a Galilean town full of artists.

Tel Aviv Museum has a large and representative collection of Israeli modern art on permanent display, along with temporary exhibitions. The Israel Museum, which has impressive collections of classic, impressionist and foreign modern art (as well as its vast collection of archaeology, Judaica and Jewish art and ethnography), somewhat neglected Israeli art before the opening in 1985 of the Ayala Zacks-

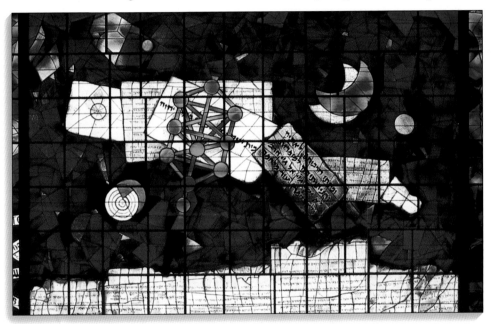

At the end of the 1970s, following in the steps of the USA and Europe, Israeli art entered the post-modernist era. The work is energetic and forceful, often containing violent images which are, perhaps, part of the post-Lebanon War reality in Israeli life. Currently, Tel Aviv artist David Reeb is among the few whose works have an overtly socio-political theme.

Museums and galleries all over the country cater to the art lover. The main ones are concentrated in two areas: Gordon Street, in central

Abramov Pavilion of Modern Art, which has become the nation's main repository of contemporary Israeli painting and sculpture.

Suzanna Landau, the curator of contemporary international art at the Israel Museum, believes in mixing Israeli and international works. The conceptual artist Zvi Goldstein, resident in Jerusalem, is among those whose work is exhibited there.

Outdoor sculpture parks have gained a big following since the Billy Rose Sculpture Garden at the Israel Museum first brought international works to the country, where they have been joined by the works of leading local sculptors, such as Yehiel Shemi.  ❏

**LEFT:** the Ha-Bima Theatre: a dream come true.
**ABOVE:** Mordechai Ardon's stained-glass windows at Givat Ram.

# CRAFTS AND JUDAICA

*Jewish arts and crafts experienced a revival with the birth of Zionism, inspiring contemporary artists to give a new twist to old traditions*

From the artists' quarter in old Safed to the seaside boutiques in Eilat, on every major city avenue and in the oriental markets, there's an almost endless array of local handicrafts. Simple straw baskets and sleek stone sculptures, ceramic and textile arts, glassware and jewellery, mass-produced religious mementos and one-of-a-kind ritual items are available everywhere. Israel is the international centre of Judaica production, and tourists – whether they're looking for something "just like grandma had" or something a bit more sophisticated – find the world's best selection of Jewish ritual arts concentrated in the shops and studios of Jerusalem.

Arts and crafts, like most things in 20th-century Israel, have their roots in the Bible. Bezalel Ben-Uri Ben-Hur, specially blessed "with the spirit of God, in wisdom, in understanding, and in knowledge" appears in the Book of Exodus to produce a divinely commissioned work of art, the Tabernacle, for the wandering Children of Israel. The order came down loud and clear: "To work in gold, and silver, and in brass, in cutting of stones for setting, and in carving of wood … in all manner of skilful workmanship." Bezalel proved worthy of the task; under his direction the desert Tabernacle was successfully completed, and from it emerged the Menorah, the seven-branched candlestick which became an eternal Jewish symbol.

When ancient Jerusalem was established, pilgrims began coming three times a year – at the major festivals of Succot, Pesach and Shavuot – to worship at the Temple. On the slopes beyond the Temple Mount they found Jerusalem's earliest art centres – special quarters for weavers, dyers, leather-workers, glassmakers, potters and goldsmiths, all turning out goods for visitors to use during their Jerusalem sojourn and to take home as keepsakes.

The destruction of the Second Temple (AD 70) and the consequent dispersal of the Jewish

**LEFT:** a *mizrach* (wall hanging) depicts Jerusalem.
**RIGHT:** brassware and tapestries for sale.

people left few opportunities for the artistic Jewish soul to express itself in the Holy Land for almost two millennia. But with the birth of the Zionist movement in the 20th century came a revival of interest in "Jewish art". Alongside the pioneers who set out to rebuild the land came a tiny group of artists, intellectuals and

craftspeople dedicated to creating a new Jewish culture. Bezalel reappeared (as Betsal'el) in the name of a fledgling art academy, and its founder, a Lithuanian Jew named Boris Schatz, proved that arts and crafts could become the touchstone of economic well-being and national pride in the Zionist settlements.

## Ritual and tradition

Today Jerusalem is again the centre of Israel's arts and crafts industry. As in ancient times, workers are to be found in their own centrally located quarters. One feature of Jerusalem's arts scene is the accessibility of its artists, enabling collectors to buy directly from the studio shops.

Jewish ritual art, the bulk of Judaica, is divided into two categories: holy vessels, directly associated with the Torah, and ritual utensils, used for tasks in the home and synagogue. While not intrinsically holy, the latter acquire a certain sanctity through their use in the performance of religious duties (*mitzvot*). If a ritual object adds an aesthetic dimension, users have the benefit of fulfilling an additional commandment, *hiddur mitzvah:* glorification of the commandment. Special value is attributed to lighting a beautiful pair of candlesticks for the Sabbath rather than simple oil wicks, though the latter would fulfil the requirement.

ritual and are accepted today as Judaica. For most of them there are no design restrictions, or even descriptions, in the Halacha.

In most cases, form and decoration followed the fashions of the time and place in which they were produced. Hanukkah lamps, from the 12th century onwards, have French Gothic windows, Moorish arches, or Italian garlands; wine cups and candlesticks are reminiscent of the Renaissance and baroque periods, a single Hebrew letter the only sign that they were used by Jews.

Symbols of the artists' surrounding cultures were given new significance when combined with classic Jewish symbols. Long-standing

## The rules of creation

Halacha, Jewish law, offers only a few rules for creating specific ritual objects. The Hanukkah lamp is perhaps the most clearly defined. It must have eight separate lights of the same height, and a distinguishable ninth light for kindling the others. They must burn, in a publicly visible spot, for at least 30 minutes past sundown. The rest is left to the artist.

Wine cups, candlesticks and spice boxes used for Sabbath and holiday blessings; cases for *mezuzot* (tiny parchment scrolls hung on every Jewish doorpost); charity boxes, festive plates, decanters, hangings – these and many other objects long ago became associated with Jewish

favourites include (Torah) crowns and double columns invoking the Temple; biblical scenes and signs of the Zodiac; lions of Judah, grape vines and pomegranates, griffins and fish and other flora and fauna; and, of course, the seven-branched Menorah. Representations of the human figure and face were generally avoided in deference to the Second Commandment ("Thou shalt have no graven images"), but they appear from time to time.

Materials were usually the best the community or individual patron could afford; lavish textiles, parchment and gold leaf, semi-precious and precious stones and metals were the ideal. When these were not available, almost anything would do: charming examples of Jewish folk art in wood, tin and paper have been preserved. (A magnificent collection is displayed in the Israel Museum, where replicas are also on sale.)

## Contemporary artists

Israel's contemporary Judaica artists, like their ancestors, favour semi-precious and precious metals, but items can be found in almost every other material, from rare woods to Lucite. Two distinct schools have recently emerged. One is highly traditional, basing its shapes and decorations on patterns from the baroque period or earlier. Many of these works are imitations or adaptations of well-known museum pieces; others are brought up to date by incorporating the lines of modern Jerusalem or devices such as whimsical moving parts. The second school is strictly, sometimes aggressively, contemporary. Form prevails over function; the artist strives to create art works which may be used in ritual.

An informal arts and crafts tour could begin at one of the two non-profit galleries which offer an instant overview of Israel's craft scene. Neither gallery sells anything but refers visitors directly to its selected artists. At the House of Quality this means going upstairs to the studios where several silversmiths, including veterans Arie Ofir and Menachem Berman, work full-time. At the Alix de Rothschild Crafts Centre the director may be on hand for tea and a chat about his latest discoveries.

Nearby, the Courtyard Gallery is the place for fibre-art fans seeking chic handmade baskets, fabrics and wall hangings. Those who prefer a strictly ethnic look can go across town to Kuzari in the Bukharim Quarter, where local women embroider everything, from tea cosies to Torah covers, in traditional patterns.

Khutsot ha-Yoster (Art & Crafts Lane) has top craftspeople like Uri Ramot (ancient glass and beads in modern settings); the Alsbergs (antique coins in custom-made jewellery); and Georges Goldstein (hand-woven tapestries and *tallitot* – prayer shawls). But the lane's greatest distinction is its concentration of outstanding silversmiths. Yaakov Greenvurcel, Zelig Segal and Emil Shenfeld are ranked among the world's top designers of contemporary Judaica,

and Michael Ende is one of the chief purveyors of the "nouveau antique" school.

Fans of the latter should also visit Yossi's Masters' Workshop (King David Street) and The Brothers Reichman (in Ge'ula). Both offer extraordinary workmanship and classic designs in fine metal. Similar style and quality characterise the ceremonial pieces by Catriel, a carver of rare woods, in Yohanan MiGush Halava. Catriel's neighbours are worth visiting: silversmiths Davidson and Amiel, calligraphic artist Korman, and jeweller Sarah Einstein, who transforms antique Middle Eastern beads into high-fashion jewellery. ❑

**LEFT:** a silversmith crafts Menorahs and other ceremonial objects.
**RIGHT:** a glassblower concentrates on his task.

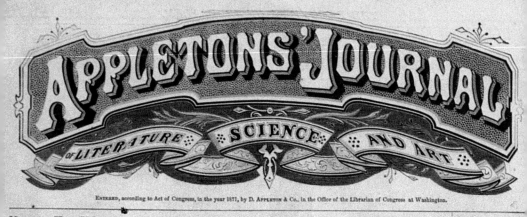

# APPLETONS' JOURNAL

## OF LITERATURE · SCIENCE · AND ART

Entered, according to Act of Congress, in the year 1871, by D. Appleton & Co., in the Office of the Librarian of Congress at Washington.

No. 99.—Vol. V.]     SATURDAY, FEBRUARY 18, 1871.     { PRICE TEN CENTS.
{ WITH SUPPLEMENT.

## THE RECOVERY OF JERUSALEM.*

THIS is the somewhat pretentious title of the narrative of recent English explorations of Jerusalem, by means of excavations conducted by Captain Wilson, of the Royal Engineers, under the auspices and at the expense of the Committee of the Palestine Exploration Fund. Without, perhaps, fulfilling the meaning of the old crusading war-cry, exact knowledge of the scenes and localities in which their religi first appeared on earth. The explorations have solved many diffic problems, and settled many fierce and protracted controversies. Sha have been sunk and tunnels made in the most secluded and mysterio parts of the sacred city, and structures brought to light that have r

WILSON'S ARCH, DISCOVERED AT JERUSALEM IN 1867.

the "Recovery of Jerusalem," it is undoubtedly a record of researches and discoveries of the highest value, and of the greatest interest to scholars, antiquarians, and, above all, to Christians who desire an

been seen by mortal eyes since the days of Titus, or perhaps of Solomon.

The beginning of this great work was the Ordnance Survey of Jerusalem, made by Captain Wilson, of the English Royal Engineers, in 1864–'65. Early in the year 1864 the sanitary state of Jerusalem attracted considerable attention; that city, which the Psalmist has described as "beautiful for situation, the joy of the whole earth," had

---

* The Recovery of Jerusalem. A Narrative of Exploration and Discovery in the City and the Holy Land. By Captain Wilson, R. E., and Captain Warren, R. E. With an Introduction by Arthur Penrhyn Stanley, D. D., Dean of Westminster. D. Appleton & Co.

# DIGGING UP THE PAST

*Israel's numerous archaeological sites provide a lively topic of discussion for a nation that loves a good argument*

**A**rchaeology is Israel's national hobby – from school child to senior citizen, from the merely curious to the serious scholar, tourists and natives alike are all encouraged to "dig in" to the land of the Bible.

With 3,500 sites in an area of approximately 21,000 sq. km (8,100 sq. miles), and finds dating back to 150,000 BC, Israel has 22 archaeological museums in addition to numerous private collections. Yet only a small proportion of Israel's potential sites have been thoroughly explored; time, money and manpower have all placed limits on the scope of, but not the devotion to, the exploration of Israel's past.

## A gentlemanly hobby

Adherents past and present to what one scholar called the "study of durable rubbish" have been drawn to biblical archaeology for a range of reasons: greed, adventure, religion and scholarship. During the Victorian period it was something of a gentlemanly hobby.

The first known "archaeologist" to work in Israel was inspired by religious belief. In AD 325 Empress Helena, the mother of Constantine the Great, the emperor who declared Christianity the official religion of his empire, ordered the removal of a Hadrianic temple to Venus built on a site which she had determined was the hill of Golgotha. Constantine erected the Church of the Holy Sepulchre to commemorate the alleged site of the crucifixion and entombment of Jesus.

During the next 16 centuries the territory, referred to variously as Palestine, the Levant, Syro-Lebanon, the Holy Land or Israel, exchanged hands numerous times. Explorers of all religions crossed its borders, armed with little more than compasses, picks, shovels, and curiosity. Stories of bribery, untimely deaths and mystical reunions with sages and prophets from time past pepper their accounts. Medieval

adventurers report that those who dared to enter the burial cavern of the patriarchs and their wives at Hebron were struck blind or senseless or worse. Such tales did not deter others.

For Western explorers, interest in the Holy Land intensified after the Napoleonic conquest of Egypt in 1798 and the subsequent discovery

of the Rosetta Stone. Scholars, amateurs and snake-oil salesmen descended on Palestine, then a sparsely populated backwater country. Some of these adventurers became the victims of this archaeological fever. For example, when the British Museum rejected as fake certain "ancient" parchments that Moses Wilhelm Shapira had bought from a Bedouin, the amateur archaeologist simply disappeared.

In 1911, Captain Montague Parker and his crew of treasure hunters barely escaped with their lives when they were discovered conducting an excavation under the Mosque of Omar on the Temple Mount. The British mission had been following the hunch of a Swedish

---

**LEFT:** an 1871 journal recounts the discovery of Wilson's Arch.
**RIGHT:** the underground city at Amatzia.

clairvoyant who insisted that this was where they would find a cache of objects from King Solomon's temple. Offended Jerusalemites rioted in the streets.

## Method in the madness

The foundations of modern archaeology as we know it were not laid until the late 19th century, and were marked by the establishment of major academic institutions sponsoring field trips and publication societies. The Palestine Exploration Fund, founded in London in 1865, is the grandfather of these groups, which include such venerable institutions as the American

Schools of Oriental Research and the Ecôle Biblique et Archaeologique Française. The work which Edward Robinson, Claude R. Conder, Sir Flinders Petrie and other giants carried out during this period continues to cast a long shadow on modern archaeology.

It was Petrie who first recognised the importance of stratigraphy, that is, the examination layer by layer of a tel, the artificial mound formed by successive settlements. He was also among the first to recognise the importance of using pottery to date each of these layers or strata. He realised that, in different periods, particular types of pottery would be associated with particular strata.

After World War I, Mortimer Wheeler and Kathleen Kenyon refined the debris analysis method of pottery dating. At about the same time a separate methodology arose, emphasising the importance of uncovering large areas to expose the architecture of a settlement. Devotees of the so-called architectural method accused those of the debris analysis school of overlooking the big picture. The latter in turn accused their colleagues of ignoring the importance of stratigraphy.

Today an eclectic approach to tel excavating prevails. Technological advances enable surveyors to provide archaeologists with considerable information before a single shovelful of earth has been removed. Carbon-14 dating has further improved the possibility of fixing an artefact in time. Archaeologists can now dig underwater, cross-reference finds on computers and learn more quickly what their colleagues have discovered. They can call on a host of specialists, including paleo-botanists, osteologists, ethnologists, philologists and biblical exegetes to interpret their finds.

Most importantly, archaeologists now emphasise that once a locus – a three-dimensional area designated for excavation – is dug and artefacts are removed, the site will have been ineluctably altered. By the very nature of their work, they destroy irreplaceable evidence in their search for remnants of the past.

## A passion for proof

Archaeology is a field whose study bolsters or threatens religious and political beliefs – as well as pet scholarly theories. In the late 1970s, for example, a small but vocal ultra-Orthodox minority tried to stop a dig at the City of David, claiming it was desecrating ancient graves. The archaeologists countered that no evidence pointed to the existence of any graves at the original site of King David's Jerusalem.

Jordan has filed formal complaints with UNESCO – largely for political reasons – against Israeli digs in East Jerusalem, although the Israeli government has done much to preserve important archaeological sites there.

Among secular, apolitical scholars the real value of the Bible in their archaeological work is hotly debated. Many doubt its utility as a historical document and a source of verifiable reference. Others cling firmly to the Bible's documentary importance and infallibility.

The careers of Israel's greatest archaeologists were hewn from this complex web of scholarly debate and political instability, plus a national passion to unearth the Jewish past. Eliezar Sukenik, his son Yigael Yadin, Moshe Dayan, Benjamin Mazar – who can think of these archaeologists except in conjunction with Israel's struggle for independence?

Mazar, who directed the 1960s excavations next to the Western Wall in Jerusalem, remembers his 1936 dig at Beit She'arim in northern Israel: "Everyone had a keen interest in the excavation, because finding Jewish antiquities reinforced the meaning of Zionism and

Despite difficulties, an impressive amount of literature has been produced, further illuminating the pages of the Bible. Archaeology may be the perfect pastime for the inhabitants of the Middle East, who have a penchant for argument and disputation.

Wherever you go in Israel you will probably meet someone who has an opinion on just who is buried in David's Tomb. Or you may stumble on to the multi-million-dollar excavation of Theo and Miriam Seibenberg, amateur archaeologists who determined that their home in Jerusalem's Jewish Quarter was planted on top of important remains. ❑

strengthened the reason for creating a Jewish state. We were... building a homeland, and Jewish antiquities were part of its foundation."

Of Sukenik's discovery in 1947 of the Dead Sea Scrolls, Yadin writes: "He found something symbolic in the thought that this was happening at the very moment when Jewish sovereignty in Palestine was about to be restored after almost 2,000 years – the very age of the parchment he had seen." That parchment is now part of the collection at the Shrine of the Book, in the Israel Museum.

**LEFT:** Theo Seibenberg examines a newly-found artefact. **ABOVE:** archaeologists debate a vital point.

## POPULARISING THE PAST

Yigael Yadin, the son of Eliezer Sukenik, followed in his father's footsteps, and has conducted many digs of his own. His books on Masada, Khatsor ha-Glilit and the Dead Sea Scrolls have dramatised the history of the "people of the book". In addition, much of his work has been popularised by others. Khatsor, a site in northern Israel with an underground water system, is the subject of James Michener's best-selling novel *The Source*. And Yadin's dig at Masada – where he discovered a ritual bath and synagogue – became the focus of a TV mini-series from which millions learned about the heroic stand of a handful of Jews against the Roman forces in AD 73.

# CONSERVING FOR THE FUTURE

*Since the State of Israel was created, forests have been planted and the land*

*regenerated, but creeping urbanisation remains a threat*

Wine, the Good Book says, "maketh glad the heart of man" (Psalm 104, 15). In Israel, where that book was written, wine-making keeps the birds happy too. That's because Israeli wine is kosher, and ancient Jewish dietary laws require all fields – including vineyards – to lie fallow every seventh year – a practice that may be one of mankind's first displays of environmental awareness.

Each year, one-seventh of Israel's viticulture production hangs unharvested. These grapes usually ripen just in time for fall migrations, so songbirds flying from Eurasia to wintering grounds in Africa can enjoy a glorious banquet on the way.

The birds' bonanza is but one of the many advantages nature enjoys in the Land of Milk and Honey. The creation of the modern State of Israel has proved highly beneficial, as special programmes have devoted energy and talent to the revival of the land and the restoration of its ecological integrity. As a result, Israel today is a cornucopia of nature, abundant and diverse, with many species of fauna and flora.

## Redeeming the land

Early in the 20th century, when the Zionist ideal was little more than a philosophical debate, the region was a desolate backwater of the crumbling Ottoman Empire. Its ecological dynamics had suffered catastrophically. Nature had been ravished. The hand of havoc had reached into the Garden of Eden.

The introduction of modern firearms was a tragedy for wildlife. Within a few decades, large numbers of the gazelles and ibex which had lived here since the days of the prophets had been ruthlessly killed. A monstrous hunting binge shot several species into extinction.

The local race of ostrich, which so perplexed Job, was blasted to nothingness. Israel's native race of Asiatic wild ass, a creature which some religious scholars identify as the animal Jesus

rode on Palm Sunday, was annihilated. The spectacular white oryx antelope, the *re'em* of the Hebrew Bible, translated in the King James Version as unicorn, suffered a similar fate. Fortunately, a few specimens were captured for breeding before the last of the wild population was exterminated.

Flora was also destroyed. For centuries Christian pilgrims had scoured the countryside for biblical wildflowers. These were picked, pressed and sent back to Europe to serve as bookmarks in family Bibles. Generations of Europeans could "consider the lilies" of the Holy Land – but these lilies were lifeless, dried, and incapable of reproduction. Today, Israel's native Madonna lily is a very rare plant.

The big disaster came a century ago, when the Ottoman Turks built a railway into the Arabian Desert, and the region's forests were levelled. The heavy timbers were used to bridge ravines, middle-sized logs became rail ties, and the smaller pieces were burned as fuel. By the

**LEFT:** kids do their bit for conservation.
**RIGHT:** ibex have been in Israel since biblical times.

time T. E. Lawrence (Lawrence of Arabia) was attacking the Ottoman trains, Israel had less than 3 percent tree cover.

With the loss of vegetation, the soil dried out, turned to dust, and was swept out to the desert by the wind. The scant winter rains had no absorbent material to hold them, and water ran quickly to the sea while the wells dried out.

Early Jewish settlers determined to recreate the biblical Land of Israel were confronted by severe problems. The land was exhausted, and could not support either a human population or its own natural processes. The ecological integrity of the land had to be restored.

2,000 sq. km (770 sq. miles) – 10 percent of the total land area of the country. With the return of the trees, winter rains were captured and channelled to the aquifers. Wells again became productive. With the return of the trees, particularly the fast-growing Jerusalem pine (*Pinus halepensis*), soil was regenerated. In many places the pines were cut once the soil was adequate and immediately replaced with apricot, almond and other fruit and nut trees.

With the return of trees, soil and water, agriculture prospered. Israel is one of the very few arid lands which grows enough food to feed itself, and which also has enough surplus to

### Plant a tree

The 15th day of the Jewish month of Shevat, Tu B'Shevat, is an Israeli Arbor Day, celebrated by planting trees in any of the scores of special planting zones in the nation's forests. Israelis plant trees on other days, too – to mark birthdays and weddings, for example. Children and parents honour each other by planting trees. In one forest about 20 km (12 miles) west of Jerusalem 6 million trees have been planted as a memorial to the Jews who perished in the Holocaust. Israeli school children visit the forest every year to plant new saplings.

Since the founding of the State of Israel in 1948, planted forests have grown to cover

count agricultural exports as its major foreign exchange product.

With the return of the trees, nature also flourished, and the land began to recover. Life processes dependent upon a good vegetative cover were regenerated. Some are hardly noticed – for example, the sprouting of orenit mushrooms in the Jerusalem forest after the first winter rains, or the growth of colourful mosaics of lichen upon fallen logs. Others are so dramatic that they are impossible to miss. The majestic golden eagles have returned to the skies, and one pair even builds its nest each year in the branches of a planted pine forest just south of Jerusalem.

## Nature reserves

There are 280 established nature reserves in Israel, covering more than 4,000 sq. km (1,540 sq. miles) – more than than one-fifth of the country's total land area. By international standards, the reserves are strictly run. They are maintained in as pristine a state as possible, and visitors are forbidden to pick flowers, camp or picnic. Administered by the Nature Reserves Authority, they serve a variety of functions. Generally, they reflect the need for humanity and nature to coexist. An example can be seen at Banias, a beautiful nature reserve at the foot of Mount Hermon, on Israel's northern border.

which flow from the slopes of Mount Hermon.

These waters give a human dimension to this nature reserve, for they are the headwaters of the Jordan River, and much of them eventually enters Israel's national water-carrier system. They flow from taps in Tel Aviv and Haifa, help irrigate the fields of the Galilee, and fill the fish ponds of the Beit She'an Valley.

Many nature reserves are established solely for the preservation of particular natural features: a seasonal pond, a secluded valley where rare flowers blossom, a sunny cliff with good nesting ledges. Some of these reserves are off-limits to human visitors because of

The name Banias is a corruption of the Greek "Panaeas", and here there are the remains of an ancient Greek temple dedicated to the god of the forests. Other archaeological treasures in the area include the remains of the ancient Nimrod Fortress and the Crusader town of Belinas.

The reserve's colourful wild oleander and thick groves of myrtle, plane and willow trees appeal to the naturalist's eye. It is a haven for a great variety of birds and mammals. The rare stone marten and wild cat live here, and otters splash with carefree abandon in the waters

**LEFT AND ABOVE:** spring flowers bloom among the cacti at Yitzrael Valley in the Galilee.

### HOLDING BACK THE DESERT

Much of the regeneration of the land has been achieved by the Jewish National Fund (JNF), Israel's afforestation agency, which was also responsible for planting the northern hemisphere's most southerly non-equatorial forest, the Yatir Forest, in the northern Negev desert.

The agency is particularly concerned with combating desert encroachment. But, despite its extraordinary achievements, the JNF comes in for criticism as well as praise. Some environmental organisations in Israel accuse it of overkill, claiming that it is trying to create European-style forests in places where a semi-arid desert environment should naturally exist.

their importance to nature and the ecological equilibrium of the region.

One of the most interesting projects is the Khai-Bar programme. Khai-Bar is a Hebrew term which simply means "wildlife", but to Israeli conservationists it also identifies an international effort to "return the animals of the Bible to the land of the Bible". Conservationists have searched the world to find remnants of the species which once inhabited these lands. Some of the discoveries were prosaic: addax antelope were found in a Chicago zoo, and a few Asiatic wild ass came from the Copenhagen Zoo.

A few of the discoveries have involved some

bilitate them to life in Israel's wild areas. One Khai-Bar reserve is deep in the Negev, about 40 km (25 miles) north of Eilat; it specialises in desert animals. Another is on top of Mount Carmel, on the Mediterranean coast near Haifa; its speciality is wildlife of the Mediterranean oak-forest region. A third Khai-Bar reserve is in the process of being set up on the Golan, to handle animals indigenous to the Galilean plains and Golan Heights.

The restoration process is comprehensive and involves years of painstaking work. Indeed, 14 years passed between the acquisition of the Asiatic wild ass from the Copenhagen Zoo, and

spectacular rescue work. Mesopotamian fallow deer, for example, were spirited out of revolutionary Iran during a howling storm, on false export papers. White oryx – the unicorns of the King James Bible – reached their ancestral home in the Negev after a globe-trotting journey of tens of thousands of kilometres. Their source was a few hundred kilometres southeast of the Negev – in the personal zoo of the late Saudi King Faisal. And a flock of ostrich chicks was air-lifted out of Ethiopia's Danakil desert when the Israeli Air Force was sent on a special mission to fetch some new immigrants to Israel.

All the animals, regardless of their origin, are first brought to special reserves set up to reha-

### UNWELCOME IMPROVEMENT

The Hula Nature Reserve in the Upper Galilee is perhaps an example of over-zealous attempts by Israel to "improve" on the existing environment. In the 1950s the Hula Swamp was drained to make way for agriculture. Of the 4,000 hectares (10,000 acres) drained, 80 hectares (200 acres) were left as a nature reserve, the habitat of water buffalo and diverse wildlife. But the farmland beneath the swamp, rich in peat, is becoming less and less fertile, and recently 400 hectares (1,000 acres) were reswamped.

This well-intentioned project has been acknowledged as a failure, and there are plans to restore the Hula Swamp in the long term.

the day when their offspring were judged tough and experienced enough to live freely in the wild. Today they are repopulating remote areas of the Negev and giving birth to wild foals.

## Ecological diversity

Despite its small size, Israel is one of the most ecologically diverse countries in the world. Two factors contribute to this: geography and topography. Geographically, Israel is at the confluence of the great Eurasian and African land masses, so any land traffic between them must pass through Israel. Many life forms have migrated through this channel; the evolutionary spread of the equines from Asia into Africa, and the migration of humanity itself from African origins through the rest of the world, filtered through this land.

Migration is still an extremely important phenomenon in Israel: twice yearly, millions of migratory birds pass through on their way to and from northern nesting grounds and southern wintering areas. More than 150 species of migratory bird are seen in Eilat alone.

Topography in Israel is a matter of spectacular contrasts. Mount Hermon, on the northern border, towers to a snowcapped 2,814 metres (9,223 ft); the Dead Sea, at 400 metres (1,300 ft) below sea level, is the lowest point on the face of the earth. Broad plains stretch across parts of the Galilee, and fringe the northern Negev with expanses of steppe grasslands. Makhtesh Ramon, a natural crater 40 km (25 miles) across, is carved from the central Negev highlands. The north–south range of the Judean Mountains forms a continuous ridge, nearly 1,000 metres (3,280 ft) high, an hour's drive east of the Mediterranean coast.

The great geographical and topographical diversity is responsible for tremendous biological diversity. There are sub-alpine meadows on the slopes of Mount Hermon, and a mere 25km (16 miles) south, at the Hula Nature Reserve, there is a lush tropical jungle: the world's northernmost papyrus swamp. Israel is a land of Eurasian oaks and African acacias, Eurasian foxes and wolves and African Dorcas gazelles and rock hyrax. It is a land of blending continents, flora, fauna and geology.

**LEFT:** a pair of scimitar-horned oryx grazing at a Khai-Bar reserve.
**RIGHT:** the Pillars of Solomon at Timna National Park.

## Encroaching urbanisation

Though Zionism has always cherished the environment, the success of the Zionist venture has proved an environmental threat. A rapidly expanding, increasingly affluent population means that more highways and cities are planned, often in some of Israel's most beautiful countryside. The Trans-Israel highway alone threatens to eat up a large swathe of land between the Negev and the Galilee, and environmentalists' urging to build railways rather than highways seems to fall on deaf ears. The attractive valley at the western entrance to Jerusalem is due to become an industrial zone.

Still, the environmentalists have won some victories in recent years, most notably in stopping a Voice of America radio relay station planned for the Negev. Its mass of antennae would have been smack in the path of millions of migrating birds. Despite US pressure and the lure of a $2 billion project, Israel declined the installation, which was built in Kuwait instead. In general, though, "green" issues are rarely on the political agenda, not because the Israelis are indifferent to them, but because issues of war and peace tend to dominate debate. Only when these matters are resolved will greater numbers of Israelis begin to protest against environmental desecration. ❑

# A HIGH-TECH ECONOMY

*Israel's high-tech economy has long tentacles, affecting sectors as diverse as diamonds and fresh foods*

In recent years the Israeli economy has enjoyed impressive rates of growth, averaging about 6 percent annually in the first half of the 1990s, making it one of the world's fastest-expanding developed economies. The austerity of Israel's formative years has been swept away by a tide of affluence as Israel's standard of living approaches that of Britain and Italy. If the stereotypical Israeli hero was once a kibbutz pioneer battling to cultivate the land or a daring paratrooper, today it is the high-tech business executive whose company provides innovative software solutions to many of the world's major computer and semiconductor corporations.

The arrival, since 1990, of more than 800,000 new immigrants from the former Soviet Union, a high percentage of them well-educated scientists, engineers and medical personnel, has helped to fuel Israel's impressive economic development. Even before this wave of immigration Israel had, for example, the highest number of physicians per capita in the world. Between 1990 and 1996 the country's 13,000 doctors were joined by an additional 15,000 among the new immigrants. Some 4 percent of the newcomers hold PhDs.

But this pattern of immigration alone is not enough to explain the country's economic success. Indeed, many newcomers need time to adjust to the Western capitalist ethos before they are able to make a valuable contribution. Two other factors, the peace process and the high-tech requirements of the modern world, have boosted Israel's economic performance and potential.

## The end of the Arab boycott

The Middle East peace process has been of crucial importance to the Israeli economy. Trade between Israel and the Arab world remains negligible and is unlikely to increase significantly in the coming years. But, more importantly, the peace process has meant the end of the tertiary Arab boycott, which meant that business corporations and governments in other countries were unwilling to do business with Israel because it would jeopardise their sales in the Arab world.

Until the Madrid Peace Conference in 1991

(after which China, India and many other Asian countries first established full diplomatic relations with Israel), dozens of major multinational corporations, such as Pepsi-Cola, and Asia-based companies, including those in Japan, South Korea and China – highly dependent on Arab oil – virtually refused to do business with Israel.

The importance of this change can be gauged by the fact that 20 percent of Israel's $20-billion-worth of exports in 1996 went to Asia, and nearly 10 percent to the countries of the former Soviet Union and Eastern Europe, who also only established diplomatic ties with Israel in the late 1980s.

**LEFT:** the Diamond Exchange, Ramat Gan.
**RIGHT:** cybernetics at the Haifa bio-med faculty.

Perhaps even more important than these diplomatic developments has been the changing emphases of the world's Western economy. It is estimated that 60 percent of Israel's exports (excluding diamonds) have some high-tech input. These range from micro-chips manufactured by the Israeli subsidiaries of major world corporations like Intel, Motorola and National Semiconductor, through to the computerised imaging systems of Scitex, which pioneered automated page layout for the world's press, and the CAT (computer assisted tomography) scanners of the Haifa-based Elscint.

The Arrow anti-missile, the first of its kind,

## Developing natural resources

Opponents of Zionism always pointed out that Israel had no natural resources and would, therefore, fail to develop economically. Proponents always claimed that the country's brain power would see it prosper. But even the latter group could never have envisaged how important ingenuity would become.

Even Israel's limited natural resources have become significant through technological developments. Israel exports more than $600 million-worth of minerals from the Dead Sea, largely because scientists found more efficient ways of extracting potash from the water, and

will also be used by the US Army when completed, while the Amos series of spacecraft has meant that Israel is now one of the few countries worldwide which is capable of launching its own satellites.

But it is in the field of computer software that Israel has really come into its own. The country is said to be the largest producer of CD-Roms and multimedia products after the USA, and in such areas as databases, CAD/CAM, internet security and education, Israeli software houses have a worldwide reputation. The country has also found substantial worldwide markets in telecommunications, data communications, biotechnology and pharmaceuticals.

### DIAMONDS ARE A HIGH-TECH TRADE

Israel may not be the first name that comes to mind when one thinks of the diamond trade, but it is the world's largest centre for cutting and polishing diamonds, exporting $4 billion-worth of the precious stones each year. The high-rise Diamond Exchange at Ramat Gan is the nerve-centre of this industry. State-of-the-art technology plays a vital role, as computers have greatly enhanced Israel's position in the field by enabling cutters to calculate the optimum way to carve up the larger stones. An aggressive marketing campaign, especially in the Far East, has opened up the Japanese market, where there has never been a tradition of acquiring diamonds.

developed uses for the bromine found there. More recently an innovative method of producing magnesium metal from the liquid deposits in the Dead Sea promises to open up lucrative export markets. A new plant has been built by Israel Chemicals in partnership with Volkswagen.

## Staying one step ahead

Even Israel's traditional exports, such as diamonds and fruit and vegetables, have major high-tech inputs. A combination of high-technology and marketing has benefited the diamond trade (see the information box, page 122)

the Israeli economy to succeed despite, rather than because of, government policies. Until the mid-1980s the country suffered from three-digit annual inflation and constant devaluation of the shekel. The more sober economic policies practised since 1986 have stabilised the currency, brought down inflation to just 4 percent per annum, and decreased the balance of payments deficit, although at the expense of rising unemployment. Despite the rise, unemployment of around 6 percent has been a major achievement in the light of the wave of recent immigration.

In addition, successive Israeli governments have dragged their feet over economic reform.

and helped Israel's export sales in fruit, vegetables and flowers. In selling to Western European consumers the country has had to stay one step ahead of Mediterranean competitors, and this has been accomplished by developing more exotic types of fruit and vegetables, such as the avocado, the persimmon, and cherry tomatoes, as well as new strains of more basic fruits and vegetables that can go onto the market when produce is scarce and prices are high.

Such ingenuity and endeavour have enabled

Between them the government and the Histadrut trade union movement still own much of the economy, and there is a tendency to wait until companies get into financial difficulties before change is brought about.

While many in positions of power in Israel – particularly in the Histadrut – are reluctant to relinquish altogether the socialist economics of the country's founding fathers, the economy is an export-oriented one and therefore market forces must inevitably be obeyed. But ultimately this is not likely to prove a problem because there seems to be an increasing demand for Israeli goods and, especially, for Israeli know-how. ❑

**Left:** an enigmatic solar energy researcher at the Weizmann Institute. **Above:** factories are essential for trade and employment.

# PLACES

*A detailed guide to the whole of Israel, with principal sites clearly cross-referenced by number to the maps*

Arriving at Ben Gurion Airport, visitors are likely to choose one of two directions: eastwards up through the Judean Hills to Jerusalem, with its history and religion, or westwards past the fragrant citrus groves to Tel Aviv, Israel's bustling, economic capital, a brash place with golden beaches and a pulsating nightlife, a city looking to its future rather than its past.

From east to west, Israel (including the Palestinian autonomous zones) is less than 100 km (60 miles) at its broadest points. Tel Aviv is at the heart of the coastal plain, a densely populated, narrow piece of land stretching from the Gaza Strip in the south to Lebanon in the north, with mild, wet, sunny winters and hot, humid summers.

The inland hills to the east offer cooler, drier climes. Jerusalem is perched on a peak 830 metres (2,700 ft) high, and other ancient cities such as the West Bank towns of Bethlehem, Hebron and Nablus are also built on hills. Here the hot, dry summers are tempered by delicious late afternoon breezes and in the winter there can even be a dusting of snow. In the spring, the best time to visit, the hillsides are ablaze with flowers. The terraced hillsides of olive groves and grapevines have a biblical charm, but otherwise the landscape has a Mediterranean familiarity.

The terrain east of Jerusalem has an alien, exotic charm, for, in addition to its social divisions, the Holy City is a continental divide. The western slopes lead down through forest and field to the Mediterranean, but to the east the land dips down dramatically through rugged desert to the Dead Sea basin, the lowest point on earth, and the northern stretch of the great Africa-Syria rift valley.

The craggy canyons and billowing beige hills of this desolate rock desert have historically attracted religious hermits, and contain concealed monasteries. The Dead Sea itself is really a lake with becalmed waters, that nestles amid a landscape of shimmering mountains and has a high salt content which enables bathers to float – a highlight of any trip to Israel.

The 500 km (300 miles) from north to south take the traveller from the majestic snow-covered peaks of Mount Hermon and the rolling hills of the Galilee to the tropical waters of the Red Sea resort of Eilat. En route are the Sea of Galilee, the Jordan Valley and Dead Sea, and the Arava Valley and Negev Desert. It is possible in the winter to ski on the slopes of Mount Hermon in the morning and go scuba diving in the Red Sea in the afternoon, where remarkable coral formations and exotically coloured fish of all shapes and sizes are a feast for the eye. Use the itineraries in the following pages to discover the best that Israel has to offer. ❑

**PRECEDING PAGES:** the Dead Sea, at the earth's lowest point; Mount Hermon; the Monastery of St George at Wadi Kelt.
**LEFT:** a street in old Bethlehem, in the West Bank.

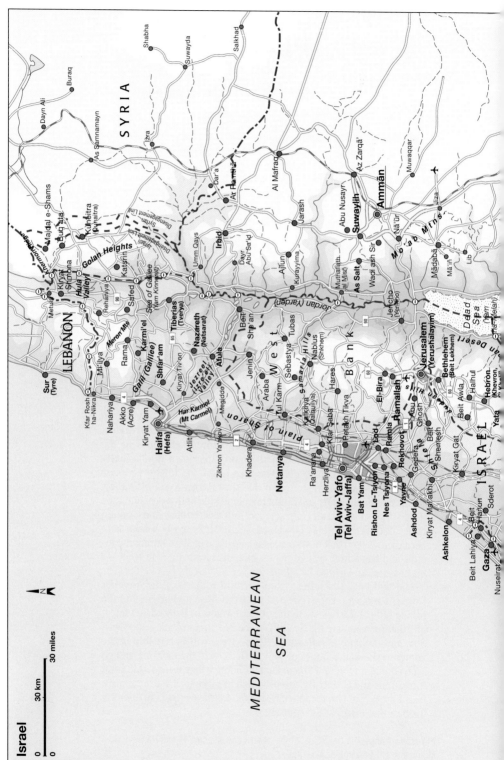

Israel

MEDITERRANEAN SEA

0  30 km
0  30 miles

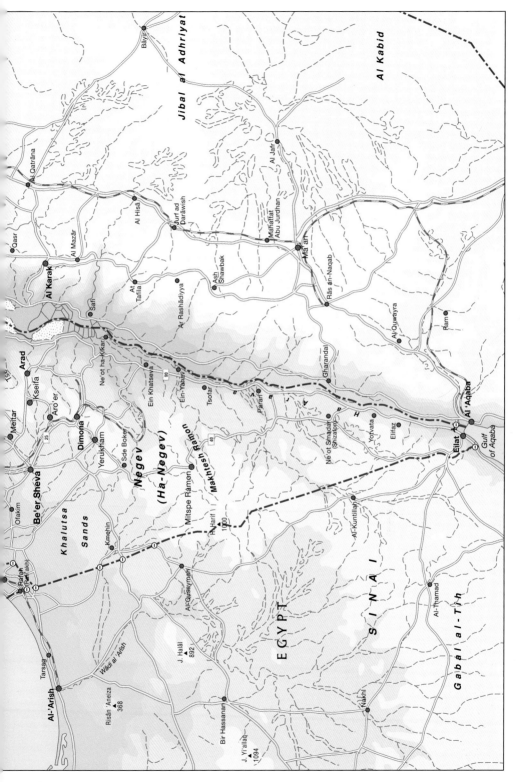

# JERUSALEM YESTERDAY AND TODAY

*The followers of three major world religions demand a say in the future of the Golden City. To appreciate why, you need to understand its turbulent past*

Map on pages 166–7

Jerusalem has been called many things: the Golden City, the Holy City, the City of David, the City of Peace. Sadly, it is also a city of strife. To Jews, it is their national and spiritual epicentre: the incarnation of ancient Israel; the place where Abraham went to sacrifice Isaac; the site of David's glory and Solomon's Temple; the eternal capital of the Jewish people. To Christians, it is the city where Jesus spent his last days on earth: the site of the Last Supper, the Crucifixion and Resurrection. To Muslims, it is Al Quds ("The Holy"), the place where Mohammed is said to have ascended to Heaven on his steed; indeed, it is Islam's third holiest city after Mecca and Medina.

From its enduring power as a spiritual symbol, to the quality of the light, Jerusalem is unique. And today, some 3,000 years after David made the city his capital, Jerusalem still has the ability to stir emotions and fire the imagination like no other city on earth.

**PRECEDING PAGES:** the Western Wall. **LEFT:** sunset from the Mount of Olives. **BELOW:** opposition to a road scheme.

## Visiting Jerusalem

Still the centrepiece of many a journey to Israel, as it has been throughout the centuries, Jerusalem continues to reward the traveller with its riches. The market-places, shrines, ruins, hotels, temples, churches and mosques are all readily accessible, and the city's tourist board is more than willing to provide directions. Yet the soul of the city is more elusive. The rhythm of daily life here is governed by prayer, usually channelled through tightly-knit religious communities, and the visitor who merely barters for *chachkas* in the Old City between hops to famous churches or museums is missing the source and substance of the place.

Also, as the seat of government for the state and a major academic centre, Jerusalem has an important secular profile, which shouldn't be overlooked.

Physically, Jerusalem is actually three cities in one, totalling over 600,000 residents. The modern part of the city, spreading out to the west, northwest and south, is West Jerusalem, a Jewish enclave since its inception in the late 1800s, and since 1948 the capital of the State of Israel. East Jerusalem comprises the city east of the old "green line" that divided it from 1948 to 1967, during which time it was Jordanian. This section is still largely Arab in population and culture. In the centre of it all is the Old City, wrapped in its ancient golden walls, containing much of historic Jerusalem and its shrines. It, too, was in Jordanian hands up to the Six Day War of 1967.

The Israeli victory that week in June 1967 not only

rolled away the barbed wire and roadblocks but also fulfilled the 2,000-year dream of returning to the Western Wall and the Old City. Israel officially annexed the Old City and East Jerusalem in 1967, and Jerusalem is once more a united city with an open flow of traffic. The Arab states still look upon these areas as occupied territory, and their return is the ultimate goal of the PLO in the peace process, but it seems unlikely that Israel will ever voluntarily part with the Old City with its thriving Jewish Quarter and the Western Wall.

## David's capital

In ancient times it was said that the world had 10 measures of beauty, of which nine belonged to Jerusalem. The city's acclaim (or immodesty) only served to make it attractive to conquerors; since its greatest hour of glory as the capital of the Israelite kingdom, it has been the object of repeated siege and conquest. In part this was due to its strategic situation on a vital trade route, at the crossroads between East and West. Ironically, however, it was later the very holiness of the city that inspired its would-be champions' relentless ferocity.

Jerusalem first crops up in biblical narrative during Abraham's migrations from Ur to Canaan. Here he was greeted warmly by Melchizedek, King of Salem, "priest of the most high God". The Israelites were already well-ensconced in the hills of Judea when David captured the city from the Jebusites around 1000 BC. Building an altar for the Ark of the Covenant on the crown of Mount Moriah, he made the city his capital, renaming it Jerusalem – the "Dwelling of Peace".

The 35 years under David's rule, and the subsequent 40 under Solomon, brought splendour to the once modest fortress town. The site of David's altar

*The Menorah at Heikhal Shlomo.*

**BELOW:** the classic panorama of the walled city.

Map on pages 166–7

saw the rise of Solomon's magnificent Temple, incorporating the much-sought-after cedar wood from Lebanon, copper from the mines at Timna, and a wide variety of rich metals and carved figures. The city was embellished with the wealth of an expansive empire, its walls reaching in an oblong shape to include David's city on the slopes of Ha-Ofel and down to the pool of Silwan below.

Around 926 BC King Solomon died, and in the absence of his authority the kingdom was split in two by his successors. Jerusalem remained the capital of the southern Kingdom of Judah, as the following centuries saw the city and its kingdom succumb to the expanding control of the Assyrians. In 586 BC Nebuchadnezzar of Babylonia plundered the city, sending its inhabitants into exile. They returned in 539 BC under the policy of the new king, Cyrus the Great of Persia, and set at once to the task of building a Second Temple.

## Greeks and Romans

Alexander the Great's conquest of Jerusalem in 332 BC initiated a brief Hellenisation of Jewish culture in the city and then in 198 BC the Seleucids took control. Deprived of religious rights, the Maccabees spearheaded a Jewish uprising, leading to the reconsecration of the destroyed Temple in 165 BC.

Hasmonean rule gave way in 63 BC to Rome, with the conquering armies of the Roman general Pompey. In 40 BC the Roman Senate conferred the rule on Herod the Great and sent him to Judea; during his reign his psychopathic behaviour was matched only by his extensive architectural endeavours, most notably the Second Temple which, according to the historian Josephus, was built by 10,000 workmen and 1,000 priests. It took eight years to complete the courtyard and another couple of years to finish the Temple itself.

*Herod the Great (King of Judea 40BC–AD4) was Jewish on his father's side.*

Map on pages 166–7

When it was completed, it was widely regarded as one of the wonders of the world. Jerusalem was still a Jewish city under Roman rule when Jesus's crucifixion was ordered by the procurator Pontius Pilate around AD 30.

The increasingly insensitive Roman administration was challenged by the Jewish Revolt of 66, which was crushed four years later by Titus, who, in the process, razed Jerusalem and plundered the Second Temple. A second rebellion was instigated by Emperor Hadrian's decree to lay the city out anew on a Roman plan and call it Aelia Capitolina; but the Bar-Kochba revolt of 132 was stamped out, and in 135 Hadrian initiated the reconstruction of the city, making it illegal for any Jew to enter its boundaries.

## Christianisation in the 4th century

The great Christianisation of Jerusalem was inaugurated in the 4th century by the Byzantine Emperor Constantine; in the 7th century the city fell to Muslim rule, and in 1099 to the bloody grip of the Crusaders for some 80 years. It once more came into its own under the Ottoman Emperor Suleiman, who rebuilt its walls from 1537 to 1541. After his death, until modern times, it fell into decline.

To this day, Suleiman's walls remain the most impressive monument to the city's multi-layered history. From stone stairways at various points in its span you can mount the restored Ramparts Walk, which follows every circuit but that by the Temple Mount. A "green belt" of lawns surrounds much of the circumference, adding to the view. The seven gates of the city are a source of fascination in themselves (*see page 164*). Just inside the Jaffa Gate, which serves as the main entrance to the Old City from West Jerusalem, is the famous Citadel, or Tower of David. In reality the structure doesn't have much to do with David; it was built by Herod, who named its three towers after his wife Mariamne, his brother Phaesal and his friend Hippicus, and was so impressive that Titus let it stand after burning the city. The Mamelukes and later Suleiman reinforced it, adding its minaret.

**BELOW:** a wall plaque in the Garden of Gethsemane.
**RIGHT:** at the Church of the Holy Sepulchre.

## Exploring the city with this guide

For practical purposes, we have divided the rest of the city into three chapters. "The Old City" (*page 143*) describes the sites within the city walls; "Outside the City Walls" (*page 157*) covers the many places of interest just outside the ancient boundaries; and both East and West Jerusalem are discussed in the chapter on "The New Jerusalem" (*page 169*).

You shouldn't hesitate to follow your own instincts in exploring this city; and do examine the possibilities of taking detours to the less obvious sites. For any guide book to attempt to describe Jerusalem in a few chapters is rather like asking a rabbi to describe the entire Talmud while standing on one foot. Probably this is just as well, for no amount of explanation can hope to capture the spirit of this complex place: the patina of gold on the Dome of the rock, the view from the Mount of Olives at sunset, the shifting moods of its houses and hills, the thoughtfulness and pride in the eyes of its citizens and the bizarre but beautiful echo of interwoven prayers – of all religions – that envelop the city walls, blowing in the wind, night and day. ❑

# JERUSALEM: THE OLD CITY

*A tour of the many sacred shrines, historic houses
and atmospheric markets contained within the
ancient walls of the Old City*

Map
on page
144

It's a museum, a bazaar, a collection of sacred shrines. It also happens to be home for ten of thousands of residents crammed within the 4-km (2½-mile) circumference of its old battlements. Its gates never close, night or day, for the 2 million overseas visitors who are drawn to the Old City of Jerusalem each year. The Jewish, Christian, Armenian and Muslim quarters of the Old City each have their own special significance, and we'll look at these as we go along.

## Around the Jaffa Gate

The main portal between the Old City and West Jerusalem is the **Jaffa Gate ❶**. The site offers a number of contemporary attractions which include the **Tower of David Museum of the History of Jerusalem ❷** (open April–Oct: daily 9am–5pm; Nov–March: daily 10am–4pm; admission charge) inside the body of the Citadel, which contains displays describing the tumultuous history of the city, figurines of Jerusalem characters, a 19th-century model of the Old City, and the multi-layered ruins of the structure itself. A multi-media show with a separate entrance describes the various moods of Jerusalem via numerous slide projectors. The walls themselves are the palette for the sound and light show presented here in a host of different languages most evenings from April to October. The Municipal Tourist Office (tel: 02-6280382) just within the gate serves as a popular starting point for walking tours.

**LEFT:** visitors to the Dome of the Rock. **BELOW:** the Jaffa Gate: the entrance to the Old City.

Also opposite the entrance to the museum is the **Christian Information Office**. About 150 metres (165 yds) in from the Jaffa Gate is the narrow entrance to the labyrinthine **Bazaar** (El Bazar) **❸**. Go straight down into the Arab souk. Aggressively friendly shopkeepers will assault you with all manner of trinkets at "special prices", but take time to distinguish the quality from the trash, because both forms abound. Prices in the stores nearest the Jaffa Gate are generally more expensive, and some shopkeepers even have the *chutzpah* to refuse to haggle. The further into the market, the better the bargains.

It's a wonderful place for bargain hunters. Palestinian pottery and Armenian tiles are attractive, but cheaper varieties have little glazing and will fade. Brass items such as coffee servers and tables should be judged by their weight: too light and it's probably plated tin. Too shiny is also suspect; a little tarnish suggests authenticity. Sheepskin jackets, gloves and slippers are popular, but in time these may smell too much like sheep, especially if they get wet. At the end of the alleyway El Bazar, just before a T-junction, a black sign overhead points right to Ha-Kardo. Turn right here and almost immediately you leave the Muslim Quarter and enter the Jewish Quarter.

## The Jewish Quarter

Inhabited by Jews as far back as the First Temple Period 3,000 years ago, the
Jewish Quarter today is a modern neighbourhood housing over 1,000 families,
with numerous synagogues and *yeshivas* (academies for Jewish studies). This
thriving little community was rebuilt out of the rubble following the reunifica-
tion of Jerusalem in the 1967 Six Day War. Families who had lived in the quarter prior to their expulsion by the Jordanians in 1948 were the first to move
back in. Religious Jews revived many of the old study houses and congregations.
Artists, attracted by the picturesque lanes, soon took up residence. Today the
Jewish Quarter is one of the city's most desirable (and expensive) areas.

Nowhere is the old-new character of the quarter more evident than in the
**Ha-Kardo** (Cardo) ➍. With its modern lamps and smart shopfronts, this sub-
merged pedestrian byway at first looks like a trendy shopping mall incongru-
ously set next to the old bazaar. Ha-Kardo was the north–south axis of the
garrison town that the Romans built after they destroyed Jerusalem in AD 70.

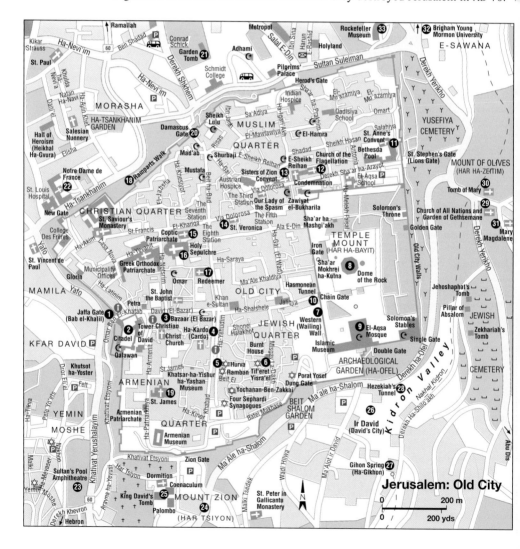

Jerusalem: Old City

Map
on page
144

Called Aelia Capitolina, the town was laid out geometrically like an army camp, with Ha-Kardo (from Latin: cardinal, or principal) as its main thoroughfare. In the Byzantine period this colonnaded avenue ran for 180 metres (300 yds) to a looming church called the Nea, built by Emperor Justinian in 543 and destroyed in an earthquake in the 8th century. Later the Crusaders used Ha-Kardo as a main market street. After they were expelled by the Muslims, Jerusalem reverted to a backwater and Ha-Kardo was eventually buried beneath 4 metres (13 ft) of rubble, to be excavated and brought to life again only in the 1980s.

Signs and diagrams posted along either side of the "new" Ha-Kardo pinpoint the remains of the various civilisations that conducted their daily commerce here. A large excavation reveals the outer wall of the city of the Judean King Hezekiah. At another point, Byzantine Corinthian-style columns have been restored, along with some roofing beams, to illustrate how shops once lined this thoroughfare.

The southern end of Ha-Kardo is open to the sky. Here the big paving stones lie bright in the sunlight, the columns exposed in all their classic beauty. It's also from this point outdoors that visitors can best appreciate the reconciliation of demands for a museum and a neighbourhood. City planners wanted to build apartments along the route, while archaeologists insisted that the historical heart of the city be exposed. The compromise: apartments standing on stilts above the ancient avenue.

## Museums and memorials

Running parallel to Ha-Kardo is **Ha-Yehudim** (Jewish Quarter Road), the site of the **Jewish Quarter Museum**, which offers a 15-minute multi-media presentation on the history of the area from the Israelite period to the present. The emphasis is on how the Jewish Quarter was lost to the Arab Legion in Israel's War of Independence in 1948; how it was subsequently regained in the Six Day War of 1967; and how it has since been reconstructed. The museum also has an unusual collection of pictures taken by *Life* magazine photographer John Phillips, both during the battle in 1948, and in 1975 when he returned to find and photograph the survivors.

A few steps away from the museum is a memorial to the fighters who fell defending the quarter. An electronic map recreates the battle, house by house.

Between the museum and the memorial is the Ashkenazi Court, a synagogue and residential complex established in 1400 by European Jews. The great **Hurva Synagogue** ❺ was burned by angry creditors in 1720 (hence its name, which means ruin). In 1856 it was rebuilt, but in May of 1948 it was blown up by the Arabs; today only the dynamic span of its front archway rises over the site.

Beneath the Hurva is the Ramban Synagogue, built shortly after the noted Bible commentator Rabbi Moses Ben Nahman emigrated from Spain in 1267, and possibly the oldest of the many houses of worship in the Jewish Quarter. Now it is used every day.

The most enchanting of the quarter's venerable houses of worship are on Ha-Kehuna in the complex known as the **Four Sephardi Synagogues**. Destroyed during the 1948 battle and used as stables during the 19-year Jordanian rule of the Old City, these

**BELOW:** buyers and sellers in an old City market.

synagogues have been lovingly restored to serve both as houses of worship and as a museum documenting their destruction and rebirth. Of particular interest are the Italian hand-carved Arks of the Law in the Stambouli and Prophet Elijah Synagogues, and the early 17th-century Yochanan Ben-Zakkai Synagogue with its cheery folk characters.

A short walk up Or Ha-Khayim, the **Khatsar ha-Yishuv ha- Yushan** (open Sun–Thur) illustrates the lifestyles of the Jewish community of the Old City in bygone days when immigrants from a particular village in, say, Poland or Hungary would cluster around one court, sharing many facilities. The grounds incorporate two courts and two synagogues.

At the end of Tif'eret Yisra'el is the most remarkable archaeological site in the Jewish Quarter: the **Burnt House** ❻ (open Sun–Thur 9am–5pm, Fri 9am–1pm; admission charge). This, apparently, was the residence of the priestly Bar-Kathros clan at the time of the Jewish revolt against Rome. Among other clues, ashes from a great conflagration indicate that the house was destroyed when Titus razed the city. The numerous finds displayed within the house include a measuring weight bearing the name Kathros, and the skeletal arm of a woman in the kitchen who was apparently struggling to escape the fire.

## The Western Wall

The wide stone steps at the end of Tif'eret Yisra'el lead down to the most important site – not only within the quarter, but in all of Jewish civilisation. This, of course, is the Kotel ha-Ma'aravi, or the **Western Wall** ❼. Clambering up and down these steps at all hours of the day and night – like so many angels ascending and descending Jacob's ladder – is a stream of worshippers, pilgrims and

**TIP**

The most popular places to eat are the cafés on David Street; the funky sweet shops along Souk Khan ez-Zeit; and Abu-Shukri's on El-Wad Street, which sells wonderful houmous.

**BELOW:** late afternoon light bathes the Jewish Quarter.

Map
on page
144

tourists. The hum from the right comes from the students of the rebuilt **Porat Yosef**, the largest *yeshiva* (religious seminary) in the quarter and the work of the noted Israeli architect Moshe Safdie. Midway down the steps is an observation platform, a good place to take in the famous postcard panorama. Below and to the left is the Western Wall plaza and the Wall itself.

## Above the Wall

The **Temple Mount** is the biblical Mount Moriah where Abraham nearly sacrificed Isaac; where the First and Second Temples once loomed, and where the golden Dome of the Rock and the silvery El-Aqsa Mosque now stand. To the right of the Temple Mount is a vast maze of archaeological excavations which lead to the Old City Wall and the Dung Gate.

The Jewish Quarter area was known in Temple times as the Upper City. The plaza below occupies the lower end of what was called the Tyropoeon Valley, the rift that cuts through the entire length of the Old City. Because this was the lowest point in the Old City, rubble and trash have been dumped here over the centuries, filling in much of the space between the upper level and the Temple Mount (and giving the Dung Gate its inglorious name).

Rising to a height of 15 metres (50 ft), the Western Wall consists chiefly of massive carved stone blocks from the Herodian era, topped by masonry from the Mameluke and Turkish periods. Contrary to popular belief, it was not a part of the Temple itself, but merely the retaining wall for the western side of the Temple Mount. But because it was the only remnant of the Temple complex to survive the Romans' sack of the city, it has inspired the reverence of Jewish people for approximately 2,000 years. Because Jews also gathered here to bemoan the

**BELOW:** praying at the Western Wall.

loss of the Temple, the place earned the evocative sobriquet "Wailing Wall".

The tunnel-like enclosure at the northern end of the Wall is the site of continuing excavations. The main arch, named after the 19th-century British explorer Captain Charles Wilson, may have supported a huge pedestrian bridge between the Temple Mount and the Upper City. Below the arch is the deep shaft dug by Wilson's contemporary, Sir Charles Warren. Archaeologists have determined that the Wall extends another 15 metres (50 ft) below ground level.

## The Temple Mount

*Turkish coffee, a legacy of the Ottoman Empire.*

Mosques and shrines dot the various quarters of the Old City, and most of the gates exhibit Islamic calligraphy, but the glories of Islamic Jerusalem are on the Temple Mount, which Muslims call **Haram esh-Sharif**, the Venerable Sanctuary, so this may be a good moment for a brief history of the Muslim impact on Jerusalem. It came essentially in three stages: the first was shortly after the death of Mohammed, when his successors spread the faith out of Arabia and wrested Jerusalem from the crumbling Byzantine Empire in 638. In this period Caliph Omar built a mosque on the Temple Mount which was later expanded to the Dome of the Rock, and in the 8th century the El-Aqsa Mosque was constructed nearby.

The second Muslim phase followed the brief Crusader occupation of the Holy Land. The Europeans were defeated by Saladin, and with the recovery of Jerusalem in 1187 the Muslims began a major reconstruction of the city and especially of the mosques. By 1249 the dominant Muslims were the Mamelukes, former slaves from Asia Minor who were highly accomplished architects and artisans. Much of the beauty of Islamic Jerusalem today is attributable to the work of the Mamelukes.

**BELOW:** celebrating a bar mitzvah at the Wall.

But corruption and dissolution marked their regime, and by 1516 the Mamelukes were easy prey for the invading Ottoman Turks. For the next 400 years Jerusalem was ruled from Constantinople. Early in this period (1520–66) Suleiman I built the city ramparts that we see today, the Damascus Gate and the greatest water system in the city from the time of Herod to the present. After Suleiman, however, the city simply stagnated until the collapse of the Ottoman Empire in World War I.

Today the Mount is the most disputed portion of this contentious city. The Arab nations are determined that an Islamic flag must fly over the site. In deference to the local Muslim authorities, Israel leaves the administration of Haram esh-Sharif entirely to Muslim officials. Israeli Border Police provide security in the area, but in cooperation with Arab policemen.

Israel's Chief Rabbinate, meanwhile, has banned Jews from visiting the Temple Mount, because somewhere on the hill is the site of the ancient Temple's Holy of Holies, the inner sanctuary which only the High Priest was allowed to enter, and even then only on one day of the year, Yom Kippur. Nevertheless, certain ultra-nationalist Israelis calling themselves the "Temple Faithful" periodically attempt to hold prayer services on the mount, an act that invariably incenses both the Arab community and other Jews.

The most eye-catching structure on Haram esh-Sharif is the **Dome of the Rock ❽**. The outside of the mosque is a fantasia of marble, mosaics and stained glass, painted tiles and quotations from the Koran, all capped by the gold-plated aluminium dome. Notable, too, are the curved pillars at the top of the steps, from which, according to tradition, scales will be hung on Judgement Day to weigh the souls of mankind.

The inside of the Dome of the Rock focuses on the huge boulder called the **Kubbet es-Sakhra**. This is the sacred rock on which Abraham was said to have prepared the sacrifice of Isaac. It is also the spot on which, during his mystical journey to Jerusalem, Mohammed is said to have mounted his steed and ascended to heaven. Appropriately enough, the heavenly interior of the famous golden dome shines down from above, a truly joyous achievement in gold leaf, mosaic and stained glass. Beneath the rock, meanwhile, is a crypt where the spirits of the dead are said to gather.

The silver-capped mosque at the southern end of the mount is **El-Aqsa ❾**, a vast complex that can accommodate as many as 5,000 worshippers. Serving essentially as a prayer hall, El-Aqsa is more functional in design than the Dome of the Rock. Probably built on the remains of a Byzantine basilica, it also straddles vast underground chambers known as Solomon's Stables.

El-Aqsa features prominently in the modern history of the region. It was on the doorstep of this mosque in 1951 that a Muslim fanatic murdered Jordan's King Abdullah in sight of his little grandson, the current King Hussein. In 1969 a deranged Australian set fire to the building, causing extensive damage (reconstruction is still under way) and sparking off inflammatory calls throughout the Muslim nations for a *jihad*, or holy war, against Israel. It was at El-Aqsa, too,

Map on page 144

**BELOW:** the monumental Dome of the Rock.

that Egypt's president, Anwar Sadat, prayed during his peace mission in 1977.

The **Islamic Museum** adjoining El-Aqsa has interesting exhibits covering centuries of Muslim life in Jerusalem, including lamps, weapons and ancient Korans. Also noteworthy are the mount's elaborately carved fountains, intricate wrought-iron gates, the miniature Dome of the Chain and the marble-and-stone *minbar,* or preaching pulpit, outside El-Aqsa.

Although this area can ignite so much political passion throughout the Middle East, it is a tranquil place, marked by sunny plazas and quiet gardens where the wind sighs through the trees.

## Troublesome tunnel

In front of the Western Wall is the entrance to the controversial **Hasmonean Tunnel** . Here archaeologists have dug out a 2,000-year-old street leading along the rim of the Temple Mount several hundred metres northwards to the Via Dolorosa as it passes through the Muslim Quarter. The Arabs have always feared that the tunnelling was a Zionist plot to get under the Temple Mount and blow up the mosques, even though excavations are not actually under Haram esh-Sharif. In fact, the tunnel has been open to visitors as a cul-de-sac for a number of years, but the opening of the northern entrance at the Via Dolorosa in 1996 sparked serious Palestinian rioting. You can reach the Via Dolorosa along Ha-Gai (El Wad), which begins to the left of the tunnel.

The southern excavations at the opposite end of the Wall contain a broad stairway where prophets harangued the crowds on their way to the Temple, the abutment called Robinson's Arch (after its 19th-century American discoverer, Dr Edward Robinson), and the remains of palatial buildings and purification

**TIP**

Tours through the Hasmonean Tunnel must be booked in advance. For details, tel: 02-6271333.

**BELOW:** a doorway on the Via Dolorosa.
**RIGHT:** a Via Dolorosa street scene.

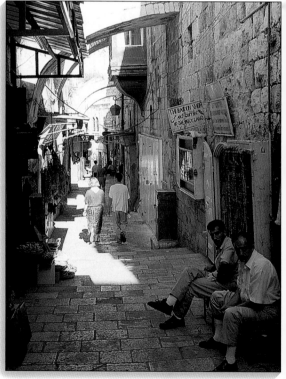

baths from Temple times. Seen from the walkway above the excavations, the site is a jigsaw puzzle of incomprehensible stone, but a licensed guide with Bible in hand makes the area come alive. New excavations, uncovered in 1996, enable the public to see the actual shop-lined street that bordered the surroundings of the Second Temple before it was destroyed in AD 70. At the southwestern edge of the Temple Mount, adjacent to the Western Wall plaza, these new findings are preserved in an archaeological park, open daily.

Map on page 144

## The road to Calvary

Rome likes to think of itself as the centre of the Christian world, and St Peter's Basilica is certainly grander than anything Jerusalem has to offer. Yet within the worn walls of Jerusalem are two places that stir the most casual Christian: the Via Dolorosa and Calvary. These names reside in the consciousness and reverberate in the vocabulary of all Western civilisation.

*Follow the Via Dolorosa.*

Archaeologists, as they are wont to do, maintain that neither the Via Dolorosa nor any of the other major sites that we identify today with the Crucifixion corresponds to historical reality. But if the Via Dolorosa that we traverse was not walked upon 2,000 years ago, some ancient road is buried underneath the present ground level. Pilgrims should not be unduly distressed that today's Via Dolorosa is a commercial street, complete with a Jesus Prison Souvenir shop and a Ninth Station Boutique. Bear in mind that the lane was a bustling city street at the time of Jesus.

The Via Dolorosa begins at St Stephen's Gate (also called the Lions' Gate) which, despite the surrounding churches, is actually in the Muslim Quarter. In the 1990s the municipality's East Jerusalem Development Corporation opened a Pilgrim's Reception Plaza here, about 30 metres (100 ft) inside St Stephen's Gate. This was the finishing touch to an elaborate and delicate project of repairing the Via Dolorosa that included the restoration of collapsing buildings and overhead arches along the route, the replacement of the 400-year-old sewage system, and proper demarcation of the Stations of the Cross. When the plaza was cleared of rubble, huge paving stones dating from the Roman period were exposed. These stones, which have been revealed at a few points elsewhere along the route, may very well have been walked on by Jesus and his followers.

**Guided tours** generally begin at the Reception Plaza, and are recommended, especially as some of the Stations of the Cross are difficult to locate in the maze of the Old City.

Directly opposite the plaza is the **Convent of St Anne ⓫**, considered to be the best-preserved Crusader church in the entire Holy Land. In addition to a crypt designated as Mary's Birthplace, the church compound contains the Bethesda Pool where Jesus performed a miraculous cure.

The **First Station of the Cross**, where Jesus was sentenced, is tucked away inside the courtyard of the Umariyah school, a Muslim boys' institution. The **Second Station**, where Jesus received the Cross, is opposite, on the street outside the **Chapel of Condemnation** and the **Church of the Flagellation ⓬**. It

**BELOW:** olive wood images of Mary and Jesus for sale.

was here that Jesus was scourged and had the crown of thorns placed on his head. The latter church also has a graceful courtyard and quiet garden.

The events associated with the first two stations are believed to have taken place in Herod's **Antonia Fortress**, remains of which are found today beneath the churches along both sides of the Via Dolorosa. In the nearby **Convent of the Sisters of Zion** ⓭, for example, is a huge underground chamber called the Lithostrotos, often said to be the place where Pilate judged Jesus; on the paving stones outside are signs of board games played by Roman soldiers.

Outside is the **Ecce Homo Arch**, which some maintain was constructed by Emperor Hadrian in the 2nd century and which takes its name from Pilate's jeer: "Behold the man!". At the end of 1985 the Sisters of Zion dedicated a Roman arch inside the church which they contend is the Ecce Homo.

Almost all of the subsequent stations on the Via Dolorosa are marked by plaques bearing the appropriate quotations from the Bible, and many are accompanied by a fan-like design in cobblestones on the street.

The **Third Station**, where Jesus fell with the Cross, is commemorated by a column in a wall on Ha-Gai (El Wad), which the Via Dolorosa traverses. Just beyond is the **Fourth Station**, where Jesus encountered Mary. On this site is the **Armenian Catholic Church of Our Lady of the Spasm**, which has a notable Byzantine mosaic in its crypt.

The Via Dolorosa at this point becomes a fairly steep and crowded commercial lane ascending to the right from Ha-Gai. The **Fifth Station**, just at the juncture of Ha-Gai and the Via Dolorosa, is where Simon the Cyrenian helped Jesus carry the Cross. A bit farther on is the **Sixth Station**, at the **House of St Veronica** ⓮, where Veronica cleansed the face of Jesus with her veil.

At the point where the Via Dolorosa bisects the souk's Khan ez-Zeit bazaar is the **Seventh Station**, where Jesus fell again. This is also believed to be the site of the Gate of Judgement from which Jesus was led out of the city to the place of crucifixion, and where his death sentence was publicly posted.

The Via Dolorosa at this point disappears; buildings cover the rest of the route to the Church of the Holy Sepulchre. But both the church and the last Stations of the Cross are close by. The **Eighth Station** is outside the **Greek Orthodox Chapel of St Charalampos**, constructed on the site where Jesus addressed the women with the words "Weep not for me, but weep for Jerusalem". At the **Coptic Patriarchate** compound ⓯ off the Khan ez-Zeit bazaar, a pillar marks the **Ninth Station**, where Jesus stumbled for the third time. This is one of the more unusual churches in the city. The monastery is a replica of an African mud-hut village, and the nearby Coptic chapel is located on the roof of the Church of the Holy Sepulchre, within which are located the final Stations of the Cross.

## The Holy Sepulchre

Experienced travellers are probably aware that the more venerated a shrine in the mind of the pilgrim, the more disconcerting the reality can be. In the case of the **Church of the Holy Sepulchre** ⓰ (open daily)

*An Armenian choir boy.*

**BELOW:** the Ecce Homo arch.

both its size and its complexity are rather bewildering. Here, at the highest point in the Old City, the Romans had a temple dedicated to Venus. Emperor Constantine the Great erected a church here in the 4th century, after his mother Helena identified the tomb of Jesus. Constantine's church was later destroyed, and the present church was built by the Crusaders in the 12th century. Much more has been added since the Crusaders left.

Map on page 144

Several Christian communities currently share the church, each maintaining its own chapels and altars and conducting services according to its own schedule. Each is responsible for the sanctity and maintenance of a scrupulously specified area. Church fathers have battled in the past over such issues as who cleans which steps. With its gloomy interior, its bustle of construction work, its competing chants and multiple aromas of incense, the Church of the Holy Sepulchre can seem intimidating. Freelance guides cluster about the doorway, offering to show visitors around for an unspecified fee. While some are competent and sincere, many have a routine in English limited to: "Here chapel, very holy. There picture, famous, famous."

Despite all this, the church maintains its magnificence. The focal points, of course, are the section built over the hillock where the Crucifixion took place (called Golgotha, from the Hebrew, or Calvary, from the Latin), and the tomb where Jesus was laid. These sites encompass the continuation of the Via Dolorosa and the final Stations of the Cross.

Stairs to the right just inside the door to the church lead up to **Calvary**. The **Tenth Station**, where Jesus was stripped of his garments, is marked by a floor mosaic. The next three stations are located at Latin and Greek altars on this same level and within a few paces of each other. They mark the nailing of Jesus

**BELOW:** a priest lights candles in the Holy Sepulchre.

Map on page 144

**TIP**

Low-priced tickets to the ramparts allow you to enter four times over two days, thereby allowing you to walk the walls at your own pace.

**BELOW:** the venerated Church of the Holy Sepulchre.
**RIGHT:** a street in the Muslim Quarter.

to the Cross, the placing of the Cross, and the removal of Christ's body. The **Fourteenth Station** is below the Holy Sepulchre: the tomb is downstairs under the church's main rotunda. Within the Holy Sepulchre are the Angel's Chapel, the rock that was miraculously rolled away from the tomb entrance, the chapel containing the burial site, and the adjacent tomb of Joseph of Arimathea.

Other notable sites within the church complex include the Catholikon, the Greek cathedral close to the main rotunda, with its stone chalice on the floor marking the centre of the world; chapels dedicated to St Helena, to Adam, and to the Raising of the Cross; and tombs of the Crusader Kings of Jerusalem. It is these side chapels and cavern-like tombs that offer contemplative visitors respite from the troops of tour groups that pour through the church. In a chapel beneath the main floor of the church one can sit in relative silence, listening to an Eastern Orthodox mass being chanted in a distant nave, or perhaps watching a solitary monk polishing a candlestick.

Outside the Holy Sepulchre are churches of most denominations. To the left of the plaza is the graceful **Lutheran Church of the Redeemer** ⓱, whose tower – open to the public – offers a magnificent view of the Old City.

The main access to the Christian Quarter is the **New Gate** – so named because it was punched through the Old City walls relatively recently, in 1887. Winding into the city from the gate are Ha-Patriarkhiya Ha-Yevanit, Ha-Notsrim and Ha-Latinim (Greek Orthdox, Catholic and Latin Patriarchate roads), all leading to their respective compounds, with churches that often contain interesting libraries and museums.

From the Church of the Holy Sepulchre the main thoroughfare northwards leads to the Damascus Gate. From here – as from most of the city gates – there is access to the **Ramparts Walk** ⓲ (open Sun–Thur 9am–5pm, Fri 9am–3pm), a walk around the top of the city walls which gives you marvellous views. To visit the Old City's remaining quarter – the Armenian Quarter – return via Muristan and David Street to the Jaffa Gate and then head southwards.

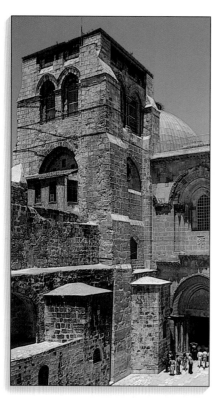

## The Armenian Quarter

**Ha-Patriarkhiya Ha-Armenit** is the street leading around the Citadel up from the David Street bazaar. Between the Christian Information Centre and the post office stand Christ Church and the Anglican Hospice, the 19th-century base for many of the British diplomats and clergymen who encouraged the exploration and modernisation of Ottoman Jerusalem.

The road passes through a brief tunnel and into the **Armenian Quarter** ⓳. A modest doorway leads to the 12th-century **St James's Cathedral**, one of the most impressive churches in the Old City. A little further on is the **Armenian Museum**, a graceful cloister housing a fascinating collection of manuscripts and artefacts. Jerusalem's 2,000 or so Armenians live in a tight community behind the cathedral-museum complex. As one of the smallest ethnic groups, they have a reputation for keeping to themselves. But in fact they are quite outgoing, proud of being descendants of the first nation to adopt Christianity, usually fluent in English, and most hospitable to visitors. ❑

# OUTSIDE THE CITY WALLS

Map
on page
144

*Just outside Jerusalem's ramparts are some of the most revered
sites in Christendom and some extraordinary
examples of excavation*

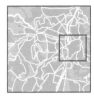

The sites surrounding the Old City walls are also redolent with religious significance. In addition, the streets just outside the Damascus Gate form the city centre of Arab Jerusalem. The **Damascus Gate ⑳**, from where you may have begun the Ramparts Walk (*see page 154*), is the grandest entryway to the Old City. Landscaped in the 1990s, its plaza offers one of Jerusalem's best forums for people-watching. The **Roman Square Museum** beneath the gate examines the Roman era of the city from the lower-level portal of that period. Also under the Old City walls close by are **Solomon's Quarries**, an ancient mine which tunnels deep below the alleys to Mount Moriah.

The **East Jerusalem Bus Station** just opposite operates buses to points in the West Bank, using independent Arab lines. From alongside the Old City, East Jerusalem's two main avenues, Derekh Shkem (**Nablus Road**) and **Salah E-Din**, lead into a cobweb of traffic. Among well-known restaurants here are the Sea Dolphin on Rashid, and Philadelphia, Dallas and Café Europa on Az-Zara.

Several hundred metres/yards to the north of the Damascus Gate, along Derekh Shkem, you will come to the **Garden Tomb ㉑** (open Mon–Sat 8am–1pm, 3.30–5pm; admission charge). Within a landscape reminiscent of a sumptuous English garden, this is a dual-chambered cave that Anglicans and other Protestants claim could have been the tomb of Jesus. The Garden Tomb is situated on a hill which, if viewed from the East Jerusalem Bus Station, suggests to many the shape of a skull, which is the meaning of the Hebrew word Golgotha.

**LEFT:** an Arab shopkeeper.
**BELOW:** the Garden Tomb.

## A vast necropolis

Golgotha aside, the whole of East Jerusalem is in fact something of a vast necropolis, and is rife with caves and burial crypts. These include **Jeremiah's Grotto**, where the prophet supposedly wrote his Lamentations over Jerusalem, and the **Tomb of Simon the Just** – a Jewish high priest alive in the 3rd century BC. The most awesome chamber is **Tomb of the Kings** – although it is misnamed, being in fact the tomb of Queen Helena of Mesopotamia, who converted to Judaism in 54 BC.

The hill to the west of the Damascus Gate is dominated by the splendid 19th-century **Hospice of Notre Dame de France ㉒**, which is opposite the New Gate. The grandiose, ornate French architecture suggests that pilgrims were not expected to suffer deprivation – and indeed the building now houses a luxury hotel with a *cordon bleu* French restaurant considered one of the best in the city. The building has a fascinating history, too. Badly damaged in the 1948 war, Notre Dame remained abandoned on the dividing line between Arab and Jewish Jerusalem. When it suffered

**TIP**

Check the *Crafts and Judaica* chapter (*page 107*) for details of recommended places to see and buy arts and crafts.

**BELOW:** graceful arches span the Coenaculum.

further damage in the Six Day War the French Assumptionists decided to cut their losses and sold the building to the Hebrew University in 1972. The Vatican was livid that such a prime piece of Catholic real estate in the Holy Land had been relinquished. Rome decided to challenge the sale in Israel's civil courts, claiming that under canon law a Catholic property cannot be sold without Vatican consent. To avoid an awkward trial the Israeli government (which owns the Hebrew University) agreed to sell Notre Dame to the Vatican, which now owns the building.

Turning left into Yafo and following the Old City walls, you can see that the new Mamila Project to the right is nearly completed. This 19th-century district of workshops and small traders has been transformed into a complex of luxury hotels, stores and apartments with some of the quarter's original buildings, such as the St Vincent orphanage, retained. Beyond the Jaffa Gate is **Khutsot ha-Yoster** (Arts & Crafts Lane), which houses the studios and shops of artists and artisans. This is especially worth visiting in August when the annual Arts and Crafts Fair is held.

Adjoining Khutsot ha-Yoster to the south is **Sultan's Pool ㉓**. This former reservoir has been converted into an amphitheatre and, located beneath the walls of the Old City, has to be one of the world's most inspiring venues for outdoor concerts.

On the far side of the Derekh Khevron bridge is the **Valley of Hinnom**. It is hard to realise that these pleasant parklands are believed, in Jewish tradition, to be the scene of child sacrifices in pagan Canaanite times, and therefore synonymous with hell, which is what the Hebrew word for Hinnom – *Gehenom* – actually means.

## Mount Zion

In contrast **Mount Zion** (Har Tsiyon) , overlooking Hinnom, although it does not exactly mean heaven, was used as a synonym for Jerusalem and came to symbolise the Jewish yearning to return to the homeland. Indeed, at the end of the 19th century Zionism was adopted as the official name of the national movement of the Jewish people. Yet inexplicably Mount Zion has been left outside the Old City walls. Legend has it that, for this oversight, Suleiman the Magnificent beheaded the chief engineer who built the 16th-century walls.

In 1948 the Old City fell to Jordan, but Israel retained Mount Zion, and from 1948 to 1967 the historic ridge was an important lookout point for the young country, as well as its closest approach to the shrines of the Old City and Western Wall. These days Mount Zion is less controversial, if no less beloved. Churches and *yeshivas* huddle side by side amid the gardens and wind-bent pipes.

Within the **Diaspora Yeshiva** complex is the site of **King David's Tomb**  (open Sun–Thur 8am–5pm, Fri 8am–1pm; admission charge). Archaeologists maintain that this is another example of a site not corresponding to historical truth, but that hasn't prevented the tomb from being venerated. The adjacent **Chamber of the Holocaust** is a memorial to the destroyed Jewish communities of Europe.

Primary among the Christian sites here is the **Coenaculum**, believed to be the Room of the Last Supper (although the Syrian Orthodox St Mark's House on Ararat Street in the Armenian Quarter makes the same claim). Today the Coenaculum is basically an elegant but bare room, empty but for the flow of daylight, and it requires considerable imagination to fill it as Leonardo did in his

Map on page 144

**BELOW:** the Church of the Dormition, on Mount Zion.

classic fresco. The Coenaculum is located on the second floor of the large, rambling complex that contains David's Tomb.

Adjacent to this building is the **Church of the Dormition**, a handsome Benedictine edifice commemorating the place where Mary fell into eternal sleep. The church has a noteworthy mosaic floor and crypt, and its basilica is the site for concerts of liturgical and classical music. The Armenians, meanwhile, are constructing a church nearby that promises to be equally splendid.

Also on Mount Zion is the **Old Protestant Cemetery**, the resting place of the British subjects who figured in the religious, cultural, archaeological and diplomatic life of 19th- and early 20th-century Jerusalem.

## Above the Kidron Valley

The **City of David** ㉖ excavations are on the steep hillside outside the **Dung Gate**. This hill is called **Ha-Ofel**, and the archaeological dig here has been the scene of violent protests by religious zealots claiming that ancient Jewish graves have been violated. The diggers dispute this, but say that in any case the site is too important to leave buried, because the Ophel is where the earliest incarnation of Jerusalem stood: the Jebusite city of more than 3,000 years ago.

Around 1,000 BC, King David captured the city and made it his capital. Although his son Solomon was to build the Temple on the high ground above it, the main residential portion of the city itself remained clinging to this slope above the Kidron Valley. It did so because at the foot of the slope is the **Gihon Spring** ㉗, at the time Jerusalem's only water supply.

Since the spring was located in a cave on the floor of the valley, Jerusalemites were in danger of being cut off from their water when the city was attacked. But

Map
on page
144

the stunning engineering project known as **Hezekiah's Tunnel** ㉘, carried out by King Hezekiah about 300 years after King David's time, managed to connect the Gihon Spring to the Silwan Pool inside the city some 530 metres (580 yards) farther down the valley. The intrepid 19th-century archaeologist Charles Warren not only explored the tunnel but also discovered a shaft reaching up through the Ophel to an underground passage from where city residents could come to draw water in buckets. In 1867 Warren had to crawl on his belly through the stream bed to explore the water system. Today visitors can study the schematics in comfort in the **City of David Archaeological Gardens**, and then stroll through the illuminated passageway to the top of Warren's shaft to peer at the water rushing below. In the Kidron Valley itself, visitors with candles can tramp along the knee-deep stream in Hezekiah's Tunnel from the Gihon Spring and through the Ophel until they emerge at the Silwan Pool.

The upper end of the Kidron Valley, also known as the Vale of Jehoshaphat, contains several Jerusalem landmarks. The slope off to the northeast is the Mount of Olives, and in the valley itself are the **Tomb of Absalom** and the **Tomb of Zekhariah**. Despite their traditional names, these stately tombs, with their graceful pillars and elaborately carved friezes, are not thought to be the resting places of David's rebellious son or of the prophet. Rather, archaeologists believe that they were part of the vast 1st-century necropolis that encircled Jerusalem, and probably served wealthy citizens or notables of the Herodian court. The handsome **Tomb of Hezir** nearby bears an inscription identifying it as the burial cave of a noted priestly family. Isolated, silent and still, the tombs at this end of the hot and dusty Kidron Valley evoke something of the mood of Egypt's Valley of the Kings.

**LEFT:** the Tomb of Zekhariah.
**BELOW:** Jewish cemetery, the Mount of Olives.

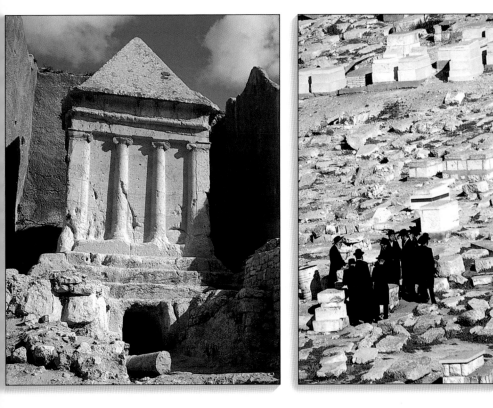

*Entrance to the Church of All Nations at the foot of the Mount of Olives.*

**BELOW:** the Dome of the Ascension.

## Mount of Olives

Wherever the historical Golgotha was located, it's agreed that Jesus made his triumphal entry into Jerusalem from the **Mount of Olives**. This hill, with its breathtaking view of the Old City, is mainly a Jewish cemetery dating back to the biblical period and still in use today. Round about the cemetery the Mount of Olives has numerous sites of significance for, in a meeting of faiths, many Jews and Christians believe that the Messiah will lead the resurrected from here into Jerusalem via the Old City's Golden Gate, which faces the mount.

Tradition has it that it was through a gate on this site that Jesus rode into Jerusalem, just as an earlier Jewish tradition says that this is how the Messiah will enter the city at the End of Days. The gate, however, is tightly sealed. It is said that a Muslim ruler decided to have it bricked up to prevent any Messiah from arriving in Jerusalem and wresting the city from Muslim hands. The reverence for this most sacred of mountains is generally reflected in a spirit of mutual tolerance and understanding. As to why the Mount of Olives is so bare and rocky: tradition has it that the Romans cut down all the olive trees to build the siege machines used in the destruction of Jerusalem in AD 70 – but that with the Resurrection, the trees will flourish again.

At the foot of the mount is the handsome **Church of All Nations**, noted for its fine Byzantine-style mosaic facade. Also known as the Basilica of the Agony, it was designed by a Franciscan architect, Antonio Barluzzi. Its 12 cupolas represent the 12 nations which contributed towards its construction. Adjoining it is the **Garden of Gethsemane ㉙**, where Jesus was betrayed – or, at least, the largest of several gardens identified as Gethsemane. The olive grove here has been verified as being 2,000 years old – although this is not particularly remarkable for olive trees. It has been suggested that it was from one of these trees that Judas hanged himself.

Next to the garden is **Mary's Tomb ㉚**, deep within the earth and illuminated by candles placed by members of the Orthodox Churches. Midway down the stairs to the 5th-century chapel are niches that are said to hold the remains of Mary's parents, Joachim and Anne, and her husband Joseph.

Among the most notable churches on the way up the mount is the Russian Orthodox **Church of Mary Magdalene ㉛**, easily identifiable by its golden onion-domes, which was built by Tsar Alexander III in 1886. Further up is the **Pater Noster Carmelite Convent**, with the Lord's Prayer in numerous languages on its interior walls; and the **Church of the Eleona**, on the site where Jesus revealed the mysteries to his followers. The small but entrancing Franciscan **Basilica of Dominus Flevit** marks the site where, according to Luke's Gospel, Jesus paused to weep over Jerusalem; built over Canaanite burial caves and a ruined Crusader church, the lovely, tear-shaped chapel was designed by Antonio Barluzzi in 1953.

On the far side of the mount, with a view of the **Judean Desert** and the red hills of Edom across the Jordan, is the **Bethpage Chapel**, from where the Palm Sunday processions to Jerusalem begin. At the crest of the hill is the **Russian Orthodox Church of the Ascension** with its landmark bell tower. Nearby,

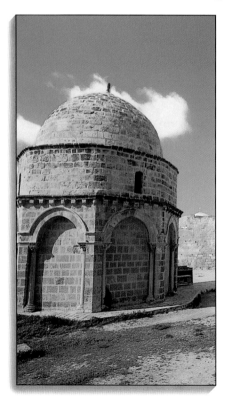

the small octagonal **Dome of the Ascension** marks the traditional site of Jesus's ascent to heaven. Converted to a mosque when the Muslims conquered the city in 1187, the structure is said to have been the architectural model for the Dome of the Rock.

From outside the **Seven Arches Hotel** is the classic picture-postcard view of Jerusalem's Old City. This is also the best place for a brief ride on one of the camels which are always lying in wait with their minders for adventurous tourists. The Arab village of E-Tur straddles the ridge of the Mount of Olives, and to the right of the steep hill (Derekh E-Tur) which leads back down to the Old City is one of Jerusalem's most aesthetically pleasing new buildings – the **Jerusalem Centre for Near Eastern Studies-Brigham Young University** ③ (tours of the campus in English Tues–Fri 10.30am, 11.30am, 2.30pm and 3.30pm; admission charge). The construction of this attractive campus and college complex, built into the hillside on eight levels, was fiercely opposed by Orthodox Jews in the 1980s. But in the interests of pluralism, the Mormons from Salt Lake City, Utah, were allowed to go ahead with their project after promising that no missionary activity will take place in Israel. Students who come to Israel for semester-long courses are warned that they will be sent home if they indulge in proselytising activities. The guided tours include the campus's splendid gardens and an inspiring view of the Old City.

Going back towards the Old City, on the corner of Sultan Suleiman, you will find the **Rockefeller Museum** ③ (open Sun–Thur 10am–5pm, Fri–Sat 10am–2pm; admission charge). It has a stately octagonal tower, a gracious courtyard and an extensive collection of archaeological finds. Still battle-scarred from 1967, it is now part of the Israel Museum.  ❑

Map on page 144

**TIP**

From the Dome of the Ascension several paths lead down to the city. Walks here, especially at dawn or sunset, are some of the loveliest experiences Jerusalem has to offer.

**LEFT:** the Pater Noster Church.
**BELOW:** camels wait for customers on the Mount of Olives.

# SEVEN GATES AROUND FOUR QUARTERS

*The Old City of Jerusalem can only be entered by seven gates while an eighth, the Golden Gate, is sealed pending the coming of the Messiah*

▷ **VENDORS AT THE GATE**
The main plaza outside the Damascus Gate is always busy, filled with Arab vendors peddling all kinds of food and drink.

Jerusalem's gates all have their own story to tell. The Jaffa Gate, as the name implies, was traditionally the main thoroughfare westwards to Jaffa (Yafo). It is known in Arabic as the Hebron Gate. The walls beside it were breached in 1898 so that Kaiser Wilhelm II of Germany could enter on horseback.

The Zion Gate, predictably, leads out to Mount Zion which was inexplicably left outside the city walls. The unfortunately named Dung Gate was the point from which the city's refuse was taken out. It offers best access to the Temple Mount and Western Wall.

St Stephen's Gate is also known as the Lions' Gate. It stands opposite the Mount of Olives, near the start of the Via Dolorosa. The Israeli army launched a surprise attack here when capturing the Old City from Jordan in 1967.

Herod's Gate, sometimes called Flowers Gate, is the least known of the gateways, and offers access to the Muslim Quarter.

The Damascus Gate is located opposite the highway which leads north to Nablus (it is called the Nablus Gate in Hebrew). It's the busiest gate linking Arab East Jerusalem and the Muslim Quarter market. The New Gate, as you would expect, is the most recent. The walls were breached in the late 19th century so that pilgrims staying in the Notre Dame Hospice opposite would have direct access to the Christian Quarter.

But the Golden Gate is special: set midway along the eastern wall of the Old City, it is blocked up. Through this gate, it is said, the Messiah will enter ancient Jerusalem after crossing a paper bridge from the Mount of Olives.

△ **AESTHETIC ARCHITECTURE**
Ornate patterns by the Zion Gate characterise the painstaking aesthetic efforts of Suleiman's architects.

◁ **HELP FROM FRIENDS**
World Jewry contributed large sums of money to the renovation of the Old City walls in the late 1960s, as this plaque by the Jaffa Gate testifies.

▽ **NO ENTRY**
The Golden Gate remains sealed, awaiting the day of redemption when the Messiah will enter the city, bringing heaven to earth.

## SULEIMAN'S GIFT TO JERUSALEM

The Old City's wall were constructed by the Ottoman sultan Suleiman the Magnificent between 1537 and 1541. The walls are 4 km (2½ miles) long, an average of 12 metres (40 ft) high and nearly 3 metres (9 ft) thick. Along the top of the wall was a patrol path for guards, now open to the public and known as Ramparts Walk.

By 16th-century standards the wall was not especially solid, and its main purpose was not so much to withstand a concerted attack as to protect Jerusalem's citizens from bandits and predatory creatures. The citadel (above), the city's main garrison, was incorporated within the walls by the Jaffa Gate, while Mount Zion was inexplicably left outside. Legend has it that Suleiman executed his chief engineer for the omission.

Suleiman supposedly embarked upon the project in the first place because of a recurring nightmare about being chased by a lion. His advisors interpreted the lion as being Jerusalem (the lion of Judah) which had been left naked (without walls) after being conquered by Suleiman's father.

◁ **GATEWAY TO PRAYER**
The Dung Gate is the most popular with Orthodox Jews due to its proximity to the Western Wall.

▽ **GUARDED BY LIONS**
St Stephen's Gate is also known as Lions' Gate because of the lions affixed to the wall outside.

▽ **GATE TO THE MUSLIM QUARTER**
Herod's Gate, to the north-east of the Old City, leads into the Muslim Quarter.

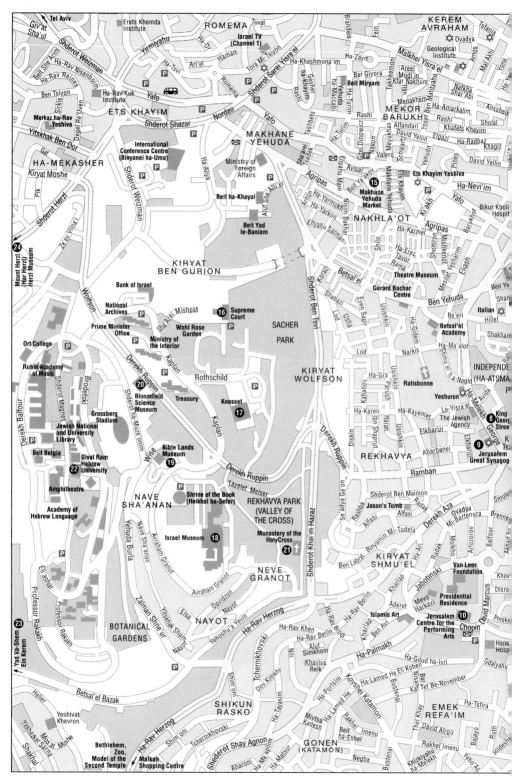

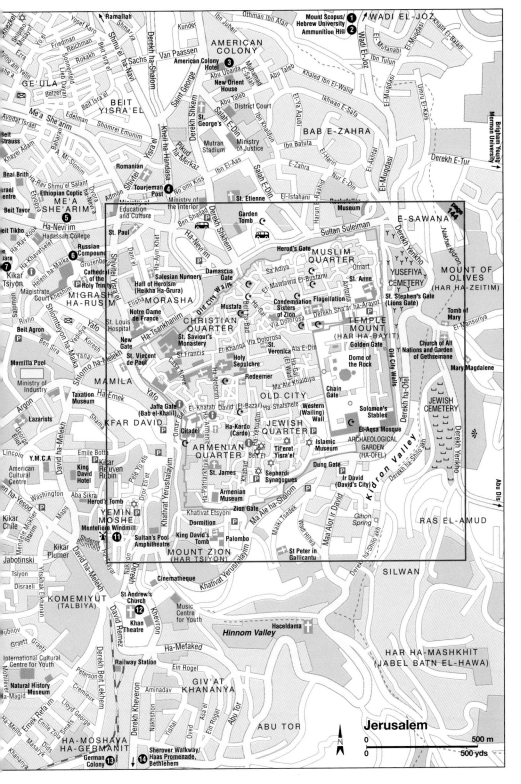

Jerusalem

# THE NEW JERUSALEM

Map
on pages
166–7

*From Mount Scopus in the east to the sombre Yad Vashem in
the west, this chapter explores the New Jerusalem,
its past history and its present development*

Throughout the ages Jews have wept, sung and prayed for Jerusalem. Above all, they prayed that one day they might return to their holy city. Yet the Jerusalem that confronted the first waves of Jews who came to start new lives here in the mid-19th century was a dismal contrast to the ideal spiritual capital they had dreamt of for so long. A backwater of the Turkish Ottoman Empire for 400 years, by 1917 the city had been left behind. It was filthy, decrepit and insanitary, cramped within the confines of its great protective wall.

Even the founder of Zionism, Theodor Herzl, during his 10-day sojourn in Palestine in 1898, noted his disgust with its squalid conditions, writing: "When I remember thee in days to come, O Jerusalem, it will not be with delight. The musty deposits of 2,000 years of inhumanity, intolerance and foulness lie in your reeking alleys. If Jerusalem is ever ours, I would begin by cleaning it up. I would tear down the filthy rat-holes, burn all the non-sacred ruins, and put the bazaars elsewhere. Then, retaining as much of the old architectural style as possible, I would build an airy, comfortable, properly sewered, brand new city around the holy places."

**LEFT:** one of the faces of the New Jerusalem.
**BELOW:** the Shrine of the Book.

## Modern metropolis

Herzl's words proved to be prophetic: Jerusalem is today every bit as sophisticated as its 19th-century predecessor was provincial. Bold geometric architecture erupts from every hillside; sleek thoroughfares lead into tree-lined boulevards; high-rises tower over church steeples and elegant city parks. There are bars, theatres and luxury hotels.

Yet the city that inspired so much Jewish yearning and Christian passion over the centuries is no less reverent for its modernity; the Christian visitor today will be struck by the vast array of churches and hospices of every denomination spread across the streets and hilltops of the city. But it is the tremendous blossoming of Jewish spirituality here that is most amazing. *Yeshivas*, synagogues and cultural institutions abound, each place of worship reflecting the specific religious or ethnic colouring of its congregation.

Shabbat is observed scrupulously; from dusk on Friday to Saturday evening all stores and buses cease their service, the streets empty, and unprepared visitors may well find themselves without food or transport, save that provided by their hotel, as Jerusalemites go to join their families for the holiday.

As the capital of the State of Israel, Jerusalem – Yerushalayim in Hebrew – holds a special meaning even for its secular residents, who gripe that the city is far less cosmopolitan and lively than Tel Aviv. The new city is still not exceptionally wealthy or grand,

but many of its structures exude a symbolic significance that outstrips their otherwise modest aesthetic merits. The domineering presence of a few undistinguished high-rises over the skyline, in particular, is jarring – if nonetheless useful for navigating one's way around. But from other perspectives the new city can be magical: old and new merge seamlessly, and Jerusalem seems as unearthly and splendid as any image its name evokes.

Perhaps the most lasting legacy of the British Mandate era is the 1918 declaration forbidding new construction to employ any material but the city's famous sandy-gold Jerusalem stone. While this has hampered architects' creativity, the result has been a rare sense of visual harmony, enhancing the city's unity while moderating the damage of its less successful architecture.

No event has had more influence on the shape of the city in recent years than its unification in the 1967 war. Not only did this clear away the barbed wire and concrete that separated East and West, it also, for a time, took Jerusalem off the front line of the Arab–Israeli conflict. As a result, since the late 1960s there has been an explosion of development. Much of it is attributable to Teddy Kollek, Mayor of Jerusalem from 1965 to 1993. He attracted new institutions into the city, conserved Old City landmarks, and presided over the colourful sweeps of new public art as well as the hideous behemoths of rapidly erected housing. Today more than 600,000 residents live within the limits of Jerusalem, and the city continues to grow, balancing, with mixed grace, the calls of the past and future.

**BELOW:** a contemporary synagogue on the university campus.

## Potent peak

Isolated and aloof atop a ridge north of the city, **Mount Scopus ❶** holds a special place in Jerusalem's history. Its prime importance is as the site of the

Map on pages 166–7

**Hebrew University**, inaugurated here under the vision of Chaim Weizmann in 1925. It was cut off from the rest of Jewish Jerusalem during the 1948 War of Independence, after a Hadassah Hospital convoy of scientists and staff was massacred in April of that year. Reabsorbed into the city since 1967, the university has enjoyed a spectacular modernisation of its campus. Among the most impressive sites here is the classical amphitheatre, which hosts concerts and lectures and, when empty, offers an awesome view of the rolling Judean Hills. Other notable monuments include a British cemetery dating from World War I.

On the far side of the government complex beneath Mount Scopus (which includes the National Police Headquarters) is **Ammunition Hill** (Giv'at ha-Takhmoshet) ❷ (open Sun–Thur 9am–4pm, Fri 9am–1pm), the scene of a bitter five-hour battle between Israelis and Jordanians in 1967. Today, the trenches and bunkers are preserved and a memorial museum honours the soldiers who died here. To the south of Ammunition Hill is the wealthy Arab quarter of **Sheikh Jarah**, which includes on its southern fringes **New Orient House**. This is a controversial Palestinian quasi-government building in which Palestinian officials hold meetings with foreign dignitaries despite Israeli government protests. On the adjacent street is the **American Colony Hotel** ❸, Jerusalem's oldest establishment and a favourite haunt of foreign journalists because of its neutral location on the border between East and West Jerusalem.

Off Kheil ha-Handasa at the old border, the **Tourjeman Post** ❹ (open Sun–Thur 9am–5pm, Fri 9am–3pm; admission charge) is a fascinating multimedia museum documenting the division of the city, within a house that served as a border post. Nearby is the site of the **Mandelbaum Gate**, which has been taken down but from 1948 to 1967 was the sole crossing from East to West.

*In the past, American writers Herman Melville and Mark Twain were among the eminent guests at the American Colony Hotel.*

**BELOW:** sunset over the city.

### Religious enclave

To the west is **Me'a She'arim** , where the mood is intense and unworldly. Over a quarter of all Jerusalem citizens are *Haredi*, or ultra-Orthodox, and these neighbourhoods reflect the rigorous religious lifestyles of their inhabitants. Me'a She'arim, meaning literally "a hundred gates", is the most famous Orthodox community. Built as early as 1875 as a refuge for Hassidic families, the neighbourhood has retained much of the intimacy and flavour of a European *shtetl*. The Orthodox Jews who live here speak Yiddish and wear the traditional styles – *peot* (side-curls), heavy, black garments for the men and shawls for the women. Signs surrounding the community warn that secular fashions, especially "immodest" female dress, are offensive and not tolerated. These admonitions should be taken seriously: immodestly dressed women are often spat at or even stoned.

Recently, more and more of these settlements have sprung up, such as the Orthodox community of **Har Nof**, on a hill just at the entrance to the city. **Ha-Bukharim Quarter**, to the northwest, dates from the 1890s and houses the descendants of this Central Asian group as well as ultra-Orthodox residents. With a phenomenally high birth-rate the ultra-Orthodox now dominate the neighbourhoods stretching to the north, including **Sanhedriya**, where the tombs of Israel's ancient judges can be found; **Ramot**, distinguished by a neighbourhood of bizarre hexagonal housing units; and right out to **Nebi Samuel** where a mosque marks the spot where the prophet Samuel is believed to be buried.

**Rehov Ha-Nevi'im** (The Street of the Prophets) runs from behind the Russian Compound to the Damascus Gate and is one of the main thoroughfares in Jerusalem; because of its congestion, planners propose to add a third traffic

*If I forget thee, O Jerusalem,*
*Let my right hand forget her cunning,*
*Let my tongue cleave to the roof of my mouth, if I remember not thee;*
*If I set not Jerusalem above my chiefest joy.*
                    *– Psalm 137*

**BELOW:** aerial view of Me'a She'arim.

Map on pages 166–7

lane. However, windows to the past will be sacrificed if the plans go ahead, since this street is famed for its historic architecture and beautiful buildings, whose wonders make a stroll down it an adventure. Where the road meets Shivtei Yisra'el, the Italian Hospital was once home to the Zionist leader Menachem Ussiskin and the author S.Y. Agnon. Today this beautiful 16th-century building houses the offices of the Ministry of Education. The **Rothschild Hospital** at the corner of Ha-Rav Kook, was built in 1887 and is now occupied by students of Hadassah Hospital for paramedical training.

On the corner of Ethiopians' Street is **Beit Tavor**, built in 1889. Since 1951 it has been home to the Swedish Theological Seminary, and the beautiful courtyard is open to visitors daily. Off the Street of the Prophets lie several religious institutions, including the Ethiopian Coptic Church.

## Russians and Prussians

**Jaffa (Yafo) Road** has long been the prime entrance-way to Jerusalem. It was paved in 1898 for the visiting German Kaiser, the Prussian Wilhelm II – for whose procession the wall between the Jaffa Gate and the Citadel was rent open. Today Jaffa Road remains the main axis for New City traffic, meandering from the gate to the northern bounds of the city, passing Makhane Yehuda, the Jewish food market, which is a colourful attraction in its own right (*see page 88*), before reaching the central bus station.

Leaving the Old City behind, Jaffa Road enters the fabric of the New at **Kikar Tzahal** (Allenby Square until 1948, then renamed to honour the Israel Defence Forces). The small street to the right, hosts another noted crafts area, while behind, to the right, loom the massive French hospices of St Louis and Notre

**BELOW:** the *Haredim* of Me'a She'arim.

Dame de France, the latter now a smart hotel, as described in the previous chapter (*see page 157*).

Further up Jaffa Road is the new **City Hall** municipal complex and plaza. Nearby is Gan Auster, with bronze plaques describing the growth of Jerusalem's population in modern times. On the left-hand side of the street are two notable buildings: the city's **Central Post Office** and, next door, Erich Mendelsohn's Anglo-Palestinian Bank, now **Bank Leumi**. With its torch-like window grilles and airy, cool interior, the late 1930s building marks a graceful union of Levantine and Bauhaus themes.

The **Russian Compound** ❻ covers several blocks to the right of Jaffa Road which were purchased by Tsar Alexander II in the wake of the Crimean War as a refuge for thousands of Russian pilgrims who flocked to the city every year, often dirt-poor and under considerable duress from their trip. Started in 1860, this complex marked the first notable presence outside the Old City; most of the buildings, including the handsome green-domed **Cathedral of the Holy Trinity** and the Russian Consulate, were completed by 1864. The compound has been largely bought by the Israeli government, and the buildings now house law courts, a police station and part of Hadassah Medical School, as well as a plethora of bars, cafés and restaurants. The **Hall of Heroism** is a small museum at the back of the complex, within what was once a British prison; it is dedicated to the Jewish underground resistance of the Mandate period.

## Downtown

Continuing towards Kikar Tsiyon (Zion Square), Jaffa Road begins to take on the bustling atmosphere of an urban centre. On the right, pleasant cafés are

*Street theatre in the city centre.*

**BELOW:** the Russian Compound.

Map on pages 166–7

interspersed with a French-language bookstore, a city tourist office, and a variety of banks. A short walk up Heleni ha-Malka will bring you to a small **Agricultural Museum** and the Jerusalem offices of the **Society for the Protection of Nature**, whose specialist Hebrew and English-language tours of the country have been widely praised.

On the other side of Jaffa Road are the winding lanes of **Nakhalat Shiv'a**, Jerusalem's second oldest residential suburb, now delightfully renovated. Founded by Joseph Rivlin in the early 1860s, the enclave had grown to hold some 50 families by the end of that decade. Now Rivlin and Salomon streets cross the old neighbourhood and, despite their decidedly narrow girths, they house quite a few of the city's favourite restaurants as well as much of its nightlife. At the end of Nakhalat Shiv'a, next to the car park, artisans sell their wares during the summer months.

At the hub of it all is **Kikar Tsiyon (Zion Square)** ❼ – always crowded, always crazy. It was called after the Zion Cinema, now long gone, a rallying spot for young Zionists in the 1930s. A bulky glass tower stands on the site now.

A block up Ha-Rav Kook, on the left, is one of Jerusalem's most unexpected little nooks – the newly restored **Beit Ticho**. In the early part of the century it was the home and office of Avraham Ticho, Jerusalem's humanitarian eye doctor, and more recently of the artist Anna Ticho.

The Jerusalem café scene really gets into its stride at **Ben Yehuda**, the five-block long pedestrian avenue that begins at Kikar Tsiyon. This is the place where everyone comes to see (and be seen), to drink and get drunk, sip cappuccino, sample pastries, and simply mingle with friends and strangers alike. Musicians, young couples and would-be prophets are always out in force, and several local characters have established their reputations here.

**TIP**

The heart of downtown West Jerusalem is defined by the triangle of Jaffa, George and Ben Yehuda, and is easily navigable.

Marking the city's main north–south axis, **Ha-Melekh George (King George V Street)** ❽, too, has its share of hubbub. The contrast between old and new is most vivid at the plaza in front of the City Tower, where the preserved doorway facade of an earlier building stands oblivious to its new surroundings. Hillel, leading back down towards the Old City, is the site of the lovely, ornate **Italian Synagogue and Museum** (open Sun and Tues 10am–1pm, Wed 4–7pm; admission charge), transported here from Conegliano Veneto, near Venice, in 1952 and dating originally from 1719; it is once more in use today. The Beit Agron, or press building, is further on, opposite the park and an ancient reservoir, **Mamila Pool**.

The Betsal'el Academy on the other side of the Tourist Office is Jerusalem's premier arts and design college and was founded in 1906.

Religion dominates Ha-Melekh George further on. The **Yeshurun Synagogue** across from the park is followed, further down the block, by the **Jerusalem Great Synagogue** ❾. The 18th-century ark covering the Torah scrolls was brought here from Padua, in Italy. The synagogue aspires to be a Third Temple, with a massive entrance-way, and the adjoining seat of the chief Rabbinate of Israel, **Heikhal Shlomo**.

**BELOW:** an earnest street musician.

*The YMCA building.*

**BELOW:** taking it
easy on Ben Yehuda
street.

## King David Street

Between Ha-Melekh George and Mamila, Gershon Agron rims the final edge of Independence Park; this quiet avenue has the world's only Taxation Museum. Nearby, David ha-Melekh (**King David Street**) hosts two of Jerusalem's most celebrated edifices. The **YMCA**, constructed 1928–33, was the work of Shreve, Lamb & Harmon, who were simultaneously designing the Empire State Building. Its 36-metre (120-ft) tower offers an outstanding view of Jerusalem and its environs, and its symmetrical rotundas reflect an elegant harmony with modern Middle Eastern form. The **King David Hotel**, opposite, was built with old-world grandeur by Egyptian Jews in 1930. It served as a British base of command in the Mandate period, and the entire right wing of the building was destroyed in a raid by the Jewish underground in 1946. In recent years it has hosted Israel's most famous visitors, including Anwar Sadat in 1977.

Below the King David, Swiss sculptor Max Bill's geometric cubes face the Old City and lead to the Khutsot ha-Yoster. Beyond the hotel an airy park holds the cavern of **Herod's Family Tomb**, where the stormy monarch buried his wife Mariamne and two sons after murdering them in a paranoid rage.

The **Jerusalem Centre for the Performing Arts** ⑩ can be reached by going up Jabotinski and turning left into Marcus. This attractive neighbourhood, known as Talbiyah, contains the city's most expensive houses. The arts complex contains the **Jerusalem Theatre** and the **Henry Crown Auditorium**; it is also a delightful place just to sit around, and to have a meal or a cup of coffee. Nearby are the **Museum of Islamic Art** and the **Presidential Residence**.

Opposite the start of Jabotinski is Shderot Blumfield which leads to the **Montefiore Windmill** ⑪, one of the city's most conspicuous landmarks, built by the

British philanthropist Sir Moses Montefiore in the 1860s. It now houses a modest museum (open Sun–Thur 8.30am–4pm, Fri 9am–1pm; admission charge). There is another windmill behind the Jerusalem Great Synagogue, but the Montefiore Windmill, which stands above the oldest Jewish neighbourhood outside the Old City, is the better known.

Until the 19th century the Old City walls effectively served as the city limits for Jerusalem's Jews – outside, intolerant Muslims and Bedouin raiders posed a threat to any adventurous stragglers. Opposite the Old City, between the Jaffa Gate and Mount Zion, the first Jewish suburb to penetrate this barrier remains in situ. Wishfully called **Mishkenot Sha'Ananim** (Dwellings of Tranquillity), the long, block-like structure was built in 1860 by Sir Moses Montefiore with the bequest of Judah Touro, a New Orleans Jew.

In the next four years Montefiore bought an adjoining plot of land and expanded the quarter, calling it **Yemin Moshe**. In the wake of the 1967 war Yemin Moshe was revitalised as an artists' colony, and today its serene walkways and stone houses command some of the highest rents of any neighbourhood in the city. Montefiore built the windmill at the edge of the quarter to provide flour for the settlement, and in 1948 it served as an important Israeli observation post.

As you head south, with the **Liberty Bell Garden** (Hapa'amon) on the right, the modern city opens onto the old. Embedded on the side of the **Valley of Hinnom** like a rugged gem, the **Cinemathèque** is a popular new landmark. Its theatres show a wide variety of foreign and alternative films, including those receiving their first screening at the annual Jerusalem Film Festival in July.

Above the cinema, the Scottish **St Andrew's Church** ⑫ has a well-regarded

**Map on pages 166–7**

**TIP**

The opening night gala for the Jerusalem Film Festival is held at the Sultan's Pool.

**BELOW:** Jerusalemites are seldom people of few words.

hospice, and a memorial to the Scottish king Robert Bruce who, on his death in 1329, requested that his heart be taken to Jerusalem (unfortunately it was way-laid en route, in Spain, and never made it). Around the corner, the **Khan The-atre**'s atmospheric archways are the venue for folk music and jazz performers, and the popular Poire & Pomme Restaurant. The railway station a block further on dates from 1892 and still offers a daily service to Tel Aviv and Haifa.

## Tree-lined boulevards

*If you have a sweet tooth, stop at one of the pastry shops offering* kanaffi, *a hot cheese and honey dessert which is wildly popular with Israelis.*

Stretching due east from Hinnom is an area of tree-lined boulevards and peace-ful homes. The area immediately east, called the **German Colony ⓭**, was founded in 1873 by German Templars and still has a subtly European air. The central street of the German Colony is Emek Refa'im, a fashionable boulevard of stores and restaurants which leads down to the large Arab-style houses of Baq'a and the Talpiyot industrial zone in the south, a less salubrious mix of discount stores and night clubs. To the east is one of the city's most delightful spots – the **Sherover Walkway** and **Haas Promenade** (East Talpiyot) ⓮. Link-ing up the Arab village of Abu Tor with the Jewish neighbourhood of East Talpiyot, these parklands offers a splendid view of the Old City and, when the summer heat haze dissipates, a breathtaking view of the Judean Desert. The promenade ends at Government House, formerly the residence of the British Governor and now the HQ of the United Nations' regional operations. This is also known as the **Hill of the Evil Counsel**, where Christian tradition has it that Judas Iscariot received his 30 pieces of silver.

Not far away, the kibbutz Ramat Rakhel also offers an inspiring view of the desert, and nearby to the south is the monastery of Mar Elias, but this will be described in the chapter on "Lands of the Bible" (*see page 281*).

**BELOW:** Montefiore Windmill.

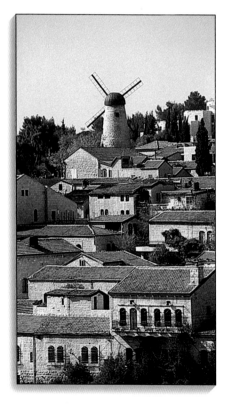

To the west is the sprawling suburb of Gilo, which overlooks Malkha. Adjacent to **Teddy Soccer Sta-dium**, home to Beitar Jerusalem, one of Israel's lead-ing teams, is the **Malkha Shopping Mall** (Kanyon). With air-conditioning in the summer and heating in the winter, the shopping mall can be a pleasant place to find gifts, entertain the children and eat a meal. The road running east of the shopping mall leads to the **Biblical Zoo** (also known as the Tisch Family Zoo-logical Gardens) (open Sun-Thur 9am–5pm, Fri 9am–2pm, Sat 10am–4pm; admission charge). The zoo is attractively landscaped into the hillside and contains animals mentioned in the Bible with the relevant quotations

Going north from the zoo, up Derekh Gan ha-Khayot and Sharet, you find the Holyland Hotel beside which is the **Model of the Second Temple** (open Sun–Thur 8am–9pm, Fri–Sat 8am–5pm; admission charge). This impressive 1:50 scale model of Jerusalem in AD 66 conveys just how vast the Second Temple complex must have been.

## The capital

The various institutions of government can be found near the western entrance to the city. But to feel the political pulse of the country, journalists often wander through the colourful **Makhane Yehuda Market ⓯** which straddles Yafo and Agripas streets to the east of the Central Bus Station. The vendors who offer a tempting array of fresh fruit and vegetables and other foodstuffs tend to lean to the right.

High on the hill above **Sacher Park**, the largest in the city, is the **Supreme Court ⓰** (open Sun–Thur 8.30am–2.30pm; admission charge). Completed in 1992, this impressive edifice uses light, shade and glass to great effect. The Supreme Court justices comprise the highest court in the land and have the power to interpret Knesset (parliamentary) legislation. The nation's Parliament Building, the **Knesset ⓱** (open Mon–Wed during debates, Sun and Thur 8.30am–2.30pm for guided tours; admission charge), is the symbol of Israel's democratic system. Be sure you take the tour of the interior, which includes a tapestry designed by Marc Chagall (you must present your passport). The carved Menorah outside was presented by the British parliament and depicts scenes from Jewish history. The **Wohl Rose Garden** above is sweetest in the spring.

The **Israel Museum ⓲** on Derekh Ruppin (open Sun, Mon, Wed, Thur 10am–5pm, Tues 4–10pm, Fri 10am–2pm, Sat 10am–4pm; admission charge) is one of those institutions that is so acclaimed it has become beyond reproach. It opened in 1965, and its boxy structure has allowed it to expand over the years; its collection today includes ethnography, period rooms, history, Jewish culture, coins, and an excellent collection of modern art. Well worth seeing is the Isamu Noguchi-designed **Billy Rose Sculpture Garden**. The **Shrine of the Book** displays the Dead Sea Scrolls in a chamber nearby. These scraps of tattered parchment represent the oldest known copy of the Old Testament.

Opposite are two more museums. The **Bible Lands Museum ⓳** (open

Map on pages 166–7

*Bust of Hadrian in the Israel Museum.*

**BELOW:** high-rise buildings surround the Knesset.

Sun–Thur 9.30am–5.30pm, Fri 9.30am–2pm; admission charge) in Avraham Granot displays artefacts dating from biblical times. The hands-on **Bloomfield Science Museum**  (open Mon–Thur 10am–6pm, Fri 10am–1pm, Sat 10am–3pm; admission charge) is imaginative and popular with children.

Beneath the Israel Museum is the Valley of the Holy Cross, a biblical landscape of olive trees dominated by the **Monastery of the Holy Cross** ㉑ (open Mon–Sat 9.30–5, Fri 9am–1.30pm, closed Sun; admission charge). Here, it is believed, grew the tree (planted by Abraham's nephew Lot after he was saved from Sodom's destruction) from which the wood was taken for the cross on which Christ was crucified. The Crusader-style monastery was built in the 7th century and belonged to the Georgian Orthodox Church until the 19th century when (for lack of funds) it was handed to the Greek Orthodox Church.

To the west of the Valley of the Cross is the **Botanical Gardens**, a small but pleasing garden of international flora, set by a lake. It is part of the **Hebrew University's Giv'at Ram Campus** ㉒, established after 1948 when Mount Scopus was cut off. The campus includes the science faculties of the university as well as the **Jewish National and University Library** (open Sun–Thur 9am–5pm, Fri 9am–1pm, closed Sat; admission charge), one of the largest libraries in the world, which counts among its treasures the actual papers on which Albert Einstein worked out his theory of relativity.

*Blooms in the Botanical Gardens.*

### Yad Vashem and Mount Herzl

**BELOW:** hands-on at the Bloomfield Science Museum.

Remembrance is a key theme of modern Judaism, and Jerusalem has no shortage of memorials. The two most potent of these lie side by side on the western ridge of the city, and provide powerful testimony to the two events which altered

the course of Jewish history in the 20th century: the Holocaust and the creation of the State of Israel.

**Yad Vashem** (Va-Shem) ❷ is the official memorial to the 6 million Jews who died at the hands of the Nazis between 1933 and 1945. It is profoundly moving. The central chamber, **Ohel Yizkor**, or the **Hall of Remembrance** (open Sun–Thur 10am–4pm, Fri 9.30am–2pm; admission charge), sits on a base of rounded boulders; inside, an eternal flame flickers amid blocks of black basalt rock engraved with the names of 21 death camps: Auschwitz, Buchenwald, Dachau, Bergen-Belsen, Sobibor, Treblinka …

Other structures include the simple shaft of the **Pillar of Heroism**; an art museum containing the work created by concentration-camp inmates, including children's drawings; and an extensive archive, the **Hall of Names**, in which the personal records of over 2 million of the victims of the Holocaust are preserved. There is also the **Valley of the Lost Communities**, dedicated to the communities throughout Europe that were destroyed by the Nazis, and several works of expressive statuary. The permanent exhibit, "Warning and Witness", documents the horrors of the era. The **Avenue of the Righteous Gentiles** leading to the memorial is lined with trees marked with the names of individual Gentiles who helped Jews during the Nazi regime.

**Mount Herzl** ❷ honours the Viennese journalist Theodor Herzl, who founded the Zionist movement between 1897 and 1904. His remains were transported to Jerusalem in 1949, and his simple black granite tomb marks the summit of the mount. Also buried in the cemetery here are Vladimir Jabotinksy and other Zionist visionaries, joined most recently by the late Prime Minister Yitzhak Rabin, assassinated in 1995. On the northern slope of the ridge lie the graves of Israeli soldiers who died defending the state. All around, the stark, rolling Judean Hills and new apartment blocks bear mute witness to their sacrifice. The **Herzl Museum** stands guard at the entrance to the mount.

## Biblical retreat

Ein Kerem, the small biblical town nestling in a valley to the west of the city proper, beneath Yad Vashem, is as timeless as the hills and well worth a whole afternoon to itself. It is rich in religious history, the most renowned sites include the **Franciscan Church of the Visitation**, designed in 1956 by the architect Antonio Barluzzi, on the spot where the Virgin Mary visited Elizabeth, John the Baptist's mother, and the central **Spring of the Vineyard** (also known as Mary's Fountain), which gave the town its name. At the **Church of St John**, mosaics and a grotto mark the traditional birthplace of the Baptist. The **Hadassah Hospital** complex just above the town is internationally known for Marc Chagall's stained-glass windows, depicting the 12 tribes of Israel. The town also has a number of galleries and restaurants.

A few kilometres south of Ein Kerem are two contemporary sites: the **Kennedy Memorial**, which is shaped like a giant tree trunk, and the **Artur Rubinstein Memorial Viewpoint**, in the shape of a huge piano keyboard. ❏

Map on pages 166–7

**BELOW:** the grief of Yad Vashem.

# THE GALILEE AND THE GOLAN

Map on pages 186–7

*This tour takes in the Christian landmarks of Nazareth,
the artists' quarter of Safed, sybaritic Tiberias
and the forbidding heights of the Golan*

**A** white-robed Druze puffing away on his pipe in a mountain top-village; a bikini-clad bather soaking in sulphuric springs at a Roman bathhouse: these are the stark contrasts typical of Israel's dynamically diverse north – the Galilee and the Golan.

Extending from the lush Jezreel Valley to the borders of Lebanon and Syria, this relatively compact region, at one moment a desolate expanse of bare rock, can suddenly explode into a blaze of blood-red buttercups and purple irises. Here Christians can retrace the steps of Jesus, while Jews can reflect on the place that produced their greatest mystics.

Lying on the main artery that linked the ancient empires, the Galilee has been a battleground for Egyptian pharaohs, biblical kings, Romans and Jews, Christians and Muslims.

More recently, Jewish pioneers established the country's first kibbutzim here. In subsequent decades the kibbutzim have mushroomed to cover much of this region where tribes of Bedouin still roam and Arab and Druze villages lie nestled in the hills.

**PRECEDING PAGES:**
the foot of Mount Tabor.
**LEFT:** Banias Waterfall.
**BELOW:** the water system at Megiddo.

## The valley

The **Jezreel Valley**, stretching from the Samarian foothills in the south to the slopes of the Galilee in the north, is Israel's largest valley. Because of its strategic location on the ancient Via Maris route, the list of great battles that have scoured this seemingly tranquil stretch is long and colourful. But the greatest battle of all has yet to be fought here. It is the one that the Book of Revelation says will pit the forces of good against the forces of evil for the final battle of mankind at Armageddon. The site referred to is **Tel Megiddo** (Mount Megiddo) ❶, a 4,000-year-old city in the centre of the valley.

Even the first written mention of Megiddo – in Egyptian hieroglyphics – describes how war was waged on the city by a mighty pharaoh some 3,500 years ago. Since then many a great figure has met his downfall on this ancient battleground. It is said of the Israelite King Josiah, who was defeated at the hands of the Egyptians around 600 BC: "And his servants carried him in a chariot dead from Megiddo" (I Kings 10, 26). In World War I the British fought a critical battle against the Turks at Megiddo Pass, with the victorious British general walking away with the title Lord Allenby of Megiddo.

In the heap of ruins that make up the *tel* (mound) of Megiddo, archaeologists have uncovered 20 cities. At the visitors' centre a miniature model of the site gives definition to what the untrained eye could see as just

a pile of stones. It is actually a 4,000-year-old Canaanite temple, King Solomon's stables (built for 500 horses), and an underground water system built by King Ahab 2,800 years ago to protect the city's water in times of siege. Steps and lighting enable easier exploration of the 120-metre (390-ft) tunnel, and of the almost 60-metre (200-ft) high shaft which was once the system's well.

## Plant a tree

The Jezreel Valley was the first and largest tract of land in what was then Palestine to be purchased by Zionist leaders close to a century ago. At he time it was uninhabitable swamp land. In draining the swamps, Jewish pioneers have planted 125 million trees over the years. The act of planting a tree came to symbolise the redemption of the Jewish homeland. Today tree-planting centres abound in Israel, with the largest one in the Jezreel Valley. The **Balfour Forest**, named after Arthur Balfour (the British foreign minister whose 1917 speech in favour of a Jewish homeland became known as the Balfour Declaration), includes a variety of trees in a sprawling forest 3 km (2 miles) southwest of Nazareth. For just a few dollars anyone can plant a tree. The centres are open on weekdays from 8.30am to 3.30pm, closing earlier on Friday.

**Afula**, the capital and the largest city in the Jezreel Valley, is the antithesis of Megiddo. There are no epic dramas to be acted out in this sleepy backwater town.

If you are interested in the early Zionist pioneer days and want an idea of the gruelling conditions which confronted these settlers, visit the **Museum of Early Agricultural Settlers** at nearby **Kibbutz Yif'at**, to the west of Nazareth.

A particularly remarkable, if eerie, site can be found on the chalky slopes of Beit She'arim, about 11 km (7 miles) northwest of the Balfour Forest. This is Israel's version of a necropolis. The limestone hills have been hollowed out to form a series of catacombs. Inside the labyrinths, vaulted chambers are lined with hundreds of sarcophagi of marble or stone (depending on the social rank of the deceased).

Northern Israel

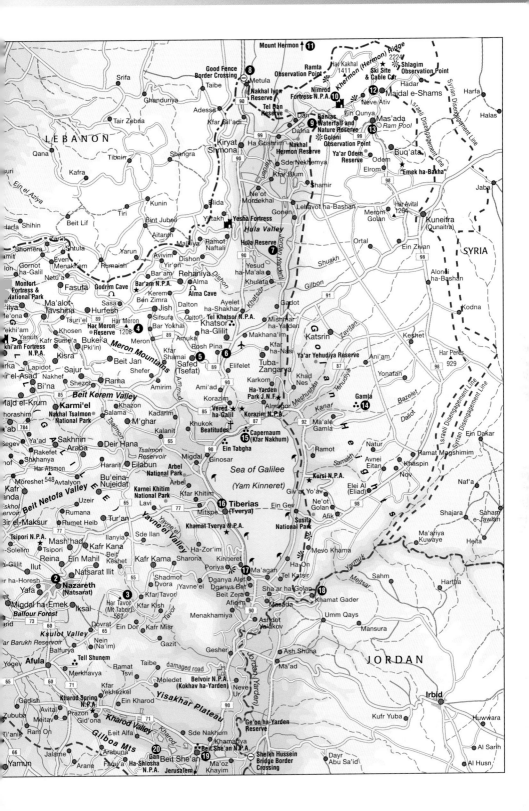

*A Franciscan waters
his garden.*

**BELOW:** the Basilica
of the Annunciation.

Each of the coffins – often elaborately engraved – weighs nearly 5 tonnes. When the Romans forbade the Jews to settle in Jerusalem, the centre of Jewish national and spiritual life moved to Beit She'arim, and this 2nd-century burial ground became a chosen spot not only for local residents but also for Jews everywhere.

Also worth visiting is Tsipori to the north, where a 2nd-century mosaic floor was unearthed in excellent condition in the late 1980s. The picture of a woman depicted on it has become known as "the Mona Lisa of the Galilee".

## Cradle of Christianity

Much more in keeping with the larger-than-life dimensions of the Jezreel Valley is **Nazareth ❷**. A strange blend of the timeless and the topical, the sacred town where Jesus Christ spent much of his life is today a bustling city of 60,000 Muslim and Christian Arabs – with a communist mayor at its helm.

"Can anything good come out of Nazareth?" (John 1, 46). This rhetorical question might seem puzzling today, particularly to millions of Christians for whom Nazareth is equated with Christianity itself. But when it was posed two millennia ago, the only feature that most distinguished this village in the lower Galilee was its obscurity.

Since then, the quaint town where Jesus grew up has become renowned. Today, of almost two dozen churches commemorating Nazareth's most esteemed resident, the grandest of all is the monumental **Basilica of the Annunciation** (open daily 8am–6pm). The largest church in the Middle East, it was completed only in 1969, but it encompasses the remains of previous Byzantine churches. It marks the spot where the Angel Gabriel is said to have

Map on pages 186–7

informed the Virgin Mary that God had chosen her to bear His son. The event has been given an international flavour, and is depicted inside in a series of elaborate murals, each from a different country. In one, Mary appears kimono-clad and with slanted eyes; in another, she's wearing a turban and bright African garb. Not to be outdone, the Americans have produced a highly modernistic Cubist version of the Virgin.

Some of the simpler churches, however, capture an air of intimacy and sanctity that the colossal Basilica lacks. This is especially so in the **Greek Orthodox Church of St Gabriel**. Upon entering the small dark shrine you hear nothing but the faint rush of water. Lapping up against the sides of the old well inside the church is the same underground spring that provided Nazareth with its water 2,000 years ago. Another very atmospheric church is the tiny Catholic one which was previously a synagogue. At one time believed to be the actual one attended by Jesus, it is now thought to have been built on the same site, probably in the 2nd century AD.

In the basement of the **Church of St Joseph** (next to the Basilica) is a cavern said to have been the carpentry workshop of Joseph, Jesus's earthly father.

A few miles outside Nazareth, nestled among pomegranate and olive groves, is the Arab village of Kafr Kana. Shortly after being baptised, Jesus attended the wedding of a poor family in this town. Here, says St John's Gospel, he used his miraculous powers for the first time, making the meagre pitchers of water overflow with wine. Two small churches in the village commemorate the feat.

**Ha Tabor ❸** rises to the east of Nazareth, but it is necessary to travel around almost four sides of a square (north, east, south, then west) to reach this huge hump of a hill. Mount Tabor offers an overview of the whole Jezreel Valley –

**BELOW:** Nazareth in the early evening light.

a patchwork of gold and green farmland. This strangely symmetrical hill, shaped like a skullcap, dominates much of the valley. It was here that the biblical prophetess Deborah was said to have led an army of 10,000 Israelites to defeat their idol-worshipping enemies. Two churches commemorate the transfiguration of Christ, which is also said to have taken place here.

When his sermons began to provoke the Jews, Jesus took three of his disciples and ascended Mount Tabor. There, the Gospels say, he "was transfigured before them – his face shone like the sun and his garments became white as light". The Franciscan **Basilica of the Transfiguration** commemorates the event, which Christians believe was a foreshadowing of his resurrection.

## Atmospheric Safed

*An Orthodox Jew in Safed.*

About 30 km (18 miles) due north of Mount Tabor are the highest peaks in the Galilee. Many people believe that they exude an inexplicable air of something eternal that makes them seem even higher than they are. **Har Meron ❹**, at 1,208 metres (3,955 ft), is the highest of the **Mountains of Meron**, whose mystique is attributed to the fascinating town that faces them: Safed.

When one of the great 16th-century poets of **Safed ❺** was returning to his town after a long absence, he was met along the way by a band of robbers who threatened to kill him. When granted a last request, he picked up his flute and began to play the haunting tune of a prayer. The melody so enchanted the robbers' camels that they began to dance, sending their bewildered owners fleeing.

Sheltered by the highest peaks in the Galilee, Safed seems also to be sheltered from time itself. Its narrow, cobble-stoned streets wind their way through stone archways and overlook the domed rooftops of 16th-century houses. Devout men, clad in black, congregate in medieval synagogues, the echo of their chants filling the streets. A modern area of Safed, with some 25,000 residents, has sprung up around the original city core.

**BELOW:** traditional themes are given a contemporary look by a Safed artist.

When the Spanish Inquisition sent thousands of Jews fleeing, many ended up in Safed, bringing with them the skills and scholarship of the golden age they had left behind in Spain. The rabbinical scholars of Safed were so prolific that in 1563 the city was prompted to set up the first printing press in the Middle East (or, in fact, in all of Asia).

The Shulchan Aroch, the basic set of daily rituals for Jews, was compiled here. But the real focus of Safed's sages was not the mundane but the mystical. Many had been drawn to the city in the first place because of its proximity to the tomb of Rabbi Shimon Bar-Yochai, the 2nd-century sage who is believed to have written the core of the Cabala, Judaism's foremost mystical text.

The efforts of Safed's wise men to narrow the gap between heaven and earth left not only great scholarly work and poignant poetry but also a legacy of legends about their mysterious powers. At one synagogue (Abohav) an earthquake destroyed the entire building but left unscathed the one wall facing Jerusalem.

Every synagogue here is wrapped in its own comparable set of legends, which the *shamash* (deacon) is usually delighted to share. Not all the synagogues are

Map on pages 186–7

medieval, many of the original ones having been destroyed and replaced by more modern structures, but the spirit of the old still lingers in these few lanes off Kikar Meginim.

The special atmosphere that permeates Safed has captured the imagination of dozens of artists who have made it their home. Like the rest of the old city, the artists' quarter of Safed remains untouched. Nothing has been added for "the benefit of the tourist" – nothing has to be. Winding your way through the labyrinth of lanes, you'll find over 50 studios and galleries as well as a general art gallery and a museum of printing.

Towering above the centre of Safed, littered with Crusader ruins, is **Citadel Hill**, an excellent lookout point, taking in a panorama that extends from the slopes of Lebanon to the Sea of Galilee.

## Revered tombs

Like the ripples that form around a stone tossed in a lake, the hills around Safed reverberate with the sanctity the city inspires. Starting in the cemetery below Safed, where the biblical prophet Hosea is said to be buried, the whole area to the Mountains of Meron is dotted with the tombs of rabbis and scholars.

At the base of Meron, in the village of the same name, is the tomb of Shimon Bar-Yochai, the revered rabbi who drew Jews to Safed in the first place. On the feast of Lag Ba'Omer in May you can still see thousands of his devout followers gather outside Safed's synagogues and make their way in a joyous procession to his grave at the foot of Mount Meron.

Ten minutes from Safed, on the road to the Lebanese border, near Dalton, is **Kerem Ben Zimra**, better known as the home of the **Dalton Winery**. Open

**BELOW:** Safed, a town of the artistic and the Orthodox.

daily for tasting, the winery has an interesting wine list, including a good Cabernet Sauvignon.

A tomb at nearby **Amuka** is the site of a pilgrimage of another sort. When Rabbi Jonathan Ben Uziel died in the 1st century, legend has it that he confided to his disciples that his greatest regret in life was not having married early enough to be fruitful and multiply. "Anyone who truly wishes to marry should pray at my tomb," said the dying rabbi, "and their wish shall be granted within a year." Over the centuries, thousands of people with marriage in mind have come here in the hope that the rabbi's promise will come true.

Also in this region is the mountainside town of **Bukei'a**, a quaint Arab village that is noted for being the only place in the Holy Land where Jews have resided continuously since Roman times.

At the outskirts of Safed flows **Nahal Ammud**. This river, which brings images of Eden to mind, leads down to the Sea of Galilee. In the summer you can wade through it, plucking pomegranates and figs along the way.

## Havens in the hills

This is rough mountainous country – stretches of bare rock interspersed with patches of pine trees, olive groves and eucalyptus. Canyons, caves and gorges abound. A number of small rivers (*nahals*) cut through this rugged region, flowing from east to west and emptying into the Mediterranean.

**BELOW:** stones piled on an ancient Jewish grave near Safed.

The wide open space of the Western Galilee acts as a haven, attracting various idealists seeking to carve their own small utopias on its slopes. So, in addition to the more common settlements like kibbutzim, Bedouin encampments and Arab and Druze villages, you'll find a community of transcendental meditationists at

Hararit who have found their nirvana on these secluded slopes. There is also a colony of vegetarians at Amirim who have set up an organic farm as well as a guesthouse where visitors can indulge in gourmet vegetarian meals.

**Karmi'el**, which has burgeoned into the largest town in the Western Galilee, is itself an unconventional experiment in urban planning – and, by all accounts, a successful one. It was established in 1964, and its population of 80,000 includes native-born Israelis as well as Jewish immigrants from 34 countries (including many Americans and, recently, Ethiopians and Russians). Clean, pretty and prosperous, Karmi'el is considered a model development town. Near its centre, against a backdrop of desolate mountains, is a series of larger-than-life sculptures depicting the history of Israel's Jewish people.

Karmi'el is set in the **Beit Kerem Valley**, the dividing line between what is considered the Upper Galilee (to the north), with peaks jutting up to almost 1,200 metres (4,000 ft), and the Lower Galilee (to the south), a much gentler expanse of rolling hills, none of which exceeds 600 metres (2,000 ft).

## Israel's "Silicon Valley"

The latest social experiment to be undertaken in this region is perhaps the boldest and broadest yet. In the midst of these isolated slopes young Israelis are busy polishing synthetic diamonds, making sophisticated electronic components and designing computer software. They have set up schools and stores, clinics and community centres in what they hope will become Israel's own modest version of Silicon Valley. The single-minded ambition that drives California's whiz kids is not found in abundance here. Infused with idealism, the young settlers of these hi-tech havens are not just out to make a buck, or so they say. They claim that it's a question of lifestyle, and that a commitment to shared values holds their enterprises together.

In some, like **Moreshet** (which means Heritage), this takes the form of strictly observing Jewish law. Others, such as **Shorashim**, share the socialistic principles of a kibbutz, with all members jointly owning the community's means of production and all receiving equal shares of the profits.

Both Moresha and Shorashim are part of the largest group of new settlements here in what is called the Segev Bloc. Set up in 1978 in the hills south of Karmi'el, it has several thousand families spread out in 18 communities. One of them, **Manof**, which is made up of mostly English-speaking immigrants from South Africa, offers guest facilities.

Weaving across the northern extremity of the Western Galilee is a highway suitably called the Northern Road. In addition to providing spectacular lookout points, this route hugs the Lebanese border for over 100 km (60 miles), sometimes running only a few yards from Lebanese farmers nonchalantly tending their orchards. While for many years the Israeli settlements along this route were frequently the target of brutal terrorist attacks, the area is today considered safe for residents and tourists alike. A worthwhile stop is **Bar'am**, where stand the exquisite columns of a 2nd-century synagogue.

**BELOW:** a statue at Karmi'el celebrates life.

*Neat rows of crops
near Kiryat Shmona.*

**BELOW AND RIGHT:**
the Galilee, as
viewed from
Khatsor ha-Glilit.

## The road to Metula

Descending eastwards from Safed is the land extending north of the Sea of Galilee which gradually narrows into what is known as the finger of the Galilee, with Metula at its tip. This is particularly pretty countryside. The east opens up into the sprawling Hula Valley, beyond which hover the Golan Heights. Towering over the valley to the west are the **Naphtali Mountains**, beyond which loom the even higher mountains of Lebanon. These picturesque peaks were in the past a source of frequent Katyusha rocket attacks on the Israeli towns below.

Apart from the beauty it offers, the road to Metula is an odyssey through the making of modern Israel. The first stop on this trek is **Rosh Pina ❻**. On the rock-strewn barren terrain they found here a century ago, pioneers fleeing from pogroms in Eastern Europe set up the first Jewish settlement to be founded in the Galilee since Roman times. They called it Rosh Pina, meaning the "cornerstone", a name which came from the passage in Psalm 118: "The stone which the builders rejected has become the cornerstone." The original 30 families who settled here were part of the first wave of Jewish immigration that began in the 1880s.

Rosh Pina, a quaint town of about 1,000, has maintained something of its original rural character. Cobble-stoned streets line the old section of the town, and 19th-century houses, though badly neglected, still stand.

Continuing towards Metula, the next stop takes you off the road of modern history, exposing instead the far more ancient foundations of the country. **Khatsor ha-Glilit** is one of the oldest archaeological sites in Israel – and by far the largest. With its 23 layers of civilisation spanning 3,000 years, it was the inspi-

Map on pages 186–7

ration for *The Source*, James Michener's best selling novel. Across the road at **Kibbutz Ayelet ha-Shakhar** there is a museum housing many of the finds. The kibbutz also runs a popular guesthouse.

This is the region of the **Hula Valley**, a stretch of lush land dotted with farming villages and little fish ponds that would seem like a mirage to someone who had stood on the same spot 40 years ago. Then you would have seen 4,000 hectares (10,000 acres) of malaria-infested swamp land – home to snakes, water buffalo and wild boar.

The draining of the valley was one of the most monumental tasks undertaken by the State of Israel in its early days. It took six years. By 1957 the lake had been emptied, leaving a verdant valley in its place but now part of the region has been re-swamped, as excessive peat in the ground is impeding agriculture. You can get an idea of what the area was like before the drainage by visiting the 80 hectares (200 acres) of swamp land that have been set aside as the **Hula Valley Reserve ❼**. There is also a museum devoted to the natural history of the region at **Kibbutz Khulata**, and a guesthouse in the northern part of the valley at **Kfar Blum**, a kibbutz with a distinctly Anglo-Saxon tone.

The nearby town of **Kiryat Shmona** (Town of Eight) is named after the heroes of Tel Hai and is, in fact, built on the site from where the Arabs used to launch their attacks. It is one of scores of development towns founded shortly after Israel became a state, in order to absorb some of the 700,000 Jews who poured into the new country. Kiryat Shmona, like many "development towns", was hardly a town at all; it began as a series of corrugated iron huts known as *ma'abarot*. Situated close to the border, it was for years the target of rocket attacks from the Lebanese mountains that overlook it. Even today the town is

subject to sporadic attacks, but development continues and it now has over 20,000 inhabitants.

## The finger of Galilee

North of Kiryat Shmona you begin to enter the narrow tip of Israel known as the "finger" or "panhandle" of the Galilee. When the end of World War I left its status unclear, Arab gangs attacked the Jews here, forcing them out of their settlements. The settlers at **Tel Khai** and **Kfar Gil'adi**, though outnumbered, held out under siege for months until their leader, Joseph Trumpeldor, was shot and killed. The incident prompted the Jews to improve their self-defence and triggered the formation of the Haganah, predecessor of the Israel Defence Forces.

The building from which the settlers defended themselves is now a museum devoted to the Haganah. Nearby is a memorial to Trumpeldor and seven fellow fighters, including two women, who died in the attack. Thousands of Israeli youths converge on the Tel Hai site on the anniversary of Trumpeldor's death. There is also a youth hostel here and a guesthouse at neighbouring Kfar Gil'adi, today a flourishing kibbutz.

Just before Metula, in the **Nakhal Iyon Reserve**, is a picturesque waterfall that flows impressively in the winter months (October–May) but is completely dry the rest of the year. This is due to a longstanding arrangement by which Israel permits Lebanese farmers to divert the water for agricultural use.

Until the Golan was captured from Syria in 1967, **Metula ❽**, the most northern point in Israel, surrounded on three sides by Lebanese land, was the target of frequent rocket attacks. Founded in 1896 by the same wave of immigrants that settled in Rosh Pina, it was for two decades the only settlement in

**BELOW:** the war memorial at Kiryat Shmona.

the area. Even today, the nearest shopping centre is some 10 km (6 miles) away in Kiryat Shmona.

Map on pages 186–7

Apart from the fresh mountain air, abundant apple orchards (most of the country's supply comes from here) and charming *pensions*, what draws tourists to this secluded town of 600 inhabitants is its now famous border with Lebanon. Every day (except Saturday) hundreds of Lebanese stream through what has come to be known as the Good Fence Border Crossing. Some, victims of the turmoil in Lebanon, come for medical care, but most of them are simply labourers commuting to jobs in Israel.

Some 10 km (6 miles) east of Kiryat Shmona, on the edge of the Golan Heights (and what used to be the Syrian border), is the archaeological site of **Tel Dan**. Situated at the northern tip of Israel, it was founded in biblical times by members of the tribe of Dan, after quarrels with the Philistines forced them to leave the southern coast. It is also notorious as one of two cities where Jeroboam permitted worship of the idolatrous golden calf.

Today the site includes various Israelite ruins, a Roman fountain and a triple-arched Canaanite gateway. In the summer, volunteers help to excavate this active and scenic *tel* where the source waters for the Jordan River emerge. The museum at **Kibbutz Dan** nearby has descriptions of the geology of the region and the reclamation of the Hula Valley below. The kibbutz also runs a very popular restaurant, the **Dag on the Dan**, specialising in fresh trout from the nearby streams.

The **Banias Waterfall ❾** (open daily 8am–6pm) is among the most popular natural attractions in the country – and has been for thousands of years. "Banias" is a corruption of the Greek *Panaeas*, and in a cave near the spring are the

*A camel peers into a camera.*

**BELOW:** most of Israel's apples come from the Metula region.

remains of an ancient temple built in honour of Pan, the Greek god of the forests.

Old Crusader ruins may also be visited in the **Banias Nature Reserve**, but the real attractions are the waterfalls and inviting pools.

Before 1967, Banias was located in Syrian territory, but just 4 km (2.5 miles) to the west, in what was and is Israeli territory, a number of other springs gurgle from the foot of Mount Hermon. The most important of these is the **Dan River**, which provides the greatest single source of the Jordan River – in fact, "Jordan" is a contraction of the Hebrew *Yored Dan* ("descending from Dan"), and that's precisely what this biblical river does. For its 264-km (165-mile) length the Jordan flows from the snowy peak of **Mount Hermon** to the catchment basin of the Dead Sea, 400 metres (1,300 ft) below sea level, and the lowest point on the face of the earth.

## The Golan

The Golan is a sombre massif doomed by history and bloodied by almost ceaseless war. It is a great block of dark grey rock lifted high above the Upper Jordan Valley, and those who have it have the power to rain misery upon their neighbours.

The Golan is a mighty fortress created by the hand of nature. During the Tertiary Age, geological folding lifted its hard basalt stone from the crust of the earth. Today it is a sloped plateau, rising in the north to heights greater than a full kilometre above sea level. It stretches 67 km (42 miles) from north to south and 25 km (15 miles) from east to west.

**BELOW:** a church in the Golan Heights.

Israel considers the Golan Heights to be part of its territory (in 1981 Israeli military occupation of this former Syrian territory was replaced with civil law and administration), although few other countries accept this *fait accompli*. Israeli justification for absorbing the Golan focused on Syria's belligerence, and the fact that it was used as a base for artillery shelling of Israeli settlements below.

Since the beginning of the peace process there has been much talk of territorial compromise over the Golan, but many people in Israel vehemently oppose such a move, in particular the 13,000 Jewish settlers in the Golan.

## Historic redoubt

The Golan has been disputed throughout history. In antiquity it was the greatest natural barrier traversed by the Via Maris, the "Sea Highway" that led from Egypt and the coastal plain across the Galilee and the Golan to the kingdom of Mesopotamia.

The Golan was allocated to the tribe of Manasseh during the biblical era, but was frequently lost and recaptured over the centuries. Under Roman rule, Jewish settlement in the Golan increased, and a few generations later, during the Jewish Revolt against Rome (AD 66), many of the descendants of those settlers met cruel deaths during the epic battle for the fortress of Gamla (*see page 201*).

The mountain range changed hands frequently during the following centuries, though archaeological evidence indicates a substantial Jewish population until the time of the Crusades; for the next eight centuries, the area was practically desolate.

At the end of the 19th century the Ottoman Turks tried to repopulate the Golan with non-Jewish settlers, to serve as a buffer against invasion from the south. Among those who put down roots here were some Druze, Circassians fleeing the Russian invasion of the Caucasus Mountains in 1878, and Turkomans who migrated from Central Asia. A village of Nusseiris (North Syrian Alawites) was also established here.

After World War I, when British troops under General Edmund Allenby drove the Ottomans off the Golan, the region was included in the British Mandate of Palestine, but in the San Remo conference of 1923 it was traded off to the French sphere of influence.

From 1948 to 1967 the Syrians used the Golan Heights as a forward base of operations against Israel. Jewish villages in the Hula Valley were shelled by Syrian artillery mounted here. Syria continued to install fortifications in the Golan throughout the 1960s, converting the region into a military zone.

War finally broke out on 6 June 1967 with Syrian army attacks on Kibbutz Dan, Ashmura and She'ar Yashuv. The attack was blunted the following day, and on 9 June Israeli troops counter-attacked. Within 48 hours all Syrian units on the Golan had either retreated or surrendered.

## The aftermath

Only six inhabited villages, with a total population of 6,400 people, remained on the Golan at the time of the Israeli victory, these including five Druze communities and one Nusseiri village at Ghajar. Within weeks, members of Israeli

Map on pages 186–7

**BELOW:** a Syrian tank rusts by the roadside.

**BELOW:** skiing on
Mount Hermon.

kibbutzim began establishing communities in the unpopulated hills, the first
being Merom Golan.

During the following years the region received new schools, medical clinics
and aid for the elderly. Modern agricultural methods vastly increased the pro-
ductivity of many crops, particularly apples, pears, peaches, almonds, plums
and cherries, and all the residents of the Golan were integrated into Israel's
wage-scale system.

Syria attacked again on 6 October 1973, the Jewish Day of Atonement, when
most Israeli troops were on leave with their families. The next day Syrian troops
occupied nearly half the Golan. Israel responded on 8 October in what was to
become the greatest tank battle in history. Within a week Syria had lost some
1,200 of an estimated 1,500 Soviet-built tanks. By 24 October, Israeli units
were within sight of Damascus when the United Nations called for peace, and
Israel complied. A dangerous legacy of minefields remains.

In recent years, the Golan has gained a new, more peaceful distinction – as the
source and soil of a new Israeli vineyard. The wine, called Yarden, is said to be
the best yet produced for export.

The Golan is not a popular tourist attraction. Most Israelis see it as a vital
buffer zone between them and Syria, an enormous bunker filling its ancient
role of blocking invasion. But visitors who do come usually tour the old Syrian fortifications that dot the area. The **Nimrod Fortress ❿** (open daily
8am–5pm) on the northern Golan, just off Highway 989, is one of these. From
this 13th-century Crusader fortress one gains a spectacular view of the Northern Galilee and the Naphtali Hills beyond, and it is easy to understand the
strategic reasons for its construction.

Map on pages 186-7

## Mount Hermon

Towering above the north end of the Golan is **Mount Hermon ⓫** (2,814 metres/9,230 ft) with several ranges radiating from it. It occupies an area roughly 40 by 20 km (25 by 12 miles) and is divided between Lebanon, Syria, Israel and several demilitarised zones under UN jurisdiction. About 20 percent of this area is under Israeli control, including the southeast ridge **Ketef ha-Hermon** (The Hermon Shoulder), whose highest point rises to 2,224 metres (7,296 ft).

The higher areas of Mount Hermon are snow-covered through most of the year, and each winter brings snow to all elevations over 1,200 metres (3,900 ft). Israeli ski enthusiasts have opened a modest ski resort on these slopes, with a chair-lift and an equipment rental shop for skis, boots, poles and toboggans. The slopes are often compared to those found in New England – not particularly lofty, but nevertheless a challenge and a pleasure to ski.

Nature on Mount Hermon is of particular interest to Israelis because it's the only sub-alpine habitat in the country. Several birds, such as the rock nuthatch and the redstart, are at the southernmost extremity of their range here, while others, such as the Hermon horned lark, are found nowhere else.

Many dolinas are scattered around Mount Hermon. These are cavities in the surface of the rock formed by karstic action on the mountain's limestone. In the winter the dolinas fill with snow, and they are the last areas to melt in the spring, thus supporting lush green vegetation long after the rest of the slope has dried out under the intense sun.

## Druze villages

At the foot of Mount Hermon is **Majdal e-Shams ⓬**, the largest of the Druze villages on the Golan. The town has good restaurants and souvenir shops, and is popular with tourists. Like all the Druze on the Golan, the residents of Majdal e-Shams have refused to take Israeli citizenship and generally use hostile language when speaking to the press about Israel.

The Druze village of **Mas'ada** to the south overlooks the **Ram Pool ⓭**, a fascinating geological phenomenon. This is one of only two extinct volcanos in the worldwhich over time has evolved into a small lake (the other is in Kenya) .

**Katsrin**, to the southwest, is the modern "capital" of the Golan and the region's only municipal centre. Established in 1977, it is designed in the shape of a butterfly and is home to the **Golan Archaeological Museum** (open Sun–Thur 9am–4pm, Fri 9am–1pm, Sat 10am–1pm; admission charge) which exhibits artefacts from the ancient settlement of Katsrin.

Another often-visited site is **Ma'ale Gamla ⓮**, but there is little joy attached to this ruined bastion. Gamla was the "Masada of the north", a fortified town of the south-central Golan which, in AD 66, was the focus of one of the early battles in the Jewish revolt against Rome. Initially, the rebels put Vespasian and three full Roman legions to shame. The over-confident Roman leader threw his troops against the Jewish bastion only to have them humbled by a much smaller and less professional Jewish force. Recovering, the embar-

**BELOW:** a Druze shopkeeper.

rassed Romans besieged the Jewish town in one of the most bitter battles of the war. Vespasian vowed that no mercy would be shown.

The Romans gradually pushed the Jews to the precipice above which this mountain-top city was built, and, when Roman victory appeared imminent, many defenders committed suicide rather than surrender. Four thousand Jews were killed in battle; another 5,000 either committed suicide or were slaughtered by the Romans after Gamla had fallen to them.

"The sole survivors were two women," historian Josephus Flavius wrote. "They survived because when the town fell they eluded the fury of the Romans, who spared not even babes in arms, but seized all they found and flung them from the citadel."

The site was reduced to rubble by the Romans and then lost to history for precisely 1,902 years. In 1968, Ma'ale Gamla was rediscovered during a systematic Israeli survey of the region. Today it is possible for visitors to stroll through the ancient streets of this community and inspect the remains of many ancient houses, and even a synagogue, all of which were constructed out of the Golan's sombre black basalt stone.

The ruins are clustered on a steep ridge, and, if you tour the area between late winter and early summer, there is a very good chance of seeing magnificent griffon vultures with a 2-metre (7-ft) wingspan soaring overhead.

Among the fields to the east of Gamla it is possible to find several prehistoric dolmens. These are stone-age structures which look like crude tables, with a large, flat stone bridging several supporting stones. They are generally considered to be burial monuments, and most are dated to about 4,000 BC. Dolmens are found at several other sites around the Golan and the Galilee.

**BELOW:** an ancient dolmen near Ma'ale Gamla.

## Jewel of the Galilee

Glowing like an emerald, its tranquil surface framed in a purplish-brown halo of mountains, the **Sea of Galilee** is probably the most breathtaking lake in the country. At 2l km (13 miles) long and 11 km (7 miles) wide, it may not be enormous by global standards, but it has, through some romantically inspired hyperbole, come to be known as a "sea". The Sea of Galilee, the Sea of Tiberias, the Sea of Ginossar are its most popular names. In Hebrew it's called Yam Kinneret because it's shaped like a *kinnor* or harp.

Not surprisingly, these bountiful shores have been inhabited for millennia, with the earliest evidence of habitation dating back 5,000 years to a cult of moon-worshippers that sprouted in the south. Some 3,000 years later the same lake witnessed the birth and spread of Christianity on its shores, while high up on the cliffs above, Jewish rebels sought refuge from Roman soldiers. The dramas of the past, however, have since faded into the idyllic landscape. Today it is new water sports, not new religions, that are hatched on these azure shores.

## Around the lake

One of the best ways to see the many sites around the lake (if you don't have access to a car) is to obtain a one- or two-day bus pass on Egged's **Minus 200 Line** (available at most major hotels), which enables you to get on and off at any of 23 stops. There are also ferry boats that go back and forth regularly from Tiberias to Ein Gev, on the east coast. For the more ambitious, swimming the same route has become a popular competitive sport.

It was in the numerous fishing villages around the Sea of Galilee that Jesus found his first followers. The village of **Capernaum** ⓫, on the northern tip of

Map on pages 186–7

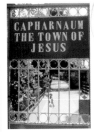

*A claim to fame.*

**BELOW:** the Church of the Beatitudes.

the lake, became his second home. Here he is said to have preached more sermons and performed more miracles than anywhere else.

It was a metropolis of sorts in its heyday, and at least five of the disciples came from here. (It is after one of them, a simple fisherman named Peter, that the Galilee's most renowned fish gets its name.) Today the site houses the elaborate remains of a 2nd-century synagogue – said to be built over the original one where Jesus used to preach. There is also a recently completed church shaped like a ship.

It was standing on a hilltop overlooking the Sea of Galilee that Jesus proclaimed to the masses that had gathered below: "Blessed are the meek, for they shall inherit the earth". This line from the Sermon on the Mount, is immortalised by the majestic **Church and Monastery of the Beatitudes** (open daily 8am–5pm). This octagonal church, set in well-maintained gardens, belongs to the Franciscan order and was built in the 1930s.

In the neighbouring town of **Ein Tabgha**, Jesus is said to have multiplied five loaves and two fishes into enough food to feed the 5,000 hungry people who had come to hear him speak. The modern **Church of the Multiplication** (open daily 8.30am–5pm) was built over the colourful mosaic floor of a Byzantine shrine in 1982. Next to it is the Church of Peter's Primacy. **Vered ha-Galil**, adjacent to the Church of the Beatitudes, is a bit of an anomaly in these parts with its Wild West-style restaurant, chalet accommodation and horseback tours.

Moving south, you will first come to the towering cliffs of **Arbel**. Today a rock climbers' haven, during Roman times they served as a hideout for Bar Kochba and his Jewish rebels.

Nearby is **Ginosar**, an especially beautiful kibbutz with a luxurious guest-

*The Vered ha-Galil ranch was founded by an Austrian prince.*

**BELOW:** the Jordan Valley at the south end of the Sea of Galilee.

Map
on pages
186–7

house. Ask some of the residents about the perfectly intact 2,000-year-old boat recently uncovered on the shores of the kibbutz.

## Lakeside resort

The capital of the lake, **Tiberias** , has become known for its "fun in the sun" spirit. A sprawling city of 60,000, halfway down the west coast, it is one of the country's most popular resorts. On its new boardwalk, lined with seafood restaurants, you can dig into delicious St Peter's fish while enjoying a stunning view of the lake. On the marina you can have your pick of water-skiing or windsurfing, or go for a dip at one of the beaches along the outskirts of the city. During summer you'll need to dunk yourself in the water one way or another.

With all the distractions available in this popular playground, it's easy to forget that Tiberias is considered one of the four holy Jewish cities. To remind you, there are the tombs of several famous Jewish sages buried here, including the 12th-century philosopher Moses Maimonides and the self-taught scholar, Rabbi Akiva, who was killed by the Romans after the Bar-Kochba uprising.

When it was founded by Herod Antipas around AD 20, Tiberias failed to attract devout Jews because it was thought to be built over an ancient Jewish cemetery and so considered impure. But eventually economic incentives, as well as a symbolic "purification" of the city by a well-respected rabbi, cleared the way for settlement. During the 2nd and 3rd centuries it reached its zenith. With a population of 40,000, it became the focus of Jewish academic life. It was at Tiberias that scholars codified the sounds of the Hebrew script and wrote the Mishnah, the great commentary on the Bible.

By the eve of the Arab conquest of 636, Tiberias was the most important

*St Peter's fish for sale.*

Christian centre outside Jerusalem. A 12th-century battle between Muslims and Crusaders destroyed the city, and, after being resettled, it was again reduced to rubble in 1837, this time by an earthquake. A few devout Jews came here to rebuild the town and lived alongside their Arab neighbours until 1948 when the Arabs of the town fled during the War of Independence.

The repeated destruction of the city has, unfortunately, left only meagre souvenirs of its vibrant past. A few remains of Crusader towers dot the shoreline, and an 18th-century mosque is crammed in between ice cream stands in the main square.

For historians and hedonists alike, Tiberias's main drawing-card is the **hot springs** situated at the southern outskirts of the city. There are many hypotheses about the cause of this natural wonder. In fact, the same cataclysmic convulsions that millions of years ago carved the Jordan Rift also created these 17 springs that gush from a depth of 2,000 metres (6,500 ft) to spew up hot streams of mineral-rich water. The therapeutic properties of the springs have been exploited for centuries.

For some contemporary healing, go to **Hamei Tiberias**. This hotel-spa offers a range of treatments, from whirlpools to electrohydrotherapy, that are reputed to cure everything from skin ailments to respiratory problems and, some claim, sterility. In the winter, a soak in these mineral-rich jacuzzis can be a soothing respite from the damp Galilee air.

You can see the original baths the Romans used in the **National Archaeological Park** across the street in a fascinating little **museum** (open Sun–Thur 10am–12 noon, 3–5pm; admission charge). Also within this national monument, which is the site of the ancient city of Khamat, archaeologists have uncov-

**TIP**

The Chinese food at Habayit (The House), opposite the Lido Beach in Tiberias, makes it one of the best restaurants in Israel.

**BELOW:** the open-air museum at Khamat Tverya.

ered a 2nd-century mosaic synagogue floor – undoubtedly the most exquisite ruins you'll find in Tiberias.

Just outside the city are the **Horns of Hittim** (Karnei Khitim) where in 1187 the Muslim forces of Saladin defeated the Crusaders in the decisive battle that brought an end to the Crusader Kingdom.

Map on pages 186–7

## Baptism in the Jordan

Shortly after Jesus left Nazareth at the age of 30, he met John the Baptist preaching near the waters of the Jordan. In the river that the Bible so often describes as a boundary – and, more figuratively, as a point of transition – Jesus was baptised. Once thus cleansed, he set out on his mission. Tradition holds that the baptism took place at the point where the Sea of Galilee merges with the Jordan River near what is today Kibbutz Kinneret.

The **Yardenit Baptismal Site** has been established just outside the kibbutz in order to accommodate the many pilgrims who still converge on the site. After the Six Day War the site was closed, except for special occasions, but it is now open for more general access. There is also a rival "Site of the Baptism" further south, near Jericho.

Around the point where the lake merges with the Jordan River in the south are three kibbutzim: **Dganya Alef**, **Dganya Bet** and **Kinneret** ⓱. Not having guesthouses, they attract fewer tourists than other kibbutzim around the lake, but they are the ones that are most worth noting because they were the first in the country. From the ranks of their members sprang many of Israel's legendary leaders, including Moshe Dayan. At the entrance to Dganya Aleph is a Syrian tank, stopped in its tracks in the 1948 War of Independence.

**BELOW:** by the lake at Tiberias.

*A tempting bunch of ripe dates.*

**BELOW:** an ostrich at Kibbutz Ha'On.

Several settlements have guesthouses and camping facilities, including **Moshav Ramot; Kibbutz Ein Gev**, site of a gala music festival every spring; **Kibbutz Ha'On**, which had an ostrich farm before they became popular in other parts of the world; and **Kibbutz Ma' agan**. Also on the east coast is the Golan Beach and its water wonderland, the Luna Gal. At **Beit Zera**, on the southern tip of the lake, are the ruins of an ancient moon-worshipping cult.

Ancient baths dating from the Roman period are found on the southern Golan at **Khammat Gader** ⑱, near the Yarmuk River. These hot baths were built over springs warmed by volcanic activity deep within the earth; when the waters emerge to the surface they're steaming hot and rich in minerals. The baths were internationally famous during Roman times, and people came from all over the empire to relax here. Israeli archaeologists have done a fine job of excavating and restoring them. Visitors are now invited to take a dip, and to inspect the fine Roman theatre, pools, plazas, mosaics and sundry inscriptions.

Epiphanius, a 4th-century monk, noted: "A festive gathering took place at Hammat Gader annually. For several days people from all over came to bathe and wash away their afflictions. But there too the Devil set his snares, since men and women bathe together." They still do – but properly attired, of course.

The ancient *tel* of **Beit She'an** ⑲ has revealed 6,000 years of civilisation. Near it sits Israel's best preserved Roman theatre which once seated 8,000, and there is an archaeological museum featuring a Byzantine mosaic floor. Beit She'an was once a member of the Roman Decapolis, meaning that it was one of the 10 most important cities in the Eastern Mediterranean. Other structures here include a colonnaded street, on the east side of which is a ruined temple which collapsed in an earthquake in the 8th century. Excavations here have revealed 18 superimposed cities, so if it's archaeological intrigue that you are after, Beit She'an should not be missed. The modern town, however, is a rather dull little place with little to offer. If you're thinking of going to Jordan, there is a crossing here called the **Jordan River Crossing**, which is sometimes known as the **Sheikh Hussein Bridge**.

Easily accessible from the highway north of Beit She'an is the impressive Crusader fortress of **Belvoir**. Perched on the highest hill in the region, it offers an extensive view of the valleys below and of neighbouring Jordan.

## The Jordan Rift

South of Beit She'an and east of the Gilboa mountain range is one of the lowest points in Israel: the **Jordan Rift**. Encompassing the Jordan Valley and the Beit She'an Valley, it is part of the same 6,500-km (4,000-mile) rift that stretches from Syria to Africa and is responsible for the lowest point on earth – the Dead Sea. Even here at 120 metres (390 ft) below sea level (it gets to 390 metres/1,280 ft further south), it's like a kiln baking under an unrelenting sun during the summer. By way of comparison, Death Valley, California, the lowest point in the United States, is only 87 metres (285 ft) below sea level. But nourished by the Jordan River, the Yarmuk River and a network of underground springs (including the Spring of Kharod), this remains a lush region, bursting with bananas, dates and other fruit. It is home to some of Israel's most prosperous kibbutzim.

**Map on pages 186–7**

A water system not quite as historic as Megiddo's but impressive in its own way can be found at **Gan ha-Shlosha** (The Garden of Three) **20**. Modern developers have managed to recreate a tiny piece of Eden in this stunning park. It is also known as Sachne, meaning "warm" in Arabic, because of the warm waters of **Ein Kharod** (The Spring of Kharod) that bubble up from under the earth to fill a huge natural swimming pool. The Spring of Kharod actually starts at the foot of the Gilboa Mountains, just east of Afula, and flows all the way to the Jordan, but for most of the way the warm waters are underground and diverted for use in local settlements. The only other spot where they surface is at **Gid'ona**, where the Israelite warrior Gideon supposedly assembled his forces 3,000 years ago, and which in more recent times served as the training spot for the forces of the Palmach, the élite fighting unit of the Jews before the State of Israel was created. There is also a memorial here to Yehoshuah Henkin, a Zionist leader, who purchased hundreds of thousands of acres of land – including this piece – for Jewish settlement.

About a mile west of Gan ha-Shlosha is **Kibbutz Beit Alfa**, where you'll find the country's best-preserved ancient synagogue floor. Discovered when kibbutz members were digging an irrigation channel, the 6th-century floor consists of a striking zodiac mosaic and a representation of the sacrifice of Isaac.

Overlooking the length of the Jezreel Valley are the **Gilboa Mountains**. Here King Saul met his untimely end at the hands of the Philistines, causing David to curse the spot forever: "Ye mountains of Gilboa, let there be no dew, nor rain upon you, neither fields of choice fruit." (II Samuel 20, 21–23). ❑

**BELOW:** the theatre at Beit She'an.

# THE CRADLE OF THREE RELIGIONS

*For some pilgrims the Holy Land bears witness to the truth of the Bible, while the more cynical see tourism turning it into a religious Disneyland*

From the historical point of view there can be no dispute. This is where Abraham first spoke of monotheism, to which Moses led the Children of Israel, and where Solomon built his Temple. During the Roman period Christ preached in the Galilee and was crucified in Jerusalem. Five centuries later Mohammed prayed in Jerusalem, and Muslims believe that after his death he came to Jerusalem on horseback before ascending to heaven.

For believers of all three religions the sites associated with all these events are sacred. For non-believers there is still a historical and archaeological fascination with the shrines.

Jews consider Hebron, Jerusalem, Tiberias and Safed to be holy cities. In Hebron the Tomb of the Patriarchs – Abraham and family – is located at the Cave of Machpelah. In Jerusalem the Western Wall, the one remaining structure from the Temple complex, is considered the holiest shrine. Tiberias was where the oral law section of the Talmud was compiled in the second century, the period in which the Cabalah, Jewish mystical texts, was written in the hills around Safed.

The principal Christian sites are the Church of the Nativity in Bethlehem, where Christ was born, the Church of the Annunciation in Nazareth, where his family lived, and the Church of the Holy Sepulchre in Jerusalem, where he was crucified and rose again.

Muslims revere the Tomb of the Patriarchs in Hebron, as Abraham was also the father of the Arab people, as well as the Temple Mount where the El-Aqsa Mosque and the Dome of the Rock are holy sites, both associated with Mohammed.

▽ **THE MOSQUE ON THE MOUNT**
The El-Aqsa Mosque on the Temple Mount was built in 705 and restored by Saladin after the Templars used it as their headquarters.

▷ **CHRIST'S HERITAGE**
The Church of the Nativity in Bethlehem is shared acrimoniously by the Catholic, Armenian and Greek Orthodox churches.

▽ **AWAITING THE MESSIAH**
Jews believe those buried on the Mount of Olives will be the first to return to life when the Messiah arrives.

◁ **CALLING THE UNFAITHFUL**
An ultra-Orthodox Jew urges his secular brethren to attend morning prayer.

## THE VIA DOLOROSA

Unlike the other Christian shrines in the Holy Land, which date back to Byzantine times, the traditional route of the Via Dolorosa was only established in the late Middle Ages. Since then Christians have re-enacted Christ's last journey, bearing a cross through the narrow, winding streets of Jerusalem's Old City. Every Friday Franciscan friars lead a procession along the Via Dolorosa from the Church of the Flagellation. These processions are especially colourful and intense on Good Friday.

There are 14 Stations of the Cross, the last five inside the Church of the Holy Sepulchre where it is believed Christ was crucified, buried and resurrected. The Catholic and Orthodox Churches do not doubt the authenticity of the Via Dolorosa and the Holy Sepulchre, but some Protestants suggest that Calvary was at the Garden Tomb site, near the Damascus Gate.

△ **FERVENT PRAYER**
The large stone blocks of the Western Wall, the last remaining vestige of the Temple complex destroyed by the Romans, attract Jewish religious fervour.

◁ **BARMITZVAH BOY**
A young Jewish boy reads from the Torah as he celebrates his barmitzvah by the Western Wall.

▷ **THE GOLDEN DOME**
The Dome of the Rock is a highly revered shrine, marking the spot from which Muslims believe that Mohammed ascended to heaven on a steed.

◁ **BAPTISM IN THE JORDAN**
The Yardenit Baptismal Site, located where the River Jordan flows out of the Sea of Galilee, receives streams of Christian pilgrims seeking baptism.

# THE NORTH COAST

*Wander into the past in ancient Akko, then travel up the lovely north coast for modern pleasures such as water sports, as well as grottoes and stunning views*

**A**kko is probably the most atmospheric place in Israel. Battered over the centuries by successive invaders, it holds its own against the flow of time and tourism. The old sea wall, built by the Crusaders, overlooks the expanse of the Mediterranean, on the northern tip of Haifa Bay, while Gothic archways and minarets mingle within the city. The ancient stone piers still give port to fishermen; the markets and cafés still overflow with friendly service and mysterious faces. Chosen as the key port of the Crusader Kingdom by Baldwin I in 1104, and successfully defended against Simon Maccabeus and Napoleon Bonaparte, Akko has left behind the glorious fury of its past. Yet if it is a backwater, it is a dramatic one, as richly eloquent as any in the Holy Land.

## Crusader capital

Akko ㉑ is among the world's oldest known seaports. It was already a major population centre when the Phoenicians dominated the northern coast. Its ancient industries include glassware (Roman historian Pliny credits Akko with discovering the art of glassmaking) and purple dyes – extracted from the *Purpura*, a sea-snail which gave the colour its name. Around 333 BC, Alexander the Great passed through the then-flourishing Greek colony; Julius Caesar came 300 years later, in the process laying the stones of the first paved road in Roman Judea – from Akko to Antioch.

The Arabs held the city from AD 636 to1104, fortifying and rebuilding much of it; yet Akko only hit its zenith during the Crusader era. The First Crusade was launched with the capture of Jerusalem in 1099. Five years later Akko fell, and the Crusaders immediately realised its value as a Mediterranean lifeline. Developed into a major trading centre by Genovese merchants, and renamed St Jean d'Acre, it became the principal port on the eastern Mediterranean rim.

Many of the most powerful and colourful Crusader orders – the Knights Templar, the Teutonic Order, the Order of St Lazarus, and the Hospitaller Order of St John – established centres here. In 1187 Saladin defeated the Europeans at the Horns of Hittim, and many Crusader cities fell into Saracen hands. Led by Philip Augustus of Spain and Richard the Lionheart of England, the knights of the Third Crusade recaptured Akko, and made it the capital of their kingdom in 1192. The remains left from the ensuing century of Crusader rule testify that this was its finest hour, before it fell once more into obscurity.

In the mid-1700s the port was revived by the Bedouin Sheikh Dahar el-Omar, followed by Akko's most notorious prime builder, the Ottoman Pasha Ahmad, known as "el-Jazzar" (the butcher) on account of his penchant for cruelty. His architectural

**PRECEDING PAGES:** the El-Jazzar Mosque. **LEFT:** an aerial view of the mosque. **BELOW:** board games in Akko.

legacies include Akko's best-known landmarks. In 1799, aided by British warships, el-Jazzar accomplished what much of Europe could not: he defeated Napoleon in a two-month siege. Turkish rule and the advent of the steamship ended Akko's importance as a port, and the town regained prominence only in the last years of the British Mandate, when its prison held hundreds of Jewish freedom fighters, including the Zionist leader Ze'ev Jabotinsky, and was the scene of a remarkable jailbreak in 1947. Since independence the city has retained its maritime character while developing its industry, and today it holds close to 40,000 residents, some two-thirds of them Jewish immigrants.

**TIP**

Remember to note the modest dress code before entering the El-Jazzar Mosque.

## Many cities in one

Like much of Israel, Akko is divided into old and new sections, and it is the old city that is of most interest. To enter the old city from the new, follow the coastal strip or the parallel Weizmann Street, where the **Tourist Information Office** stands. Either route takes you through the dry moat and city walls, built by the Crusaders and later refortified. You can climb the wall here, and visit the northeastern command post, the Burj el-Kommandar, with a strategic view and a restored promenade which continues on to Land Gate, at the bay.

As you enter the city, the first prominent structure is the elegant **El-Jazzar Mosque Ⓐ** (open dawn to dusk; admission charge), built in 1781–82 by "the butcher", and now the site of his tomb and that of his adopted son, Suleiman. Ringed with domed arcades and swaying palms, the mosque is considered the finest in Israel, and serves as a spiritual centre for Israel's Muslim community. Except for a shrine containing a single hair from the beard of the prophet, the interior is as stark as it is magnificent.

**BELOW:** the mosque and the harbour.

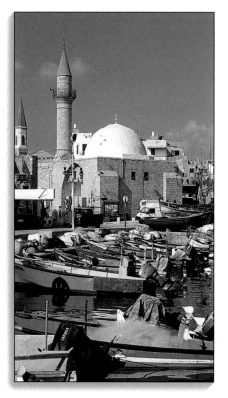

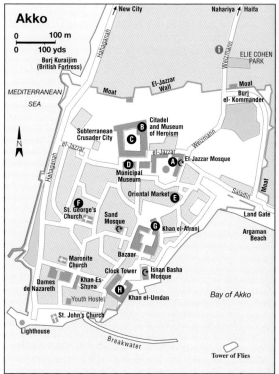

Map on page 216

On the right-hand side of Weizmann Street, dominating the old city skyline, is the towering **Citadel and Museum of Heroism** ❸ (open Sat–Thur 9.30am–5pm, Fri 9.30am–noon; admission charge). Built by el-Jazzar on Crusader ruins, the fortress has been used variously as an arsenal and a barracks and, since Turkish times, as a prison. This was the centre for the incarceration and execution of Jewish underground fighters during the British Mandate, and exhibits in the museum document this unsettling period.

Abutting the Citadel is the most interesting site of all, the dank and dramatic **Subterranean Crusader City** ❸ (open Sat–Thur 9am–4.30pm, Fri 9am– 12.30pm; admission charge). While not excavated in their entirety, the halls of the sprawling complex contain such unusual historical testimony as carved fleur-de-lys insignia. Now reclaimed, the halls are the venue for the autumn **Akko Theatre Festival**, which brings together the best of Israel's experimental companies.

As you emerge from the subterranean city, turn off a small lane into a restored Turkish bathhouse, which is now the **Municipal Museum** ❶ (same hours as Crusader city; tickets valid for both). The museum contains exhibits on archaeology, Islamic culture, folklore and weaponry.

Wandering deeper into the maze-like streets of Akko, you may stumble across the Sand Mosque, off the **Souk**, the fascinating **Oriental Market** ❸. Further in is the **Greek Orthodox St George's Church** ❸, dedicated to two British officers who fell at Akko in 1799 and 1840. Of special interest are the *khans* (inns) that grace the port-side area. These include the imposing **Khan el-Afranj** (Inn of the Franks) ❸, near the **Bazaar**, and the unequalled **Khan el-Umdan** (Inn of the Pillars) ❶. The lower storeys of the latter were used as stables and

*Oriental spices for sale in Akko.*

**BELOW:** calling the faithful to prayer.

its upper ones as lodgings. Its geometric courtyard is memorable, and the clock-tower (minus its clock ) offers a glimmering view of the port.

Beneath the tower, wander by the fishing port, and up along the sea wall, which houses one or two lovely cafés among its layered arches. The youth hostel is here, and, further on, the lighthouse, and from this corner you can take in the sunset view of the sea wall heading north to the new city, the old stone houses huddled in its tired embrace.

## North to the border

Arching north from Akko along the coast lies the final architectural gift from el-Jazzar, the austere, self-contained spine of the **Turkish Aqueduct**, which once ran 15 km (9 miles) to the spring at **Kabri**, now a picnic and camping site.

Further on, the **Bahá'í Tomb and Gardens** mark the burial site and villa of Mirza Hussein Ali, an early leader of the Bahá'í faith, known also as Baha Ulla – Glory to God. Surrounding the tomb is a lovely formal Persian garden.

Just north of the gardens is **Nahariya** ㉒. A clean and modest resort community founded in 1934 by German Jews, it offers many amenities for water sports, and a fine coastline on which to enjoy them. Its most noticeable landmark is the quiet stream, the Ga'aton, which flows down the centre of the main street. Nahariya has built an image as the national honeymoon hideaway, and in spring offers discounts to newlyweds, and occasionally to other couples. Its reputation is rooted in its association with a Canaanite fertility goddess.

The honeymooning really gets into high gear during the celebration of Lag b'Omer – the one day in the six weeks following Passover that Jewish law allows couples to wed. Some 5 km (3 miles) northwards along the coastal road

**TIP**

For information, maps and tours when travelling to inaccessible spots such as Monfort Fortress, contact the Society for the Protection of Nature, tel: (02) 6232936 (Jerusalem); (03) 6375063 (Tel Aviv); or (04) 8664136 (Haifa).

**BELOW:** view of the Rainbow Arch.

are the ruins of **Akhziv** ㉓, once a thriving Phoenician port, now a thriving Club Med resort. For non-members there are also a holiday village, a campground, and a sparkling beach, equipped with shower facilities. The site is excellent for underwater fishing, and contains small tidal pools to explore.

From here continue northwards, passing the **Akhziv Bridge**, or Gesher Ha-Ziv (Bridge of Glory), where l4 young Haganah men were killed in 1946 while trying to blow it up in order to cut British communication links. The tragedy is memorialised in the name of the local kibbutz, and in a roadside monument.

Inland at the Shlomi junction lies an intriguing piece of nature. The **Rainbow Arch** was formed when a section of the cliff edge dissolved, leaving a large, almost perfect arch. Today, abseilers rappel down this beautiful natural arch to the lush valley below. From the roadside the marked footpath is a gentle uphill stroll to the arch and a panoramic view. Some 15 km (9 miles) east of the coast, atop a steep ridge, and accessible only by footpaths, lies **Monfort Fortress** ㉔, the most important of a string of Crusader forts, now set in a National Park.

Some 9 km (5 miles) north of Nahariya towers the rocky border point of **Rosh ha-Nikra** ㉕, Israel's northernmost coastal limit. The view from the chalk-white cliffs set off against the crashing azure waves is entrancing, but it is Rosh ha-Nikra's **grottoes**, formed by millennia of erosion, that are the prime attraction. A new cable car (April–June & Sept daily 8.30am–6pm, July–Aug 8.30am–11pm) takes you down over the pounding tide, and a footpath is also there for the determined. Atop the cliff, the southernmost edge of the range known as the **Ladder of Tyre**, is a cafeteria, and a view over the now walled-up railway tunnel that once led to Lebanon. On a clear day, looking south, one can just make out the port of **Haifa** ㉖ (*see page 223*). ❑

Map
on pages
186–7

*Cable cars take you to the grottoes.*

**LEFT AND BELOW:**
Rosh ha-Nikra: the
grottoes and the
snowy-white cliffs.

# HAIFA

*Haifa is a busy working port where Jews and Arabs live in harmony. The dome of a Bahá'í shrine, promoting a common world language and religion, is the most prominent landmark*

Maps:
Area 186
City 226

In 1750 the Bedouin Sheikh Dahar el-Omar destroyed a squalid coastal village because its inhabitants neglected to pay homage. The town lay in ruins for eight years, until, having made his point, the sheikh rebuilt it and improved its natural harbour. **Haifa** ㉖ grew from that unpropitious beginning, and has since evolved into a bustling port city and maritime centre.

Today Haifa is Israel's third-largest city, the centre of the nation's renowned high-technology industries. From its original cradle on the narrow coastal strip between the Mediterranean and the Carmel Range, Haifa has marched up Mount Carmel, settling itself lazily among the gentle slopes. The city is built on three levels, rising from its original location along the waterfront. The second level, in the Carmel foothills, is Hadar Ha-Karmel, the central business district and the oldest residential area. The newest neighbourhoods have climbed all the way to the crests of the peak, and cling to its sides, connected by a network of excellent roads. At the very apex is the Carmel Centre, where some of the city's most attractive homes and classiest hotels and shops are located.

**PRECEDING PAGES:** a bird's-eye view of Haifa. **LEFT:** the Bahá'í Temple. **BELOW:** Haifa is now a thriving modern port.

## Historic port

Haifa had been known since the 2nd century as a safe haven for passing ships, situated as it was along one of the Mediterranean's oldest sea lanes, but at the time of its premature destruction in the mid-18th century it was little more than an assemblage of huts, with fewer than 250 inhabitants. Reborn, it thrived, and by 1890 some 8,000 people lived within its limits. Yet it took a combination of railroads and war to catapult the city into significance in the 20th century.

The two causes were interlinked: under the impending pressures of war, the Ottoman Turks built the Hejaz Railroad connecting Haifa to Damascus in the north, while the British started the Sinai Military Railroad, which was later to link Haifa to Qantara on the Suez Canal. At the end of the war, when the British controlled Palestine under a League of Nations mandate, they gradually modernised Haifa's port.

With a steady increase in maritime traffic, and a continuing stream of immigrants, the population reached 25,000 by 1918. By 1923 it had more than doubled, and by 1931 doubled again to exceed 100,000. After Israel's independence in 1948 further development of the port became essential. Israel's land borders were sealed, and Haifa's port became the Jewish state's only opening to the world.

## Blue-collar city

Today the port, monitored by a centralised computer system, bristles with massive electronically-operated

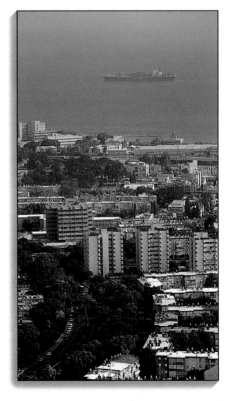

*Proud of their industrious image, Haifa residents like to say that while Tel Aviv plays and Jerusalem prays, Haifa works.*

cargo-handling equipment, berths the world's sea-going mammoths, and was Israel's premier maritime centre, although it has now been overtaken by Ashdod. But Haifa has also become a versatile industrial centre. Known affectionately as the "Red City" because of its long-standing identification with the nation's labour movement, it is essentially a blue-collar city.

At the northern edge of the city, an industrial zone accommodates a very extensive petrochemical industry, oil refineries and many small manufacturing units. Israel's high-technology companies are centred in a new science-based industrial district at the southern entrance to the city. Some 70 percent of the area's 120,000 wage-earners (out of a total population of over 300,000) are employed in industrial enterprises, excluding civil service and tourist-related jobs. Haifa's blue-collar character is mitigated by the presence of two major academic institutions, the Technion and the University of Haifa, whose faculties and students total about 50,000.

## Religious communities

Haifa's religious population lives in distinct communities contiguous with secular neighbourhoods in the heart of the city, near Hadar. The atmosphere around Yosef Street, near the municipal theatre, around Ha-Ge'ula, near the Glory of Israel religious school or in Ramot Wishnitz, just below Derekh ha-Rupin, is as rich in intensity and devotion to tradition as are comparable communities elsewhere in Israel. But in Haifa they never throw stones. This is due in part to the sensible implementation of a policy promulgated in 1947 by David Ben Gurion. Known as the Status Quo Agreement, it guaranteed the preservation of the status quo on religious issues as it was at the time the state was established. In other

**BELOW:** Haifa's university dominates the skyline.

municipalities the amorphous agreement has become a platform for squabbling, but prosaic Haifa managed to transform it into a workable arrangement.

This amicability means that, although cinemas are closed on Friday evenings, theatres, discos, restaurants and nightclubs operate as usual. Haifa's zoo and most museums are open on the Sabbath, but are not allowed to charge admission fees, and hotels ask departing guests to pay their bills before Friday evening.

Maps:
Area 186
City 226

## Arab communities

A Saturday bus service is unusual in Israel. The fact that it happens in Haifa reflects the formative influence of its Arab citizens on the city's social patterns. There has always been a significant Arab presence in Haifa, and Jews and Arabs here have a long history of mutual give-and-take. Israeli Arabs constitute about 10 percent of Haifa's population, and the city attracts thousands more every day from the surrounding villages. Although there are some mixed areas, most Arabs have remained in their own neighbourhoods, in many cases in the same places where their families have lived for generations.

There are two distinctive Arab communities in Haifa; **Wadi Nisnas** is one of the area's oldest neighbourhoods, adjacent to Hadar, near Bet Ha-geffen, Haifa's Arab–Jewish community centre. With its buildings of massive sandstone blocks, window grilles and arched doorways, its prevalence of Arabic and Middle Eastern music, and the range of exotic food and clothing for sale, Wadi Nisnas is a graphic reminder that Haifa stands with one foot firmly planted in the Levant.

In sharp contrast to Wadi Nisnas, **Kababir**, perched high on a ridge overlooking the Mediterranean, is an Arab neighbourhood of sumptuous dwellings

**BELOW:**
sharing opinions.

*A cheerful young resident.*

and lush gardens. Established as an independent village in 1830, the community opted for annexation to Haifa when the State of Israel was established in 1948, anticipating the benefits of schools, health services, water and sewage systems. The majority of residents are Ahmdya Muslims, a small Islamic sect distinct from the larger Shi'ite and Sunni groups in Wadi Nisnas. Although fully integrated into the Haifa municipality, Kababir is administered locally by a committee of six elders elected annually by the men of the community. A new mosque, completed in 1984, is the only one of its kind in the Middle East.

## The Carmel slope

The **Carmel Centre** (Ha-Karmel) **Ⓐ** is where most of Haifa's hotels are located. Here, atop towering Mount Carmel, panoramic scenes of the city, sea and mountains burst into view at every turn. Modern shops line Shderot ha-Nasi along with sidewalk cafés and restaurants specialising in kosher, Chinese, Italian and Middle Eastern foods.

Atop the crest of Mount Carmel loom the contemporary features of the **University of Haifa**, its distinctive tower thrusting resolutely against the sky. Founded in 1972, the university serves the entire northern district, and has branches in some of the more remote areas. The 25-storey **Eshkol Tower**, designed by the Brazilian architect Oscar Niemeyer, offers an unparalleled view of northern Israel. To the east are the fertile valleys of the Galilee and the brooding outline of the Golan Heights, while down below miles of yellow-sand beaches stretch like satin ribbon along the Mediterranean shore. To the north are Haifa Bay, Akko, and the white cliffs of Rosh ha-Nikra. On a clear day it's all visible: a living map, sparkling with sun and sea. At night, harbour lights vie

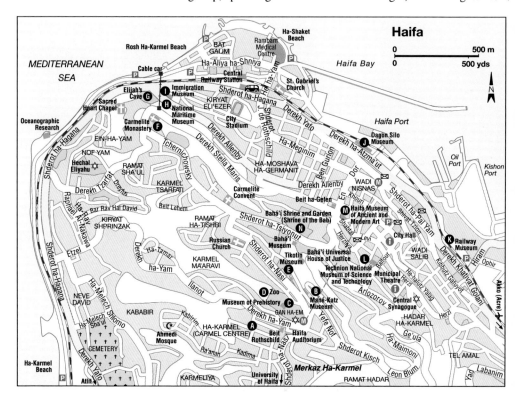

Map on page 226

with the stars, and the city marks its place with a million glinting shadows.

Tucked within the mountainous folds of upper Haifa are a number of hidden treasures. On the slope near the Promenade is the **Mané-Katz Museum** ⓑ (open Sun–Thur 10am–1pm, 4–6pm, Sat 10am–1pm; admission free) is housed in the building where the Jewish-French expressionist lived and worked in his later years. Besides his paintings and sculptures, the display also includes his personal collection of Judaica and antique furniture. A short distance away is the Edenic Mothers' Garden, the biggest of Haifa's parks – and there are nearly 400 of them. Among curving paths, flowers and picnicking families is the **Steke-lis Museum of Prehistory** ⓒ (open Sun–Thur 8am–2pm, Sat 10am–2pm; admission charge), displaying finds of the Carmel area, which way back then was home to Neanderthal Man.

A little farther on is the pleasant, well-maintained **Haifa Zoo** ⓓ, and in the far corner of the park an open-air restaurant specialising in Middle Eastern foods. Israel's only museum of Japanese art, the **Tikotin Museum** ⓔ (open Sun–Thur 10am–5pm, Sat 10am–2pm; admission charge), is in the heart of the Carmel Centre, at 89 Shderot ha-Nasi.

Going down the slope, past the Promenade, you reach that part of the city known as **French Carmel**, an expensive but cosy residential district. At the end of this area, Mount Carmel levels off into a promontory, and this is the site of the **Carmelite Monastery** ⓕ (open daily 6am–1.30pm, 3–6pm), the world centre of the Carmelite Order. Situated at the end of the mountain, along Stella Maris Road, the church commands one of the most spectacular views of the city. The site was selected in the 12th century by a small band of Crusaders who settled there to devote themselves to asceticism, solitude and prayer. The order

**BELOW:** Elijah's Grotto, below the Carmelite Monastery.

which grew from that beginning was officially founded by St Brocard in the 13th century. The church was built in the 18th century, over a grotto associated in the Jewish and Christian traditions with the prophet Elijah and his disciple Elisha. The interior dome depicts events in their lives, and a small museum displays local archaeological discoveries.

**Elijah's Cave G** (open Sun–Thur 8am–5pm) can be reached by a footpath from the monastery. The prophet is said to have rested and meditated here in the 9th century BC, before his momentous encounter with the Baalists on one of the peaks of the Carmel Range. After leaving the cave, he is said to have climbed to the top of Mount Carmel, where an altar had been erected by the worshippers of Baal and other Phoenician deities. Elijah challenged their priests to light a flame under a sacrifice by means of their religious powers.

According to tradition, the pagan priests failed; Elijah called upon the Lord and the flames were instantly ignited. Ahab, the Jewish king who had angered the Lord by worshipping Baal, was witness to the event. Rejecting paganism, he ordered the massacre at the Kishon River of all the Baalists. The event is recorded in detail in I Kings 18, 17–46. Some Christians believe the cave to have sheltered the Holy Family on the way back from Egypt, and know it also as the **Grotto of the Madonna**.

## Along the seafront

Opposite the monastery itself, a sinuous platform marks the upper terminal of Haifa's cable car system. Delayed for more than a year due to controversy surrounding its intended operation on the Sabbath, the system ferries passengers from the Carmel heights down to the seaside Bat Galim Promenade. It is an easy

*The quickest way to sea level.*

**BELOW:** the Dagon Grain Silo.

Map on page 226

walk to the **National Maritime Museum**  (open Sun–Thur 10am–4pm, Sat 10am–1pm; admission charge) and the **Museum of Clandestine Immigration** ❶ (open Sun–Thur 9am–4pm, Fri 9am–1pm; admission charge). The immigration museum includes the tiny ship in which Jewish immigrants sought to evade the British Mandatory government's blockade in the years before the State of Israel was declared.

Adjacent to the port area, a short bus ride from the prophet's retreat, is the **Dagon Grain Silo** ❶ – probably one of the only architecturally pleasing silos in the world. Besides its commercial use for receiving and storing grain from ships anchored in the port, the silo houses a **museum** (guided tours Sun–Fri 10.30am; admission charge) devoted to the history of bread- and beer-making. An assortment of old implements is displayed with explanatory photographs, murals and mosaics, and there is a working model of the silo's own mechanised system.

Hugging the waterfront, the **Railroad Museum** ❶ (open Sun–Tues and Thur 10am–12 noon; admission charge) opposite 40 Hativat Golani Street is a tribute to the importance of the railway in Haifa's history. Steam engines that hauled freight from the hinterlands to the port are preserved, along with luxury passenger cars, ornate sleeping cars, and wood-panelled dining cars. Visitors are encouraged to climb aboard and try out the accommodation.

## Hadar

In Hadar, the level above the waterfront, the original edifice of the country's pre-eminent **Institute of Technology**, the **Technion** ❶, has been preserved as an architectural landmark and is now the home of the exciting hands-on **National**

**BELOW:** a spooky glow lights up the Technion.

**Museum of Science** (open Sun–Thur 9am–6pm, Fri 10am–3pm, Sat 10am–5pm; admission charge). The magnificent old building, constructed in 1924, was designed by Alexander Baerwald, combining European lines with an eastern dome, crenellated roofs and intricate mosaics. The Technion recently expanded into a large new campus in the Neve Shannon neighbourhood; free tours are offered daily.

*There's plenty of decorated pottery for sale.*

The **Haifa Museum of Ancient and Modern Art**  (open Sun–Thur, Sat 10am–1pm, Tues, Thur, Sat 6–9pm; admission charge) at the southern edge of Hadar, on Shabtai Levy Street, is crammed with displays. Comfortable viewing from good vantage points isn't always possible, but the variety and quality of the collections make a visit worth the effort. Special exhibitions are occasionally held. Work by contemporary Israeli artists is exhibited at the **Chagall Artists' House** at 24 Hazionut Blvd (open daily; admission free).

## One world religion

From the Haifa Museum, go uphill on Shderot Ha-Tsiyonut to the **Bahá'í Shrine and Gardens** (open daily: shrine 9am–12 noon; garden 9am–5pm; admission charge). The gold-domed **Shrine of the Bab**, with its Corinthian-style columns, is Haifa's best-recognised landmark, and the world centre of the Bahá'í faith. Founded in Persia by Mirza Ali Mohammed, the sect was proscribed and its leader publicly executed there in 1850. Claiming over 3 million adherents worldwide, the faith is based on brotherhood, love and charity. Its followers view Moses, Christ, the Buddha and Mohammed as messengers sent by God to different parts of the world in different eras, but all preaching a similar philosophy. They advocate a common world language and religion.

**BELOW:** the Bahá'í Gardens.

## Food and fun

Pavement cafés are everywhere in Haifa, ranging from a couple of tiny tables on a sidestreet, where excellent Viennese coffee can be bought, to the umbrella-shaded elegance near the Cinématique at the Rothschild Centre on Hanassi Street. Haifa also has a wide variety of restaurants, ranging from dinner-and-dancing in the Rondo Grill of the Dan Carmel Hotel to a Middle Eastern evening of folk-dancing at Al-Pasha on Hamman-al-Pasha Street. More local flavour can be sampled at The Pleasant Brothers, an unassuming place on the corner of Moriah and Pica streets in the Ahuza neighbourhood. This is a long-time local favourite, popular for its *shish kebab*, *shishlik* and salads. After dinner, have a cup of coffee in one of the many coffee houses around the corner on Pica Street.

Evening entertainment in Haifa is often a matter of luck. There is the usual range of discos, pubs and bars, but the most popular places depend on their patrons to join in the singing and dancing. An evening stroll along Panorama in the Carmel Centre, or Balfour and Herzliya streets in Hadar, will reveal where the fun is.

## Israel's only subway

One block up the hill from the *felafel* stands of He-halutz is the Hadar entrance to the **Carmelit**, Israel's only subway. While most visitors are accustomed to subways, the Carmelit is one of a kind. Its tunnel, hacked through the interior rock of the mountain, operates on the same principle as San Francisco's cable cars: one train hurtling down from the Carmel Centre at the top of the mountain hauls the other train up the steep incline from sea level. Even the cars are designed at an angle. From top to bottom, the trip takes seven minutes. ❑

Map on page 226

**TIP**

For informal eating, try *felafels*, bought at any of the kiosks lining He-halutz Street in Hadar. Standing up alongside the kiosks, people buy the basic felafel (fried chick-pea balls in pitta bread) and then help themselves to hot peppers, sauces, olives, pickes, salad and aubergine.

**BELOW:** a Carmel souvenir shop.

# CENTRAL AND SOUTH COAST

*Crusader ruins, pioneer settlements and citrus groves line
the coast, but for most people the sand and the surf
are the major attractions*

Map
on page
236

From the environs of Caesarea in the north to Ashkelon in the south, Israel's central and south coast is citrus country – the fertile Sharon Plain. In Hebrew the word for citrus, *hadar*, is the same as the word for "splendour", and in the proper season both meanings are equally appropriate as the entire strip from seashore to foothills grows lush with orchards and ripe, hanging fruit. However, Israel's growing population means that the orange groves are being transformed into housing estates, industrial zones and shopping centres. Yet the citrus crop was never indigenous to the area, and well into the 19th century the central coast was a miasma of malarial swamps. By the turn of the century, however, the development of pumps which could raise the buried groundwater to the soil surface harnessed the land to the needs of its pioneer settlers, who set about draining the marshes and cultivating new orchards.

Today, citrus is Israel's most valuable agricultural export. The varieties under cultivation run the spectrum, with the sweet "Jaffa" oranges and their kin dominating along the coast, and grapefruit mainly thriving in the thicker, river-washed soil further inland. The citrus harvest is from November to April, and this is when the fruits are at their most intoxicating, swinging ripely off their evergreen branches, their scent wafting out over the road to the sea.

**PRECEDING PAGES:**
the beach at
Herzliya.
**LEFT:** planting a
seedling at a
coastal kibbutz.
**BELOW:** enjoying
the beach.

## The Carmel Range

The Carmel Range takes its name from the words Kerem-El, meaning "Vineyard of God". It runs for about 25 km (16 miles) along the coast, rising to some 500 metres (1,650 ft) and falling steeply to the Mediterranean. The Kishon River flows at its feet. Today it contains **Mount Carmel National Park ❶**, Israel's largest national forest preserve, which is lush with hilly woodlands, well-marked hiking trails, picnic facilities and breathtaking vistas. Almost one-tenth of the 8,500-hectare (21,000-acre) park is a nature preserve where deer and gazelle roam freely.

Just beyond the park, tucked among the slopes and valleys of the Carmel Range, are the Druze villages of **Daliyat el-Karmel** and **Isfiya ❷**. Surrounded by tawny precipices plunging to verdant valleys carpeted with tangled foliage, the villages are easily accessible by car or bus. The market places offer traditional handicrafts and pleasant cafés where Turkish coffee and succulent pastries can be enjoyed under the trees. The **Carmelite Monastery** at **Muhraka**, nearby, stands over the site where Elijah defeated the Baalists.

Winding down through the mountainside, the roadarcs through the gorges of a severe, astonishingly attractive landscape: the region is known as **Little Switzerland**. Kibbutz Beit Oren tucked between the pines here operates a guesthouse. At the crest of the

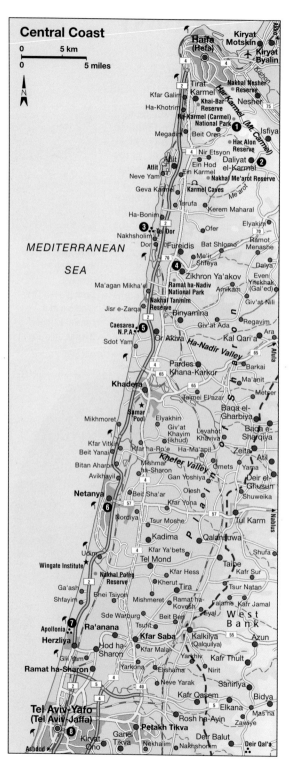

**Central Coast**

0        5 km

0              5 miles

N

MEDITERRANEAN
SEA

ridge lies the ultimate view of the Carmel coast.

Just to the south, you will come to one of three caves inhabited by Neanderthal Man 50,000 years ago and discovered in 1929. The caves contained flint tools and dozens of skeletons that provided anthropologists with revelations about the lifestyle of these early hunters. Ensconced amid gnarled olive trees and Moorish arches, the artists' colony of **Ein Hod** was conceived in 1953 as a rugged oasis of creativity, and today provides living and working space for some 200 artisans. The gallery and restaurant in the town centre warmly welcome company.

## The Carmel Coast

Down on the coast you will come to the the imposing Crusader fortress of **Atlit**, perched wearily on the rocks above the Mediterranean. At present the ruins are off-limits to the general public. A modern-day fortress, the prison in which Israel held Shi'ite prisoners during its war in Lebanon, is visible nearby.

Slightly further south, past Ha-Bonim beach and the moshav of the same name, you come to one of Israel's most active on-going archaeological sites: **Tel Dor 3**. The excavations have as yet only unearthed a fraction of this sprawling ancient city, but the ruins on display, including Canaanite, Israelite and Hellenistic finds, indicate a vast metropolis of tens of thousands of inhabitants. Archaeology aside, this is a site of enormous natural beauty, the lagoons and water washing against the cliffs complementing the rolling hills of Mount Carmel inland.

Abutting the *tel* just to the south is the lovely beach of **Nakhsholim** (Breakers), and there is a kibbutz of the same name with a roomy guesthouse and a friendly atmosphere. In the grounds is an illuminating **Maritime Museum**, housed in a turn-of-the-century building which was once a glass factory. This rocky portion of the Carmel coast, along a major ancient shipping lane, is the site of hundreds of undersea wrecks, which were the focus of a major underwater excavation in 1985. The museum holds a selection of these treasures culled from the depths, and their exhibits range from Phoenician catapult balls to relics dating from Napoleon's naval misadventures off this shore in 1799.

Map on page 236

Along the length of this coast, rows of vegetables sheathed in white plastic dot the roadsides, often under the stately presence of towering cypress or eucalyptus trees. Towards evening, when the hues in the sky drift into violet, lilac and pale orange, the landscape looks as if it had been painted by Claude Monet.

Take a turning inland just after Nakhsholim, and after a short distance (passing the tranquil Arab town of Fureidis (Paradise) you will reach the town of **Zikhron Ya'akov** ❹, which was established in 1882 in memory of James (Jacob) Rothschild, the father of the great benefactor of Israel's first settlers, Baron Edmond (Benjamin) de Rothschild. The **Aaronson House and Museum**, just off the main street, details the lives of Aaron and Sarah Aaronson. Aaron was a botanist who, in the early 1900s, isolated durable strains of wheat for cultivation in Palestine. He and his sister are enshrined in legend because of their role in organising the pro-British "Nili" spy ring during resistance to the oppressive Turkish regime. Caught by the Turks, and afraid she would give away information, Sarah shot herself in her home in 1917.

*Beach apartments at Nakhsholim.*

Like Rishon Le-Tsiyon further south, Zikhron Ya'akov is one of the original homes of the Carmel Oriental Vineyards, and tourists are welcome to take a free tour of the facilities, capped off with a complimentary wine-tasting break.

A minute's drive to the south is **Rothschild's Tomb**, built in the 1950s to house the remains of the Parisian banker and his wife Adelaide. Situated amid a fragrant garden of date trees, sage, roses and other flowers, this sensuously designed landscape opens up to a magnificent panorama of the Upper Sharon, while a concrete map indicates the locations of the settlements made possible by Rothschild (whose generosity lingers today in the barroom phrase "put it on the Baron's account"). The tomb itself is contemporary and tasteful; the site, all told, is one of the most significant in Israel.

**BELOW:** the coast at Tel Dor.

Two kilometres (1 mile) further south is **Binyamina**, also named after the great benefactor. This lower portion of the Carmel Range bears the name **Ramat ha-Nadiv** – Benefactor's Heights – and has been designated a National Park.

Heading south towards Caesarea, one immediately enters the area of the excellent birdwatching country of the **Kabara Marshes**, where some of the early Zionist settlements were established at the turn of the century. The Crocodile River bears testimony to the once intimidating nature of the terrain, but the last crocodile here died in 1910.

## Crusaders at their best

Although its greatest historical importance was as a Roman colony, it is to the Crusader ruins at **Caesarea** ❺ that tourists flock by the busload today, and truly they are as impressive as any in Israel. It takes a good half day just to take in the site, while the visual impact of Crusader arches, crumbling walls and smashed Roman pillars is constantly disarming, and attests to

the layered history of habitation here. Despite being one of Israel's most lauded archaeological sites, Caesarea is still difficult to reach via public transportation, which means that individual tourists must either rent a car, stay overnight nearby, or join a tour.

While settlements in the region date back as far as Phoenician times, the history of the city only really began with the Romans in 22 BC when the royal master-builder Herod the Great founded it, naming it in honour of the emperor Augustus. Around the year 6 BC it was designated the official residence of the governors of Judea, and for some 500 years Caesarea was to remain the capital of Roman administration in Palestine. At the time of Jesus, Pontius Pilate lived here, and St Paul was imprisoned here for two years before being sent to Rome from this port.

The great Jewish Revolt in AD 66 began in Caesarea, and in the struggle that followed the city's prisons saw the torture and execution of many captive Jewish zealots. In AD 70 the Roman general Vespasian was crowned emperor here. With the Bar-Kochba uprising, many notable Jews once again met their deaths here, among them the great sage and spiritual leader Rabbi Akiva, in 135. (The rabbi is commemorated in the nearby community of Or Akiva.)

During the period of Pax Romana, the city was a centre of Hellenistic and, later, Christian culture. The Crusaders, under Baldwin I, captured the city in 1101, and during the next 200 years Caesarea changed hands with confusing frequency. King Baldwin believed it held the Holy Grail which Jesus sipped from at the Last Supper, but the massive fortifications that so commend it today were only added after 1254, with the reconquest of the city by Louis IX. Muslim forces captured the city in 1265 (and again in 1291), and Caesarea never

**BELOW:** view of the Mediterranean from the Carmel range.

regained its importance, being pillaged over the centuries by successive rulers.

The contemporary visitor to Caesarea enters the **Crusader City** (open daily 8am–6pm, except Fri 8am–5pm; admission charge) through a vaulted gatehouse, after passing over a bridge across a wide moat. The walls around the city, which slope down precipitously from an imposing height, are perhaps the most awe-inspiring monument here; walking the breadth of this imposing redoubt, imaginative tourists can easily picture the spectacle of hand-to-hand combat that took place here time and again. Inside the city are numerous ruins of Crusaders' homes and streets. Along the waterfront, Roman pillars used as foundation stones by the Crusaders jut out among the waves.

Outside the entrance to the Crusader City, a Byzantine Street of Statues represents the city that preceded the Crusaders, its headless figures pondering the passing of their power. Some 500 metres (550 yards) south of the city walls is the restored **Roman Amphitheatre** (hours as for the Crusader ruins). This arena witnessed mass executions in Roman times. More recently it has hosted popular summer concerts by such virtuosi as Pablo Casals and Isaac Stern, and rock stars such as Eric Clapton.

The handsome Roman aqueducts stretching north from the city once conducted fresh spring water; today they provide shade for lounging bathers. Inland from the ruins is the only golf course in Israel, in the grounds of the elegant and pricey **Dan Caesarea Hotel.**

**Kibbutz Sdot Yam,** just south of Caesarea, is worth special note as the former home of the Jewish poetess-martyr Hannah Sennesh. Joining the young kibbutz after escaping from Hungary at the outbreak of World War II, she parachuted back behind Axis lines in 1944. Shortly afterwards she was caught, tortured and executed at the age of 23. A modest archaeological museum here is named in her honour.

## Cities of wealth and taste

The region just north of Netanya is the Valley of Hefer (Emek Hefer, in Hebrew), and although it isn't really a valley the area gets a mention in the Old Testament. This marshy plain is inextricably linked to the efforts of the pioneers of the 1930s, whose sweat and foresight revitalised the land, enabling it to be as productive as it is today. Kfar Vitkin was among the first of these new settlements and today it is among the largest moshavim (collective farming settlements) in the country.

About 12 km (7 miles) south of Caesarea is **Mikhmoret** beach, beautiful and seldom crowded. Here you can find sandy coves to nestle in and extraordinary sunsets from atop the cliffs. **Khadera,** the city inland of the beach, serves as a transfer point for visitors to the northern Sharon.

Scarcely 10 km (6 miles) south lies **Netanya** ❻, the capital city of the Sharon region. Founded as a citrus colony in 1929, Netanya has blossomed. It has an attractive beach and promenade, a population upwards of 150,000 and a galaxy of expensive and not-quite-so-expensive hotels, often filled to capacity with both Europeans and Israelis. Most of the hotels are clustered along King David and Machnes streets,

Map on page 236

*Modern sculpture at Caesarea.*

**BELOW:** archaeologists sift through rubble at Caesarea.

by the beachfront, while the bus station is situated on the main thoroughfare, Herzl Street, a few blocks' walk away.

All three avenues come together at Independence Square (Kikar Ha'Atzmaut), where a kiosk houses the Tourist Information Office, which will give information about Israeli folk dancing, horseback riding and various recreational sports, visits to a citrus packing plant (in season) and a "Meet the Israelis" programme whereby a tourist can visit the home of a native Netanyan for a cup of coffee and exchange of views. The boldly modernistic concrete beach facilities and pleasantly landscaped greenery make Netanya a fine place to spend a lazy afternoon.

## Centre of the diamond trade

Netanya is also the hub of Israel's formidable diamond industry, the country's second most important export after high-tech electronics. Inaugurated by immigrants from Belgium and The Netherlands in the early years of the state, the business has grown to the extent that, since 1974, Israel has held the title of world's number-one exporter of polished diamonds (the raw stones being imported from Asia and Africa).

Heading south from Netanya, we pass over the Nahal Poleg (Poleg River), at one time set in an unpleasant morass, now tamed as the **Nakhal Poleg Nature Reserve**. Close by stands the Wingate Institute, Israel's premier centre for sports and physical training instruction. It is named after Charles Orde Wingate, a British officer who served in Palestine from 1936 to 1939, and who helped instruct the Jewish police force in defensive fighting techniques that would later prove invaluable in the War of Independence. Wingate reputedly carried a

**TIP**

Several companies offer opportunities to buy diamonds. Taub & Company, the largest, has an extensive showroom of precious stones. Guided tours include the chance to see the diamond craftsmen in action.

**BELOW:** graceful ruins by the sea.

Bible with him, reinforcing the Jews' knowledge of their land through appropriately quoted passages.

Just before you reach Herzliya (some 20 km/12 miles south of Netanya) the ruins of a Crusader fortress and an ancient Hellenistic city, **Apollonia**, overlook the water. It is said the beach still contains visible remnants of the ancient coloured glass that was once produced here.

Map on page 236

## High living

The city of **Herzliya** ❼ (pop. 110,000) includes among its inhabitants the élite of Israeli society, and anyone who has money to play with, from wealthy real estate developers to industrial moguls to members of the intelligentsia such as Abba Eban. It is a favourite with diplomats and ambassadors, who are only too happy to take advantage of the stylish beaches and company, and whose villas stud the slopes above the shore amid such ritzy five-star hotels as the Sharon, Accadia and Daniel.

Reflecting the general opulence, some of the nicer beaches charge an admittance fee. This is the scheme in Herzliya-by-the-Sea, at the town centre. Along the highway the city puts on a different face: a haven for high-tech entrepreneurs. Numerous well-known company names – Scitex, Elbit, Digital – glow brightly with futuristic logos, their office complexes complementing the city's reputation as the base of Israel's communications industry.

The coastal highway from Herzliya to Tel Aviv winds past modest memorials. On the shore side of the highway a faded ship's hull commemorates immigrants who died attempting to gain refuge in Palestine in the final years of the British Mandate. A short way on, a metallic rectangle standing atop a layered curve of

*Herzliya beach lookout point.*

**BELOW:** the beach at Herzliya.

a pedestal commemorates the 34 people killed in a 1978 sea-launched terrorist attack. Another monument lies inland in **Ramat ha-Sharon**: the Memorial to the Fallen Members of Israel's Intelligence Community.

## The South Coast

The Mediterranean coast means many things to the Israelis. It is, first and foremost, the spine of the country, in terms of population as well as geography. The coastal plain is the site of the country's most luxurious hotels, and some of its most important ruins. It is a prime transportation corridor and the location of the fertile Sharon Plain, the source of Israel's citrus industry. Its harbours service industry, military and tourist needs alike.

For the average Israeli the Mediterranean coast means one thing: recreation. From April to October, from Yad Mordekhai in the south to Rosh ha-Nikra at the northern tip, thousands of bronzed sabras flock in droves to the sands, to bake in the sun, play paddle-ball along the water's edge, swim, wade, run, sail, tan, and then watch everyone else do the same. While many of the best-known beaches are a kaleidoscope of human activity in the summer, there are lesser-known ones which offer fewer facilities but equally pleasant access to sun and sand. Because of the density of resources, it's not unusual to take a dip against a backdrop of an ancient aqueduct, or the looming silhouette of a power plant.

## Israel's first communities

**BELOW RIGHT:**
the Mameluke
tower at Yavne.

Israel's southern coast stretches from **Tel Aviv** ❽ (*see page 251*) to the tip of the Gaza Strip. The whole area from Tel Aviv to Ashdod is historically known as Darom (the South). In ancient times it was a seat of wisdom, thanks to Yavne

(*see below*), and in the 20th century it became the location of some of the new country's first, and southernmost, communities.

The coastal road from Tel Aviv runs through the resort-suburb of Bat Yam and then, to reach two of these early communities, you must turn inland. The more important of the two is **Rishon Le-Tsiyon** ❾, meaning "First in Zion", which was founded in 1882 by Polish and Russian Zionists.

After struggling for five years, the community was given new life in 1887 by Baron Edmond de Rothschild who, in one of his first acts as Israel's benefactor, established vineyards here. He imported shoots of grape vines from Beaujolais, Burgundy and Bordeaux, and the vineyards flourished, producing mainly sweet wines for Jewish ceremonial occasions. After years of Rothschild ownership, the company became a cooperative in 1957, and today the Carmel Oriental Vineyards produce a variety of lovely dry whites and table wines. After touring the wine cellars and the old Rothschild offices, the visitor can enjoy a free wine-tasting, courtesy of Carmel.

Also to Rishon Le-Tsiyon's credit are the first synagogue built in Israel in modern times (1885), the first kindergarten to teach in Hebrew, and the first Hebrew cultural centre, where the national anthem *Ha-Tikva* (The Hope) was composed and sung for the first time.

The second community is **Nes Tsiyona**, founded in 1884, and said to be the first place where the now familiar blue-and-white flag of Zion was unfurled.

As you continue south, the next place of note is **Yavne** ❿, a town which proffers a rich history. The legend goes that in AD 70, when the fall of Jerusalem seemed imminent in the war against Rome, the renowned Rabbi Yohanon Ben Zakkai appeared before the Roman general Vespasian to request permission to

Map on page 242

*A small garden contains all seven of the trees mentioned in the Bible – fig, date, grape, pomegranate, olive, palm and carob.*

**BELOW:**
a rabbi enjoys those good vibrations.

found an academy here, predicting that one day the general would become emperor. The prophecy came true shortly afterwards, and the request was granted. Whether or not the legend is true, Yavne did become the site of a great academy in subsequent years, and is known as the site where the Mishna, the great commentary on the Bible which adapted Judaism to a modern framework, was started.

The *tel* of Yavne today consists of a lone Mameluke tower, built on Crusader ruins on top of a ridge. More recently, Yavne is notable as the site of a small atomic research reactor, Israel's first, built in 1960 by architect Philip Johnson. Just north of here, where the Sorek River winds into the sea, is the site of the ancient port of Yavne, Yavne Yam, and the swimming beach of Palmakhim, said to offer Israel's finest surfing, as well as the site where Judas Maccabeus gained a victory over Greek forces in the 2nd century BC.

*Flowers bloom on a coastal kibbutz.*

## Philistine cities

Still on the coast, some 10 km (6 miles) south, is **Ashdod** ⓫ with its concrete skyline. Its Philistine history now long behind it, Ashdod is a burgeoning man-made harbour, Israel's most important port, and, if not much of a gift to tourism, a striking example of commercial success.

Re-founded only in 1957, Ashdod grew in four decades to a city of over 120,000 people, and is virtually bursting at its seams with rugged vitality. With a prospering economy based on the new deep-water port, Ashdod is a major immigrant absorption centre. Its populace includes Arabic-speaking Jews, Indian Jews, sabras and ex-Soviet Jews, among them a large community from Georgia, known as "Gruzinim". From Memorial Hill, just below the lighthouse, there is a clear view of the port, with great ships lined up to carry away exports such as potash and phosphates.

**BELOW:** Roman pillars in the sea at Ashkelon.

Outside the city, to the southeast, lies the grave of the ancient metropolis, **Tel Ashdod**. The site is quite literally a *tel* (mound), as little remains other than a hillock and the scattered shards of Philistine pottery. Returning towards the highway, keep an eye out for the sycamore trees which dot the environs, and which bear a sometimes edible fruit.

Ashdod marked the northernmost advance of the Egyptian army in 1948, and supposedly hosted Gamal Abdel Nasser himself. At the point where the road crosses the stream-bed, just east of the city, two relics of that period can be found. The first, the railroad bridge parallel to the road, is a reconstruction of the original, which was blown up by the commandos of the Israeli Givati Brigade, whose nickname was the Foxes of Samson. To the west of the bridges a small white pillbox, built by the British in World War II, stands in lonely vigil.

## Ancient trading post

One of the world's oldest cities, **Ashkelon** ⓬, some 40 km (25 miles) south, has retained far more of its Philistine heritage. Situated on a crest of dunes above the sea, Ashkelon is an amalgam of industrial plants, contemporary apartment towers and lovely beaches. But it is the archaeological park that makes it special,

Map on page 242

and thoughtful preservation has ensured that the area is rewarding for visitors.

The multi-layered ruins of this strategic harbour city attest to the diversity of the people who have lived here over the centuries. Lying along the famous Via Maris, the roadway linking Egypt and Syria, the city was a trading centre from its earliest days, its exports including wine, grain, and a variety of local onion which is now known as a scallion, after its place of origin. In the early 12th century BC the town was conquered by the Philistines, in their sweep of the southern coast, and in the following years it grew to become one of the five great Philistine cities – the others being Ashdod, Gaza, Gath and Ekron.

The next two centuries witnessed bitter rivalry between the Philistines and the Israelites, and although the Jews never took the city it filtered into Jewish history through the story of Samson, whose exploits included his victory with the jawbone of an ass, the episode in which he set fire to the Philistine fields by tying torches to foxes' tails, and his famed ill-fated romance with Delilah.

When King Saul died at the hands of the Philistines, it prompted David's oft-quoted lament: "Tell it not in Gath, publish it not in the streets of Ashkelon, lest the daughters of the Philistines rejoice." (II Sam 1, 20). Three centuries later Ashkelon was still a Philistine stronghold, provoking the wrath of the prophet Zephaniah, who, in one of the final books of the Old Testament, proclaims: "For Gaza shall be forsaken, and Ashkelon a desolation: they shall drive out Ashdod at the noonday, and Ekron shall be rooted up." (Zeph 2, 4).

Eventually, of course, they all were. Taken in the ensuing centuries by Assyrians, Babylonians and others, Ashkelon once more experienced growth in the years of Greek and Roman rule. Herod the Great was supposedly born here, and contributed greatly to the city. Ashkelon fell to the Arabs in the 7th

**BELOW:** tetrapods in Ashdod's port.

Map
on page
242

*Dagon – the name of one of Ashkelon's hotels, is Hebrew for mermaid.*

century, and briefly to the Crusaders in 1153, and, in the process, was pillaged of its monuments and stones. In 1270 the city was destroyed completely by the Sultan Baibars.

Today most of the city's antiquities are encompassed within the **National Park**. Here one can ramble by the ruins of Herodian colonnades and ancient synagogues, along a Roman avenue presided over by the headless statue of Nike, goddess of victory, in and a long-abandoned Roman amphitheatre. The site is surrounded by a grass-covered Crusader wall while, on the beach below, fallen pillars rest forlornly against the pressing of the tides.

The modern city consists of two distinct residential areas: **Midgal**, a former Arab town, to the east, and **Afridar**, a newer suburb, along the shore, founded in 1955 by Jews from South Africa. Distinguished by its tall, fenestrated clock-tower, Afridar is the pleasant downtown area where one can find the commercial centre and Tourist Information Office, and two preserved Roman sarcophagi. There are a number of hotels here, including the fancy King Saul and Swissotel, and the affordable self-contained Dagon. The beaches are fine for bathing, and enjoy such biblical names as Samson Beach, Delilah Beach, Bar-Kochba Beach, and so on. Other notable sights include the Roman-era **Painted Tomb**, and, in Barnea to the north, the remains of a Byzantine church and 5th-century mosaic. On the coastal highway, on the way in from Ashdod, you will have passed an access road to **Nitsanim**, opposite which is a fine strip of beach.

## The end of the road

Some 16 km (10 miles) north of the Gaza Strip lies the kibbutz of **Yad Mordekhai** ⑬. Named after Mordekhai Anilewitz, who died leading the Jews in their uprising against the Nazis in the Warsaw Ghetto in 1943, the kibbutz was founded that same year by Polish immigrants, and played a pivotal role during the Israeli War of Independence. Attacked by the Egyptian army as it made its advance north in May 1948, the settlement managed to hold out against vastly superior Egyptian forces for six days, thereby allowing Tel Aviv to muster adequate defence.

Several structures at the kibbutz commemorate the heroic episode; the morbid but effective battlefield reconstruction includes cut-out figures of the advancing Egyptian soldiers, and a taped narration describes the course of events.

Close by, the imposing **museum** houses displays about the fighting and the four kibbutzim that stood together here, and a memorial to the Polish-Jewish community which was annihilated during the Holocaust. On a ridge nearby are the graves of those who fell defending the young settlement.

Overlooking today's community, the statue of Anilewitz stands in defiant pose, grenade in hand, while behind him rests the fallen water tower, its rutted surface preserved in commemoration of all it withstood. The overall effect of Yad Mordekhai is unquestionably sobering rather than joyful, yet it does provide a potent insight into the mentality of this small nation, which has time and again been besieged by hostile forces. ❏

**BELOW:** a statue of Anilewitz guards Yad Mordekhai.

# Gaza

The sandy strip of **Gaza** ⑭ is a small one. It is only 6 km wide and 45 km long (4 miles by 28 miles), is home to over 800,000 Palestinians, and is thus one of the most densely populated areas in the world, with one of the world's highest birth rates. It begins at the Shikma River in the north and extends to the Egyptian border at Rafah. Gaza was once a part of the seafaring Philistine federation; it was here that the illustrious Samson met the beguiling Delilah, who turned out to be his nemesis.

According to Arab tradition, Samson is buried under the site of the Great Mosque, a structure built by the Crusaders in 1150 and transformed into a mosque by the Mamelukes. Gaza has hosted (not always willingly) Muslims, Crusaders, Ottoman Turks, the British, and even Napoleon's soldiers, since Samson's time. In 1948 Egyptian soldiers were perched on this gateway to Palestine, and Egypt retained control after Israel's independence.

About a fifth of the 800,000 Palestinian Arabs who were displaced by the 1948 fighting ended up in Gaza. Egypt's President Nasser organised the first *fedayeen* (underground fighters) and encouraged guerrilla warfare against Israel. Israel responded in 1956 with the Sinai Campaign, during which it briefly occupied the Sinai Peninsula and the Gaza Strip. In the Six Day War of 1967, Israel seized the territory from Egypt again.

In May 1994 Gaza at last gained self-rule in areas of civil government. Along with Jericho it was the first of the Occupied Territories to benefit from the Middle East Peace Accords. Subsequently, the PLO moved its headquarters from Tunis to Gaza, and its chairman, Yasser Arafat, is based there.

But the prospects for this impoverished strip of land did not turn round overnight, in spite of the tremendous optimism of the inhabitants and promises of investment by international organisations. For close to 40 years Palestinian refugees had lived in UNRWA camps, designed for temporary accommodation, and although 90 percent of households

have electricity, conditions remain squalid. Furthermore, some 60 percent of Gaza's adult residents are unemployed. A hopeful sign was the opening of an airport in 1998.

Poverty creates fertile ground for Hamas, the Islamic Resistance Movement fiercely opposed to the PLO–Israeli Peace Accords and a rival to the PLO for control of the area. One of the biggest challenges for Palestinian security forces is to prevent further acts of terrorism by Hamas members.

Before travelling to Gaza, it is important to keep abreast of current political events and to heed security measures. There is little to see in the way of tourist sights, but the street life is an attraction. Arab women in long black robes, plastic baskets balanced on their heads, walk through the streets and camps, passing children in crisp school uniforms, emblazoned with the Palestinian flag. The city centres are busy with merchants selling a variety of wares: cotton clothing (the word "gauze" comes from Gaza), terracotta pottery (a speciality), wicker furniture, and mounds of camel-hair carpets. ❑

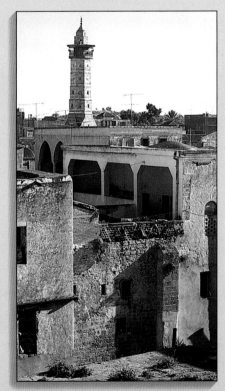

**RIGHT:** the city of Khan Yunis.

# TEL AVIV

*This detailed tour of Israel's capital of style finds a biblical flavour in Old Yafo, funky shopping in Sheinkin and superb arts venues all over town*

Maps:
Area 236
City 252

A century ago, who would have predicted **Tel Aviv** ? It sprang out of the desolate sand dunes north of Yafo almost overnight, when a group of local residents purchased some land in 1909 and raffled it off among themselves. They intended to build a garden suburb in which to find respite after a day's work in noisy, crowded Yafo, but they also had hopes of creating the first new Jewish city for 2,000 years. They named it Tel Aviv (Hill of Spring), symbolising hope for a new future to be built on the ruins of the past. A *tel* in Hebrew is an artificial hill, created on the accumulated debris of past; *aviv* means spring, connoting new life.

## City of style

The first houses were completed before the year was out. By the eve of World War I the suburb had grown to 20 times its original size, and Yafo's Jewish institutions began draining into the new city to the north. When the war began the Turkish rulers expelled the Jewish population of Yafo and Tel Aviv to other parts of the region, but after the British occupation in 1917 the settlers drifted back to their homes. Over the following decades they continued laying out their new city. By the middle of the century the fledgling metropolis had blossomed with tree-lined boulevards and spanking-new international-style apartments, and had already overtaken Jerusalem in population and vitality.

In the city's early days people built their own dwellings, infusing their own vision and hope into the city they were moulding. The first residents built houses which reminded them of their origins in Europe, inspired by neo-classical buildings in Vienna, Odessa or Warsaw. Local architects tried to introduce European styles by softening the symmetrical corners with rounded balconies, or by adding domes, arched entranceways, and wall decorations depicting biblical motifs. In the 1920s and 1930s, Tel Aviv became an eclectic collection of styles and influences. Its staid neo-classical structures were jazzed up with art nouveau, Middle Eastern and kitsch elements.

In the 1930s the International building style, inspired by the Bauhaus in Germany and such architects as Le Corbusier and Erich Mendelsohn, took over. The symmetry and colonnades made way for clean, minimalist lines, and severe functionality became the name of the game. Tel Aviv was the only city in the world to be dominated by the International style. In later years the "White City", as it was dubbed by poet Nathan Alterman, was peeling, and its buildings were repainted in various colours, partly in reaction to the severe style. But city streets are still characterised today by roof gardens and apartment

**PRECEDING PAGES:** the beach at Tel Aviv. **LEFT:** catching up on the gossip. **BELOW:** pointing the way in Yafo.

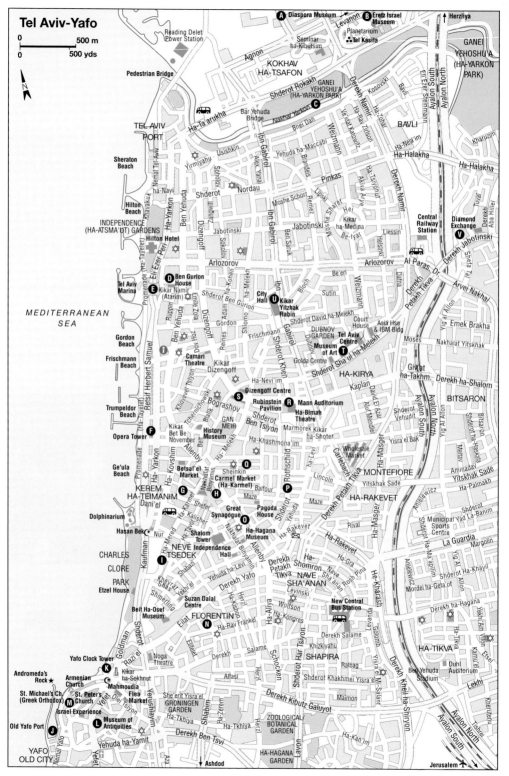

# Tel Aviv-Yafo

0       500 m

0       500 yds

blocks raised up on columns, and many of the newer apartment complexes going up are once more sparkling white.

Today Tel Aviv is Israel's centre of culture, business, haute couture and nightlife. Its white beaches, sunny weather and smart hotels make it a year-round tourist resort. While the city itself holds only 350,000 residents, Tel Aviv's sizeable metropolitan district contains over 2 million people – approximately one-third of the country's population. With celebrated cafés and sleek new office towers, the world's first modern Jewish city is as contemporary as it is boisterous, combining the *joie de vivre* of a Mediterranean people with the style and sophistication of Europe's most fashionable cities.

Tel Aviv is part of the greater city of Tel Aviv-Yafo, the two being combined officially in 1950 after years of merging into one another. While Tel Aviv was born with the 20th century, Yafo is ancient and still has its own rich history.

## Orientation

The most important streets to get to know are Ben Yehuda, which runs parallel to the shoreline and serves the various hotels along that strip, and Dizengoff, which runs from the Mann Auditorium complex and the famous hub of Dizengoff Circle down to the intersection with Ben Yehuda at the northern tip of the city. These routes are both conveniently serviced by buses number 4 and 5, respectively, which in turn run all the way to the Central Bus Station, a brand new, six-storey building to the southeast of the city, replacing what was arguably the ugliest, seediest bus station of them all. Allenby is the final important connecting street, passing through most of the downtown area to Ben Yehuda, where it turns left for two blocks before terminating at the beachfront.

In terms of its residential structure Tel Aviv is infamous for its north–south divide. The trim, neatly maintained streets of North Tel Aviv are home to many of the country's rich, while the impoverished streets of South Tel Aviv house the nation's poorest. Ramat Aviv in the north of the city is synonymous with affluence and also contains Tel Aviv University. With a campus dominated by neatly manicured lawns, this is the country's largest university.

No visit to Israel would be complete without calling at the **Bet Hatefusoth** on the university campus. Founded in 1979, the **Museum of the Jewish Diaspora** Ⓐ (open Sun–Thur 10am–5pm, Fri 9am–1pm; admission charge) is known throughout the Jewish world. It is also, in concept and methodology, a radical departure from the accepted notion of a museum, for, apart from a few sacramental objects, Bet Hatefusoth contains no preserved artefacts. Its principal aim is reconstruction.

The body of the main exhibit is handled thematically, focusing on general themes of Jewish Life in the Diaspora: family life, community, religion, culture, and the return to Zion. Its striking displays include a collection of beautifully intricate models of synagogue buildings from across the globe. A memorial column in the central atrium commemorates Jewish martyrdom through the ages. An audio-visual depiction of the migrations of Jews is presented in the hall known

Map on page 252

*Tel Aviv was also the name given to the Hebrew translation of Theodor Herzl's book* Altneuland *(Old-new Land), in which he conceived of the Jewish State.*

**BELOW:** model of a Florentine synagogue at Bet Hatefusoth.

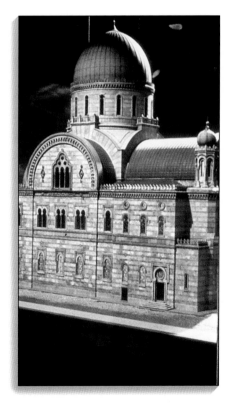

as the **Chronosphere**. Four video study-areas enable visitors to view documentary films selected from a catalogue, while a computer system allows them to trace their own lineage. Special exhibitions highlight topics related to Jewish communities around the world.

Nearby in **Ramat Aviv**, the sprawling **Eretz Israel Museum**  on University Street (open Sun–Thur 9am–2pm, Sat 10am–2pm; admission charge) comprises the most comprehensive storehouse of archaeological, anthropological and historical findings in the region. Its spiritual backbone is **Tel Kasila**, an excavation site in which 12 distinct layers of civilisation have been uncovered, its finds including an ancient Philistine temple and Hebrew inscriptions from 800 BC. The complex consists of 11 pavilions, including exhibits of glassware, ceramics, copper, coins, folklore and ethnography, and a planetarium.

*The national flag flies over many public buildings.*

Defining the northernmost limit of the city proper is the **Nakhal Yarkon** , which once marked the border between the tribes of Dan and Ephraim. Today the river is lined with rambling **parkland** and serves to accommodate scullers who row along it in the cooler hours of the day. Near the river's western rim can be seen the dome and chimneys of the Reading Power Station, while the greenery of the city's exhibition grounds marks the river's eastern limit.

To the south of the Yarkon River is the trendy quarter known as **Little Old Tel Aviv** where the city's three major north–south roads begin – Ha-Yarkon, Ben Yehuda and Dizengoff. There are a large number of cafés, restaurants and bars in this quarter where Tel Aviv's disused port was located. To the south stretches **Independence Gardens**, a strip of green offering a stirring view of the Mediterranean from its cliffs. Alternatively, there is a path on the promenade below. Independence Gardens hides among its shrubbery various archaeological

**BELOW:** boating on the Yarkon.

finds, and in the evening it is the gathering spot of the city's gay community. Just inland, in Ben Gurion Boulevard, **Ben Gurion House** , formerly the home of Israel's first prime minister and today a public museum housing the personal mementos of David Ben Gurion and a 20,000 volume library.

## Hotels and best beaches

The seaside promenade is dotted with cafés, restaurants, ice-cream parlours and the like, all offering free sea air and costly refreshments. On summer nights the promenade is clogged with people on foot and in cars, manoeuvring for some sea breeze after the day's oppressive heat or queueing up outside the **Planet Hollywood** restaurant or the **Yotvata** dairy restaurant synonymous with chocolate milk and great dairy products from a kibbutz-based enterprise.

The **marina**, the largest in the Middle East, rents out sailing and motor-boats, and equipment for windsurfing, seasurfing, water-skiing and other water sports.

You can't get away from **Kikar Namir** (still known locally by its former name, **Kikar Atarim**) **E**, a concrete monstrosity squatting over the marina, at the end of Ben Gurion. This open-air mall offers concrete mushroom sunshades, tourist items and a chance to lose one's way. Its cafés, pizzerias and restaurants, tolerable in the sunlight, turn seedy at night.

The city's main hotel district lies along the coast here. From the north of the city to the south, the coastline is dominated by an imposing row of hotels lined up like dominoes, including (among others) the Hilton, north of Arlozorov, and the Carlton, Moriah, Holiday Inn, Ramada, Sheraton and Dan. The **Opera Tower** **F** to the south of the hotels is a distinctive building which houses apartments, restaurants, shops, jewellery stores and a cinema.

Map on page 252

**TIP**

In front of the Carlton and Marina hotels is Tel Aviv's large sea-water swimming pool. Aerobic exercise sessions are held on the beach in the summer, and a roller-skating rink operates in the evening near the pool.

**BELOW:**
Kikar Namir at dusk.

Each hotel has its own beach strip (the beaches are all public), most of them quite civilised, with showers, easy chairs and refreshment facilities. Marking the end of the hotel line to the south, across from the Dan Panorama, is the **Dolphinarium**, a white elephant, now unused, obscuring the magnificent view of Old Yafo from Tel Aviv's coast. There is, however, a free outdoor reggae gig every Friday, Saturday and Sunday in summer.

## Levantine lifestyle

Just inland is the **Kerem ha-Teimanim** (Yemenite Quarter) , its exotic winding streets a jolt back in time, preserving the look and feel of the Yemenite community which settled here a century ago. Here, in Arab-style stone houses, is the best place to sample the spicy, pungent Yemenite cuisine. Pundak Shaul, Zion, Pninat Hakerem and Maganda are among the best Yemenite restaurants in the country. Like the Yemenite Quarter, Tel Aviv's market-places are an inseparable part of the Levant. The biggest and best known of these is the **Carmel Market (Ha-Karmel)** , off Allenby. Always crowded with shoppers and hagglers, the market is a medley of colours, smells and sounds. A large variety of exotic fruits, vegetables and herbs can be found here, as well as clothes, shoes, pickled foods and pitta bread at bargain prices.

To the left of the entrance to the Carmel Market on Allenby street is a pedestrianised street called **Nakhalat Binyamin**. Here, on Tuesdays and Fridays, arts and crafts traders bring their wares to parade and sell. A great place for present-shopping, as the artisans combine jewellery with juggling, cactus plants with camel bags, and wood carvings with wonderful art.

Between the Yemenite Quarter and Neve Tsedek, on the fast road to Yafo, is

**BELOW:**
vegetables for sale
in Carmel Market.

the **Hasan Bek Mosque**, contrasting sharply with the contemporary high-rise near it. Built in 1916 by Yafo's Turkish-Arab governor, the mosque was intended to block the development of Tel Aviv towards the sea. During the War of Independence the mosque served as an outpost for Arab snipers. In 1992 it was sold by its local Muslim owners to a Tel Aviv businessman who planned to open a nightclub there. After protests of outrage from the Arab world the mosque was purchased by the Egyptian government, which has attractively refurbished both the exterior and interior.

Map on page 252

## Neve Tsedek

The oldest quarter in the city, **Neve Tsedek ❶**, was founded in 1887 as a suburb of Yafo, and is a picturesque maze of narrow streets flanked by low-built Arab-style houses. At the time the quarter was considered a luxury suburb, despite the crowded housing and less-than-sanitary conditions. In recent years the quarter's quaint old dwellings have taken the fancy of artists and well-to-do families, who have restored them and replanted the inner courtyards.

The **Neve Tsedek Theater**, otherwise known as the Suzan Dalal Center, which specialises in avant-garde drama, opened in the building of the city's first girls' school, which was also the first all-Hebrew school in Israel. This is also the home of the **Batsheva Dance Company** and the **Inbal Dance Company**. With the theatre's opening in a magnificent plaza dotted with orange trees, several colourful galleries, restaurants and nightclubs popped up, lending a new vitality to the century-old streets. On the border of Neve Tsedek and Tel Aviv, at the intersection of Lilienblum and Pines streets, stands Israel's first cinema. The **Eden Cinema** was built in 1914, seating 600 viewers who marvelled at the silent movies accompanied by a not-always-synchronised orchestra.

*When talking pictures arrived at the end of the 1920s, the cinema management, successfully pressurised by the powerful Labour Federation, continued paying the unemployed orchestra members' wages for 18 months.*

**BELOW:** Tel Aviv's coast, viewed from Yafo.

## Yafo, where it all began

Neve Tsedek stretches southwards to Yafo, the place where it all began. It is said that when God got fed up with his creatures, he brought the Great Flood on the world to wipe the slate clean and start afresh. After the flood subsided and Noah's Ark landed on Mount Ararat, Noah's youngest son Japheth found a pleasant hill overlooking a bay and settled down, naming the site "Yafo", Hebrew for beautiful. One of the world's oldest cities, Yafo has retained its biblical flavour, spiced by centuries of historical events and myths. The famous Cedars of Lebanon to be used by King Solomon in building the Temple in Jerusalem were shipped to Yafo – even then an important Mediterranean trading port. The miracle of raising Tabitha from the dead was performed by the Apostle Peter when he stayed at the Yafo house of Simon the Tanner (Acts 9, 36–42).

Some 3,400 years ago Yafo was conquered by the Egyptians. Subsequently Alexander the Great, Herod, Richard the Lionheart, Napoleon, and the Turks (among others) all passed through, alternately destroying and building. The British took over from the Ottomans at the end of World War I, and Yafo returned to Israel during the War of Independence in 1948.

Jewish residence was resumed in Yafo long before that, in 1820, when a Jewish traveller from Constantinople settled here. Soon after came a larger community, mainly North African merchants and craftsmen, who merged with the local Arab community. By the time of Israel's independence the city had close to 100,000 residents, over 30,000 of them Jewish. Modern Yafo has retained its Eastern flavour, and today holds a colourful medley of immigrants from North African and Central European countries.

## Old Yafo today

Old Yafo was reconstructed and renovated in 1963, with cobbled paths and winding alleys twisting through the massive stone fortifications surrounding the city. Today it sports an artists' colony, art galleries, craft shops, tourist shops, seafood restaurants and nightclubs. The **Old Yafo Port ❿**, destined for demolition (and eventual reconstruction as an exclusive marina), is still the home port of the local fishermen, who haul in their catch every dawn. Their findings end up in the cauldrons of the town's many restaurants, three of which are located right in the old port, overlooking the pier and bobbing boats.

Looking seawards one can make out a cluster of rocks, the largest of which is said to be Andromeda's. But recent renovation of the pier, which included the bombing of some of the formation, may have blown the rock out of existence. For the rest, time seems to have stood still. Primitive ovens still churn out an infinite variety of oriental-spiced pitta breads, and the ancient streets hum with aggressive shopkeepers, pastry vendors and meandering passers-by.

Old Yafo begins at the **Clock Tower ⓚ** on Yefet, built in 1906 and facing the local police station. The tower's stained-glass windows each portray a different

*Greek mythology holds that Andromeda, daughter of the King of Yafo, was chained to a rock just off Yafo's port to appease the wrath of a sea monster (subsequently being rescued by Perseus on his winged white horse).*

**BELOW:**
Old Yafo Port.

chapter in the town's history. Opposite the tower, past an arched entranceway, is a large courtyard, once the Armenian Hostel which served as a central station for travellers going to Jewish settlements throughout the country. Walk past the police station and, on your right, an entrance leads to the **Mahmoudia Mosque**, built in 1812 and named after Yafo's Turkish governor.

Turning right from Yefet onto Mifrats Shlomo, towards the renovated section of Old Yafo, one passes the **Yafo Museum of Antiquities** ❶ (open Sun, Mon, Wed, Thur, Fri 9am–1pm, Tues 4–7pm, Sat 10am–2pm; admission charge), where archaeological exhibits from many years of excavations trace the city's development. Erected in the 18th century, the building was the Turkish governor's headquarters and local prison. Later it won acclaim throughout the Middle East as the soap factory of the Greek Orthodox Damiani family.

The Franciscan **St Peter's Church** ❿ is further along, on one side of Keddumim Square. The **St Louis Monastery** in the courtyard was named after the French king who arrived at the head of a Crusade and stayed here in 1147. The monastery later served as a hostel for pilgrims to Jerusalem and was known in the 17th century as "The Europeans' House". Napoleon also relaxed here after conquering Yafo.

A little way north and towards the sea is the minaret of the **Jama El-Baher Mosque**, located next door to the first Jewish house in Yafo, built in 1820. The **Armenian Convent** and church here mark the site of a 17th-century pilgrims' inn. A magnificent renovated Turkish mansion behind the museum, once a Turkish bath house, has been converted into a nightclub and restaurant, **El-Hamam**.

At the top of the hill, past the Pisgah Park, **Horoscope Path** begins to wind its way through the Yafo wall. It goes all the way to the lighthouse at the wall's

Map on page 252

*Romantic dining at Yafo.*

**BELOW LEFT:** Yafo Museum of Antiquities.
**BELOW:** St Peter's Church.

*Stone head in Yafo.*

southern entrance, on the corner of Shimon Haburski. At the centre of the renovated section is a square called **Kikar Kedumin**, in which the Yafo excavations present a reconstruction of the city's multi-faceted history; this is also one of Tel Aviv's most popular evening spots.

On the southern side of the wall, along Pasteur, a modern structure rather spoils the beauty of the ancientd walls. This is the **Israel Experience**, a tourist centre comprising an auditorium for a multi-media show, a shopping area and a restaurant. The main show combines computerised projection systems on giant screens by means of 40 slide projectors, accompanied by special light and sound effects. Further along Pasteur Street is the **Horace Richter Gallery**.

Back on Yefet, turn left and walk down the hill crossing the road. Just before the traffic lights is **Abu Elafiah**, Yafo's first pitta-bread establishment (dating back to the 1880s). It reputedly does its briskest business on Passover and Yom Kippur when droves of bread-craving Israelis queue outside. The area is especially lively after dark, when Tel Aviv's night owls descend on Yafo.

Yafo's famous **Flea Market** lies in the next complex of alleys just east of here. It specialises in antiques, copperware ("antique" specimens made while you watch), jewellery and second-hand junk. It isn't open on Saturdays.

To the northeast of Yafo lies **Florentinn**, an ugly ramshackle neighbourhood, which is nevertheless considered the city's most trendy and bohemian quarter, with a flourishing nightlife. East of Florentin is the new Central Bus Station, a vast complex of shops, offices and eateries. Other than stopping to grab a quick, great-value *felafel* with as much salad as you want, it is advisable to board your bus as quickly as possible. The area to the north, the old bus station, is even more seedy, and is best avoided.

**BELOW:**
modern buildings,
modern man.

Map on page 252

## Financial district

Immediately north of the Bus Station is the city's financial district. The streets are overlooked by the **Shalom Tower**, on Herzl, for many years the tallest building in Israel but recently superseded by the three high-rise towers of the Azrieli Centre overlooking the Ayalon highway. The tower soars 35 floors – and 140 metres (460 ft) – above the city, an austere white rectangle. Its main significance lies in its location. Here stood one of the first buildings to be erected in Tel Aviv – the Herzliya Gymnasium (High School). Built in 1910 on the first thoroughfare, the school was a symbol of pioneering and became the cultural and economic nucleus of the town. It was torn down in 1959. All that remains of it is a huge fresco on the wall of the tower, created by artist Nahum Gutman.

The tower holds some 34 office floors. Its top floor is open to the public and presents a multi-media information system on the history of Tel Aviv-Yafo and a magnificent view of the area, reaching on a clear day from Mount Carmel in the north to the Negev in the south, with Jerusalem visible to the east.

One of the most impressive buildings remaining in Tel Aviv's financial district is the **Pagoda House** in King Albert Square. It was built in 1925 for an American, Joseph Bloch. The house had a pagoda-like structure at the top of its three floors, and the first passenger lift in Tel Aviv. It is currently under renovation. Opposite is an excellent restaurant/bar, **Nakhmani 22**.

Continue down Nakhmani, passing the **Gesher Theatre** on your left. Founded in 1991 (but now in a new location), it is Israel's first Russian-speaking theatre and is testament to the growing influence of the 800,000 or so immigrants from the former Soviet Union. The building was also used, in pre-state days, as a centre for the Haganah forces (the Jewish underground).

**BELOW:** beating the traffic on Rothschild.

Turn right and first left until you reach **Allenby**, named after the British general who liberated Tel Aviv from the Turks in 1917. Turn left and cross the road, continuing on Allenby until you reach the impressive **Great Synagogue** , built by Rav Kook, first Chief Rabbi of Tel Aviv-Yafo. He boycotted the placing of Tel Aviv's foundation stone, on the grounds that they had not located a site for the synagogue. He made it his personal mission to get the project accomplished, and within a few years it was the dominant building on Allenby Street. On Yom Ha'atsma'ut (Independence Day) there is a massive service in the presence of the Chief Rabbi, the mayor, prime minister and other dignitaries. Although a secular place at face value, Tel Aviv is home to a large Orthodox community. Unlike Jerusalem, there is no segregation in living quarters and therefore very little antagonism between secular and religious residents. For example, the headquarters of the ultra-Orthodox Lubavitchers is situated on Sheinkin Street, possibly the epitome of the modern secular Israeli.

*For home thoughts.*

## Rothschild Boulevard

Built in 1910 over a dried river-bed, **Rothschild** was once Tel Aviv's most elegant address. It's still lovely, its central promenade dotted with trees, benches and refreshment kiosks, and its buildings embrace a jumble of styles. At number 13 the Betsal'el style (named after the Betsal'el Art School in Jerusalem) combines European and Oriental design.

The public museum, **Independence Hall**, is at number 16, the former residence of Tel Aviv's first mayor, Meir Dizengoff. The Declaration of Independence was signed here on 15 May 1948, and it was also the first home of the Knesset (parliament) until it moved to the Opera Tower building on the beach,

**BELOW:** part of the Sheinkin scene.

Map on page 252

then to Jerusalem. The second and third floors comprise the **Bible Museum** (open Sun–Fri 9am–1pm, Sat 10am–2pm; admission charge).

Across the road is the **Israel Defence Forces** (Ha-Hagana) **Museum** (open Sun–Thur 9am–3pm, Fri 9am–12.20pm; admission charge), located in the former residence of Haganah commander Eliahu Golumb. Here, and dotted around the city are square brown signs that refer to the original use of the buildings. Before Israel's independence the resistance forces fought underground from these positions, against both the British and the Arabs. The IDF (Israel Defence Forces) headquarters is still located in Tel Aviv at the Kirya, originally a German Templar settlement, turned into their headquarters by the British, before being taken over by the IDF. This explains where Saddam Hussein was aiming for when his forces fired Iraqi missiles at Tel Aviv in the 1991 Gulf War.

**Breuer House** at number 46 was built in 1922; it has tiny decorative balconies, a pagoda-like wooden roof, a minaret, and a large enclosed garden. On the verge of demolition in 1948, it was saved when the Soviet ambassador requested it for his headquarters. It served as the Soviet Embassy until 1953, when diplomatic relations with the USSR were severed.

Typical Bauhaus-style buildings may be seen at numbers 89, 91 and 140, and on nearby Engel, recently converted into a pedestrian mall.

**Sheinkin** ❑ is the bastion of Israel's young and trendy, leftist and secular community. The local equivalent of London's Soho or New York's Village, Sheinkin is only just being discovered by tourists. Stretching from Allenby all the way east to Yehuda ha-Levi, it is a street that has it all. On Friday it is closed to traffic to allow shoppers to buy wallpaper, furniture or home appliances; to discover a second-hand fake-fur coat, bind a book, buy eggs in a shop selling only farm-fresh produce, have their hair done, and wind up over coffee in a Bohemian café with trees growing in it. The latter is **Café Tamar**, a veteran establishment that locals affirm has always been there.

Sheinkin is renowned for its leading fashion designs, and hip Tel Avivians who can be seen flaunting their funky outfits and the latest chic hairstyles. At the western end of Sheinkin is the Betsal'el Market, reputed to have the best *felafels* in Israel, as well as the usual discount quality fashion items and bric-a-brac.

## A walk on Bialik

Further west along Allenby, **Bialik** is another pleasant street dating from the city's early days. At number 14 is **Beit Reuven**, the former residence of Israeli artist Reuven Rubin; a short walk from here is the **Beit Biali**, once the home of Israel's national poet, Haim Nahman Bialik. Built in 1925, it has a little tower and dome, a prominent pink balcony and arched columns, like those of the Doge's Palace in Venice.

At the end of the street is **Skura House**, containing the **Museum for the History of Tel Aviv-Yafo** (open Sun–Fri 9am–1pm, except Tues 4–7pm; admission charge). Built in 1925, this housed the City Hall from 1928 to 1968, when it moved north to Ibn Gabirol Street. Next to the building, stairs lead down to Idelson Street, near **Gan Meir** (Meir Garden), one of the prettiest in town. Across the park, up King George

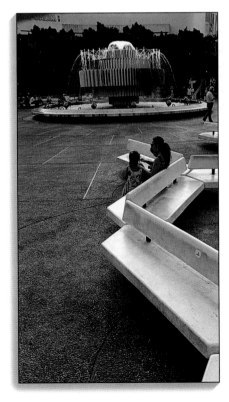

**BELOW:** the fountain in Dizengoff Circle.

Street (Ha-Metekh George), lies Tel Aviv's shortest street, **Simta Almonit** (Anonymous Alley), sister to the nearby **Simta Palmonit** (Unknown Alley). These two alleys were built as academics' residences in American Colonial style for American and British immigrants in the 1920s.

## The modern city

To the east of this neighborhood, at the northern end of Rothschild and the eastern extremity of Dizengoff, is Tel Aviv's premier cultural complex including the **Ha-Bimah Theatre**, the **Mann Auditorium** and the **Rubinstein Pavilion** . During the Russian Revolution a group of young Russian-Jewish actors formed a collective and dreamed of a Hebrew theatre. The dream came true in Tel Aviv, dozens of years later. The **Ha-Bimah Theatre** (ha-Bimah means "the stage" in Hebrew), built in the square of the same name, originally had creaking wooden chairs and lousy acoustics: today it has two theatres (one seating 1,000 and a smaller one with seats for 300), revolving stages, and simultaneous translation into several languages during the high season.

Just next to the theatre is the **Mann Auditorium**, the home of the Israel Philharmonic Orchestra. Tickets here are highly prized and hard to get. The third building in this complex is the **Rubinstein Pavilion**, a branch of the Tel Aviv Museum, which specialises in modern art exhibitions. The little park in the middle of the complex hides the chic brass-and-chrome **Apropos Café**.

## Dizengoff's cafés

**BELOW:** Dizengoff's Hard Rock Café.

This arts complex is at the start of **Dizengoff** ⑤, once the city's most fashionable thoroughfare and although less grand today, still one of Tel Aviv's princi-

pal streets. Café-going is a major part of any self-respecting Tel Avivian's way of life. Some people go to cafés for their first coffee of the day; others conduct business meetings or entertain guests; retired people spend their mornings over cappuccinos and croissants. On a sunny day you may get the impression that the entire city is on holiday, sipping coffee at sidewalk cafés.

Map on page 252

Much of Israeli café activity still takes place along Dizengoff, although Sheinkin is more trendy, and pedestrianised Nakhalat Binyamin a more convenient café loction. Young, upbeat and action-packed, this street is a constant parade of beautiful people, window shoppers, tourists, actors, models and in-vogue popstars, vagabonds, soldiers and business people. A seat in a Dizengoff café is an excellent vantage point for observing the human panorama.

At no time is Dizengoff more glamorous or crowded than on Friday afternoons, when groups of Tel Avivians congregate to unwind from the long work week with friends, try to chat up girls, catch up on gossip, and learn of the night's best parties.

A block north of the Ha-Bimah complex is the **Dizengoff Centre**, a modern multi-level shopping complex offering everything from offbeat pets to oriental carpets, complete with cinemas, restaurants, sports shops and banks. Those who like to combine sightseeing with food can then eat their way along this end of Dizengoff which is crowded with snack bars and restaurants, offering everything from fruit juice, pizza and hamburgers to Hungarian *blintzes* and *shwarma*.

*The Opera House.*

The raised piazza with the sculpture-fountain spouting in its centre is **Kikar Dizengoff**. Originally a traffic roundabout, the pedestrian level has since been lifted above the street, creating a peculiar urban hub but allowing the free flow of people above and traffic below.

**BELOW:** Asia House and the flowing IBM Building.

Map on page 252

The next street to cut across Dizengoff is Gordon, known as **Gallery**. Works of the great masters, such as Picasso and Chagall, are displayed here beside paintings by leading Israeli artists like Agam, Gutman and Kadishman.

The serious café scene really begins in the north of Dizengoff with "respectable" veteran establishments like Café Afarsemon and Batya. Eminent literary figures and the Austro-Hungarian set used to favour the former Café Stern a little way down, today the Stern-Dolphin Fish Restaurant. On the corner of Ben Gurion Boulevard is Café Cherry, particularly popular as a meeting place on Fridays.

## More arts off Ibn Gabirol

*Outside the Museum of Art.*

Ibn Gabirol also runs north through the city from the Ha-Bimah Theatre. To the right of Ibn Gabirol on Sha'ul ha-Melekh Street, a rival cultural complex, the **Tel Aviv Museum of Art ❼** (open Sun–Thurs 10am–9.30pm; admission charge), has four central galleries, an auditorium which often features film retrospectives, numerous other halls, a sculpture garden, a cafeteria and a shop. There are exhibitions of 17th-century Dutch and Flemish masters, 18th-century Italian paintings, Impressionists, post-Impressionists, and a good selection of 20th-century art from the USA and Europe, in addition to modern Israeli work. Next to the Museum the **Tel Aviv Centre for Performing Arts** was recently inaugurated. This attractive new building includes the New Israel Opera and a theatre and auditorium.

At the corner of Sha'ul ha-Melekh and Weizmann are the most striking modern edifices in the city, the most unusual being **Asia House**, created by architect Mordechai Ben-Horin in gleaming white to resemble a horizontal series of giant rolling waves. Its entrance hall holds a permanent exhibit of sculpture under a pastel-coloured mosaic ceiling. The **IBM Building** next door towers above, a three-sided cylinder supported on a mushroom-like shaft. Designed by Israeli architects Yasky, Gil & Silvan, it creates a handsome profile for the city skyline. Across the street, the red slated roofs of the **German Templar Colony** (1870–1939) provide one more architectural style in a city of contrasts.

**BELOW:** the Tel Aviv corniche.

Ibn Gabirol itself leads to the central square of the city, next to the headquarters of the municipality. It was here, at Kikar Malchei Yisrael (the Square of the Kings of Israel), on 4 November 1995 that Prime Minister Yitzhak Rabin was assassinated after a huge demonstration in support of the peace process. The square was immediately renamed **Yitzhak Rabin Square (Kikar Yitzhak Rabin) ⓤ**, and there is an unusual memorial close to the spot where he fell, at the northern end of the square, just behind the steps to the City Hall. Portraits, paintings and graffiti cover the area as the people's memorial to a man respected by many of differing convictions.

As you move east along Jabotinski, a dense forest of high-rise buildings suddenly looms on the horizon. Technically speaking the Diamond Exchange district is in adjoining Ramat Gan rather than Tel Aviv. The gleaming office blocks contain not only the diamond traders, who handle some $5-billion-worth of diamonds each year, but also many of the country's most successful high-tech enterprises. The **Diamond Exchange ⓥ** has a museum (open Sun-Thur 10am-4pm, Fri 8am–noon; admission charge), which tells the story of diamonds. ❑

# Nightlife

In the late 1980s an advertising campaign for Tel Aviv's nightlife revolved around the slogan "The City That Never Stops". The label has stuck. Tel Avivans are proud of their energy and stamina, working hard by day and playing hard at night. Nightlife in Tel Aviv, as throughout Israel, starts late. The restaurants don't get busy until after ten, and the bars, cafés and nightclubs start filling up from midnight onwards. But if night birds start late in terms of time they start early age-wise. Parents will often take small children to bars and cafés at midnight, while unaccompanied 14-year-olds roam the streets well into the early hours. Israeli parents take the relaxed attitude that there is nothing youngsters can do at three in the morning that they couldn't do at three in the afternoon.

In any event, Tel Aviv's streets are jammed with pedestrians of all ages, as well as cars, well into the early hours of the morning, especially at the weekends (remember that the weekend days off are Friday and Saturday).

At night tourists might do well to stick to the seafront. Tel Aviv's Mediterranean coast stretches from the fashionable restaurants of Little Old Tel Aviv in the north, through the male gay pick-up venue in Independence Gardens (Gan Ha'atsma'ut), to the cafés popular with teenagers to the south of the hotel district, and the sleazy red-light district behind the Opera Tower. Further south there are the restaurants of the Yemenite quarter and then Yafo with its nightclubs and fish restaurants. Perhaps the latter are the most delightful night-time experiences. Taboun is the pick of these. Enjoying a meal with the sound of the sea lapping against the shore is not only romantic but also a delicious relief from the city's stifling humidity.

But humidity aside, those who want to search inland for the core of Tel Aviv nightlife are also not starved of choice. Culture fiends tend to hang out in the vicinity of the Ha-Bimah Theatre/Mann Auditorium complex at the beginning of Dizengoff. Further north on Dizengoff, near the junction with Gordon,

**RIGHT:** romantic tryst, the beginning of an enchanted evening.

Israelis like to stroll around at night popping into art galleries and sipping coffee at nearby cafés. Gallery crawling is also the done thing in Old Yafo.

Dizengoff, however, is no longer the main after-dark attraction. The trendiest neighbourhood is Sheinkin, a narrow street to the north of the financial district which runs eastwards from the Yemenite Quarter. Sheinkin offers an abundant choice of small restaurants, cafés and bars. If Sheinkin is trendy, then Florentin to the south (northeast of Yafo) is bohemian – a particularly Israeli mixture of the seedy and the avant-garde.

Remember that the essence of Tel Aviv nightlife is outdoors. As elsewhere in the Mediterranean there is a fine dividing line between a café and a bar and it is acceptable to just have a drink in a café, or go to a pub for a meal or a soft drink or coffee. Nothing is nicer than to find an outdoor table and watch the world go by. The night crowds can be noisy and lively but drunkenness is very rare. Indeed, Israelis are infamous for spending long hours in bars nursing one beer. ❑

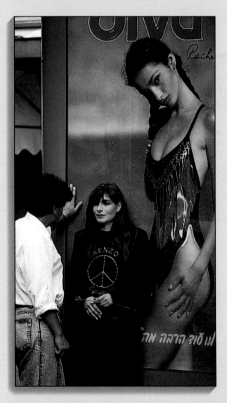

# THE INLAND PLAINS

Map on page 272

*Don't rush through the plains between Tel Aviv and Jerusalem
or you'll miss the monasteries, caves and splendid views
of the Judean foothills*

It is not the most acclaimed tourist area in the Holy Land, nor is it the most famous for its ruins, and many visitors pass through this region, from Tel Aviv to Jerusalem and back, never bothering to venture from the main roads. Yet the consistent flow of conquerors, immigrants, wayfarers and settlers has left its mark on the landscape, and the area – still the central crossroads of the nation – is rich in history.

Rising from the flat coastal plain into the gently rolling Judean foothills, this area has always been one of the most densely populated in the country. Some of the first modern Jewish settlements in the 1880s and 1890s were established here. Today several of these villages have grown into small towns; others, with their lush vegetation and smell of cow dung, convey an air of tranquillity at odds with the hectic pace of so much of modern Israel.

## Ground-breaking research

Start your journey at **Rekhovot ❶**, about 20 km (12 miles) south-east of Tel Aviv. This is the home of the **Weizmann Institute of Science**, the research and development centre named after Chaim Weizmann, the country's first president. Weizmann was also an organic chemist of international renown, and for many years the leader of the Zionist movement. His scientific research assisted the British war effort during World War I, towards the end of which he was instrumental in securing the Balfour Declaration. Founded in 1934, the Weizmann Institute originally concentrated on local agriculture and medicine, but in 1949 it was transformed into a world-class research institute. Today it has a staff of 1,500 researchers and graduate students, with over 400 research projects in the pipeline in such fields as cancer cures, hormones, immunology, ageing, cell structure, computer science, geophysics, lasers, atomic particles and astrophysics.

The centre's moving spirit in its early years was Meyer Weisgal, an American showbiz impresario who, in addition to raising millions of dollars for the institute, used to pace the grounds picking up discarded cartons, plastic bags and even matchsticks. The institute is still one of the tidiest places in Israel. There are daily guided tours of the grounds. The view from the top of the futuristic atomic particle accelerator is good, and Weizmann's house, designed by Erich Mendelsohn in 1936–37, is worth seeing.

Opposite the Weizmann Institute is another prestigious academic campus: the **Hebrew University's Faculty of Agriculture**, one of the world's leading research centres in this discipline, which has played an important role in the development of the country's leading-edge farming capability.

**PRECEDING PAGES:** young pines in the Judean foothills. **LEFT:** the railway from Tel Aviv to Jerusalem. **BELOW:** the greenhouse effect.

Slightly north of Rekhovot lie Ramla and Lod (Lydda). They were originally Arab towns, but many of their inhabitants fled during the War of Independence in 1948. Today they are two of the few mixed Jewish–Arab communities in Israel. **Ramla ❷** has three important mosques: the **White Mosque**, dating from the 8th century; the **Mosque of the Forty**, built by the Mamelukes in 1318; and the **Great Mosque**, constructed on the site of the Crusader Cathedral of St John. The **Vaulted Pool**, an underground cistern in the town's centre, dates from the 9th century. Finally, the **Open House** organises activities for Jewish and Arab youth in an attempt to bridge the gap between the cultures.

*Thorny bloom in the Judean foothills.*

North of **Lod** is **Ben Gurion Airport**, the country's busy international terminal, named after Israel's first prime minister. Lying today in the shadow of soaring jetliners, Lod was an important town during the biblical and Second Temple periods. Visit the ancient **Sheikh's Tomb** built over the ruins of a 12th-century Crusader church, in the basement of which is the **Tomb of St George**.

## The Judean foothills

East of Ramla, in the Jerusalem foothills (take road 443), is the site of **Modi'im**, the birthplace of the Hasmonean family, leaders of the 2nd-century BC revolt against the Syrian-Greek empire which then controlled Judea. The revolt began in Modi'im when an official ordered the people to sacrifice a cockerel on a pagan altar, in accordance with the imperial policy of fostering Hellenisation and repressing Judaism. Mattitiahu, a local priest, and his five sons killed the official and his military escort, triggering the conflict. The revolt, led by Judas Maccabeus, the third son, expanded all over Judea, resulting in the recapture of the Temple and the restoration of Jewish worship in Jerusalem.

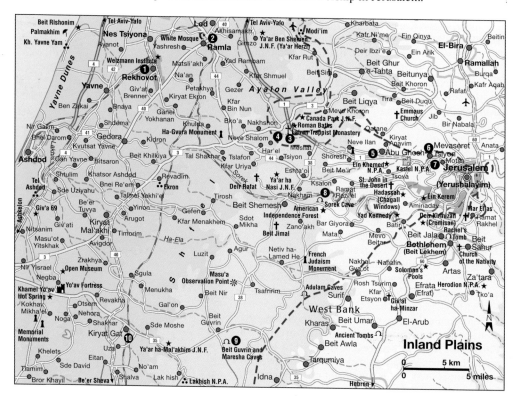

---

Map on page 272

Not much remains of ancient Modi'im, but an attractive park has been laid out, with a model of a village of the period of the revolt. Visitors can bake pitta bread in the ancient-style ovens, handle replicas of ancient agricultural implements and spin yarn. At Hanukkah, the festival commemorating the revolt, a torch is lit at Modi'im and carried in relays to Jerusalem to light candles at the Western Wall. Today, Modi'im is being built into a major city to help house Israel's growing population.

Now return to the main road to Jerusalem, which enters the gorge of **Shaar Hagai**, west of Latrun, then climbs steeply through the wooded hills. They weren't always so green; when the first Jewish pioneers arrived they saw a hilly desert stripped of trees by centuries of abuse. The early forests were made up almost entirely of indigenous Jerusalem pine, which still dominates, but foresters are diversifying for both ecological and aesthetic reasons, planting cypress, acacia, eucalyptus, pistachio, carob and varieties of the local scrub oak.

Nearby is the French Trappist **Monastery of Latrun** ❸ (just across the old border with Jordan). The monks make and sell wine, which complements the locally produced cheeses. The remains of a 12th-century Crusader fortress called **Le Toron des Chevaliers**, and an almost perfectly preserved Roman villa and bath house, are also located nearby.

A little to the north is **Canada Park**, a recreation centre with vineyards, almond orchards, ancient fig trees and adventure playgrounds. In the park are the ruins of a village thought to be the Emmaus of the New Testament, where according to St Luke's Gospel the risen Jesus was seen. Emmaus was also the site of one of the greatest victories of the Hasmoneans.

If you take the road southwest from Latrun you will shortly come to **Neve Shalom** ❹, a heartening experiment in Jewish–Arab coexistence. The only settlement founded specifically for people of the two groups to live together, it runs special courses where Jewish and Arab schoolchildren learn about each other's cultures.

Back on the main road you may be surprised to see dozens of ruined vehicles by the roadside, painted brown to prevent them from rusting. They are the remains of burnt-out armoured vans and buses which carried supplies to besieged Jerusalem in the 1948 war, and which sit permanently at the spots where they were destroyed. Jutting out from a hilltop farther ahead is the more formal Monument to the Road Builders, its aluminium spars pointing compellingly to the capital beyond. The nearby settlements of Shoresh, Neve Ilan, Kiryat Anavim and Ma'ale ha-Khamisha offer guesthouses with stunning views of the Judean hills; all of them have attractive swimming pools and comfortable accommodation.

A little further along are three Arab villages, each of them with features of interest. The largest, **Abu Ghosh** ❺, is named after the Arab family which still comprises the majority of its inhabitants. It has two fine churches and a French Benedictine monastery. A sacred spring, where Jesus is said to have drunk, is situated in a garden of towering pines and old palm trees. Some great local Arab restaurants offer tasty spiced pitta bread, *hummus* and *tahina*.

**BELOW:** the Monastery of Latrun.

Nearby **Ein Naquba** is the only Arab village built by the State of Israel from scratch; it was constructed for villagers whose homes were taken over by new immigrants after they fled from their village of Beit Naquba in the 1948 war.

Although most of its fruit trees and vegetable plots are watered by modern methods, neighbouring **Ein Rafa** has an irrigation system that dates back to biblical times. Some 4 hectares (10 acres) of land are watered by a natural spring, which flows into the individual plots according to a traditional eight-day rota system, stringently observed by the villagers.

*The church at Abu Ghosh.*

Between the two villages and the main road is **Ein Khemed** (or Aqua Bella), a landscaped camping site and nature reserve with a stream flowing through it and a restored Crusader farm. Up the hill is the suburb of **Mevaseret Tsiyon ❻**, formerly **Kastel**, an important Arab town and site of a key battle for Jerusalem in 1948. Part of the village has been preserved as a memorial to those who died, and some bunkers and pillboxes have been restored. There are magnificent views of the surrounding Judean Hills and the gleaming expanse of Jerusalem.

Continuing in the direction of Jerusalem you will come to the village of **Motsa ❼**, and the stump of **Herzl's Cypress**. Planted by the founder of modern Zionism on his visit to the Holy Land in 1898, the tree became a place of pilgrimage, and was later cut down as an anti-Zionist gesture. A glass case has been built around the stump, and it is traditional for presidents of Israel to plant a tree in the surrounding garden as a symbol of the continuing growth of Zionism.

## The Jerusalem corridor

**BELOW:** stalactites in Sorek Cave.

Take the secondary road to Beit Shemesh and, about 20 km (13 miles) west of Jerusalem, you will reach the spectacular **Sorek Cave ❽** (open for tours

Sun–Thur 8am–4pm, Fri 8am–2pm; admission charge), which extends across some 6 hectares (15 acres) of the **Avshalom Nature Reserve**. Discovered by chance during routine quarrying, it is by far the largest cave in Israel and contains stalactites and stalagmites of breathtaking beauty.

Map on page 272

Just to the south is the **Valley of Elah**, where David killed Goliath, the Philistine from Gath. The battle is described in I Samuel 17. The actual site of the encounter is not marked; today a kibbutz and a TV satellite receiving station stand in the valley.

South of here, on the road to Kiryat Gat, is the ancient site of **Beit Guvrin ❾**, opposite a modern kibbutz of the same name. There are many Crusader ruins here, but it is the **Maresha Caves** that are of special note (open for tours Sun–Thur 8am–4pm, Fri 8am–2pm; admission charge). There are hundreds of these bell-shaped caves, caused by ancient Roman quarrying. Some of them are even earlier, dating to Greek and even Phoenician times.

## A haven for immigrants

Continue west for about 18 km (12 miles) to the development town of **Kiryat Gat ❿**. Founded in 1954 as the centre of the Lachish Region, the city marked Israel's first attempt to deal in an organised way with the immigrants who poured into the country in the late 1940s and early 1950s. Earlier settlement had been realised haphazardly, but here a team of experts created a whole area of coordinated settlement. The new immigrant villages were integrated with existing kibbutzim, grouped around four regional centres providing various facilities and services. In the centre was Kiryat Gat, with cotton mills, sugar refineries and other industries based on local agriculture. ❑

*According to the Bible, David rejected the armour given to him by King Saul, "and chose him five smooth stones out of the brook", one of which he slung at the giant warrior, killing him.*

**BELOW:** a Roman cave at Beit Guvrin.

# THE WEST BANK

*This remains a contentious area, but its holy sites and
ancient cities still draw both pilgrims and tourists*

**H**ugging the Jordan River to the east and the amber-hued walls
of Jerusalem to the west, stretching out over the cities and
valleys of Samaria to the north and the tumbling Judean Hills
to the south, the West Bank is perhaps the geographical centre of
the Middle East, and the epicentre of all the tensions which that
area has come to represent. It lies at the very heart of the Holy
Land, holding such revered sites as Bethlehem, Hebron, Shilo and
Jericho within its domain.

For centuries, Jews, Christians and Muslims have paid homage here,
and today pilgrims still flock to its shrines. Scattered throughout the
region, these places are often claimed by more than one religion, and
such spots lend a physical immediacy to age-old conflicts. More than
a millennium has not erased the tension in this contested land.

The West Bank was occupied by Israel in 1967, making 300,000
Palestinians into first-time refugees while another 150,000 picked
up their belongings for the second time. Many moved to Jordan. In
1977 the new Likud coalition decided to populate the West Bank,
particularly Samaria, where there were sizeable Arab populations.
When the Labour government took office in 1992 the growth of the
new settlements was frozen, although existing settlements were
greatly expanded. The Likud government continued this policy when
itreturned to power in 1996.

In 1994 the first tentative steps were taken to restore the Occupied Territories to the Palestinian people, beginning with the town of
Jericho and the Gaza Strip. Since then, and in accordance with the
1993 Oslo Agreements, Israel has handed over all of the major Arab
towns in the West Bank, except for the western half of Hebron.
Owing to its place in Jewish history – it is the site of the Cave of
Machpelah (Tomb of the Patriarchs), resting place of Abraham, Isaac
and Jacob – militant Jewish settlers have complicated the retreat of
Israeli forces there.

Before venturing into the West Bank, check on the prevailing political climate. (Modest dress (no shorts) is recommended.) Several
companies offer group tours of the region, though these invariably
express a Jewish nationalistic theme.

Between the army outposts, Jewish settlements and refugee
camps, a trip to the West Bank necessarily provokes political
awareness. But much of the landscape appears unchanged since
the days of Abraham, David, or Jesus. With the political and spiritual both so firmly entrenched here, your sense of wonder is sure
to be heightened. However, in this period of negotiations, and especially since the return of the Likud Party to power in 1996, the area
is to be approached with caution. ❏

**PRECEDING PAGES:** a shepherd at work in the West Bank.
**LEFT:** a Jericho tourism official tries to be optimistic.

# LANDS OF THE BIBLE

*Bethlehem is the high spot for many visitors to the West Bank,
but the pastoral landscapes of the Bible also have
many other interesting sites to explore*

Map
on page
282

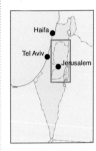

Israelis call the northern part of the West Bank by its biblical name Samaria (Shomron in Hebrew), while south of Jerusalem is known as Judea (Yehuda). The road running through the heart of the West Bank, along the ridge of the mountain chain 800–1,000 metres (2,625–3,280 ft) high, is known historically as the King's Highway and was an alternative trading route to the Via Maris (Mediterranean coastal road) linking Mesopotamia to Egypt 5,000 years ago. These mountain ridges, with a cooler, less humid climate, attracted much of the region's population, and the King's Highway passes through five of the eight West Bank towns under autonomous Palestinian rule, as well as Jerusalem. Known today as Route 60, the highway is a worthwhile trip for the adventurous, passing through stunning countryside and pastoral biblical landscapes as well as the Palestinian urban enclaves. Clearly, when the security situation is tense it is impracticable to travel this route.

Highway 60, which comes down from the Galilee, enters the West Bank through the Jezreel Valley about 14 km (8 miles) south of Afula. The most northerly of the Palestinian autonomous zones is the sedate but otherwise unexceptional town of Jenin, to the south of which is the picturesque Dotan Valley dropping dramatically to the west. It was here, so the story goes, that Joseph was sold to Egyptian traders by his jealous brothers.

## Omri's stately capital

A little over 10 km (6 miles) north-west of Nablus and 30 km (18 miles) south of Jenin is the site of one of the most impressive ruins in the Holy Land: **Sebastya ❶**. Once called Samaria, it was the capital of the northern Kingdom of Israel upon King Omri's accession to power in 887 BC. He and his son, the ill-tempered Ahab, built magnificent palaces and temples inside a circular protective wall. Ahab incurred the wrath of the Lord by adding temples to Baal and Astarte, cult figures favoured by his wife, Jezebel.

The remains of **Ahab's Palace** adjoin the impressive steps which led to Herod's **Temple of Augustus**, constructed *circa* 30 BC. Herod's grandiose style is not lost in the rubble, and parts of many of his massive constructions still stand. In addition to Herod's work, Sebastya's ruins include an enormous hippodrome, the acropolis, a basilica, and many remains of Israelite and Hellenistic walls. The colonnade-lined street is a majestic reminder of Sebastya's opulence.

In the village of Sebastya, just outside the Roman wall, lie the ruins of a Crusader cathedral. It is reputed to stand over the tombs of the prophets Elisha and Obadiah and of John the Baptist. This site is included in the **Mosque of Nabi Yaya**, in which a small chamber is believed to hold the head of John the Baptist.

**LEFT:** harvesting wheat in Samaria.
**BELOW:** the Palestinian flag.

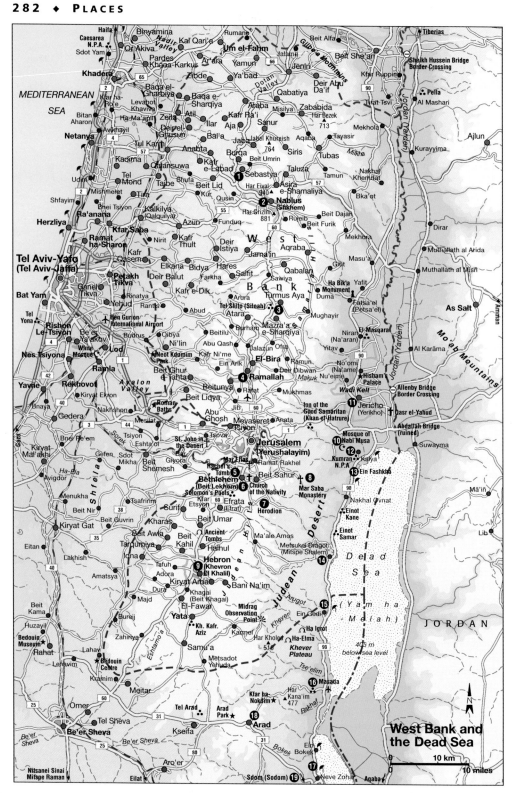

West Bank and the Dead Sea

Some 10 km (6 miles) further south is **Nablus**  ❷ (Shkhem in Hebrew), which is many things to many people. The largest city in the West Bank, with an estimated population of over 100,000, it is chock-full of sites with biblical resonances. From a distance, Nablus looks like a *pointilliste* painting: innumerable blue doors dot houses neatly spread across a hillside. Within earshot there's a cacophony of sounds: honking car horns, the majestic *mu'ezzin* calling the Muslim faithful to prayer, and the ululations of Arab women.

Rich in history, the area just outside today's city centre is mentioned in Genesis as the place where Jacob pitched his tents. **Jacob's Well**, located here, is still in use by Nablus residents. According to St John's Gospel (4, 25–26), Jesus stopped here for refreshment, weary from his travels. He spoke to a Samaritan woman who drew water from the well. "I know that the Messiah cometh, which is called Christ," she told him, whereupon Jesus responded: "I that speak unto thee am he." Adjoining this structure is a Greek Orthodox convent built on the remains of a Crusader church.

Nearby, the **Tomb of Joseph** is a shrine reputed to hold the great man's bones, "in a parcel of ground which Jacob bought of the sons of Hamor the father of Shkhem" (Joshua 24, 32). (Defying scripture, there is another cenotaph for Joseph at the Tomb of the Patriarchs in Hebron.) Under the Oslo Agreements the Tomb of Joseph compound has remained under IDF control while extremist *yeshiva* students are also domiciled here, making it the most sensitive flashpoint outside Hebron. In 1996 a dozen Israeli soldiers were killed during violent riots.

During the time of the Judges, Abimelech, the son of Gideon, had himself proclaimed king here; some 200 years later, in 928 BC, the 10 northern tribes called on Jeroboam to be king, and for several years Shkhem served as the capital of the new northern kingdom of Israel. Going farther back into biblical history, Abraham probably stopped in Shkhem just after he arrived in Canaan, and some believe that this was the place where he was given the covenant between God and man.

## The Samaritans

Standing like gate-posts at the south-eastern entrance to Nablus are two historic peaks, **Har Eival** and **Har Grizim**, named by Moses as the mountains of cursing and blessing. After the conquest, Joshua built an altar on Har Eival and from this point read the law to the people.

Har Grizim is the centre of the Samaritan religion. The sect's origins date back to 720 BC when Assyria swept through the northern kingdom. Returning from exile in 538 BC, the Jews shunned the Samaritans for their intermarriage with the conquerors, although the Samaritans claimed strict adherence to the Mosaic Law. Today, about half the 500 remaining Samaritans (they were tens of thousands strong during the Middle Ages) celebrate the Passover holiday.

In Biblical times the city of **Shilo** (Siloah) ❸ stood equidistant between Nablus and Bethel. According to the Bible, it was at Siloah that the main division of the Promised Land among the 12 tribes was made and

*It is not uncommon in these parts to see a lone Bedouin tent with an incongruous TV antenna protruding from its centre and a pick-up truck parked outside.*

**BELOW:** pillars and poise in Sebastya.

*Tenacious flora.*

where the cities were allocated. In the 11th century BC it was the religious centre for the Israelite tribes, and for over 200 years it was the sacred ground for the Ark of the Covenant. It was here that the great prophet Samuel's mother Hannah prayed for his birth. In time, the Philistines defeated the Israelites, captured the ark, and burned Siloah to the ground. Today the *tel* of Siloah spans less than 3 hectares (8 acres), although archaeologists have unearthed remnants of civilisations dating to the Bronze Age (1600 BC). There is also a large modern Jewish settlement nearby.

As you travel south of Nablus en route to Ramallah, limestone terraces climb up and down the hills, retaining all the mineral-rich soil they can. Knotty olive trees edged with flora grace the landscape. These olives are harvested by the local farmers, who transport them to the villages for pressing. Twelve km (7 miles) north-west of Ramallahh, **Bir Zeit** is the largest of the five major Palestinian universities in the West Bank. Constructed by the Israelis in 1972, it is an active centre of hostility to the Israeli government; Israeli and self-imposed closures often occur.

Just north of Ramallah, two towns atop nearby hills serve as natural landmarks: **Bethel** and **Ai**. Bethel is prominent in early biblical narratives as the site where Jacob dreamed of a ladder ascending to Heaven. At this spot he made an altar and called it Beit El, or House of God. This is also where the Ark of the Law remained until the time of the Judges. Ai was one of the earliest cities captured by Joshua and the Israelites during their military conquest of Canaan.

The Palestinian town of **Ramallah** ❹ sees itself as the capital of the West Bank. Much smaller than Nablus, and without the historical significance of Jerusalem, Ramallah is most remarkable for its affluence. Streets and streets of

large, luxurious villas testify to the town's wealth. While adjoining El Bira is predominantly Muslim, Ramallah itself is mainly Christian, and almost every Ramallah family has immediate relatives living in the USA. Ramallah provides much of the intellectual fervour and financial fuel for the Palestinian national movement. The town's status has been further enhanced by the fact that Yasser Arafat's wife Suha is a Christian from Ramallah (she converted to Islam before marrying the Palestinian leader), and the Palestinian Authority (in essence the government) frequently meets here as an alternative to Gaza. Demographically speaking, Ramallah is in effect part of the Jerusalem conurbation, as the southern suburbs of Kalandia lead into the northern neighbourhoods of Israel's capital – Atarot (which has Jerusalem's airport as well as a large industrial zone), the affluent suburb of Beit Ha'nina and the Shu'afat refugee camp.

Bethlehem is in the same manner also part of the Jerusalem metropolitan area. The southern Jerusalem neighbourhood of Gilo almost touches the town of Christ's birth, while somewhere within Jerusalem's city limits, Samaria becomes Judea.

Map on page 282

## Judea

There is no clear boundary marking the transition of the hills of Samaria to those of Judea, as both are part of the same central range of high ground, reaching from above Ramallah in the north through the Judean cities of Bethlehem and Hebron. Yet the **Judean Hills** have sustained a body of legend as a wellspring of the Old and New Testaments. To the east, marking the descent of the range into the Jordan Rift Valley, lies the **Judean Desert**, which over the centuries served as a place of refuge for prophets, monks and kings. Judea is as elusive as it is revered; all around, the arid rolling hills remind you that this is the land of the Bible, and belie the tensions below the surface.

The approach to Bethlehem, just south of the border within the Palestinian autonomous zone, holds **Rachel's Tomb ❺**, where the wife of the Patriarch Jacob and mother of Joseph and Benjamin is said to be buried. The shrine is one of the holiest in Israel, a place of worship for Jews and Muslims. The modest dome over the site was rebuilt by the British philanthropist Sir Moses Montefiore in 1841, at the place where, it is said, "Jacob set a pillar upon her grave".

**BELOW:** St Catherine's Church in Bethlehem.

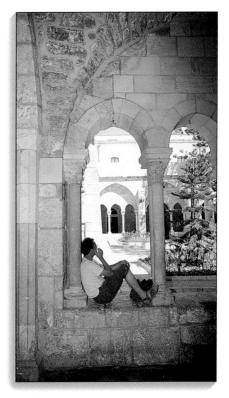

## Shrines of Bethlehem

Centuries after Rachel, Boaz married Ruth after she gleaned his fields. (Their great-grandson David, became the poet-king of Israel.) On the eastern edge of **Bethlehem ❻** lies the **Field of Ruth**. It is near the Arab village of **Beit Sahur** (House of the Shepherd), and is believed to be the field where the angel appeared to the shepherds "keeping watch over their flock by night" to announce the birth of Jesus.

On **Manger Street**, which leads directly into the hub of the town, up a flight of stairs, you'll find three huge water cisterns hewn out of rock, said to be **David's Well**. When he was battling the Philistines in their garrison here, thirst prompted David to cry: "Oh, that one would give me water to drink of the well of Bethlehem, which is by the gate!" But, offered the water drawn from the well of his enemies, he refused to drink it.

Today, music, bells and churches grace the town. The area teems with pilgrims during the holidays, and the festivities don't stop after Christmas and Easter. The pomp, ornate decor and beautiful displays continue year-round.

Christ was born in Bethlehem. The exact routes taken by the Nazarene in life remain unknown, and the Gospels do not even agree on chronology, but over the ages there has been a broadening consensus on the exact site of his birth. Following the road into Manger Square, you come to the **Church of the Nativity** (open daily dawn–dusk), entered by stooping through a small entrance, reduced to such a size by the Crusaders for defence purposes. The original basilica was built in 325 by Emperor Constantine the Great. The foundation for it is the cave revered in Christian tradition as the place where Jesus was born, which is mentioned in the writings of St Justin Martyr just 100 years after Christ.

*A sign to the Grotto.*

Beyond the vestibule is the nave; much of this interior, including the towering wooden beams, dates from Emperor Justinian's rebuilding in the 6th century. At the front of the church, downstairs, is the **Grotto of the Nativity**, where the altar features a barely discernible 12th-century mosaic. But the eye is riveted to a gleaming star on the floor of this small space, inscribed in Latin *Hic de virgine Maria Jesus Christus natus est* (Here Jesus Christ was born of the Virgin Mary). Next to the ornate and gilded grotto is the **Chapel of the Manger**, where Mary placed the newborn child.

**BELOW:** the Milk Grotto Church.

The Church of the Nativity adjoins several churches of varying Christian denominations. The most celebrated on Christmas Eve is **St Catherine's**, from which Bethlehem's annual midnight Mass is broadcast worldwide.

A few minutes' walk down Milk Grotto Street will take you to the **Milk Grotto Church**. Its milky white colour gives it its the name; the legend is that while Mary was feeding the newborn Jesus, some of her milk splashed to the stone floor and permanently whitened it. Today stone scrapings are sold to pilgrims to improve breastfeeding.

Map on page 282

Outside the churches and shrines, countless self-appointed tour guides promise to show you all you wish to see. They often know some interesting tidbits about the history of the town, but you must pay for this "freely" offered information or be hounded around Manger Square and its environs. All over town, but particularly in the square, vendors offer a wide array of religious articles and artefacts. They are freshly minted but traditionally inspired, often of olive wood, ceramics or Jerusalem stone. If you are persistent but not too pushy, you can bargain and take care of all your Christmas shopping in one go.

As you look northwards, steeples rise from the hillside maze of houses, proclaiming the city's continued sanctity to the 20,000 Arab Christians who live here. Among the various religious institutions is an Arabic-language university directed by the Catholic Order of the Brothers of Christian Schools; known as **Bethlehem University**, it was established with Israeli assistance.

## Castles in the wilderness

Some 8 km (5 miles) east of here is the desert citadel of **Herodion ❼**, perhaps the most outstanding of Herod the Great's architectural conceits. A monstrous circular protective wall struck with four watchposts guarded Herod's living space; included in the layout were hot baths, arcades, a synagogue, and numerous other luxuries. The banqueting hall of the palace is as immense as a football stadium, and the structure caps an elevation of 800 metres (2,500 ft) above sea level or 100 metres (330 ft) above the desert floor.

Even more remote, dug into the canyon walls overlooking the Kidron River to the northeast, is the blue-domed **Mar Saba Monastery ❽**. St Sabas used this serene niche in the desert as a retreat for study and worship, and in AD 492 he established the monastery named after him. In the 7th century, Persians and Arabs ruined the monastery and murdered the monks; it was rebuilt, however, and early in the 8th century John of Damascus came to the site. The writing he completed here made an important contribution to Christianity and is representative of Christian/Islamic differences at the time. Today the most prominent feature of the hermitage is the huge protective wall surrounding the complex. Among the finds displayed inside are the robed remains of St Sabas himself, returned here in 1965 from Venice, where they had been preserved for over 700 years. Also on view are the skulls of the hundreds of monks killed by the Persians in 614. Women are not allowed to enter the monastery.

Along the path to Mar Saba is the church of **St Theodosius**, where the three wise men are said to have rested after worshipping the infant Jesus, and where St Theodosius died in 529 at the age of 105.

Roughly 8 km (5 miles) from Bethlehem, as you

**BELOW:** the citadel of Herodion.

head south towards Hebron, lie the dark-green cisterns known as **Solomon's Pools**. Tradition attributes them to the great Jewish king in the 10th century BC; archaeology suggests they date from Roman times. In either case, an aqueduct carried water from here to the population of Jerusalem, and today the cisterns still serve as a source of water for the city.

## Passionate Hebron

*The Mar Saba area is inhabited by Bedouin, who claim to descend from the monastery's ancient caretakers, who came here from Byzantium.*

Close to 25 km (15 miles) south of Bethlehem is the ancient city of **Hebron ❾**. The city represents layers of history, but its agricultural and urban community is progressive. Farmers, goat-keepers, shepherds and food packers have made great strides in production by mechanising their tasks.

The town also has a major **Islamic University**, which enrols nearly 2,000 Arab students. In existence since 1971, this institution is noted for promoting Palestinian culture and nationalism, much to the chagrin of the Israeli authorities who close the facility every so often, citing anti-Israel activity.

Hebron is definitely not the place to sport your knowledge of Hebrew – but any attempt to speak a few words of Arabic is appreciated by the local people. The chances are that you'll be beckoned into a web of merchants' stalls or to a private home for a cup of tea. Turning down such an invitation will offend, but steer clear of controversy. Debating the merits of Israel's presence on the West Bank, for example, is ill-advised, especially since this is the last Arab town, under the Oslo Agreements, from which Israel has not fully retreated. Hebron remains volatile, with a Jewish enclave in the south-eastern part of the city.

**BELOW:** Mar Saba Monastery.

Meander through the criss-cross of alleyways in the Hebron *kasbah*. Here you will find a variety of artisans crafting pottery, compressing and sculpting

Map on page 282

olive wood, and blowing the colourful glass for which Hebron is widely known. A variety of fresh fruits can be bought all along the roadsides and in the souk. Hebron-grown peaches, pale and sweet, are in demand all over the Middle East, and Hebron's produce, including dried and fresh fruits as well as different types of vegetables, is transported (with Israeli agreement) to Arab countries by way of the Allenby Bridge.

The Jewish presence in Hebron dates back to when God gave Abraham his son Isaac as well as Ishmael. Abraham chose this airy hill as the burial ground for his family, and today the **Tomb of the Patriarchs** dominates the city and is visited by both Jews and Muslims. According to the Book of Genesis, Abraham bought the Cave of Machpelah from Ephron the Hittite as the burial site for his wife Sarah.

Here all three Patriarchs and their wives are believed to be buried, and their cenotaphs compose the centre of the edifice: Abraham and Sarah in the centre, Jacob and Leah on the outer side of the enclosure, and on the other side, within the mosque area, Isaac and Rebecca. More expansive folklore further contends the site holds the graves of Adam, Eve, Esau, and all 12 sons of Jacob as well.

Just outside the structure is **Joseph's Tomb**, at least in name; according to the book of Joshua (24, 32), Joseph's bones were laid to rest instead at Shkhem (Nablus) after their transport from Egypt.

The entire rectangular building gives the impression of a massive fortress, and was built with typical architectural confidence by Herod the Great. The Arabs later made a mosque of it, and the Crusaders made it a church during their stay, adding the roof-top crenellations. In 1188 it was taken by Saladin and once more converted into a mosque.

Eight hundred years after Abraham, David was crowned King of Israel in Hebron, and later made it his capital. With David's capture of Jerusalem from the Jebusites in around 1000 BC the capital was shifted, although Hebron remained one of the four holy cities of Israel, along with Jerusalem, Tiberias and Safed. The city's Jewish community survived the destruction of both Temples and remained until the year 1100, when it was expelled by the Crusaders. The population increased and dwindled alternately over the centuries. In 1929, and again in 1936, the community was wiped out in anti-Jewish riots, and after that it was not until 1967 that Jews re-entered Hebron. In 1968 a group of Jewish settlers gained *de facto* rights to settle in the area, although not in Hebron's Arab centre. The result is a suburb called **Kiryat Arba** (Hebron's name in biblical times), overlooking the city from a nearby hill.

## Today's tensions

Both Jews and Muslims claim descent from Abraham, and the Hebron area (particularly the Tomb of the Patriarchs) is a centre of separate worship and mutual confrontation. Adding to the friction is the fact that a mosque covers part of the site, which had at one time been a synagogue.

The situation in Hebron has been tense ever since the 1967 War, and Israeli soldiers are on constant

**BELOW:** a politically correct vegetable seller.

patrol in the area. Violent clashes between Jews and Arabs have riddled the town. Due to sporadic unrest here, it is best to consult the Israeli Government Tourist Office in Jerusalem before travelling to Hebron. Be sure you plan your return trip in advance, however: Hebron is the one place in the West Bank where you should not spend the night.

On the outskirts of Hebron stands the gnarled but living **Oak of Abraham**, believed to be some 600 years old. It is reputed to be on the site where Abraham was visited by three angels who told him of Isaac's impending birth. It is owned by Russian monks, who have a small monastery here. The ancient name for this place is Mamre; Abraham supposedly built an altar and a well here, and Herod's structure on the site was where Bar-Kochba's defeated troops were sold into slavery.

North of Hebron, along the road to Bethlehem, lies the **Etsyon Bloc**, where the agricultural-religious community of Kibbutz Ha-Dati was founded in 1926. Abandoned in the Arab riots of 1929, it was resettled only to be disturbed again in the riots of 1936–39. In 1948 its settlers were wiped out in the War of Independence. The Etsyon Bloc and the surrounding Hebron Hills were retaken by the Israeli army in June 1967, and several months later **Kibbutz Kfar Etsyon** was resettled by children of the original kibbutznikim.

From Kfar Etsyon the highway leads directly back to Jerusalem, some 14 km (8 miles) away, through a newly constructed series of tunnels and bridges that bypasses Bethlehem. Just off the highway is the kibbutz of Ramat Rakhel which offers an inspiring view of the desert, and nearby to the south is the 11th-century Crusader monastery **Mar Elias**. Elijah supposedly slept here when fleeing from Jezebel. Close by, Israeli archaeologists recently uncovered a Byzantine

**BELOW:**
the Monastery
of St George.

church. It has attractively preserved mosaics, and, more importantly, the Greek Orthodox Church recently proclaimed that the large flat stone in the 4th-century complex is to be called "The Mary Stone". The belief is that the pregnant Mary rested on this rock on her way south to Bethlehem.

To reach Jericho travel the new highway down from French Hill to Ma'ale Adumim, a huge outer suburb of Jerusalem and the largest Jewish entity in the West Bank. Then follow the highway down through the inspiring and billowing stone hills of the Judean Desert to the lowest point on earth.

Map on page 282

## Hidden hermitage

On the road northeast of Jerusalem to Wadi Kelt, the silence is so pure that it creates a ringing in your ears. For 1,600 years, since the age of the Patriarchs, monks have inhabited this surreal place, where the **Wadi Kelt River** meanders through a dramatic gorge in the canyon between Jericho and Jerusalem. This 35-km (22-mile) stretch includes ruins on top of ruins, monasteries, eerie hermits' caves and surprising watering holes. These sights appear as adornments on the earth's crust, which forms hills, cliffs and ravines – a photographer's delight. Honeycombing the rock face are hollowed-out niches which serve as cells for monks, who live off the fruit of the land. The **Greek Orthodox Monastery of St George** is just over a century old, but its community long precedes it. Hasmonean, Herodian and Roman remains line this circuitous course.

South of Jericho, off the Jerusalem–Jericho highway, is the **Mosque of Nabi Musa ❿**, astounding to the eye. It appears out of nowhere in the middle of nowhere. Here Muslims worship at the Tomb of Moses. The Mamelukes constructed the mosque in the 13th century, providing a high cenotaph for Moses.

*A Greek Orthodox monk.*

**BELOW:** a detail at Hisham's Palace.

*Was Moses buried at Nabi Musa? The Bible states that he was "buried in a valley in the land of Moab, but no man knoweth of his sepulchre unto this day". However, tradition places the tomb here.*

It is open during the times of Muslim prayer, and all day Friday. Only Muslims are admitted in April, when thousands make their pilgrimage. The Muslim route to Nabi Musa intersects the procession of Christians making their Easter pilgrimages to al-Maghtes on the Jordan River, and clashes have resulted.

## The walls of Jericho

The northern border between Israeli-held land and the Palestinian autonomous zone of Jericho is marked not by an international frontier but the **Oasis Casino**. The casino, a huge investment by an Austrian leisure chain, was opened in 1998 just inside Palestinian territory. Such gambling is illegal in Israel, and the casino is aimed at Israelis who otherwise would have to travel to Egypt or Turkey to satisfy their craving. Even though the casino can hold 2,000 people at a time, it is not uncommon for long entrance queues to form at weekends and holidays.

Jericho must have been a prime spot for the earliest city-dwellers on earth some 10,000 years ago. Widely considered to have sprouted the first agricultural community, the town today is once more centred on agriculture, although on a less historic scale. Jericho is ensconced in an oasis in the midst of barren land; its Jericho's greenery is nurtured by underground springs, the secret of the town's endurance. It was the first Arab town in the West Bank to be handed over to the Palestinian Authority.

In times past, rulers used this spot as a warm-weather retreat. One such was Hisham, the 10th Umayyid caliph, who built the fabulous **Hisham's Palace**, about 3 km (2 miles) from the city, in the 8th century. An enormous aqueduct supplied water from the nearby Ein Dug Springs to a cistern, which then doled it out to the palace as needed. The carvings and monumental pillars are awesome, and the palace floors contain examples of the finest Islamic mosaics.

**BELOW:** Yasser Arafat is a permanent presence in Jericho.

A few kilometres south of the palace is **Elisha's Spring**, a fountain which the Jews believe was purified by the prophet after the populace claimed it was harmful to crops: it is referred to by Arabs today as Ein-es-Sultan. Nearby is the preserved floor of a 6th-century synagogue, featuring a mosaic menorah in its centre, within the walls of a Jericho home.

Ancient **Jericho ⓫**, which lies under Tel es-Sultan, is where the walls came tumbling down on the seventh day after they were encircled by Joshua and the Children of Israel. Archaeological excavations confirm that settlements here date to 8,000 BC, when the population of hunters and gatherers completed the transition to sedentary life, becoming the earliest practitioners of agriculture and animal husbandry.

Jericho today is a sleepy town of 7,000 people, with most of the activity confined to its centre. Here, men and women gather to sit on rattan stools, talk, sip coffee, or play backgammon. The markets are ablaze with fruit and vegetables, and huge bunches of dates and bananas swing from their beams. The cafés offer authentic Middle Eastern foods and refreshment.

In the stark wilderness outside this small town, Jesus tempted by the devil on a peak the Bible calls the **Mount of Temptation** (also called Qarantal). Hinged to the rock face here is a **Greek Orthodox**

Map on page 282

**Monastery of the Temptation**, constructed in front of the grotto where Jesus was said to have fasted for 40 days and nights.

## Along the River Jordan

Some 10 km (6 miles) east of Jericho, at a ford north of the Dead Sea known as **al-Maghtes**, Jesus is said to have been baptised: "And it came to pass in those days, that Jesus came from Nazareth of Galilee, and was baptised by John in Jordan" (Mark 1, 6–9). Not surprisingly, this **Site of the Baptism** is one of the places favoured today by Christians as a baptism place.

The American writer Mark Twain described the Jordan River as "so crooked that a man does not know which side of it he is on half the time. In going 90 miles it does not get over more than 50 miles of ground. It is not any wider than Broadway in New York". It is true that the symbolism attached to this stream – its muddy waters barely flowing in winter – far exceeds its actual size.

The **Allenby Bridge** is the river crossing from the West Bank to Jordan. During the 1967 war it was reduced to scaffolding and jammed with Palestinians fleeing to Jordan. It has been rebuilt, and its traffic is strictly monitored by Israeli security. It is the gateway for West Bank produce into the market places of the Arab world. Visits are exchanged by families and friends on both sides of the Jordan, and many West Bank residents go to Amman for banking and commercial links. Although Israel and Jordan are officially at peace, the Palestinian community living between the two still constitutes a security threat. Stationed at the bridge's western side are Israeli soldiers who meticulously search travellers' personal belongings. Similarly, the Jordanian armed checkpoints at the border just beyond are potent reminders that peace remains tentative. ❑

**BELOW:** the Tomb of the Patriarchs.

# THE DEAD SEA

*Float in the salt water and bathe in the therapeutic mud at the lowest spot on earth, then visit Masada, Israel's most spectacular archaeological site*

Map on page 282

hristian pilgrims travelling here over the centuries were aghast at the lifelessness they encountered and gave the **Dead Sea** its name. It's an apt one, for the most saline body of water on the face of the earth contains no life of any sort, and for most of its history there has been little life around it either. Yet today it is a source of both life and health: the potash contained in its bitter waters is an invaluable fertiliser, exported all over the world, while the lake and the springs that feed it are said to have cured everything from arthritis to psoriasis since ancient times. Sun-worshippers from Scandinavia and health fanatics from Germany fill its spas and hotels, seeking remedies and relaxation. Tourists and Israelis come here to breathe in the abundant oxygen, float on the water's salty surface, and marvel at the rugged panoramas.

Situated some 400 metres (1,300 ft) below sea level in a geological fault that extends all the way to East Africa, the Dead Sea is the lowest point on the face of the globe, and is surrounded by the starkest scenery the world has to offer. Steep cliffs of reddish flint rise sharply to the west, contrasting with beige limestone bluffs and the blinding white salt flats of the plain. Across the shimmering gold surface of the water to the east, the mauve and purple mountains of the biblical Moab and Edom are almost indistinguishable in the morning, gaining visibility throughout the day. In late afternoon their wadis and canyons are heavily shadowed, forming a spectacular backdrop of ragged earth.

Mild and pleasant in winter, the Dead Sea basin is an oven in summer. The hot air has an almost solid presence, and the glare from the sun is ferocious.

The southern part of the Dead Sea has partly dried up, due to the use of the waters of the River Jordan by both Israel and Jordan. On the Israeli side, dykes built for the potash plant form a network of artificial lakes designed for the extraction of chemicals; they are also used by bathers.

The **Judean Desert**, the area between the hills of Judea and the Dead Sea, was a region of hermits, prophets and rebels. David hid here from Saul. The Hasmoneans, who raised the banner of Jewish independence from the Syrian-Greek empire in the 2nd century BC, regrouped here after their initial defeat. Jesus retired to the desert to meditate, and the Essenes established a community in its desolate wastes. The Jewish War against Rome of AD 66–73 started with the capture of the Judean desert fastness of Masada.

Israel's pre-1967 border with Jordan ran just north of Ein Gedi, about halfway up the western shore of the Dead Sea, so only the southern half of the Judean desert was in Israel. Some of the sites described here became accessible to Israelis only after the Six Day War, and may revert back to Arab administration.

**PRECEDING PAGES:** covered in Dead Sea mud. **LEFT:** buoyant reading. **BELOW:** young mud larks.

*Fun in the mud.*

## The scrolls of Kumran

On the northwest shore of the Dead Sea is the Essene settlement of **Kumran** ⑫, where the Dead Sea Scrolls were found. The Essenes, an ascetic Jewish sect of the Second Temple period, deliberately built their community in this inaccessible spot. It was destroyed by the Romans in AD 68.

In the early summer of 1947 a Bedouin shepherd stumbled across the most exciting archaeological discovery of the century: scrolls, dating from the first centuries before and after Christ, preserved in earthenware jars. Some of these documents were acquired by Israel in rather dramatic circumstances. Eliezar Sukenik, Professor of Archaeology at the Hebrew University, was offered by an Armenian dealer the chance of buying a collection of ancient scrolls. He was shown a fragment briefly and was impressed by its antiquity – but, to see the collection, he had to travel to Bethlehem. It was the period just prior to the establishment of the State of Israel, and Jerusalem was a war zone; Bethlehem was in the Arab-controlled area, and dangerous for Jews. Sukenik approached his son Yigael Yadin for advice. Yadin, an archaeologist himself, and at that time Chief of Operations of the new Israel Defence Forces, replied: "As an archaeologist, I urge you to go; as your son, I beg that you do not go; as chief of operations of the army, I forbid you to go!" Sukenik did go to Bethlehem, at considerable personal risk, and managed to buy three scrolls. He could not complete the purchase of the other four, which were eventually taken to the United States and later re-purchased for Israel by Yadin.

**BELOW:** a cave at Kumran.
**RIGHT:** traditional local transport.

Subsequent searches of the caves unearthed other scrolls and thousands of fragments, most of which are now on display in Israel, either in the Shrine of the Book at the Israel Museum in Jerusalem or in the Rockefeller Museum. They

Map
on page
282

have revolutionised scholarship of the Second Temple period and thrown new light on the origins of Christianity, indicating that Jesus may have been an Essene, or at least was strongly influenced by the sect. The scrolls have revealed the mood of messianic fatalism among the Jews of that time, explaining both the emergence of Christianity and the fervour of the Jewish rebels in their hopeless war against Rome. The scrolls have also disclosed much about the nature of the Essene way of life and their beliefs, ritual and worship.

The partly reconstructed buildings of Kumran are on a plateau some 100 metres (330 ft) above the shore and are well worth a visit. Numerous caves, including those where the scrolls were found, are visible in the nearby cliffs, but are not accessible to the tourist. Near the caves is a tourist centre, run by the neighbouring **Kibbutz Kalya**, which also offers accommodation.

## Salt baths

The oasis of **Ein Fashkha** ⓮, where the Essenes grew their food, is 3 km (2 miles) to the south. Today it is a popular bathing site, where visitors can swim in the Dead Sea and then wash off the salt in the fresh water of the springs. Bathing here is a unique experience: the swimmer bobs around like a cork, and it's possible to read a paper while sitting on the surface. The salinity of the water – 10 times that of the oceans – can make it very painful if you have a cut or scratch. Emperor Vespasian threw manacled slaves into the sea to test its buoyancy. Most modern bathers go in voluntarily. Non-swimmers can float easily, but must be careful to maintain their balance. The bitter taste of even a drop can linger all day, and a mouthful of Dead Sea water should be avoided.

Some 19 km (12 miles) south of Kumran is the new kibbutz of **Mitspe**

**BELOW:** the ruins of an Essene village.

**Shalem** . The original site, on a cliff overlooking the sea, has been converted into a field school, **Metsukei Dragot**, which offers desert safaris in jeeps, rock climbing and rappelling. Past the school there is access to the steep-sided **Murabbat Canyon**, which contains caves where other 1st- and 2nd-century scrolls were discovered. The canyon descends to the Dead Sea, but at that point it is sheer and unscalable. A walk down the canyon from the field school is a memorable experience, but not to be undertaken alone. Would-be hikers are advised to go in a group from the school, with expert guides.

Also found in the Murabbat caves were fragments relating to a later revolt against Rome in AD 132–35, led by Simon Bar Kochba, including a letter written by Bar Kochba himself to one of his commanders.

*Birdwatching in the desert.*

## Where David hid from Saul

Less than 15 km (8 miles) further south is the lush oasis of **Ein Gedi** ⑮, site of a kibbutz, a nature reserve and another field school. A particularly beautiful spot, with the greenery creeping up the steep cliffs beside the springs, Ein Gedi is the home of a large variety of birds and animals, including gazelles, ibex, oryx, foxes, jackals and even a few leopards.

The most popular site for hiking and bathing is **David's Spring**, which leads up to a beautiful waterfall, fringed in ferns, where tradition says David hid from King Saul, when he was the victim of one of the king's rages. "Then Saul took three thousand chosen men out of all Israel, and went to seek David and his men upon the rocks of the wild goats." (I Sam 24, 2). According to the biblical account, David crept up on Saul as he slept and cut off a piece of the king's robe, proving he could have killed him but desisted. A tearful reconciliation followed.

**BELOW:** cooling off at Ein Gedi.
**RIGHT:** the free-roaming ibex.

Map on page 282

On most days, summer and winter, the area around David's Spring is thronged with visitors, so the more energetic may prefer to hike along the course of **Nakhal Arugot**, a kilometre south. This canyon is full of wildlife and has deep pools for bathing. Both Nakhal David and Nakhal Arugot are nature reserves.

Kibbutz Ein Gedi runs a guesthouse and a spa for bathing in the Dead Sea water and nearby sulphur springs and mud baths. A camping site, youth hostel and restaurant are situated on the shore below the kibbutz.

A little further south is the canyon of **Nakhal Khever**. Of particular interest here are two caves: the **Cave of Horror**, where 40 skeletons dating from the time of the Bar Kochba revolt were discovered, and the nearby **Cave of Letters**, in which 15 letters written by Bar Kochba to his commanders were found. As with Murabbat, visitors are not advised to climb to the caves alone.

## Masada

About 20 km (12 miles) south of Ein Gedi, towering almost 300 metres (1,000 ft) above the Dead Sea shore, is the rock of **Masada ⑯**, the most spectacular archaeological site in Israel. Part of the line of cliffs which rise up to the Judean desert plateau, Masada is cut off from the surrounding area by steep wadis to the north, south and west.

It was on this desolate mesa, in 43BC, that Herod the Great seized an existing fortress and used it as a retreat from his potentially rebellious subjects. Visitors to the site can wander through the magnificent three-tiered palace which extends down the northern cliff; the Roman bath house, with its ingenious heating system; the vast storehouses; the western palace with its fine mosaics, and the huge water cisterns hewn in the rock. They can appreciate the view of the remarkable

**BELOW:** the fortress of Masada.

desert landscape from the summit, which can be climbed easily from the west via the Roman ramp, ascended by cable-car from the east or, more energetically, climbed via the Snake Path, also from the east. These features alone make the fortress worth a visit, but it is the story of the epic siege of the fortress in the Jewish War against Rome which has made Masada a place of pilgrimage second only to the Western Wall.

In AD 66 a group of Jewish rebels known as Zealots, and also called the Sicarii – named after the *sica* (dagger), their favourite weapon – seized Masada from its Roman garrison, triggering the Jewish War against Rome. Securing their base there, the Sicarii proceeded to Jerusalem, where they took over the leadership of the revolt. In bitter in-fighting between the rebel groups their leader was killed, and they returned to Masada to regroup.

The new Sicarii leader, Elazar Ben-Yair, waited out the war at Masada, joined from time to time by other groups. He was still in possession after the fall of Jerusalem in AD 70. Three years later the Roman Tenth Legion arrived to put an end to this last Jewish stronghold. With its auxiliaries and camp followers, the legion numbered over 15,000. Defending Masada were fewer than 1,000 Jewish men, women and children. Herod's store-rooms were still well supplied. The Romans destroyed the aqueduct feeding the cisterns from dams in the wadi, but the cisterns had enough water for a prolonged period and were accessible from the summit.

The legion constructed a wall around the rock which blocked the main possible escape routes, reinforced by camps, and then built an earth ramp, reinforced by wooden beams and shielded by stone, which pointed like a dagger at the perimeter wall of the fortress.

**BELOW:** the cistern at Masada.

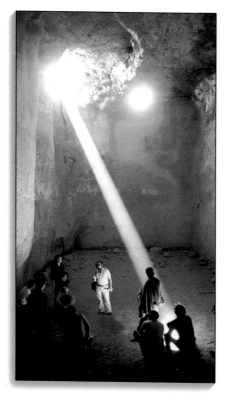

The final defences were set on fire, and when the blaze died down the Romans entered Masada to discover the bodies of the defenders laid out in rows. Repudiating defeat and refusing slavery, the men had first killed their own families and then themselves, drawing lots for a final 10 to carry out the act, one last electee killing the other nine and finally committing suicide.

The account in *The Jewish War* by Flavius Josephus has become one of the legends of modern Israel. In recognition of the symbolic importance of the site, young soldiers being inducted into the armed forces today swear their oath of allegiance atop the fortress and vow: "Masada shall not fall again!"

The excavations by Yigael Yadin in the 1960s uncovered the magnificence of Herod's fortress and palaces, but the most moving finds were of the Zealots' living quarters in the casement wall, their synagogue and ritual baths, the remains of the fire, and fragments of their final meal. The skeletons of a man, woman and child were uncovered in the northern palace; more were found in a nearby cave, where they had apparently been thrown by the Romans.

The country caught its collective breath when the discovery was announced of a set of inscribed pottery shards, which may have been the lots cast by the defenders to decide who would kill the others. One of them was inscribed "Ben-Yai".

Map on page 282

## Sodom's soothing spas

Ensconced along the shore just north of biblical Sodom, the resorts of **Ein Bokek** and **Neve Zohar**  attract health-seekers from across the globe, with a wide range of accommodation based around the mineral springs. Famous since the 1st century AD, the healing waters are believed to cure a spectrum of ailments, from skin disease to lumbago, arthritis and rheumatism. The clinics, run by medical staff, offer sulphur baths, mineral baths, salt baths, mud baths, massage and exercise programmes. The prices range from reasonable to expensive, the latter in five-star hotels where the spas are actually on the premises.

Don't miss the mud if you do stay; Cleopatra is said to have sent slaves here to fetch it for her, and today Dead Sea Mud has once more become a sought-after export as a natural moisturiser.

*Spa hotel at Ein Bokek.*

## Arad, old and new

Between the spas and the chemical plant a road wends its way westwards into the mountains, climbing over 1,000 metres (3,300 ft) in less than 25 km (15 miles), to **Arad** ⓲, Israel's first planned town.

Arad has a history of human habitation going back 5,000 years, but while the modern town is constructed on an elevation near the Dead Sea to ensure a mild climate, the historic settlement is set in farming land 8 km (5 miles) further west. The ancient mound of **Tel Arad** has been excavated and partly reconstructed. Sections of a Canaanite town of the 3rd millennium BC have been found, with pottery from the First Dynasty in Egypt, indicating trade between the two nations at that time.

A 10th-century BC fortress from the time of King Solomon was the next settle-

**BELOW:** waiting for the mud to work.

**Black Mud** a natural sediment from the DEAD SEA

Makes you feel young and full of energy, relaxes tensions and soothes pains. Application of Mud stimulates the metabolism and blood circulation. Keeps your skin young and fresh. Can be applied to the entire body, to painful parts, as a beauty face-mask or as a means for strengthening hair growth.

° Contents: The solid part (57.4%) Montmorillonite, Caolinite, Illte, Quartz, Calcite, Feldspars, Organic material.
Liquid part (42.6%): (W/W₃) Na-3%; K-1%; Ca-1.72%; Mg-3.52%; Sr-0.03%;
Li-0.0012%; Cl-18.1%; So₄-0.34%; Hco₃-0.28%; Br-0.42%;

בוץ שחור משקע טבעי מים המלח

להרגשה צעירה וליחניות, לרגיעה ממתחים ומכאוב. מריחה של הבוץ מזרחת את פעילות חלוף החומרים ומחזור הדם.
לצעירות העור ורעננותו. ניתן למריחה על הגוף כולו, על חלקיו גוף כואבים, כמסיכת יופי לפנים ואמצעי לחזוק השיער.
° תכולה: החלק המוצק (57.4%): מונטמורילוניט, קאולניט, אילט, קוורץ, קלציט, פלדספים, חומר אורגני.
(W/W₃) Na-3%; K-1%; Ca-1.72%; Mg-3.52%; Sr-0.03%; (42.6%) החלק הנוזלי
Li-0.0012%; Cl-18.1%; So₄-0.34%; Hco₃-0.28%; Br-0.42%;

Map
on page
282

ment. Far smaller than the original Canaanite city, the enclosure contained a sanctuary modelled on the Temple in Jerusalem, with a courtyard, an outer chamber and a Holy of Holies, the only one of its kind ever discovered.

Archaeologists found the remains of a burnt substance on two smaller altars inside the Holy of Holies. Analysis showed it to be traces of animal fat, indicating sacrifices. This is consistent with the denunciations of the prophets, recorded in the Bible, of continuing sacrifices on the "high places". King Hezekiah, who ruled Judah from 720 to 692 BC, heeded the advice and "removed the high places and broke the images".

Modern Arad, founded in 1961, was the most ambitious new town project of its time. It was meant to provide housing, health services and tourism facilities plus regional industries. It was well placed to utilise the natural resources, and mineral spas at the Dead Sea, and offered dry desert air, suitable for asthma treatment. Architecturally, it was conceived as a fortress against the desert: the buildings were grouped around squares; the paved walkways were shaded by houses; greenery was planted in small concentrations which did not require too much water. The six basic neighbourhoods and the town centre were less than a mile across. Arad is an interesting example of theory being changed by practice. It was initially assumed that the inhabitants would wish to cluster together in the desert environment, but this did not prove to be the case, and the planners were forced to modify their designs to meet demand for more space. Arad is the epitome of planned pioneering: the rational creation of a town, adapted to the desert and utilising its resources. King Uzziah, the Bible records, "built towers in the wilderness". Constructed only a few miles from where the king's buildings stood, Arad's apartment blocks are Israel's new towers in the desert, a symbol of today's Israel: a modern community arising where an ancient one used to exist.

**BELOW:** cult basin at Tel Arad.
**RIGHT:** visiting the caves at Ein Bokek.

### City of sin?

From Arad, take the road back to Neve Zohar, then south to **Sodom** (Sdom) ⓭. There is a peaceful atmosphere about modern Sodom which, despite its oppressive heat, makes it an unexpectedly calm place to swim, stroll or sunbathe. This is in stark contrast with the "cities of sin", Sodom and Gomorrah, which were destroyed with fire and brimstone for the decadence and sexual perversion of their inhabitants. The Bible is rather coy regarding the exact nature of these "sins", but homosexuality and buggery are implied (originating the term "sodomite").

According to the story, God allowed Lot, Abraham's nephew, to escape with his family, but his wife, disobeying instructions, looked back, and was turned into a pillar of salt. On the Dead Sea shore there is a cave with a hollow tower. Called **Lot's Wife**, the pillar is said to be the remains of that unhappy lady. Take a walk inside, lick your finger, and taste the salt.

Further south, the conveyor belts, funnels and ovens of the **Dead Sea Mineral Works** grind and roar day and night. Articulated trucks move ponderously out of the yard, hauling the potash, magnesium and salt down the Arava to Eilat, or up the ridge to the railway and Ashdod ports. ❑

# FOUR SEAS KEEP VISITORS IN THE SWIM

*The Med, the Red and the Dead – and, of course, the Sea of Galilee: Israel's four seas offer a wide variety of pleasures and experiences*

According to the map, Israel has four seas, but in reality there are only two. The Sea of Galilee and the Dead Sea are actually lakes, relatively small bodies of water linked by the River Jordan. Also known as Lake Tiberias, the Sea of Galilee is a mere 230 sq. km (88 sq. miles) in size. Surrounded by the picturesque hills of the Galilee and the Golan, the lake is edged by artificial beaches. Although only some 100 km (62 miles) further south, the Dead Sea lies amid a barren, majestic sweep of mountainous rocky desert. Set at the lowest point on earth, 400 metres (1,300 ft) below sea level, it has a unique mineral composition, including a 30 percent salt content which makes bathers float. The sea has now split in two as a result of evaporation and excessive mining of potassium and bromides.

The Red Sea, another 200 km (125 miles) to the south, a northern finger of the Indian Ocean, is the closest that tropical waters come to Europe. Beneath the surface, fish of all shapes, sizes and colours, and exquisite coral formations, can be seen. At Coral World Underwater Observatory a submarine – yellow, of course – takes those who can afford it on underwater sightseeing trips.

Sandy beaches dominate the 200-km (125-mile) Mediterranean coastline from Rosh ha-Nikra to Ashkelon. The beaches are beautiful but can get very crowded at weekends with Israelis escaping the city heat.

### THE VEST OF LIFE ▷
There is absolutely no divine protection against drowning in the Holy Land. Taking precautions is wise: many don't, and there are more than 100 deaths by drowning every year.

### △ GALILEAN SEA
The Sea of Galilee is in fact a vast reservoir providing Israel with more than one third of its drinking-water.

### RED SEA LIFE ▷
The Red Sea has exotic tropical marine life, guaranteed winter sunshine and opportunities for a wide range of water sports.

### ◁ FLIPPING OUT AT THE BEACH
Israel's glorious Mediterranean beaches turn some people head over heels with enthusiasm.

### ▽ EIN BOKEK
Bathers at Ein Bokek on the Dead Sea enjoy an oxygen-rich atmosphere and sunbathing that is free of ultra-violet rays.

### △△ HISTORIC PORT
At Yafo Port, Jonah set sail on his ill-fated voyage, and Solomon imported cedars from Lebanon to build the Temple.

### △ DIVERS' PARADISE
Israel has the highest number of qualified divers per capita in the world, with over 50,000 registered.

## MUD, MUD, GLORIOUS MUD

Despite its slimy, salty nature, the Dead Sea is extremely therapeutic. The fashionable and fun way to let the sea's minerals work wonders on your body is by covering yourself in Dead Sea mud. Among the minerals found in the water are bromine, which soothes the nerves, and iodine and magnesium which ease arthritis, rheumatism, psoriasis and skin problems as well as respiratory complaints. The mud can be applied professionally by medical staff in the region's hotels within the framework of comprehensive treatment, or simply slapped on by the sea.

There are also sulphur baths available at Ein Gedi and Ein Bokek. Other health advantages to the Dead Sea region include the high level of oxygen in the low-altitude air, and evaporating gases which rise from the sea and create a filter which takes out the sun's harmful ultra-violet rays. Thus the cancerous risks of sun-bathing are reduced, despite searing summer temper-atures of 40°C (104°F). The winter average is a delightful 21°C (70°F).

# THE NEGEV

*King Solomon's Mines and the market at Be'er Sheva are not the only sights in the Negev – there are magnificent craters, nature reserves, and a high-tech university*

Map on page 312

The very name "Negev" conjures up an image of the rugged outdoors, jeeps, camels, frontiersmen – an unforgiving expanse of bleak wastes, sunlight and sharp, dry air. It is every bit as vast and intimidating as it sounds, containing 60 percent of Israel's land area but less than 10 percent of its population. Yet the Negev is far from barren: it supports successful agricultural communities, a sprawling "capital", a complex desert ecosystem, and – since Israel relinquished the Sinai in 1982 – a variety of defence activities.

The Hebrew word means "parched", and the Negev is indeed parched, with rainfall varying from an annual average of 30 cm (12 inches) in the north to almost zero in Eilat. But don't expect white sand and palm trees. The northern and western Negev is a dusty plain slashed with wadis: dried-up river-beds which froth with occasional winter flash floods. To the south are the bleak flint, limestone, chalk, dolomite and granite mountains, with the Arava Valley to the east dividing them from biblical Edom, today part of Jordan.

**PRECEDING PAGES:** the stark hills of the Judean Desert. **LEFT:** the visitor centre at Mitspe Ramon. **BELOW:** rare blooms.

## History

The Negev is saturated with history. In Abraham's time, around 2,000 BC, the area was inhabited by nomadic tribes. When the Children of Israel left Egypt (around 1280 BC) the warlike Amalekites blocked their path to the Promised Land. Joshua eventually conquered Canaan and awarded the Negev to the tribe of Simeon, but only the northern part was settled. King David extended Israelite rule over the Negev in the 10th century BC, and his son Solomon built a string of forts. Solomon also developed the copper mines at Timna, and the port of Etzion Geber (Eilat). After the division of the kingdom into Israel and Judah the area was occupied by the Edomites, who were expelled by the Nabateans in the 1st century BC.

In the Middle Ages the Negev was an important Byzantine centre. In subsequent centuries it remained the domain of nomadic Bedouins until the start of Zionist immigration in the 1880s. But it was not until 1939 that the first successful kibbutz, **Negba**, northwest of Be'er Sheva, was established. Three other outposts in the western Negev were created in 1943, and a further 11 were thrown up on a single day in 1946.

The Jews fought hard for the inclusion of the Negev in the new State of Israel, and the UN partition plan awarded most of it to the Jewish state. The rest was won in the War of Independence of 1948, when the Egyptian and Transjordanian armies were expelled.

David Ben Gurion, Israel's first prime minister, believed passionately in the development of the Negev, and went to live in what was then a tiny isolated kibbutz, Sde Boker, when he retired.

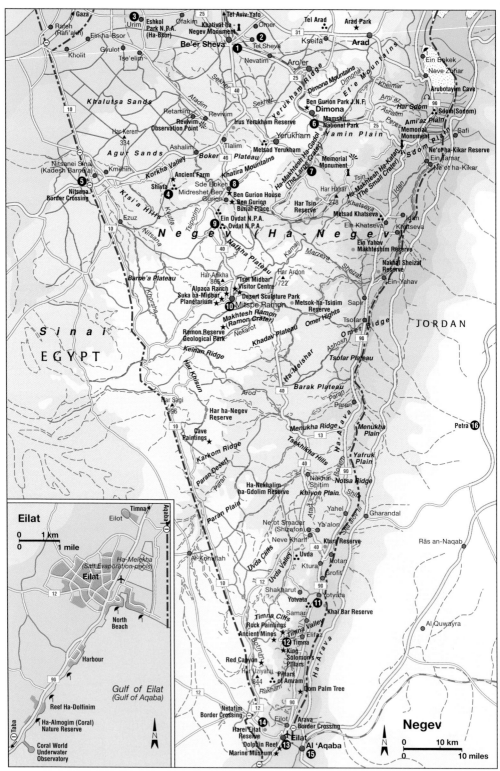

**Negev**

*Eilat*

0 — 1 km
0 — 1 mile

Gulf of Eilat
(Gulf of Aqaba)

N

0 — 10 km
0 — 10 miles

## Capital of the Negev

Although it has become comparatively civilised, **Be'er Sheva ❶** still possesses something of its old frontier atmosphere: brash, bustling, and bursting with energy. Big trucks park in the main streets; open jeeps drive through the centre; sunburned men with scuffed boots and dust in their hair drink beer in the sidewalk cafés; young soldiers sip their colas, wait for rides and monopolise the public telephones. You don't see too many suits or ties here.

Map on page 312

Despite planners' efforts to create a new centre further east, the old city remains the real centre of the town. The unusual rectangular formation of its streets was the work of a German engineer who served with the Turkish army in the years before World War I. The rest of Be'er Sheva, a monument to the great improvisation phase of Israel's development, is laid out like an English garden city, without consideration for climatic and topographical conditions.

But the town, thrown up hastily while Israel was doubling its population with an influx of immigrants, couldn't have been built in any other way. There was no time for proper planning. Today, with a population of 150,000, a flourishing industrial base, a university, hospital, medical school, music conservatory, dance school, an orchestra and arts centre, Be'er Sheva is Israel's fourth largest city. If it's a mess, it's a triumphant mess. Be'er Sheva is the capital of the Negev, providing services for the surrounding population. The regional offices of the companies extracting potash, phosphates, magnesium, salt and lime are all here, alongside new factories for everything from ceramics to pesticides.

The town accommodates people from over 70 countries, the earlier immigrants from Romania and Morocco rubbing shoulders with more recent arrivals from Argentina and the former Soviet Union. An Arab town until 1948, it is now a predominantly Jewish community, but several hundred Bedouin have moved here from the surrounding area and form an important part of the population.

**BELOW:** a Bedouin trader at the weekly market.

## City sights

Every Thursday morning there is a **Bedouin market** on the southern edge of town, for which a special structure has been built. The Bedouin still trade their camels, sheep and goats here, but in recent years the market has become a tourist attraction, providing opportunities to buy all kinds of arts and crafts.

The name Be'er Sheva means "well of the swearing", in memory of the pact sworn between the patriarch Abraham and a local ruler, Abimelech, in which Abraham secured the use of a well to water his flocks. There is a dispute as to the location of the actual **Well of the Swearing**. The traditional site is at the bottom of the main street in the old town, but more recently archaeologists have suggested that it is the 40-metre (130-ft) well excavated at the site of Tel Be'er Sheva, some 6 km (4 miles) east of the modern city.

The **Ben Gurion University of the Negev**, founded here in 1969, is one of Israel's largest universities, with a student population of 10,000 studying courses in, among others, humanities, sciences, engineering and medicine. In this respect the university has transformed the town from a desert backwater into a modern community, with its own sinfonietta orchestra and

light opera group. Its contribution to the surrounding environment should not be overlooked. Impressively, the university is researching projects on water resource management and carrying out magnesium research and arid zones studies. The **Be'er Sheva Museum**, housed in a former mosque in the old town, has a good display of archaeological artefacts. The city has a youth hostel, hotels of all standards and several good restaurants, including ones specialising in Moroccan, Romanian and South American cuisine, which reflect the make-up of the population.

About a mile to the northeast, overlooking the city, is the **Khativat ha-Negev** Monument to the Palmach, which captured Be'er Sheva in the War of Independence. Designed by sculptor Dani Karavan, who spent five years on the project, its trenches, bunkers, pillboxes and tower (through which visitors are encouraged to climb and crawl) create a claustrophobic atmosphere evocative of a siege. The sinuous concrete edifice is a worthy commemoration of the bitter battle for the Negev between the Egyptian army and the fledgling Israeli forces backing the kibbutz outposts during the 1948 war.

South of the monument is Israel's only animal hospital, attached to the life sciences department of Ben Gurion University. It includes a camel clinic.

Southeast of the hospital, next to ancient Tel Be'er Sheva, is **Tel Sheva ❷**, a modern village built for the local Bedouin. It is the first of five Bedouin villages in the Negev gradually replacing the traditional tented camps of the nomads which, as a rule, are spread out over a large area. High-walled courtyards separate the houses, in an attempt to preserve as much privacy as possible.

The concept was developed by an Arab architect, and its logic seemed unassailable, but in fact the Bedouin were not keen on Tel Sheva, and subsequent

**BELOW:**
the futuristic library at Be'er Sheva's Ben Gurion University.

Map on page 312

developments have encouraged the former nomads to build their own homes. Israel's Bedouin claim large tracts of the desert over which they formerly grazed their herds, but the lands were never registered, and this has led to disputes with the government. In most cases the Bedouin have been given title to the land around their camps. Where the land has been appropriated by the government, as in the case of the **Nevatim Airforce Base** east of Be'er Sheva, monetary compensation has been awarded.

## The western Negev

West from Be'er Sheva the Negev is flat and dull, more suitable for settlement than for tourism. It is an area of cotton and potatoes as well as extensive wheat fields, irrigated by the run-off from the National Water Carrier, which ends in this area.

The first Negev kibbutzim were built in this region in the 1940s, and, after the peace treaty with Egypt, some of Israel's northern Sinai settlements were moved to Pit'hat Shalom (the Peace Region) next to the international border in 1982. East of these communities lies the **Eshkol National Park** (Ha-Bsor) ❸, 300 hectares (750 acres) of trees, lawns and playing fields with an amphitheatre, a swimming pool and a natural pond, surrounded by cat-tails and cane and stocked with fish.

The Western Negev road, which goes south from this region, is designated as a military area, as it is right on the Egyptian border, and travellers using it have to fill in forms provided by the military. Since the peace treaty with Egypt in 1978 it is not regarded as dangerous, but the army wants to know who is using it so that travellers are not stranded there after dark. The southern sector of the

*Most Bedouin children receive elementary education, and recently a Bedouin high school was built. The first Bedouin doctor to graduate in Israel, Yunis Abu-Rabia, is in charge of the region's health service.*

**BELOW:** camels quench their thirst.

road winds attractively through the Negev mountains, providing some spectacular views of Sinai to the west and the Negev to the east.

There is a road (number 222) from Eshkol to the junction at Mash'abei Sade, just past the Revivim Observation Point. From here, follow the road towards the Egyptian border and you will come to **Shivta** ❹, in the Korkha Valley, a Nabatean city later rebuilt by the Byzantines in the 5th century. An Arab tribe, the Nabateans dominated the Negev and Edom in the first centuries BC and AD. Although less accessible than Ovdat (*see page 319*), Shivta is still relatively well-preserved, with three churches, a wine press and several public areas still intact. There is also a direct route from Be'er Sheva to Shivta.

**Nitsana** ❺, 25 km (16 miles) further west at the intersection of the western highway, is one of three active border crossings to Egypt. The village also located at Nitsana – a desert outpost which now has a thriving seminar centre dedicated to desert flora and fauna – was founded in 1987 and lies just next to the border. It was here that the government issued a proposal for a new settlement to encourage some 50,000 or so of the bulging population to settle part of this vast uninhabited desert. Ben Gurion was firm in his belief that "unless we conquer… the desert… we cannot succeed in the tasks of immigration and re-settlement". Some 50 years on it seems that the call is finally being heeded – although the plan is still in its infancy.

To reach Eilat from Nitsana you can continue down the road which hugs the Sinai border, but there are two other main routes to the pleasure resort on the Red Sea. From Be'er Sheva the main highway leads down the eastern side of the Negev, through the **Ha-Arava**, and that is the one to take if your aim is simply reaching the sunny beaches. Alternatively, a narrow, beautiful, scenic road goes

**BELOW:** the ancient site of Mamshit.

right through the middle of the desert. The traveller may well feel that the Negev between Be'er Sheva and Eilat is a mythical badland dividing Israel from the Red Sea paradise to the south, but there is plenty to see on both routes.

Map on page 312

## The Arava

The eastern route takes you past the moshav of **Nevatim**, settled in the early 1950s by Jews from Cochin in southern India. Even within the kaleidoscope of the Israeli population these beautiful, dark-skinned people stand out as "more different" than others. In the past few years they have become famous for growing winter flowers, exported by air to Europe. This industry, which takes advantage of the mild desert climate, has been taken up by others and become a major Israeli export.

Further east, the development towns of **Yerukham** and **Dimona**, built in the mid-1950s, were settled primarily by immigrants from North Africa. Yerukham has a new park, 10 km (6 miles) south of the road, which should one day become a startling green patch in the arid grey-brown wasteland, but so far the dust tends to dominate the man-high trees. Nearby is an artificial lake, created by a dammed wadi, fed by the winter rains. A huge variety of birds migrate across the Mediterranean coast from Africa to Europe in the spring and return in the autumn; Israel is one of their favourite way-stations.

**Dimona** is home to the fierce harsh desert climate which many thought would prove too much for people to live and work in. The few original settlers have now blossomed into a town of 28,000. Although it's called the "Flower of the Desert", Dimona is known more for its nuclear plant and Black Hebrew community than for its flora. A small Indian Jewish community also resides here, and their delicatessens supply great Indian spices and poppadums.

Between Yerukham and Dimona, the dome of Israel's Atomic Research Station looms in the plain behind its numerous protective barbed-wire fences.

Just past Dimona is the site of **Mamshit ❻**, called Kurnab by the Arabs. A fine example of a Nabataean site of the 1st century AD, it contains the remains of two beautiful Byzantine churches and a network of ancient dams. Nearby is the **Camel Farm** of Mamshit, home to the original ships of the desert. It is still worth a visit even if this alternative mode of travel is not to your taste. Safaris, 4-wheel-drive tours, rappelling and hiking are among the other options.

South of the road is **Ha-Makhtesh Ha-Gadol (The Large Crater) ❼**, a spectacular geological fault. Further east, **Ha-Makhtesh Ha-Katan (The Small Crater)** is less extensive but more beautiful, with geological layers in some locations exposed like a rainbow cake. Their origin is unknown. One theory ascribes the Negev craters to volcanic activity; another suggests the fall of large meteors in the distant past.

The old road south – today a dirt-track – cuts through the desert south of the small crater, connecting with the Arava Valley via **Scorpions' Pass**. The most spectacular road in the southern desert, it plunges down a series of dizzying loops that follow each other with frightening suddenness. To the right

**BELOW:** an immigrant from Cochin works with winter flowers.

**BELOW:**
an observatory at Mitspe Ramon.

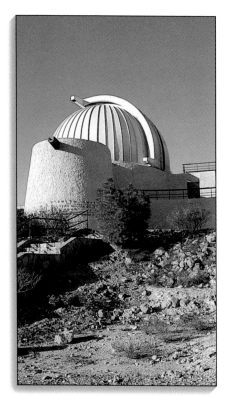

are the heights of the Negev, great slabs of primeval rock, slammed together. Below are the purple-grey lunar formations of the **Tsin Valley**, with the square-shaped hillock of **Ha-har** rising up from the valley floor. Be warned: the rusty metal drums that line the road have been unable to prevent accidents.

The main road from Mamshit reaches the Arava Valley south of the Dead Sea, at the Arava Junction, near the moshav farming village of **Neot ha-Kikar**. Situated in the salt marshes and utilising brackish water, it has become one of the most successful settlements in Israel, exporting a variety of winter vegetables to Europe. In the 1960s Neot ha-Kikar was settled by an eccentric group of desert lovers, who established a private company. As initial attempts at farming the area proved less than successful, they set up a desert touring company for trips by camel and jeep to the less accessible locations of the Negev. Those initial settlers eventually abandoned the village, but their company (still called Neot ha-Kikar) continues to thrive, with offices in Tel Aviv and Eilat.

Similar tours are run by the Society for the Protection of Nature in Israel, which, among its noteworthy spectrum of activities, offers a four-day camel tour starting at **Ein-Yahav**, a moshav some 80 km (50 miles) south.

The road through the Arava is bordered by the flint and limestone ridges of the Negev to the west; 19 km (12 miles) to the east tower the magnificent mountains of **Edom** in Jordan, which are capped with snow in winter. These mountains change colour during the day from pale mauve in the morning, to pink, red and deep purple in the evening, their canyons and gulleys etched in grey.

To the south lies the **Paran Plain**, the most spectacular of the Negev wadis, which runs into the Arava. The road twists through the timeless desert scenery before joining the southern stretch of the Arava road on its way to Eilat. You can continue on this route, taking in the Khai Bar Nature Reserve and Timna (*see page 321*), but we will return to Be'er Sheva and take the central desert road through the Negev Plateau.

## The Negev Plateau

The most interesting route south is also the oldest and least convenient, but it passes a number of interesting sites, the first of which is **Sde Boker** ❽, some 50 km (30 miles) south of Be'er Sheva. The kibbutz was the final home of David Ben Gurion, Israel's first prime minister, and his wife, Paula. Their simple, cream-coloured tombstones, which overlook the Wilderness of Tsin, form a place of pilgrimage for Israeli youth movements and foreign admirers. The old man is said to have selected his burial place, with its view of beige and mustard limestone hills, the flint rocks beyond, and the delicate mauve of Edom in the hazy distance.

The **Sde Boker College**, south of the kibbutz, is divided into three sections: the Institute for Arid Zone Research coordinates desert biology, agriculture and architecture; the Ben Gurion Institute houses the prime minister's papers and records, and the Centre of the Environment runs a field school and a high school with an emphasis on environmental studies.

South of the college is **Ein Ovdat**, a steep-sided canyon with freshwater pools fringed with lush vegetation. Rock badgers, gazelles and a wide variety of

Map on page 312

birds inhabit this oasis, where the water is remarkably cold even in the heat of summer. A swim can be refreshing, but the water is deep and sometimes it is difficult to climb out onto the slippery rocks. Lone hikers should not take the risk, and parties of visitors should take it in turns, leaving some out of the water to haul out their companions. There are paths up the sides of the cliffs, with iron rungs and railings in the difficult parts.

A few kilometres further south is **Ovdat** ❾, the site of the Negev's main Nabatean city, built in the 2nd century BC. Situated on a limestone hill above the surrounding desert, Ovdat was not only excavated but also partly reconstructed in the early 1950s. With its impressive buildings, burial caves, a kiln, workshop and two Byzantine churches, it is one of the most rewarding sites in the country; but what makes it fascinating is the reconstruction of Nabatean and Byzantine agriculture.

With their capital at Petra (today in the Kingdom of Jordan), the Nabateans' achievements in farming the desert are unsurpassed. Their technique was based on the run-off systems of irrigation. Little rain falls in this part of the desert, but when it does, it is not absorbed by the local loess soil; it cuts gulleys and wadis, running in torrents to the Mediterranean in the west and the Dead Sea and the Arava in the east. The run-off system collects this water in a network of fields and terraces, fed by dams, channels and slopes. Variations include gently sloped fields in which each tree has its own catchment area. A botanist, Michael Evenari, working with archaeologists and engineers, has reconstructed Ovdat and two other farms, growing a variety of crops without the help of piped water: fodder, wheat, onions, carrots, asparagus, artichokes, apricots, grapes, peaches, almonds, peanuts and pistachios are among them.

*Sculpture at Ovdat.*

**BELOW:** ruined villa at Ovdat.

What started as research into ancient agriculture has proved to be relevant to the modern era, as the system could provide valuable food crops in arid countries of the third world using only existing desert resources, thus preserving the delicate ecological balances. Indeed, although the ancient Nabateans managed to grow grapevines here 2,000 years ago, they didn't irrigate them with salt water. New scientific research using saline water has begun to reap rewards in the form of Cabernet Sauvignon and Sauvignon Blanc.

A half hour south of Ovdat is the development town of **Mitspe Ramon** , perched at an elevation of 1,000 metres (3,300 ft) along the northern edge of the **Makhtesh Ramon** – the largest of the three craters in the Negev (40 km/ 25 miles long and 12 km/7 miles wide). Despite its vast size, the crater comes into view quite suddenly: an awesome sight. Among the finds have been fossilised plants and preserved dinosaur footprints dating back 200 million years to the Triassic and Jurassic periods. Mitspe Ramon has an observatory, connected with Tel Aviv University, which takes full advantage of the dry desert air. In the Makhtesh Ramon a geological trail displays the melting-pot of minerals present in the area, evident from the patches of yellow, ochre, purple and green that tint the landscape.

From here the road snakes south, joining with the eastern route near the Jordanian border just before Ktura. The next stop is at **Kibbutz Yotvata**, with the fascinating **Khai Bar Nature Reserve** ⓫. At this unusual game park, conservationists have imported and bred a variety of animals mentioned in the Bible which had become extinct locally: wild asses, ostriches and numerous varieties of gazelle. A holiday village, with modest but comfortable accommodation, swimming pools and a mini-market, is on-site, as is the **Arava Visitors' Centre**

**TIP**

Kibbutz Yotvata produces some of the best dairy products in Israel. Try some at the cafeteria beside the petrol station.

**BELOW:** the giant Mushroom Rock.

with a museum and audio-visual display of the desert. **Ktura**, a kibbutz 16 km (10 miles) to the north, offers horse-riding.

**Timna** , 24 km (15 miles) further south, is the site of **King Solomon's Mines**, a little to the south of the modern copper mine. The ancient circular stone ovens for roasting the copper ore look simple enough, with stone channels to the collection vessels for the metal, but the air channels were skilfully angled to catch the prevailing north wind which comes down the Arava. The late archaeologist Nelson Glueck, who excavated the mines, called the ventilation system "an ancient example of automation".

The area surrounding the mines is being developed as a national park, with an artificial lake and a network of roads – including a fine scenic route in the northeast of the park to facilitate touring. Highlights include **King Solomon's Pillars**, a natural formation of Nubian sandstone, and the redoubtable **Mushroom Rock**, a granite rock shaped like a mushroom. The time-worn remains of a settlement, a fortress and two Egyptian sanctuaries used by the ancient mine-workers can also be seen. From here, it's a mere 30 km (18 miles) to Eilat and the Red Sea.

## Off the beaten track

Further into the desert lie the venerable walls of some 40-odd strongholds built by King Solomon to guard his route to Timna and his port of Etzion Geber. After the peace treaty with Egypt, 20 of these fortresses were partly excavated in a rescue operation mounted by the Department of Antiquities. The fortresses were destroyed shortly after King Solomon's death, and never rebuilt. It is advisable to visit such sites in the company of a trained guide. ❑

*Map on page 312*

*Nitsanei Sinai (Kadesh Barne'a), on the Sinai border, was the only one of Solomon's fortresses to be rebuilt.*

**BELOW:** King Solomon's Mines at Timna.

# EILAT

Map on page 312

*Eilat is a hedonistic playground, a birdwatcher's delight, and a jumping-off point for visits to Jordan to see the great Nabataean city of Petra, and to the Sinai in Egypt*

Remote from the rest of Israel, **Eilat ⓭** is searing hot and parched dry. The city's cultural diversions are negligible, and a geological fault runs through the town. There's neither casino nor racetrack nor concert hall.

Nevertheless, Eilat is one of Israel's most popular tourist resorts. Holiday-makers migrate instinctively, like tens of thousands of lemmings, to its sun-burnt shores and soothing seas. What's more, a good percentage of them are Israelis who know the best places in the country for spending a holiday.

Some Israelis going to Eilat claim they're vacationing *hutz l'aretz* (abroad). Others simply say they're off to *sof olam* – the end of the world. And anyone who drives from the populated central part of Israel across that "Great Bald Spot" known as the Negev Desert might be inclined to agree with them.

Eilat is Israel's southernmost community. It is the state's flipper-hold on the Red Sea. It is also a mecca (if such a word can be used in Israel) for snorkellers, scuba-divers, windsurfers, water-skiers, swimmers, sailors, sandcastle builders, sun-worshippers, tropical-fish fanatics and birdwatchers.

Eilat's single significant industry lies in assisting visitors to do nothing productive. It is a sensual city which caters for people who like magnificent natural beauty, lazy afternoons, spicy food and cold beer.

**PRECEDING PAGES:** Eilat's Dolphinarium. **LEFT:** diving off the Coral Reef. **BELOW:** the North Beach.

## First city

Eilatis whimsically call their town Israel's "First City", because it was the first piece of land in what is now Israel to be occupied by the Children of Israel after the Exodus from Egypt (Deuteronomy 2, 8). But Moses was only a tourist; he moved north to find milk and honey soon afterwards.

A few centuries later King Solomon built a port here and called it Etzion Geber. With the help of his friend King Hiram of Phoenicia, he sent a fleet of ships east to the land of Ophir, "and fetched from thence gold, four hundred and twenty talents, and brought it to King Solomon" (I Kings 9, 26). Since there were about 3,000 shekels to the talent, and about a half-ounce to the shekel, the sailors must have lugged some 20 tonnes of gold back to Jerusalem.

Eilat changed hands many times during the following centuries. The Edomites grabbed it for a while, and then King Uzziah took it back for the Israelites. The Syrians later wrested it away from him. A succession of conquerors marched through – Nabateans, Greeks, Romans, Mamelukes, Crusaders, Ottoman Turks and others. The Crusaders left behind their 12th-century fortress at Coral Island, just south of Taba. The celebrated Colonel T. E. Lawrence, popularly known as Lawrence of Arabia, trekked through here after his conquest of Aqaba across the bay.

*Eilat's busy port.*

The most recent army to conquer Eilat was the Israel Defence Forces, which swooped down on this exotic pearl during Operation Uvda in March 1949 and scared the daylights out of several sleepy lizards and a tortoise living in the ruins of Umm Rashrash, an otherwise uninhabited mudbrick "police station" which stood all alone in what is now the centre of the town. Although the United Nations had allocated Eilat to Israel in its partition plan, the capture of this corner of the Promised Land in the War of Independence was so hastily organised that Israeli troops arrived without a flag to proclaim it as part of their new state. So, a soldier with artistic talent was issued a bed sheet and a bottle of blue ink with which to produce an Israeli flag of appropriate dimension and design.

## Development town

The new flag didn't fly over very much, but the Israeli authorities knew that Eilat was located in a highly strategic position, and rapid steps were taken to create a town. It was strategic because it provided Israel's only access to the Indian and Pacific Oceans, and trade with Asia, East Africa, Australia and the islands, including vital oil supplies from pre-revolutionary Iran. Holding on to Eilat also meant a break in land continuity between Egypt and Jordan, thus offering a military advantage to the defence forces.

In the rush to create a city on the Red Sea, Eilat's builders didn't invest much in fine architecture. Instead, they went for fast, simple, sturdy construction of apartments to house immigrants trickling in from the horrors of Nazi-occupied Europe, and the expulsions by Arab states such as Iraq and Yemen. Visitors to Eilat can see some of the older 1950s apartment buildings still standing like concrete bastions on the hillside. They're still quite serviceable and are occupied

**BELOW:** Eilat, the "First City".

by Eilati families who have affectionate nicknames for them, such as "Sing Sing" and "La Bastille".

As the city expanded, other neighbourhoods grew further up the slopes of the Eilat Mountains. Improved architecture didn't spare them from satirical nicknames. One neighbourhood built about a kilometre up a steep hill west of the centre of town is locally know as the "Onesh" district. In Hebrew, *onesh* means "punishment", and anybody who walks this distance from the centre of town on a hot day will appreciate the appropriateness of this sobriquet. In recent years, prosperity has produced colonies of villas around the town, unleashing a new generation of nicknames which are still to stand the test of time.

Map on page 312

## Crisis and boom

Egypt's President Gamal Abdel Nasser also realised the strategic value of Eilat and its potential as a multi-million-dollar tourist playground. He planned to make Eilat one of his first conquests in the 1967 war.

In May of that year he imposed a blockade on Eilat and shut down its shipping – including the vital oil supplies from Iran. Next, he ordered the UN peacekeeping forces out of Sinai and moved his own army into the mountains north-west of Eilat, within clear view of Jordan. With one quick push he could have cut off Eilat, linked up with the Jordanian Arab Legion and created a solid, integrated southern front against Israel. Eilat was in an extremely vulnerable position for a few days, until the Israeli pre-emptive strike against Egyptian air fields deprived Nasser of the vital air cover his troops would need. The following six days witnessed Israel's lightning conquest of Sinai, and the removal of military threats against Eilat.

Shortly after the Six Day War, terrorist infiltration from Jordanian territory near Eilat caused apprehension. There were several incidents, and people were killed. Eilat remained unattractive for tourism, immigration and development until the charismatic Moshe Dayan flew there to make a speech intended for the ears of Jordan's King Hussein. Further infiltration of terrorists from Jordan, he said, would indicate to Israel that the Jordanian armed forces were incapable of maintaining a secure border. If this became the case, he added, the Israel Defence Forces would have to do the job for them by entering Jordanian territory – including the port city of Aqaba – to stem the incursions.

The Jordanian monarch got the message, and border security improved immediately. Assured of security, Eilat blossomed. The past decade has catapulted the city into success, with an ever-expanding tourist business, a population of close to 50,000 and a busy downtown area, with a modern art museum, a sheltered lagoon and marina, and a shorefront lined with hotels.

Most of the tourists are Israelis, who drive the four-hour trans-desert trek from Jerusalem and Tel Aviv for their holidays. But many others, especially in winter, are foreigners who take charter flights from Europe directly to Eilat. Arkia, Israel's domestic airline, also operates several flights a day from here to other cities in Israel, and the Sinai.

## Plenty of rocks

An adage grew up among Eilatis: "If we could export rocks, we'd all be millionaires." The key to Eilat's tourism has been to twist the adage to bring the foreigners to the rocks. Nearly all of these rocks are pre-Cambrian, formed by the forces of the Earth in the epochs before the beginning of life on the planet.

**TIP**

Eilat is a free-trade zone, which means it has no sales tax. As a result, many items are cheaper than elsewhere in the country.

**BELOW:** windsurfing at dusk.
**RIGHT:** camping out at Taba.

Map on page 312

Aeons ago they covered the land facing the north, where the ancient Tethys Sea flowed over what is now the state of Israel. To the south extended the primordial megacontinent of Gondwanaland. Gondwanaland eventually drifted apart to form India, Africa, South America, Australia and Antarctica, and the bed of the Tethys Sea was pushed up to form the bedrock of Israel.

Geologists are forever pottering about the Eilat Mountains, picking at chunks of granite, gneiss, quartz-porphyry and diabase. In some places they are after an attractive bluish-green malachite which merchants in town call Eilat Stone, a type of copper ore which can be shaped and given a high polish. In fact, this stone has been used in jewellery-making in the region for thousands of years, and is still very evident in many Eilat tourist shops.

For those who like to see their rocks in the rough, there are the Eilat Mountains, spectacular ascents of colourful stone. In some areas it appears as if their volcanic genesis was fast-frozen, and their flowing magmas interrupted in full flood. Erosion here has taken some bizarre and incredibly beautiful courses. In places it is possible to walk through narrow canyons with walls towering hundreds of metres vertically, but just a metre or two apart. The harsh desert wind has carved monumental pillars among the mountains, particularly in the sandstone regions, such as the **Pillars of Amram** (named after the father of Moses), some 9 km (5 miles) north of Eilat and 3 km (2 miles) west of the main highway. The site is laced with lovely ravines and clusters of imposing natural columns.

About 4 km (2½ miles) south of Eilat, along the coastal highway leading to Sinai, is the entry to **Solomon's Canyon**, a popular hiking area. A dusty granite quarry at the mouth of the canyon tends to obscure the formations lying

**LEFT:** a sun-worshipper.
**BELOW:** camels wait by the marina.

beyond, but those following the path markers in the **Harei Eilat Nature Reserve**  will be treated to an exotic geological adventure. As you enter the canyon, **Ha-Metsuda** (The Stronghold) rises to the left. This great rock was vital to Eilat's defences against invasion from the Sinai coast. The path then leads another 16 km (10 miles) up into the mountains, twisting and turning along the route of the canyon. Hikers pass first beneath **Har Yehoshafat**, then **Har Shlomo**, and then **Har Uziya**, each of which towers more than 700 metres (2,300 ft) overhead.

Eventually the trail crosses the paved **Moon Valley Highway** which leads into central Sinai. Across the highway, the trail continues on to the spectacular cliffs and oasis at **Ein Netafim** (the Spring of the Drops), which trickles across a barren rock into a picturesque pool at the foot of an imposing cliff. Further along is **Red Canyon**, another impressive natural wonder of erosion-sculpted sandstone.

*Welcome to the Dolphinarium.*

## Seaside sojourning

Beaches are a year-round attraction in Eilat. Even in the summer, when temperatures can range well above baking at 40°C/105°F, the waters of the Red Sea are cool and soothing. Midwinter swimming, however, is usually left to the Europeans and Americans, while native Eilatis stare from the shore, bundled up in parkas to dispel the wintry gusts, which usually hover at around 15°C (roughly 60°F).

**BELOW:** an underwater world.

Eilat has five distinct and attractive beaches, spanning 11 km (7 miles), ranging from fine sand to gravel. **North Beach**, close to the centre of the town, is the local hangout for sun-worshippers. The bay is protected, the swimming is easy, and dozens of hotels line the shore. The eastern end of North Beach also has inexpensive bungalows and even camping facilities for those on a tight budget.

Further south is the **Dolphin Reef** (open daily 9am–5pm; admission charge), a private beach where you can swim with the dolphins. If you have a licence you can hire diving equipment and dive with them too. There are qualified guides to accompany divers. The dolphins are very friendly – so much so that they are sometimes used in therapeutic programmes for children with disabilities.

A little further down the coast, past the navy station and port facilities, is **Ha-Almogim Nature Reserve**. This reserve includes a fine sandy beach and a truly spectacular coral reef. Here visitors can rent diving masks, snorkels and flippers from the reserve's office and swim along any of three marked routes which lead over different parts of the coral reef. Special markers set into the reef itself identify different types of coral and plants growing there, as well as some of the more common fish.

The reserve also has changing rooms, showers, snack and souvenir stands and other tourist amenities. But tourist-friendly though it may be, this is a monitored nature reserve. Swimmers must be very careful not to bruise any of the coral. Removal of any pieces of coral is taken very seriously indeed and will result in the culprit paying a visit to the local judge.

Further south is the **Coral World Underwater Observatory** (open Sun–Thur 8.30am–5pm, Fri 8.30am–3pm; admission charge), an unusual commercial aquarium and undersea observatory. Here the visitor walks out on a long pier to the observatory building, which is set into the reef itself. Descending the spiral staircase within the observatory, one emerges into a circular room with windows facing out into the coral reef at a depth of 5 metres (16 ft). All sorts of fish swim freely about outside the window, and the many colours and shapes of the living reef are astonishing sights which should not be missed. There is also a yellow submarine, the *Jacqueline*, which will take you on one-hour underwater trips. Nothing quite as lovely has been seen since Captain Nemo retired the *Nautilus*.

Those who abjure actually going into the water might be more inclined to ride on it instead. A large marina and lagoon at North Beach is the mooring for many boats and yachts, from expensive charter schooners to more affordable windsurfing craft. There are also several glass-bottomed boats for reef-viewing, and a number of water-skiing speedboats available for charter. Licensed diving clubs which will rent diving equipment and offer diving courses include Lucky Divers, Red Sea Divers, and Eilat Aqua Sport.

## For the birds

Birdwatching too, is a year-round attraction in Eilat, and several dozen species of resident bird can be found in the mountains and deserts, by the seashore and among the fields of neighbouring **Kibbutz Eilot**. The spring migration season, however, is particularly dazzling and is the best time to be here. Millions upon millions of migratory birds fly across the Eilat region on their northward journeys from warm wintering havens in Africa to their breeding grounds scattered

Map on page 312

**TIP**

You can learn to dive while in Eilat: several schools advertise prominently in the town.

**BELOW:** two ways of hitting the water.

across Eurasia. Great waves of eagles and falcons fill the sky – and highly respected ornithologists keep producing reports giving strangely precise figures such as 19,288 steppe eagles, 26,770 black kites and 225,952 honey buzzards in the course of a single migration season.

Sharp-eyed birdwatchers will also pick out booted eagles, snake eagles, lesser spotted eagles, imperial eagles, marsh harriers, sparrowhawks and osprey. And then come the pelicans and storks in their tens of thousands.

The Nature Reserves Authority has established special hiking trails and observation hides in the region. A dedicated information centre is maintained by the **Nature Reserves Authority** in the **King Solomon Hotel** to provide information for birdwatching, registration for tours, rental of field glasses, sale of literature and lectures and nature films about the region.

*The King Solomon Hotel.*

For those looking for a leisurely holiday there are scores of restaurants ranging from inexpensive pizza parlours and *felafel* stands, through reasonably-priced places selling very good seafood, to high-priced haute cuisine in the Eilat Centre, the New Tourist Centre and the Hotel District. Several hotels also have nightclubs, discos and other entertainments. The **Red Sea Jazz Festival** has become an annual summer fixture, drawing thousands of jazz fans to several nights of live entertainment by local acts and international stars.

## Jordan's rose-red city

In the wake of the Middle East peace process Eilat has become a popular base for visits to Sinai in Egypt and Petra in Jordan. The region is marketed as a "Middle Eastern French Riviera" and its region's tourist industry is flourishing.

**BELOW:** the rosy facades at Petra.

The **Arava Crossing** to Jordan, northeast of Eilat, has offered access to the

**Maps: pp 312 and 333**

Hashemite Kingdom since the peace accord was signed with Israel in 1994. The frontier can be reached along a road running eastwards off the main Arava highway several kilometres north of Eilat, not far from Kibbutz Eilot. The Arava Checkpoint is open Sun–Thur 6.30am–10pm and Fri–Sat 8am–8pm. It is closed on Yom Kippur and Id el Fitr. Passport holders can enter Jordan without a visa upon payment of a small charge. It is not yet possible to take vehicles from Israel into Jordan. There is no public transport (only taxis) between Eilat and the border crossing.

The town of **Aqaba** ⓯ is unexceptional. Sitting alongside Eilat on the northern shore of the Red Sea, Aqaba is Jordan's only outlet to the sea and therefore a busy port. The tourist infrastructure here is much less significant than in Eilat, making the beaches quieter. The name Aqaba was given to the town in the 14th century by the Mamelukes, and it was the first town captured from the Turks in 1917 by the Arab forces led by T. E. Lawrence – Lawrence of Arabia.

By far the most popular excursion into Jordan involves travelling northwards some 120 km (75 miles) to the fabulous Nabatean city of **Petra** ⓰. Reached through a narrow canyon, Petra is best known for the dramatic tomb and temple facades carved into the Nubian sandstone mountains. The pink, red and purple-hued mountain walls would be exquisite enough, but in addition there are the romance and history of the location, which lay forgotten for nearly 2,000 years until "rediscovered" by the Swiss explorer Ludwig Burckhardt in 1812.

*In 1845 Petra was immortalised in a poem by the English cleric John W. Burgon, in which he described it as "a rose-red city, half as old as time".*

## Visiting the Sinai

The Sinai was captured by Israeli forces in 1967 and returned to Egypt in 1982 under the Camp David peace treaty. It remains a popular playground for Israelis

**BELOW:** St Catherine's Monastery, in the Sinai.

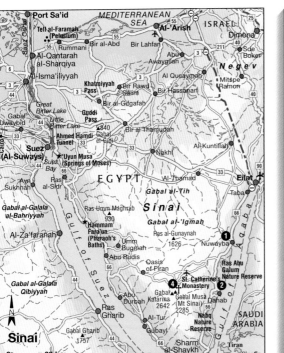

Map on page 333

who built up a tourist infrastructure along the Red Sea coast during the years when they held the territory. Since then the Egyptians have greatly expanded the region's tourist facilities, but vast stretches of the Sinai remain gloriously isolated. It is more rugged and spectacular than the Negev, and everything here is on a grander scale.

The Sinai can be reached from the **Taba Border Crossing**, 10 km (6 miles) south of Eilat. The Taba enclave itself, which has a Hilton Hotel with a casino, is technically in Egyptian territory, but is open to all who can produce valid passports. The crossing into the Sinai is open 24 hours a day, seven days a week, closing only for the Jewish festival of Yom Kippur and the Muslim festival of Id el Fitr. Visas for a two-week stay in the Sinai peninsula only are given at the frontier itself for a small fee, but people wishing to visit the rest of Egypt must obtain a visa from an Egyptian consulate in Eilat or elsewhere. Bus number 15 will take you to the border, and there are buses and taxis on the Egyptian side running through Sinai and on to Cairo. Passenger cars can be taken into the Sinai for a modest fee.

There are three major resorts along the Sinai's Red Sea coast: **Nuwayba ❶**, 60 km (38 miles) south of Eilat, **Dahab ❷**, 135 km (85 miles) south of Eilat, and **Sharm al-Shaykh ❸**, 225 km (140 miles) south of Eilat. You can stop en route to eat fresh fish in one of the coastal villages. Desert safaris to nearby wadis and oases are offered from all these locations, but an even bigger attraction than the stunning desert landscapes is the marine life, and especially the coral reefs.

The Sinai is considered one of the world's premier locations for divers. Generally speaking the coral formations are more remarkable to the south, with Sharm al-Shaykh being the favourite choice of seasoned divers. Conservationists are inceasingly concerned about the harm caused to coral at Ras Mohammed National Park; this is mainly due to over-harvesting and damage from ships' anchors, but also to illicit souvenir-hunting.

### St Catherine's and the burning bush

The other major attraction of Sinai is **St Catherine's Monastery ❹** (open daily 9.30am–noon; closed public holidays). reached from a road running southwest for 35 km (21 miles) from a point midway between Nuwayba and Dahab. Built by funding from the Byzantine ruler Justinian in the 6th century, on a site where some believe the burning bush spoke to Moses, the monastery is today home to Greek Orthodox monks. It has a magnificent basilica and a splendid fresco depicting the transfiguration of Christ. The tiny Chapel of the Burning Bush stands on the spot where the biblical event is said to have taken place.

The nearby summit at an altitude of 2,640 metres (8,660 ft) offers a breathtaking view of the desert.

All-inclusive tours to both Sinai and Petra involving overnight stays are available from the many travel agents in Eilat. As the price and content of these tours vary quite a lot, it is worth shopping around for the best value. ❑

**BELOW:** rugs for sale in the Sinai.
**RIGHT:** gliding above the gulf.

# INSIGHT GUIDES
# Travel Tips

*Insight Guides* portray destinations in depth, providing the complete picture and the top photography

*Insight Pocket Guides* focus on the best choices for places to see and things to do and include large fold-out maps

*Insight Compact Guides'* portability makes them the perfect books to carry with you for on-the-spot reference

# Three types of guide for all types of travel

**INSIGHT GUIDES** Different people need different kinds of information. Some want *background information* to help them prepare for the trip. Others seek *personal recommendations* from someone who knows the destination well. And others look for *compactly presented data* for on-the-spot reference. With three carefully designed series, Insight Guides offer readers the perfect choice. Insight Guides will turn your visit into an experience.

**The world's largest collection of visual travel guides**

# CONTENTS

# Getting Acquainted

## The Place

**Area:** 21,000 sq. km (8,110 sq. miles) including administered territories and Palestinian autonomous zones.
**Capital:** Jerusalem
**Highest mountain:** Mount Hermon (2,766 metres/3,962 ft)
**Longest river:** River Jordan (264 km/ 165 miles)
**Population:** 6.05 million: Jerusalem 620,000; Greater Tel Aviv 2,000,000; Greater Haifa 600,000.
**Languages:** Hebrew and Arabic
**Religion:** 80 percent Jewish, 15 percent Muslim, 5 percent Christian and Druze
**Time zone:** GMT plus 2 hours
**Currency:** New Israeli shekel
**Weights & measures:** Metric
**Electricity:** 220 volts AC, single phase, 50 cycles
**National anthem:** *Ha-Tikva* (The Hope)
**National emblem:** The Star of David
**International dialling code:** 00 972 (2 Jerusalem; 3 Tel Aviv; 4 Haifa; 6 Galilee; 7 Eilat and the South)

## Climate

Israeli summers are long (lasting from April to October), hot and virtually rainless. During these months Tel Aviv and the coast are humid, while the atmosphere in hill towns such as Jerusalem is drier and cooler. The winter season (from November to March) is generally mild, but quite cold in hilly areas. Spells of rain are interspersed with brilliant sunshine. During the winter the Tiberias area on the Sea of Galilee, the Dead Sea and Eilat (all searingly hot in summer) have ideal warm, sunny weather.

The weather in Israel allows for year-round bathing: from April to October along the Mediterranean coast and around the Sea of Galilee; and throughout the year, though especially enjoyable in winter, along the Dead Sea shore and the Gulf of Eilat.

The best time to visit is early spring, when the hillsides are ablaze with flowers and the weather is still mild. Late autumn is also very pleasant, while Eilat and the Dead Sea are best appreciated in the winter. The hot summers are strictly for those who enjoy high temperatures and know how to handle the heat (i.e. drink lots of liquid, use sunscreen, move slowly and stay in the shade).

## Mean Temperatures

Minimum–Maximum

|  | Jan | April | July | Oct |
|---|---|---|---|---|
| **Jerusalem** | | | | |
| °C | 6–11 | 12–21 | 19–29 | 16–26 |
| °F | 43–53 | 53–69 | 66–84 | 60–78 |
| **Tel Aviv** | | | | |
| °C | 9–18 | 12–22 | 21–30 | 15–29 |
| °F | 49–65 | 54–72 | 70–86 | 59–84 |
| **Haifa** | | | | |
| °C | 8–17 | 13–26 | 20–30 | 16–27 |
| °F | 46–63 | 55–78 | 68–86 | 60–81 |
| **Tiberias** | | | | |
| °C | 9–18 | 13–27 | 23–37 | 19–32 |
| °F | 48–65 | 56–80 | 73–98 | 65–89 |
| **Eilat** | | | | |
| °C | 10–21 | 17–31 | 25–40 | 20–33 |
| °F | 49–70 | 63–87 | 78–103 | 69–92 |

## Annual Rainfall

Jerusalem and Tel Aviv: 550mm (22 inches)
Galilee: 650mm (26 inches)
Eilat: 20mm (0.79 inches)
All rain falls between October and April, with most of it concentrated in December, January and February.

## The Economy

Israel's biggest exports are polished diamonds, high-tech and electronics equipment, fruit and vegetables, petrochemicals and minerals from the Dead Sea. Exports amount to over $30 billion a year. In addition, Israel receives nearly $2 billion a year from tourism, a further $2 billion from donation by World Jewry and other supporters of Israel, and over $3 billion from US aid. Israelis also receive around $500 million a year from Germany in compensation for Nazi atrocities.

Imports comprise mainly manufactured goods (from cars to compact discs) as well as oil, coal and raw diamonds. In the early 1990s the gross domestic product rose by about 6 percent a year, while inflation averaged 10 percent. In recent years growth has risen to 2 percent a year and inflation to 7 percent, but unemployment has climbed by 9 percent.

## The Government

Israel is a democracy with a 120-member single chamber Knesset (parliament) elected every four years by all citizens aged 18 and over. Seats are allocated by proportional representation. In 1996 the prime minister was elected directly by the voters for the first time, but must still command a majority in the Knesset. The president, elected every five years by a secret ballot of Knesset members, is a titular head of state, rather like the British monarch. Israel has no formal constitution, but the Supreme Court has the power to interpret Knesset legislation.

## David Ben Gurion

Israel's first prime minister, when it became an independent state in 1948, was David Ben Gurion, leader of the socialist Mapai Party. He was widely respected, and his memory is honoured in street names throughout the country, as well as by Ben Gurion Airport and the Ben Gurion University of the Negev in Be'er Sheva.

# Planning the Trip

## What to Bring

Dress in Israel is informal by Western standards. Few people wear jackets and ties in the summer except for business occasions. However, even in the summer Jerusalem can get quite cool in the evenings. Be sure to bring some conservative clothes for visiting religious sites.

Suggested packing lists might include the following:

**Summer** (April to October): slacks, shorts and open-necked shirts for men; plenty of light cotton daytime dresses and a slightly smarter dress for more formal occasions for women; light shoes, sandals and more solid shoes for touring; sunglasses, hat, swimsuit and beachwear; a light coat, jacket or sweater for cool evenings in the hills.

**Winter** (November to March): warm coat, sweaters, raincoat and hat, walking shoes, overshoes; shirts, slacks, sports jacket; woollen or heavy suit, blouses, skirts and slacks, long dress or evening skirt for women; lighter clothing and swimsuit for Eilat and the Dead Sea coast.

If you forget anything, you will find that the shops in Israel have high-quality clothes for all occasions.

Everything is available in Israel, but the cost of living is high, roughly 10 to 20 percent more expensive than in Western Europe, so it is advisable to bring films and other holiday necessities with you.

**Note:** the sun's rays are extremely powerful in Israel even in the winter so bring a broad-brimmed hat, lots of sunscreen and a water canteen.

## Visas & Passports

Tourists are required to hold passports valid for Israel. Stateless persons require a valid travel document with a return visa to the country of issue.

Citizens of the USA, Canada, the European Union, Australia and New Zealand do not need a visa to enter Israel, only a valid passport.

## Landing-for-the-Day

If you visit Israel on a cruise ship you will be given a Landing-for-the-Day card, which permits you to remain in the country for as long as your ship is in port, and you need not apply for a visitor's visa.

This applies only to people wishing to enter Israel for travel purposes.

### Visa Extensions

Those entering Israel on vacation can only stay for three months and are not allowed to work for money. Anyone wishing to enter the country for work, study or permanent settlement must apply for the appropriate visa at an Israeli Diplomatic or Consular Mission before leaving their own country. Due to a rise in illegal workers in Israel, even visitors from North America and Western Europe may be refused entry if they do not have return tickets, sufficient funds for their stay or an Israeli citizen to vouch for them.

### Entry & Exit Formalities

All visitors to Israel, including diplomats, are required to fill in an entry form, AL-17, upon arrival. Visitors who intend continuing to Arab or Muslim countries (except Egypt and Jordan) after their visit to Israel should ask the frontier control officer to put the entry stamp on this form instead of in their passports, as they may subsequently be refused entry into countries hostile towards Israel if an Israeli stamp appears on the passport itself.

### Extensions of Stay

Tourists who wish to stay in the country for longer than three months must obtain an extension of stay. This applies also to citizens of those countries which are exempt from entry visas, and generally requires the stamping of your passport. The extension may be obtained through any district office of the Ministry of Interior.

The main offices are located at:
**Jerusalem**, General Building, Shlomtsiyou ha-Malka, tel: (02) 6290222.
**Tel Aviv**, Shalom Meyer Tower, Visa Department, 9 Akhad ha'am, tel: (03) 5193333.
**Haifa**, Government Building (opposite Municipality), 11 Hassan Shukri, tel: (04) 8616222.

## Customs

Every adult tourist may bring into the country, without payment of duty, the following articles, provided that they are for personal use: eau de Cologne or perfume not exceeding 0.2 litres (0.44 pint), wine up to 2 litres and other alcoholic drinks not exceeding 1 litre; tobacco or cigars not exceeding 250 grams or 250 cigarettes; gifts up to US$200 (about £350) in value, including assorted foodstuffs not exceeding 3 kg (6½ lb), on condition that no single type of food exceeds 1 kg (2¼ lb).

Gift parcels sent unaccompanied – by post or by any other means – are liable to full import duties and Value Added Tax.

Portable, expensive electronic items such as cameras, video cameras and lap-top computers may be taken into the country duty-free on condition that they are taken out on departure. These are meant to be for your use in Israel. You may have trouble explaining why you need to use a fax machine or VCR, and there are stiff fines (usually equal to the value of the item) for those attempting to smuggle such goods into Israel. The red–green customs clearance system is in operation at Ben Gurion

Airport. Tourists bringing in the goods mentioned above may choose the Green Channel and leave the airport. Tourists bringing in other goods, even if they are exempt from duty, must use the Red Channel.

The following articles are subject to declaration and deposits of duties and taxes, and the Red Channel must be taken: professional instruments (which can be held in the hand during operation) up to a value of $1,650; boat (rowing, sailing or motor) and a caravan trailer; scuba-diving equipment, portable and appreciably used; records in reasonable quantities.

### Customs Deposits

The customs authorities are entitled to demand deposits or guarantees on any article brought in by a tourist or sent separately. This is usually enforced only for very expensive professional equipment or other costly items. The guarantees or deposits are returned to tourists when they leave the country and take the articles out with them. Since the formalities take some time, it is advisable to make all arrangements a day or two before departure, and preferably at the port of entry of the goods, so that the return of the guarantee can be carried out more conveniently.

For further information contact: The Department of Customs and Excise, 32 Agron, POB 320, 91000 Jerusalem, tel: (02) 6703333.

## Health

There are no vaccination requirements for tourists entering Israel except if they are arriving from infected areas. By far the biggest health problem affecting visitors stems from a lack of respect for the sun. Sunburn and sunstroke afflict bathers, while dehydration plagues those who over-exert themselves sightseeing. Tourists should acclimatise gradually, apply suntan lotions liberally, keep indoors or in the shade between 10am and 4pm in the late spring, summer and early autumn, and wear light, comfortable clothes that cover legs and arms,

and a hat and sunglasses.

Most importantly of all, it is vital to drink continually even if you do not feel thirsty. Research has shown that the average person who is exerting him or herself in the heat of the day during an Israeli summer needs to drink 1 litre (over 2 pints) every hour to replace the body liquids lost through sweat.

The first symptoms of dehydration are tiredness, headache and lack of appetite. Advanced dehydration can express itself in unpleasant symptoms, from migraines and fever to diarrhoea and vomiting. Medication will not help. Recovery will come about through rest and sipping water, possibly with some salt added, though it is probably best to consult a doctor to ensure that the problem really is dehydration.

Upset stomachs are also common. Here, too, rest and a diet of water are the best medicine. Tap water is as drinkable as anywhere in the developed world, though mineral waters are available everywhere. The country has a sophisticated but expensive medical infrastructure, so health insurance is a must.

### Aids

The number of cases of Aids in Israel is considerably lower than in the countries of Western Europe, but is nevertheless on the increase. The usual precautions should be taken. The Ministry of the Interior requires all visitors seeking to extend their stay beyond three months to take an Aids test.

## Money

Tourists may bring an unlimited amount of foreign currency into Israel, whether in cash, travellers' cheques, letters of credit or State of Israel Bonds. They may also bring in an unlimited amount of Israeli shekels. They are not required to declare, upon arrival, the amount of foreign currency in their possession, and currency exchanges are not recorded. It is also possible to convert excess shekels back into foreign currency.

### Local Currency

The currency is the New Israeli shekel (NIS), which officially succeeded the old Israeli shekel in 1985. The shekel is divided into 100 agorot. Bills are issued in four denominations: 10 NIS (orange with a portrait of former Prime Minister Golda Meir – but this note has now virtually faded out in favour of a coin), 20 NIS (grey with a portrait of former Prime Minister Moshe Sharett), 50 NIS (purple with a portrait of Nobel Prize-winner Shmuel Agnon), 100 NIS (grey with a portrait of former President Yitzhak Ben Zvi), 200 NIS (reddish-brown with a portrait of former President Zalman Shazar). Change comes in coins of 5 agorot, 10 agorot, ½ shekel, 1 shekel, 5 shekels and 10 shekels.

Exchange rates are the same in all banks and *bureaux de change*. The NIS is stable and floats freely against the world's major currencies, with a revised exchange rate each day according to supply and demand. Vendors are prepared to accept the world's better-known currencies but offer inferior exchange rates.

## CREDIT CARDS & CHEQUES

Visa, MasterCard/Euro Card, American Express and Diners' Club are honoured virtually everywhere. The cash machines outside almost every Israeli bank will dispense money against these cards (so remember your personal identification number); this can save waiting around in crowded banks. Travellers' cheques and Eurocheques are widely accepted,

## Lost & Stolen Cards

Should your credit card get lost or stolen while you are in Israel, telephone one of the following numbers immediately:
**American Express,** tel: (03) 5242211.
**Visa & Diners' Club,** tel: (03) 5723572.
**EuroCard/MasterCard,** tel: (03) 5764444.

though banks take a commission on each cheque so it is cheaper to bring them in higher denominations.

## Useful Addresses and Information

### Tourist Information Abroad

**Canada:** Suite 700, 180 Bloor Street West, Toronto, Ontario, tel: 416-964-3784.
**United States:** 350 Fifth Avenue, 19th Floor, New York, tel: (212) 5600650.
**United Kingdom:** 18a Oxford Street London WIN 9DJ, tel 0171 299–1111, fax: 0171 299–1112.

## Getting There

### BY AIR

Ben Gurion International Airport is situated in Lod (Lydda), near the Mediterranean coast, 20 km (12 miles) southeast of Tel Aviv, 50 km (30 miles) west of Jerusalem and 110 km (68 miles) southeast of Haifa, and is the main hub for international air traffic. Its facilities include a Government Tourist Office, open around the clock, providing information and helping to arrange accommodation, tel: (03) 9711485. The airport also has a bank and post office, both open 24 hours except for holidays and the Sabbath (*Shabbat*), plus a cafeteria, shopping area and First Aid post. The El Al Lost & Found department, also open 24 hours, can be reached at tel: (03) 9712541. Airport arrivals information in English on tel: (03) 9723344.

About 40 percent of the international flights in and out of Ben Gurion International Airport are operated by the government-owned El Al Israel Airlines, which carries over 2 million passengers a year.

Other major airlines with regular flights to Ben Gurion International Airport include Air France, Alitalia, Austrian Airlines, British Airways, Delta, Iberia, KLM, Lufthansa, Sabena, SAS, South African Airways, and Swissair.

There are also regular charter flights to Ben Gurion International Airport by El Al, by Arkia, another

Israeli carrier, and by overseas companies including Monarch and Tower.

### BY SEA

The main ports are Haifa and Ashdod. The Stability Line and Sol Line offer sailings from Greece and Cyprus to Haifa port, and many Mediterranean cruises include Israel in their itineraries. Official ports of entry for foreign yachts and boats, in addition to these, include Eilat and the Tel Aviv Marina.

### BY ROAD

#### From Jordan

Following the signing of a peace agreement between Israel and Jordan in 1994, communications between the two countries have improved considerably (Israel now recognises Jordanian stamps in passports and visas, and vice versa). Visitors now have several border crossings to choose from: the Allenby Bridge, the Jordan River Crossing (near Beit She'an) and the Arava Checkpoint (between Eilat and Aqaba).
**Allenby Bridge**, near Jericho, some

## Checking Advice

Things change rapidly in Israel, and it is advisable to check the advice given here before travelling. Israel's Ministry of Tourism can provide the latest information, tel: (02) 7548111.

40 km (25 miles) from Jerusalem, is the main crossing-point. For information tel: (02) 9941038

The visa requirements are the same as those at any other point of entry into Israel (it is not possible to get an Israeli visa upon arrival at the bridge and, as yet, it is still not possible to get one in Jordan). The bridge is open Sunday–Thursday 8am–4pm and on Friday and the eves of holidays 8–11am. It is closed on Saturday and on Jewish holidays. At Allenby Bridge a Tourist Information Office is open at the same time as the bridge. Other facilities are: currency

exchange, post office, public telephones, cafeteria, toilets, porters and *sherut* (service) taxis to Jerusalem, Jericho, Bethlehem, Hebron, Ramallah and Gaza.

For opening hours and restrictions at points of entry between Jordan and Israel check details with Israel's Ministry of Tourism, or contact the border:
**Jordan River** (near Beit She'an): (06) 6586448. Sunday–Thursday 6.30am–10pm Friday–Saturday 8am–8pm, closed Yom Kippur and Id el Fitr.
**Arava Checkpoint** (near Eilat): (07) 6336812.
**Buses:** There are bus services from Amman to the three border crossings with Israel which meet up with buses from Jerusalem. There is a direct bus service from Amman to Tel Aviv's Central Bus Station.

#### From Egypt

Points of entry open between Israel and Egypt are Nitsana, Rafah and Taba, open 363 days a year (exceptions are Yom Kippur and the first day of Id el Fitr).
**Nitsana**, the main point of entry, is about 60 km (37 miles) southwest of Be'er sheba, and is open between 8am and 4pm, tel: (07) 6555867.
**Rafah**, 50 km (30 miles) southwest of Ashkelon, is open between 8.30am and 5pm, tel: (07) 673 4205
**Taba**, just south of Eilat, is open 24 hours a day, tel: (07) 637 2104.
**Buses:** There are bus services from Cairo to Tel Aviv and Jerusalem and to the Taba border point near Eilat.

## On Departure

### BY AIR

#### Confirming Reservations

You must confirm your scheduled departure with your airline at least 72 hours in advance.

#### Procedures on Departure

Departing passengers should arrive at the airport 2–3 hours prior to their flight's departure time (but see below for a short cut) and prepare the following documents:

passport, flight tickets and money (Israeli currency preferred) for payment of the airport tax, approximately $10. This tax is usually included in the price of the air ticket.

## Porter Service

The Israel Airports Authority offers a day-before check-in service for your baggage which saves the hassle of security checks at Ben Gurion Airport. Your suitcases are transported to the airport and instead of arriving 2–3 hours before your flight you need only arrive 1 hour 15 minutes in advance. A charge of about $2.50 per person is made for this service. You can hand your baggage in at the following locations:

**Jerusalem:** 7 Kanfei Nesharim, Giv'at Sha'ul
**Tel Aviv:** North Railway Station, Arlozorov.
Dan Panorama Hotel, Kaufman Street.
**Haifa:** International Conference Centre, 2 Pliman Street.
Haifa Airport.
**Eilat:** Eilat Airport.
**Be'er Sheva:** Beit Noam, 21 Shazar Street.
**Rishon Le-Tsiyon:** 33 Lazarov Street (near Kanion Hazahav).
**Rosh Pina:** Mahanaim Airport.
**Kiryat Shmona:** Airport.
For information about opening hours and appropriate times to take in your baggage tel: (03) 9723388.

### Security Checks
These are for your protection. Be prepared to unlock your luggage and submit yourself and your carry-on bags to a careful but courteous examination. To avoid spoiling any precious records of your visit, make sure to empty your camera of film.

### Getting to the Airport
**From Tel Aviv:** By United Tours Bus number 222 from the Railway Station, Arlozorov, to Ben Gurion Airport every hour, year round, from 4am–noon. For details tel: (03) 7543410.
By Egged Buses, every 15

minutes, 6am–11.30pm.
**From Jerusalem:** By Egged Buses, from 6.15am to 7pm, approximately every 20 minutes. By Nesher *sherut* taxi: book in advance at 2I Ha-Melekh George, tel: (02) 6257227.
**From Haifa:** By Egged Buses, from 7am to 6pm, every 45 minutes. By Aviv *sherut* taxi service, at 5 Allenby, tel: (04) 8666333, every hour from 6am–5pm.

### Travelling On
**To Jordan**
When crossing from Israel to Jordan you must possess a passport valid for at least six months and a Jordanian visa (obtainable at the Jordanian checkpoint), and pay an exit tax. This is a revenue stamp which can be purchased at post offices in Israel as well as at the Bridge. Private vehicles (including cycles) may not cross the bridge (the Arava Checkpoint is open to vehicles).

## Border Crossings

### Allenby Bridge
**From Jerusalem:** By *sherut* taxi service from Damascus Gate.
**From Jericho, Bethlehem, Hebron, Ramalla and Gaza:** By *sherut* taxi from the centre of each town. If leaving by other means of transport you must coordinate your departure with the Tourism Staff Officer, Judea and Samaria, tel: (02) 9955318, or with the Allenby Bridge Tourist Information Office, tel: (02) 9941038.
**From Tel Aviv:** A Dan bus now runs direct from the Central Bus Station in Tel Aviv to Amman twice daily (except Saturday) at 7am and 2.30pm. Contact Dan Buses for the latest information (03) 6394444.

### Jordan River Crossing:
**From Beit She'an:** By bus16 – daily (except Saturday) – departing 8.20am, 9.20am, and 2.20pm.
**Arava Checkpoint:** Taxis only.

### To Egypt
Passengers to Egypt pay a tax of $8. Visitors departing via the land

crossing-point at Nitsana pay a tax approximately equivalent to $2, payable at the Bank Leumi branch at the terminal. Visitors departing via Rafah pay approximately $8. It can be paid at any branch of Bank Hapoalim to the order of the Israel Airport Authority, account number 566-05-39710.

Tourists crossing from Taba to Egypt can obtain a visa (for up to 7 days) on presentation of a passport and payment of a $5 tax. Travel is permitted to the tourist sites in the southern Sinai only, and you must return to Israel via Taba. The AL-17 Israel entry form is required.

If you're not going through Taba, an Egyptian visa must be obtained in advance. You need your passport and the AL-17 entry form. Private vehicles may be driven into Egypt, and documentation must be obtained in your own country. Rented cars may not cross the border. Southern Sinai may also be entered by sea through Sharm Al Shaykh. Free visas for a 48-hour stay obtainable in advance from the Egyptian Consulate in Eilat.

### Getting to the Border
**From Jerusalem:** By *sherut* service from Damascus Gate.
**From Tel Aviv:** By *sherut* service from the Central Bus Station. Tourist agencies in Israel also offer inexpensive round-trip bus service in air-conditioned buses, leaving daily except on *Shabbat*.

Both El Al and Air Sinai also offer several flights to Cairo each week. Far more expensive than the bus, but cuts the travel time down from 10 hours to less than an hour.

The Egged Bus Co-op runs a regular service from Tel Aviv to Cairo. Buses depart Sunday–Thursday from the Central Bus Station at 8.30am. Visas cost approximately $15 and can be obtained from the Egyptian Consulate in Tel Aviv, at 54 Basel, Tel Aviv 62744, tel: (03) 5464151. A transit tax is payable when leaving through the land borders.

# Practical Tips

## Backpacking

Israel is a backpacker's paradise. It is customary for Israelis, after completing their army service, to spend six months, or even a year, hitchhiking around the world, and so backpackers are generally warmly received in Israel and rarely frowned on as undesirables.

Hitchhiking is as common as catching a bus, and hitchhiking stops, rather like bus stops, can be found at every major junction. But competition is tough in urban areas where dozens of Israelis vye for car space, including soldiers, who receive priority.

Buses are relatively cheap, and there is a 10 percent discount on inter-city routes for holders of international student cards.

Youth hostels abound, and their representatives often wait at bus stations to approach backpackers. Sleeping on the beach or in public parks is also usually permitted. Eating is incredibly cheap and healthy at *felafel* stalls, where you can take as much salad as you want along with your pitta bread and *felafel* for just $2.

Backpackers also like Israel because there is usually plenty of casual employment. Strictly speaking this is illegal, and wages are poor, but a week or two's pay for washing dishes or working on a construction site can be useful for those travelling around the world on a shoestring budget.

## Travelling with Children

Israelis love children, who are expected to be seen and heard. Restaurants, hotels and cafés are very flexible in meeting children's fussy food needs, and many hotels operate baby-sitting services.

Children under 5 travel free on buses. Children under 4 must be harnessed into special seats when travelling in cars (except taxis).

## Gay Travellers

Homosexuality between consenting adults (aged 18 and over) became legal in Israel in 1988, when the Law of Equal Rights in the Workplace was also amended to ban discrimination against gay people. Tel Aviv has a Community Centre housing support and study groups, a library and art gallery. Independence Park in Tel Aviv is the country's main gay pick-up point, and gay clubs abound in the city. Jerusalem also has a gay scene, albeit smaller.

## Students

**Youth Tours**: The Israel Student Tourist Association (ISSTA) arranges low-cost flights to and from Israel and offers young visitors a variety of tours, including safaris and work camps. The association also issues and renews International Student Identity Cards. The ISSTA representative at Ben Gurion Airport answers queries on kibbutzim, archaeological digs, hotels and hostels, buses, taxis, inland flights, and discounts. (Also see the section on Backpacking.)

ISSTA offices are located in Israel's three main cities:
**Tel Aviv**: 109 Ben Yehuda, tel: (02) 6247164/5.
**Jerusalem**: 5 Eli'Ashar, tel: (02) 6225258.
**Haifa**: Hakranot, Herzl, tel: (04) 8669139.

## Etiquette

After receiving some service or purchase, it is polite to say *toda* (thanks) or *toda raba* (thanks very much). Often the response will be *bevakasha* (please) or *alo davar* (it's nothing). The standard hello or goodbye is *shalom*. "How are you?"

## Religious Etiquette

Of obvious sensitivity is religious etiquette. When visiting holy sites, women should dress conservatively (no bare legs or shoulders), and men should wear shirts and long trousers. When visiting Jewish shrines or memorials it's also standard for men to cover their heads; if you don't have a *kepah* or hat, a cardboard substitute is often provided. In some religious neighbourhoods, especially in Jerusalem, these conservative rules of dress apply as general practice. While not all Israelis are observant, you should be aware that religious Jews see the Sabbath as a holy day and smoking or other behaviour can be considered offensive.

is *Ma Shlomcha?* to a man or *Ma Shlomech?* to a woman. "See you" is *lehitra'ot*.

But generally Israelis can be curt, not bothering to say please or thank you, though increasingly greater efforts are being made to be polite to tourists. This is all part of Israel's famous casual attitude, in which formalities are often dispensed with. Do not judge Israelis harshly by their lack of courtesy. If you are really in trouble, they will often surprise you by their painstaking and generous efforts to help.

Israelis can be very physical, looking strangers hard in the eye and doing a lot of touching. This is usually done out of friendliness rather than sexual forwardness, but the situation can be confusing for a female tourist coming into contact with a strange man.

## Business Hours

### Banks

Sunday and Thursday 8.30am–1pm and 4–6pm; Monday, Tuesday and Wednesday 8.30am–1pm only; Friday and eves of holy days 8.30am–12 noon.

Branches in the leading hotels

usually offer convenient additional banking hours.

### Offices
Sunday–Thursday 8am–12 noon.

### Stores
Sunday–Thursday, 9am–7pm; Friday mornings only and sometimes Saturday night. Some smaller stores may, however, take a siesta.

## Tipping

In restaurants, if a service charge is not included, then 10–15 percent is expected. Israelis do not tip taxi drivers, but drivers will expect a small tip from tourists. Hotel staff such as porters (bell hops) will be happy with a few shekels for each item of baggage.

## Religious Services

Jews and Muslims will have no problems finding synagogues and mosques, which are virtually on every street corner in some neighbourhoods.

### JEWISH
Jerusalem Great Synagogue,
56 Ha-Melekh George.
Tel: (02) 6247112.
Chabad Synagogue,
16 Yirmiyahu, Jerusalem.
Tel: (02) 5814755.
Centre for Conservative Judaism,
4 Agron, Jerusalem.
Tel: (02) 6223539.
Union for Progressive Judaism,
13 David ha-Melekh, Jerusalem.
Tel: (02) 6232444.
Tel Aviv Great Synagogue,
110 Allenby.
Tel: (03) 5604905.
Beit Yisrael,
Independence Square, Netanya.
Tel: (09) 8624345.
Haifa Central Synagogue,
Rabbi Herzog.
Tel: (04) 8660599.

### MUSLIM
The best-known mosques in Israel are the El-Aqsa Mosque (tel: (02)

6281248) on Jerusalem's Temple Mount, the El-Jazzar Mosque in Akko and the White Mosque in Ramla. There are also many mosques in Arab towns and villages throughout Israel.

### CHRISTIANS
While Israel has much to offer every tourist, for the Christian pilgrim a trip to Israel is more than just a journey because here the pilgrim has the unique opportunity of tracing the footsteps of Jesus and the early Christians and visiting sites significant to the life and teaching of Jesus: Bethlehem, his birthplace; Nazareth, the town of his boyhood; the Sea of Galilee, scene of miracles and his ministerial teaching; Mount Tabor, site of the Transfiguration; the Garden of Gethsemane and Jerusalem, where he spent his last hours of prayer and agony; and Latrun, the site of a Trappist monastery, near the biblical Emmans Jesus appeared after the Resurrection.

### JERUSALEM
Armenian Cathedral of St James.
Tel: (02) 6284549,
Monday–Friday 3am–3.30pm;
Saturday and Sunday
2.30am–3.15pm.
Coenaculum Franciscan Chapel.
Tel: (02) 6713597,
7am–noon, 3pm–sundown. Ring bell.
Christ Church – Office.
Tel: (02) 6282082, 8–10am,
4.30–6pm.
Dominus Flevit.
Tel: (02) 6285837,
6.45am–11.30am, 3–5pm.
Ein Kerem: St John's.
Tel: (02) 6413639, 5.30am–noon,
2.30–6pm (winter 2.30–5.30pm).
Ein Kerem: Visitation.
Tel: (02) 6417291, 9am–noon,
3–6pm.
Flagellation.
Tel: (02) 6282936, 6am–noon,
2–6pm (winter 2–5.30pm).
Garden Tomb.
Tel: (02) 6283402, 8am–1pm,

3–5pm (winter 8am–12.30pm and 2.30–4.30pm). Sunday closed.
Gethsemane, Church of Agony and Grotto.
Tel: (02) 6283264, 8.30am–noon,
3pm–sundown (winter
2pm–sundown).
Holy Sepulchre.
Tel: (02) 6273314, 4am–8pm
(winter 4am–7pm).
Lithostrotos-Ecce Homo.
Tel: (02) 6282445,
8.30am–4.30pm; Sunday closed
(winter 8.30am–4pm).
Lutheran Church of the Redeemer.
Tel: (02) 6282543, 9am–1pm, 2–5
pm, Friday 9am–1pm; Sunday for services only.
Monastery of the Holy Cross.
Tel: (02) 5634442, irregular hours –
phone in advance.
Russian Cathedral.
Tel: (02) 6284580, by appointment.
St Mary Magdalene.
Tel: (02) 6282897, irregular hours –
phone in advance.
St Anne's, Bethesda.
Tel: (02) 6283258, 8am–noon,
2.30–6pm (winter 2–5pm).
St George's Cathedral.
Tel: (02) 6282253 or 282167,
6.45am–6.30pm.
Church of the Dormition.
Tel: (02) 6719927, 7am–12.30pm,
2–7pm.
Abu Ghosh Crusader Church.
Tel: (02) 6539798, 8.30–11am,
2.30–5pm.

### OUTSIDE JERUSALEM
Bethlehem Nativity Church.
6am–6pm.
Bethlehem St Catherine.
Tel: (02) 6742425, 8am–noon,
2.30–6pm.
Bethlehem Shepherds' Field.
Tel: (02) 6742423, 8am–11.30am,
2–6pm (winter 2–5pm).
Capernaum "City of Jesus".
Tel: (06) 6721059,
8.30am–4.30pm.
Emmaus Qubeibeh.
Tel: (04) 9952495 ext: 4,
6.30–11.30am, 2–6pm.
Latrun Monastery.
Tel: (08) 9420065, 7.30–11.30am,
2.30–5pm.
Mount of Beatitudes,

tel: (06) 6720878, 8am–noon, 2–4pm.
Mount Carmel Stella Maris, tel: (04) 8523460, 6am–noon, 3–6pm (winter 3–5pm).
Nazareth: Basilica of the Annunciation & St Joseph's, tel: (06) 6572501, 8.30–11.45am, 2–6pm; Sunday 2–6pm (winter 2–5pm).
Tabor Transfiguration, tel: (06) 6567489, 8am–noon, 3–5pm.
Tabgha: Multiplication of the Bread, tel: (06) 6721061, 8am–4pm.
The **Christian Information Centre**, inside the Old City's Jaffa Gate, opposite the Citadel (tel: 02-6287647), offers information on all churches, monasteries and other Christian shrines. The office also issues certificates of Christian pilgrimage.

## BAPTISMAL SITES

An organised baptismal site has been erected at Yardenit at the mouth of the River Jordan, 8 km (5 miles) south of Tiberias. Descent is by steps or wheelchair-accessible ramp. There is ample space for groups. The site is open during daylight hours. Al-Maghtes, near Jericho, also claims to be the site of Christ's baptism, and is accessible to pilgrims.

## Public Holidays

Public holidays fall on the Jewish festivals listed here. On Rosh Hashana (New Year), Yom Kippur (Day of Atonement), the first and last day of Succot (Tabernacles), the first and last day of Pesach (Passover) and Shavuot, all shops and offices are closed and there is no public transport. On Holocaust Day, Memorial Day and Tisha B'Av all places of entertainment and restaurants are closed.

In Arab areas, such as Nazareth and Bethlehem, Christian and Muslim festivals are observed, though most shops remain open on Friday and Sunday, the Muslim and Christian Sabbaths.

## The Sabbath & Festivals

Israel observes a solar–lunar year in accordance with Jewish religious tradition, with the New Year occurring in September/October, with the festival of Rosh Hashana. But the standard Gregorian system is also in daily use everywhere.

The working week runs from Sunday to Thursday, and most businesses are also open on Friday mornings. From sunset on Friday to sunset on Saturday, however, everything shuts down in observance of the Jewish Sabbath, or *Shabbat*.

This includes all banks and public services, including buses and other forms of transportation. In Tel Aviv and Haifa, however, small mini-buses run along the main bus routes and inter-city *sheruts* (communal taxis) also run some services. On Saturday evening, most of the transport and other public services are resumed.

The Hebrew calendar is a lunar calendar with a leap month added every two to three years to ensure that the year is also a solar one. Jewish holy days, therefore, fall on different dates in the general calendar each year, so exact dates cannot be given. The months only are indicated in the following list.

## Calendar of Jewish Holidays

| | |
|---|---|
| **Rosh Hashana** | Sept/Oct |
| **Yom Kippur** | Sept/Oct |
| **Succot** | Sept/Oct |
| **Simhat Torah** | Sept/Oct |
| **Hanukkah** | Dec |
| **Tu B'Shevat** | Jan/Feb |
| **Purim** | Feb/Mar |
| **Pesach** | Mar/Apr |
| **Independence Day** | Apr/May |
| **Lag Ba'Omer** | May |
| **Jerusalem Liberation Day** | May/June |
| **Shavuot** | May/June |
| **Tisha B'Av** | July/Aug |

## MUSLIM HOLY DAYS

Friday is a holy day for Muslims, and places of worship are closed to

## Yom Kippur

Yom Kippur ends the 10-day period of penitence which begins at Rosh Hashana. It is a 25-hour period of complete fasting for the observant Jew, and the entire country comes to a standstill – no transport, no restaurant service, no museums. Visitors who do not fast should check with their hotels about arrangements for meals.

visitors during prayers on that day, as they are on all holy days. The Muslim calendar comprises 12 lunar months, so that, say, the month of Ramadan rotates backwards through the seasons. Muslim holy days are decided in accordance with the appearance of the new moon, thus falling on different dates in the general calendar each year. The most important are:
**Id el Adha, Sacrificial Festival** (four days).
**New Year**
**Mohammed's Birthday**.
**Feast of Ramadan** (one month).
**Id el Fitr, Conclusion of Ramadan** (three days).

## CHRISTIAN HOLY DAYS

Sunday is, of course, the Christian Sabbath, but different Christian denominations celebrate festivals on different dates. For example, the Catholic and Protestant Christmas is 25 December, the Orthodox Christmas 6 January, and the Armenian Orthodox Christmas 14 January. During some years all denominations celebrate Easter together, while at other times the Orthodox Easter falls a week after the Western Easter.

## Media

Access to news is very important for Israelis, due to their unique geo-political situation. Listening to hourly news updates on the radio in taxis and buses, as well as in private homes, is part of the daily

## Direct Line

Jerusalem has a fax number direct to heaven: c/o The Western Wall, (02) 5612222. The telephone company places your fax in the cracks of the wall.

routine. There is some censorship, but only in security matters.

### Print

Israelis are prolific newspaper readers. With several dozen daily newspapers and countless weekly and monthly magazines, they read more newspapers per head of the population than almost any other country in the world. Most of these newspapers are in Hebrew, the two largest being the afternoon journals *Yediot Ahronot* and *Ma'ariv*, which each sell over 500,000 copies of their Friday (weekend) edition. This is a very high number when you consider that there are only 6 million Israelis.

The *Jerusalem Post* is published in English six days a week (except Saturday). Founded in 1932, the paper was originally owned by the Histadrut Trade Union Movement and supported the Labour Party. But in 1990 it was sold to Conrad Black's Canadian-based Hollinger Corporation for $17 million. Hollinger also owns Britain's *Daily Telegraph* group. Under new management, the *Jerusalem Post* now supports the right-wing Likud. The *Time Out* section of the Friday paper is the only English listing of what's going on in the arts, music, theatre, television and radio. The paper also carries useful information about medical services, religious services, etc.

The *Jerusalem Report* is an English-language fortnightly magazine that gives comprehensive news and features insights into Israeli life. It offers a more centre-left alternative to the *Jerusalem Post*. The *International Herald Tribune* is published daily in Tel Aviv, together with an English translation

of the Hebrew daily *Ha'Aretz*.

There is also a dynamic Arab press with over 20 publications, including six dailies and six weeklies. The Israeli Arab press is based in Haifa, while journals printed in East Jerusalem are aimed at a readership in the West Bank and Gaza.

The size and impact of the recent waves of immigration from Russia can be measured by the press. There are a dozen national papers printed in Russian, most of which are dailies. In addition there are several weeklies in French, Spanish, Amharic, Hungarian, Romanian and many other languages.

Many of the leading newspapers and magazines from Western Europe and North America are available at newsagents the day after publication.

## Broadcast Media

The Israel Broadcasting Authority (IBA) is a government-run organisation modelled on Britain's BBC and has two channels. Programmes include a 15-minute news bulletin in English (currently at 6.15pm). Channel 2 is a commercial station, and then there is cable television which offers subscribers 30 channels including BBC World Service, CNN and Sky.

In addition, Israel can receive broadcasts from all its neighbours, including two English language stations, Middle East Television, broadcast from Lebanon, and Jordan's Channel 6.

The IBA has a comprehensive radio service broadcasting on six networks. On the foreign language service there are English-language news bulletins at 7am, 1pm and 5pm. Other Israeli stations include the BBC World Service, Voice of America and Jordan's English-language radio station.

## Post & Telephone

### Postal Services

Israel's post offices have many branches and can be identified by a

logo of a white stag leaping across a red background. Post boxes are red for out-of-town and international mail, and yellow for letters within the city. Letters take 7–10 days to reach Europe and America. Express service takes half the time, and Super Express (which is very expensive) about one-third of the time.

Post office hours are 8am–12.30pm and 3.30–6pm. Major post offices are open all day. On Friday afternoon, Saturday and holidays post offices are closed all day.

### Telephone

Phone books are in Hebrew only. Numbers can be obtained from Information (tel: 144), which operates an English-language service, though callers are charged the cost of one unit for each enquiry.

Public telephone booths can be found throughout the country. Most function when telephone cards are inserted. These cards can be bought at post offices and newsagents. Restaurants, cafés and bars usually have coin-operated phones which are more expensive than card-operated ones. At major tourist sites some telephones accept international credit cards, and this can be a convenient way of making overseas calls. Many private companies lease out cellular phones for about $5 per day, but the cost of calls on cellular phones is much cheaper than in Western Europe and North America.

Overseas calls can be booked through the post offices listed below, or the international operator (tel: 188). International phone calls from hotels are often very expensive (perhaps three times the actual price). Alternatively, using the 177 toll-free number you will be connected to an operator abroad who can place reversed-charge calls or debit your credit card or subscriber account.

The numbers to call are:
**Canada**: tel: 177-430 2727.
**UK**: British Telecom, tel: 177-440 2727.

**USA:** AT&T, tel: 177-100-2727; MCI, tel: 177 150-2727; Sprint, tel: 177-102-2727.

Three Israeli telecom companies offer international calls: Golden Lines, Barak, and Bezeq. To phone abroad first dial 012 (for Golden Lines), 013 (for Barak) and 014 (for Bezeq), then the country code (44 for Britain, 1 for the USA and Canada, etc.), then the area code (omitting any initial zeroes) followed by the number.

Each of the three companies offers flat-rate tariffs 24 hours a day, 7 days a week. However, tariffs, though relatively inexpensive, vary considerably from company to company and it is worth using the following toll free

## Telephone Area Codes

| | | |
|---|---|---|
| 02 | – | Jerusalem |
| 03 | – | Tel Aviv |
| 04 | – | Haifa |
| 06 | – | The Galilee and North |
| 07 | – | The South, including Eilat, Be'er Sheva and Ashkelon |
| 08 | – | Ashdod, Rekhovot |
| 09 | – | Herzlija, Netanya |
| 051 | – | Pelephone cellular phone network |
| 053 | – | Cellcom cellular phone network |
| 054 | – | Partner/Orange cellular phone network. |

numbers to clarify which telecom provider is cheapest. Barak, for example, offers the cheapest calls to the UK, while Golden Lines is cheapest to the USA.

> Golden Lines 1-800-012-012
> Barak 1-800-013-013
> Bezeq 188

These numbers will also give details of discounts for frequent callers. Post offices with international telephone call facilities:

**Jerusalem:** 3 Koresh.
Tel: (02) 6249858
**Tel Aviv:** 13 Frischmann.
Tel: (03) 5244365
**Eilat:** The Old Commercial Centre, Hatamarim Boulevard.
Tel: (07) 6372323

**Tiberias:** Pedestrian Mall.
Tel: (06) 6739218

### Recorded Messages

By dialling (03) 5160259 tourists can receive information on events in the Tel Aviv area. Tourists can also leave messages if they have any questions, and they will have their calls returned the next day by a member of staff. This service operates Sunday–Thursday after 6pm, and Friday after 3pm.

Jerusalem has a similar service: tel: (02) 6754863, Sunday–Thursday after 6pm, and Friday after 2pm.

Haifa has a 24-hour "What's on in Haifa" service, tel: (04) 8640840.

## Internet Information

Israel's Ministry of Tourism has an excellent site offering information about the country, accommodation, restaurants, transport etc. at: http://www.israel-mfa.gov.il/sites.html (under "sites" choose "tourism").

Information about Israel can be found from the Foreign Ministry's site: URL:http//www-mfa.gov.il

Alternatively, information about Israel and Jerusalem can be found at the following net sites: http://www1.huji.ac.il/jeru/moreinfo.html and http://www1.huji.ac.il//jerusalem.html

## Tourist Information

**Akko**, El-Jazzar Street.
Tel: (04) 991 1764.
**Allenby Bridge**.
Tel: (02) 9922471.
**Arad**, 28 Ben Yair Street.
Tel: (07) 9954409.
**Ben Gurion Airport**.
Tel: (03) 9711485.
**Bethlehem**, Manger Square.
Tel: (02) 741581.
**Eilat**, Yotam Street.
Tel: (07) 6372111.
**Haifa**, 106 Hanassi Avenue.
Tel: (04) 8374010; 20 Herzl **Boulevard**.
Tel: (04) 8666521/2.

## Useful Numbers

**Police:** 100.
**Ambulance:** 101.
**Fire Service:** 102.
**Collect calls:** 142.
**Information:** 144.
**Telephone Repairs:** 166.
**Overseas Operator:** 188.
**Direct Dialling Information:** 195.
**Telegrams:** 171.

**Jerusalem**, 17 Yafo.
Tel: (02) 6258844.
**Jaffa Gate**.
Tel: (02) 6280382.
**Nahariya**, City Hall Building.
Tel: (04) 9879800.
**Nazareth**, Casa Nova Street.
Tel: (06) 6573003.
**Netanya**, Ha'atzmaut Square.
Tel: (09) 9573003.
**Safed**, Municipal Building.
Tel: (06) 6927414.
**Tel Aviv**, New Central Bus Station.
Tel: (03) 6395660.
**Tiberias**, 23 Habanim Street.
Tel: (06) 6725666.
All these offices are open Sunday–Thursday 8.30am–5pm, Friday 8.30am–12am.

## Embassies & Consulates

Most embassies are closed on Sunday.

### Jerusalem

**UK Embassy**,
19 Nashabibi, Sheikh Jarah.
Tel: (02) 5828281/5828482; fax: (02) 5322368.
**US Embassy**,
16 Agron.
Tel: (02) 6253288 (West Jerusalem); 27 Derekh Shkem.
Tel: (02) 6282452 (East Jerusalem).

### Tel Aviv

**Australian Embassy**,
37 Shderoths Sha'ul ha-Melekh, Tel Aviv.
Tel: (03) 6950451.
**Canadian Embassy**,
220 Rehov Hayarkon,
63405 Tel Aviv.
Tel: (03) 5272929.

Visa section, 7 Khavakuk ha-Navi.
Tel: (03) 5442878.
**Embassy of The Republic of South Africa,**
Dizengoff 50 (Dizengoff Tower).
Tel: (03) 5252566.
Fax: (03) 5253230.
**UK Embassy,**
192 Ha-Yarkon, Tel Aviv 63405.
Tel: (03) 5249171;
Consular Section, 1 Ben Yehuda.
Tel: (03) 5100166.
Fax: (03) 5101167.
**US Embassy,**
71 Ha-Yarkon,Tel Aviv 63903.
Tel: (03) 5197575.
Fax: (03) 5103830.

*Other Useful Addresses*
**American Cultural Centre,**
Keren ha-Yesod 19, Jerusalem.
Tel: (02) 6255755.
**British Council Library,**
3 Abu Ovadja, Jerusalem.
Tel: (02) 6283021;
140 Ha-Yarkon, Tel Aviv.
Tel: (03) 5222194.

## Emergencies

### Security & Crime

Israel has a high rate of non-violent crimes (theft of homes, cars, property, pickpocketing, etc.) but little violent crime (mugging, murder and rape). Do not leave valuables in hotel rooms, or cars, or leave wallets sticking out of pockets. Take all the usual precautions.

In terms of violent crime the security situation is the most pressing problem, but incidents are few and far between. Under no circumstances leave unattended baggage lying around in a public place. Police sappers will blow it up within a few minutes. You should report all suspicious packages.

Before taking trips to the West Bank or Gaza you should ask about the prevailing security situation there.

To contact the police, tel: 100.

### Drug Offences

Hashish is illegal, but prosecutions are rarely brought. Because neighbouring Lebanon supplies much of the world's hashish, the

drug is widely available in Israel, with peddlers frequenting bars. The use of heroin, also grown in Lebanon, is regarded much more seriously by the Israeli authorities.

## Legal Representation

If you need a lawyer there are bound to be many who have emigrated to Israel from your country of origin, and most lawyers speak English. Your consulate can probably suggest some names.

## Lost Property

Egged Lost Property (buses), tel: (02) 5304766. Otherwise phone the local police station (tel: 100).

## Medical Services

Visitors are advised to have medical insurance because in a worst-case scenario hospital bills can reach astronomical levels. Israel has a highly developed medical system in which the most advanced techniques from laser surgery to laparoscopic procedures are routine. Even before the recent influx of new immigrants, Israel had the highest ratio of doctors in the world.

## Medical emergencies

Dial 101 to summon an ambulance or for information about the nearest hospital receiving casualties. If you want to see a doctor urgently, you can go to a **Magen David Adom** ambulance station at night, or the emergency room of any hospital (remember 101 will give you details).

If in pain, Israelis tend to be expressive. So if you are sitting in the emergency room of a hospital with an appendix that is about to burst, go ahead and yell. If you stoically play the strong silent type, then staff will tend to assume you are not really in pain and others will be treated before you.

Most doctors will be happy to see patients privately for about $40 a consultation. The tourist magazines are usually filled with adverts for medical services provided by US- and European-trained doctors.

### Medical Equipment

Visitors temporarily in need of such medical equipment as oxygen tanks, wheelchairs, vaporisers and a large number of other items can obtain them on loan, at no charge, at the Yad Sarah Organization for the Free Loan of Medical Equipment, Jerusalem. Book at least two weeks before your visit, Yad Sarah, 43 Ha-Nevi'im Street, 95141 Jerusalem, tel: (02) 644444; fax: (02) 6244493; Internet: www.yadsarah.drg.il; E-mail: info@yadsarah.org.il.

### Dentists

There are numerous dental surgeries in all the main towns, so if you stroll around the area near your hotel you are bound to come across one. The majority will speak some English, and your hotel may be able to offer recommendations.

### Pharmacists

Most pharmacists are helpful and used to dealing with tourists. The *Jerusalem Post* will tell you which pharmacy is on all-night or weekend duty. Routine prescription drugs like antibiotics are frequently sold over the counter, even though this is illegal.

### Public Toilets

Public toilets are few and far between, although there are usually some in the most popular tourist spots. If you can't find one, don't feel shy about nipping into a hotel or bar.

# Getting Around

## From the Airport

An El Al airport bus leaves Ben Gurion Airport Terminal in Tel Aviv (some 20 minutes away from the airport) approximately every hour from 6am to 10pm, and in accordance with the arrival of planes at other hours as well.

Egged buses leave for Tel Aviv every 15 minutes 5am–11.10pm; for Jerusalem (one hour away) about every 20 minutes from 7.15am to 6pm; for Haifa (1½ hours away) from 7am to 6pm, approximately every 20 minutes.

United Tours Bus number 222 travels between the airport and the Railway Station, Arlozorov, Tel Aviv, every hour year-round. The service operates from 4am to midnight. The bus stops at the Palace, Diplomat, Sheraton and Dan hotels. For further details, tel: (03) 7543410.

*Sherut* (communal) taxis take less than an hour to reach the centre of Jerusalem. Ordinary taxis are available to almost any point in the country. The fare is fixed, and you may ask to be shown the official price list. The cost of a taxi to Tel Aviv is approximately $10–15, and to Jerusalem about $22–30.

## Internal Airports

Ben Gurion International Airport, tel: (03) 9710111.
Eilat, tel: (07) 6373333.
Haifa, tel: (04) 8722084.
Herzliya, tel: (09) 9502373.
Jerusalem, tel: (02) 5850980.
Rosh Pina (North), tel: (06) 6936478.
Sde Dov, Tel Aviv, tel: (03) 6991058.
Uvda, tel: (07) 6339442.

## Internal Flights

The following airlines offer internal scheduled flights:

- Arkia Israeli Airlines Ltd, Sde Dov Airport, Tel Aviv, tel: (03) 6992222.
- Israir, 6 Eliar, Ramat Aan tel: (03) 6136564.
- El-Rom Airlines Ltd, Sde Dov Airport, Tel Aviv, tel: (03) 5412554.

## Public Transport

### Buses

Buses are by far the most common means of transportation for both urban and inter-urban services. Services are regular and the fares are reasonable, though prices have risen substantially in recent years due to the withdrawal of government subsidies.

Most buses in Israel are operated by the Egged Bus Cooperative, one of the largest bus companies in the world. Buses are air-conditioned, and Egged operates all urban and inter-urban services except within Tel Aviv. Services are punctual and, if anything, impatient drivers tend to leave half a minute before time. If travelling to Eilat, it is advisable to reserve seats several days in advance.

An intra-urban flat fare ticket costs about $1.25 and a Jerusalem–Tel Aviv ticket costs $6. Tel Aviv–Eilat costs $25. Return tickets are cheaper, and there are tickets allowing unlimited travel anywhere in Israel over a period of 7, 14 or 21 days or a month.

Buses do not run from Friday before sundown until Saturday after sundown. Inter-urban bus services start around 6am and finish in the early evening except for the Tel Aviv–Jerusalem and Tel Aviv–Haifa lines which continue until midnight. Urban services run from 5am to midnight.

### Egged Information:

Jerusalem: tel: (02) 5304555.
Tel Aviv: tel: (03) 5375555.

A number of other companies operate charter flights (3–10 passengers) to various parts of the country. Further particulars may be obtained from travel agents.

El-Rom Airlines operate air taxi services from Be'er Sheva to Tel Aviv, Eilat, Jerusalem and Haifa, and from Tel Aviv to Mitspe Ramon and Sodom.

Haifa: tel: (04) 8549555.
Eilat: tel: (07) 6373148.

The Jerusalem Central Bus Station is in Yafo, near the western entrance to the city. The Tel Aviv Central Bus Station is a vast shopping mall complex on Levinski in the south of the city, and the Haifa Central Bus Station is on the Tel Aviv highway at the city's southern entrance.

For information about Dan bus lines in Tel Aviv, tel: (03) 6394444

### Trains

Israel Railways run from Haifa and Nahariya in the north and from Tel Aviv to Jerusalem, on a daily basis. Fares are considerably lower than bus fares, and seats can be reserved in advance for a small extra charge.

Most of the trains are rather old, but all of them have buffet cars and service. The trip from Tel Aviv to Jerusalem is a particularly lovely train route, winding through the scenic Sorek valley.

There is no train service on the Sabbath, or on Jewish holidays.
**Train information:**
tel: (03) 6937515.
**Main Railway Stations:**
Haifa: Bat Galim.
Tel: (04) 8564564.
Jerusalem: Kikar Remez.
Tel: (02) 6733764.
Tel Aviv: Central Station, Arlozorov.
Tel: (03) 5421515.
**Student Discount**: A 10 percent discount on all inter-city Egged Bus Company trips and 25 percent on Israel Railways are available on presentation of a student card.

### Metro

Israel's only subway operates in Haifa. This recently renovated system is in fact an underground cable car. It is also the quickest way of getting about Haifa. The train runs from Central Mount Carmel to downtown Haifa every 10 minutes and makes six stops. The trip takes 9 minutes. It operates Sunday–Thursday 5.30am–midnight, Friday 5.30am to 1 hour before the Sabbath, and Saturday from sunset to midnight.

### Taxis & Sherut

Taxis offer a quick and convenient mode of travel in Israel. You can phone for a taxi in any major city, or hail one in the street.

All urban taxis have meters, whose operation is compulsory. If the driver wants to turn off the meter he may be trying to take you for a ride in more ways than one. Tipping is not compulsory, but is often greatly appreciated.

Prices are pre-fixed between cities, and the driver will tell you your fare in advance, or show you the official price list if you ask for it. The *sherut* is Israel's own indigenous mode of transportation, operating in and between main cities every day but *Shabbat*; some private companies or owners operate on *Shabbat* as well. Individuals share a van or cab, which accommodates up to seven people, at a fixed price usually equivalent to the bus fare for the same route.

*Sheruts* between cities leave from near the central bus station, and, in Jerusalem, from near Kikar Tsiyou (Zion Square). In Tel Aviv and some other cities, local *sheruts* follow the main bus routes, making similar stops in quicker time.

## Private Transport

### Driving

Israelis drive with Mediterranean creativity. There is a lot of horn honking, overtaking on the inside and general improvisation. But life on the road is not as chaotic as in many other Mediterranean

countries. With well over one million vehicles on the roads, Israel has one of the world's densest road systems. There are around 500 fatalities each year from road accidents, which is comparable with death rates on Western European roads.

Laws are strictly enforced, and it is necessary to wear seat belts at all times and strap children under four into appropriate seats. Speed limits are 90–100 kph (55–60 mph) on highways and 50–70 kph (30–40 mph) in urban areas. Keep your passport, driver's licence and other papers with you at all times. Police tend to be lenient with tourists but can take you straight in front of a judge if they wish.

Fuel is cheaper in Israel than in Western Europe but more expensive than in America. In Eilat, a VAT-free zone, you do not pay the usual 17 percent VAT charge on fuel.

### Parking

Parking is very difficult in the major city centres and it is best to look for a parking lot. These can cost $1.50 an hour in Jerusalem, and up to $3 per hour in parts of Tel Aviv. If a kerbside is marked in blue and white you need a ticket, which you can purchase in batches

## Car-hire Companies

**Hertz:** 18 David ha-Melekh, Jerusalem.
Tel: (02) 6256334;
144 Ha-Yarkon, Tel Aviv.
Tel: (03) 5223332.
**Avis:** 22 David ha-Melekh, Jerusalem.
Tel: (02) 6249001/3;
113 Ha-Yarkon, Tel Aviv.
Tel: (03) 6884242.
**Eldan:** 24 David ha-Melekh, Jerusalem.
Tel: (02) 6252151;
Tel Aviv. Tel: (03) 6394343.
Internet: http://www.eldan.co.il.
**Reliable:** 14 David ha-Melekh, Jerusalem.
Tel: (02) 6248204/5;
112 Ha-Yarkon, Tel Aviv.
Tel: (03) 5249764.

of five from kiosks, lottery kiosks and stores. Each ticket costs about 90 cents and allows you to park for an hour. You must tear out the right time, month and day and display the ticket on the kerbside window. These tickets must be displayed from 7am to 7pm. Outside these hours, parking is usually free, though it is prohibited in some residential areas of Tel Aviv.

If you fail to display a ticket, or the ticket has expired, you are liable for a $20 fine, though this need not be paid for several months.

Do not ignore red-and-white marked kerbsides or No Parking signs. Here you may be clamped with a "Denver boot" or towed away. In either instance it will cost you $20 (or more) and a lot of wasted time in redeeming your car.

### Hiring a Car

Many of the world's principal car-hire companies, including Hertz, Avis, Euro-Car, Inter-Rent, Budget and Thrifty, have outlets in Israel. Israel's largest car-hire company, Eldan, also has offices overseas. These companies can supply you with a car at the airport and allow you to leave it there on departure. They have a network of offices around the country. In addition, if you break down a new car is almost immediately at your service.

Car hire is expensive (at least $300 a week for a small 1200cc or 1300cc saloon). Traffic is usually heavy, and parking is difficult in Israel's big cities. Also, hiring a car is not really necessary for the centre of the country which has good bus and taxi services.

However, it is worth hiring a car for touring the Galilee or the Negev, and it can be cheaper off-season (between October and April) or if you do a deal with one of the many local, smaller companies. But in general it is much cheaper to book a car as part of a package deal (flight, hotel, car) with your travel agent overseas.

As everywhere in the world, carefully check that there is no damage to the car, that the spare wheel, jack and other equipment are in place, and that oil and water are sufficient before accepting a car.

Car-hire companies require an international driving licence or will accept national licences if written in English or French.

## On Foot

### Pedestrians

Drivers cannot be relied upon to stop at pedestrian crossings. And pedestrians can't always be relied on not to wander casually into the road. The safest place to cross, of course, is at traffic lights when the pedestrian light is green. Beware at right-turn filters where the pedestrian light is green but traffic may still pass. In Jerusalem, police hand out fines to pedestrians who cross at red lights.

## Specialist Tours

So much history gets missed without an expert guide to explain the significance of each site, so it is well worth joining an organised tour. Major tour bus companies include:

**Egged Tours**.
Tel: (02) 5304868.
**United Tours**.
Tel: (02) 6251287.
**Galilee Tours**.
Tel: (toll free) 177-0222525.
Fax: (02) 6231341.
**Camel Riders**.
Tel: (07) 6373218.
Fax: (07) 6371944.
Desert sites by camel, and Bedouin-style accommodation.

# Where to Stay

## Accommodation

There is a wide choice of accommodation in Israel, from deluxe suites in high-class hotels through to budget hotels and youth hostels. But there is a certain sameness about Israeli hotels, most of which were built between 1960 and 1980, offering modern comfort and convenience without much character. Unique Israeli forms of accommodation include kibbutz guesthouses (relatively expensive rural retreats) and Christian hospices (more luxurious than they sound, usually with a 19th-century European ambience), both of which offer an unusual taste of Israel.

## Kibbutz Guesthouses

Visitors wanting a truly Israeli experience should try a kibbutz guesthouse. They usually offer all the facilities of a luxury hotel plus the chance to get acquainted with kibbutz life at first hand. Though many of these guesthouses are in isolated rural areas, especially in the northern Galilee, others are located in the countryside but just 20 minutes or so by bus or car from Jerusalem or Tel Aviv.

For further information, contact **Kibbutz Hotels Chain**, 90 Ben Yehuda, Tel Aviv 61031. Tel: (03) 5243358. Following is a list of recommended kibbutz guesthouses.

**Mitspe Rachel**,
Kibbutz Ramat Rachel (near Jerusalem).
Tel: (02) 6702555.
Fax (02) 6733155.
Though within the city limits the kibbutz grounds offer a stirring view of the Judean Desert. **$$**

**Neve Ilan**,
D.N. Hare Yehuda (near Jerusalem).
Tel: (02) 5348111.
Fax: (02) 5348197.
Pleasant country club atmosphere 20 minutes by bus from Jerusalem with view of coastal plain. **$$**

**Shfayim Guesthouse**,
Kibbutz Shfayim.
Tel: (09) 9523434.
Close to the Mediterranean coast and a short bus ride away from Tel Aviv. **$$**

**Kfar Blum Guesthouse**,
Kibbutz Kfar Blum.
Tel: (06) 6943666.
Fax: (03) 6948555.
Beneath the snowcapped Mount Hermon in the Upper Galilee. The River Jordan flows through this kibbutz. **$$**

## Price Bands

**$** – under $90
**$$** – $90-$150
**$$$** – above $150

These prices are for double rooms and usually include breakfast.

## Christian Hospices

Another fascinating Holy Land experience is the broad array of Christian hospices. Originally designed principally for pilgrims, and owned by churches, these hospices cater for allcomers, including many Israeli Jews on vacation, who enjoy the old-world European charm of these establishments.

The term hospice is misleading. Some, like Notre Dame in Jerusalem, owned by the Vatican, resemble luxury hotels. Others reflect the ethnic origins of their founders. The Sisters of Zion convent in the Jerusalem suburb of Ein Kerem resembles a pension in Provence, while St Andrew's Church in Jerusalem could be a guest house anywhere in Scotland and even serves mince pies and mulled wine at Christmas.

## IN JERUSALEM

**Notre Dame,**
opposite the New Gate.
Tel: (02) 6281223.
Fax: (02) 6282397.
Luxurious accommodation, splendid 19th-century architecture and one of Jerusalem's best (non-kosher) restaurants. Superbly appointed opposite the Old City walls. Owned by the Vatican. **$$**

**YMCA,**
David ha-Melekh.
Tel: (02) 6253433.
Stylish 1930s building opposite the King David Hotel. Recently refurbished and made more up-market. **$$.**

**St Andrew's Scots Memorial Hospice,**
(opposite the railway station).
Tel: (02) 6732401.
Intimate guesthouse atmosphere in central location. No kippers, but there is sometimes haggis. **$**

**Our Sisters of Zion,**
Ein Kerem.
Tel: (02) 6415738.
Fax: (02) 6437739.
Delightful Provençal-style pension in Ein Kerem. Spacious gardens filled with olive trees and grape vines and comfortable accommodation. **$$**

## Hotels

Until recently, Israel's Ministry of Tourism graded hotels from one to five stars according to size, service and facilities. This system has now been discontinued.

Hotels require guests to check out by midday but on Saturday and holidays guests are entitled to retain possession of their rooms until the Sabbath or holiday finishes in the evening. Check-in is usually after 3pm.

Prices can be more expensive during the high season, which is Easter/Passover, July to August, Jewish New Year and Christmas. But there is a wide range of hotels catering for every pocket down to youth hostels which charge about $10–15 a night.

Hotel rates are generally quoted in dollars and include a 15 percent service charge. If you pay in foreign currency you are exempt from 17 percent VAT. In Eilat there is no VAT charge.

## Price Bands for Hotels

**$** – under $90
**$$** – $90-$150
**$$$** – above $150

These prices are for double rooms and usually include breakfast. Holidaymakers can save up to 33 percent on hotel prices by booking a package deal overseas.

## AKKO

**Palm Beach,**
Sefat Hayam.
Tel: 04-9815815.
Fax: 04-9910434.
The hotel has its own private beach and is a 20-minute walk from Akko's Old City. **$$**

## BE'ER SHEVA

**Hilton,**
4 Henrietta Szold.
Tel: 07-6405444.
Fax: 07-6405445.
Unexceptional accommodation, but a convenient stop-over if you want to get to the Bedouin market early.

## DEAD SEA

**Hyatt Regency Dead Sea Resort and Spa Hotel,**
Ein Bokek.
Tel: 07-6591234.
Fax: 07-6368811.
This large hotel offers therapeutic treatment based on the Dead Sea's minerals and has a range of recreational facilities. **$$$**

**Tsell Harim,**
Ein Bokek, Dead Sea.
Tel: (07) 6584121.
Fax: (07) 6584666.
Cheap and comfortable the hotel is located by the sea. **$**

## EILAT

**King Solomon's Palace,**
North Beach.
Tel: 07-6363444.
Fax: 07-6334189.
Elegantly designed hotel overlooking the marina with an excellent choice of restaurants. **$$$**

**Princess Hotel,**
nr Taba border crossing, Eilat.
Tel: (07) 6365555.
Fax: (07) 6376333.
Well away from the town and near the Egyptian border, this hotel is a self-contained complex of swimming pools and restaurants. **$$$**

**Royal Beach,**
North Beach, Eilat.
Tel: (07) 6368888.
Fax: (07) 6368811. Large hotel with a diverse array of restaurants and pools. **$$$**

**Lagoona,**
North Beach, Eilat.
Tel: (07) 6332089.
Tranquil location north of the city, on the lagoon, with a good view of the Red Sea. **$$**

**Red Rock,**
POB 306, Eilat.
Tel: (07) 6373171.
Great location by the beach and near the centre of town; otherwise comfortable but unexceptional. **$$**

**Etzion,**
1 Sderot Hatamarim, Eilat.
Tel: (07) 6370003.
Far from the beach, but in the town and near the central bus station. **$**

**Moon Valley,**
POB 1135, Eilat.
Tel: (07) 6333888.
Cheap, clean and comfortable. It's as well the hotel has its own swimming pool because it is a 10-minute walk from the beach. **$**

**Red Sea Sport Club,**
Coral Beach.
Tel: (07) 6382222.
Fax: (07) 6382200. Compact and comfortable: this is the place to be if you enjoy diving. The hotel also offers courses for beginners. **$**

## HAIFA

**Dan Carmel,**
85–87 Hanasi Boulevard, Haifa.
Tel: (04) 8306211.
The city's most stylish hotel located on Mount Carmel with a breathtaking panorama of Haifa Bay and the azure-coloured Mediterranean. **$$$**

**Dvir,**
124 Yefe Nof.
Tel: (04) 8389131.
Fax: (04) 8381068
Compact and convenient, the hotel offers a breathtaking view of Haifa bay and the azure Mediterranean. **$**

## HERZLIYA

**Dan Accadia,**
Derekh Hayam.
Tel: (09) 9597070.
Fax: (09) 9597090.
One of Israel's oldest and most elegant luxury hotels, this is the pick of the accommodation in this up-market resort to the north of Tel Aviv. **$$$**

## JERUSALEM

**American Colony,**
Nablus, Jerusalem.
Tel: (02) 6279777.
Fax: (02) 6279779. Jerusalem's oldest hotel has much character and charm and is favoured by the foreign press corps on account of its location between West and East Jerusalem. **$$$**

**Hilton,**
1 David ha-Melekh.
Tel: (02) 6211111.
Fax: (02) 6211000. This recently opened hotel is attractively designed and well appointed, near the Jaffa Gate and downtown Jerusalem. **$$$**

**King David Hotel,**
23 David ha-Melekh, Jerusalem.
Tel: (02) 6208888.
Fax: (02) 6232303.
Israel's premier hotel, where political leaders and, the rich and famous stay. It has style and an old-world ambience, but in terms of quality of service its newer rivals try harder. Has beautiful gardens overlooking the Old City. **$$$**

**Laromme,**
3 Jabotinski, Jerusalem.
Tel: (02) 6756666.
Fax: (02) 6756777.
Overlooking the Liberty Bell Garden, this delightfully designed hotel has attracted some world leaders away from the King David. **$$$**

**Hyatt Regency,**
32 Lekhi, Mount Scopus, Jerusalem.
Tel: (02) 5331234.
Fax: (02) 5323196.
Stylish interior, Commands a splendid view of the Old City. **$$$**

**Dan Pearl,**
POB 793, Jerusalem.
Tel: (02) 6226666.
Fax: (02) 6226649.
Superbly located opposite the Old City walls near the Jaffa Gate. **$$$**

**Holiday Inn Crowne Plaza,**
Givat Ram.
Tel: (02) 6588888.
Fax: (02) 6527097.
Landmark high-rise building at the entrance to the city, opposite the Central Bus Station, this hotel offers luxury accommodation for modest prices. **$$**

**Holyland Hotel,**
Bayit va-Gan, Jerusalem.
Tel: (02) 6437777.
Fax: (02) 6437744.
Away from town near the Second Temple model, with a laid-back ambience and great view of West Jerusalem. **$$**

**Reich Hotel,**
Beit ha-Kerem, Jerusalem.
Tel: (02) 6523121.
Fax: (02) 6523120.
Located in the leafy suburbs of Beit ha-Kerem, the hotel is not far from the city and the Bus Station. **$$**

**Windmill Hotel,**
3 Mendele Mekher Sfar, Jerusalem.
Tel: (02) 5663111.
Fax: (02) 5610964.
Comfortable and convenient, and well located for walks into both the New and Old Cities. **$$**

**Caesar Hotel,**
208 Yafo, Jerusalem.
Tel: (02) 5005656.
Fax: (02) 5382802.
Modern and non-descript, but right by the Central Bus Station, this hotel is ideal for itinerant tourists. **$**

**Itzik Hotel,**
141 Yafo.
Tel: (02) 6233730.
Fax: (02) 6243879.
Newly opened, comfortable and clean, with interesting location in the heart of the Makhane Yehuda fruit and vegetable market. **$**

**Palatin Hotel,**
Ha-Melekh George, Jerusalem.
Tel: (02) 6231141.
Fax: (02) 6259323.
A clean and comfortable hotel, with a central location in West Jerusalem. **$**

**Ron Hotel,**
Kikar Tsiyon (Zion Square), Jerusalem.
Tel: (02) 6253471.
Fax: (02) 6250707.
Smack in the centre of West Jerusalem, this hotel has an old-world charm. Its balconies are sometimes rented out to politicians for addressing political rallies. **$**

## NAZARETH

**New Grand,**
New Grand Road.
Tel: (06) 6573020.
Fax: (06) 6576281.
Good value accommodation about 15 minutes' walk from the Basilica of the Annunciation. **$**

## NETANYA

**King Solomon,**
11 Hma'apilim, Netanya.
Tel: (09) 8338444.
Fax: (09) 8611397.
Pick of the budget-price hotels in Netanya. Near the beach and centre of town. **$$**

**Yahalom Hotel,**
11 Gad Machness, Netanya.
Tel: (09) 8635345.
Located in Netanya's hotel district opposite the sea; makes a pleasant base for seeing the country. **$**

## SAFED

**Howard Johnson Plaza Ruta Rimon Inn,** Artists' Quarter, Safed.
Tel: (06) 6920665.
Fax: (06) 6920456; 177-022-7676 (toll free).

## Price Bands for Hotels

$ - under $90
$$ - $90-$150
$$$ - above $150

These prices are for double rooms and usually include breakfast. Holidaymakers can save up to 33 percent on hotel prices by booking a package deal overseas.

The best hotel in the Galilee, with relaxing hillside views. **$$$**
**Central Hotel,**
37 Yerushalayim, Safed.
Tel: (09) 6972666.
In the heart of Safed by the artists' colony and synagogue neighbourhood. Makes a good base for seeing the Galilee. **$**

---

## TEL AVIV

**Carlton,**
10 Eli'Ezer Peri.
Tel: (03) 5201818.
Fax: (03) 5271043.
Overlooking the marina, the hotel offers excellent views of the Mediterranean. **$$$**
**Dan Tel Aviv,** 99 Ha-Yarkon.
Tel: 03-5202525.
Fax: 03-5249755.
The city's veteran luxury hotel offers excellent sea views and is renowned for comfort, style and convenience. **$$$**
**Dan Panorama,**
10 Kaufmann.
Tel: 03-5190124.
Fax: 03-5171777.
Well away from the rest of the hotels, the Dan Panorama is conveniently close to Yafo and offers the best value of all the luxury hotels. **$$$**
**Tel Aviv Hilton,**
Independence Gardens, Tel Aviv.
Tel: (03) 5202222.
Fax: (03) 5272711.
Generally accepted as the city's most luxurious hotel. Very fashionable with Tel Aviv high society, with prices to match. **$$$**
**Tel Aviv Sheraton,**
115 Mokher Sfarim, Tel Aviv.

Tel: (03) 5211111.
Fax: (03) 5233322.
Challenges the Hilton's claim to be the city's paramount hotel. **$$$**
**Adiv Hotel,**
5 Mendele Ha-Yarkon, Tel Aviv.
Tel: (03) 5229141.
Fax: (03) 5229144.
Friendly, comfortable and convenient with self-service restaurant. Situated just over the road from the seafront and beach. **$$**
**Imperial Hotel,**
66 Ha-Yarkon, Tel Aviv.
Tel: (03) 5177002.
In the heart of the city's hotel district, this comfortable hotel is well located for the beach and walks to the Dizengoff shopping and nightlife district. **$$**
**Metropolitan,**
11/15 Trumpeldor.
Tel: (03) 5192727.
Fax: (03) 5172626.
Well located for the beach and centre of town, this hotel is comfortable and convenient but otherwise ordinary. **$$**
**City,**
9 Mapu.
Tel: (03) 5246253.
Fax: (03) 5246250.
Near the beach and centre of town, this clean and comfortable hotel puts a roof over your head. **$**
**Deborah Hotel,**
Ben Yehuda, Tel Aviv.
Tel: (03) 5278282.
Pleasant hotel and location in the northern part of the city though it's a 5-minute walk from the beach. **$**

---

## TIBERIAS

**Howard Johnson Plaza,**
1 Eliezer Kaplan, Tiberias.
Tel: (06) 6792231.
Fax: (06) 6792320.
On the lakeside in Tiberias, this is one of the city's oldest and most stylish hotels. **$$**
**Aviv,**
66 Hagalil.
Tel: (06) 6720007.
Fax: (06) 6723510.
Good value accommodation within easy walking distance of the lake. **$**

## Bed & Breakfast

With the exception of the Galilee, there is a very limited amount of B&B accommodation in Israel, partly because Israelis live in relatively small apartments, so rarely have rooms to offer.
**Good Morning Jerusalem**.
Tel: (02) 6511270.
Located in the International Congress Centre opposite the bus station, gives information on all available B&Bs in the city. Overnight prices are no more than $60 per couple.
**Moshav Amirim** in the Galilee.
Tel: (06) 6989572.
Fax: (06) 6980772.
Offers B&B with vegetarian meals. In fact, Amirim is a vegetarian village with a great view of the Sea of Galilee.
**Garden of Eden,**
14 Rotemim, Eilat.
Tel: (07) 6371306.

## Holiday Apartments

For a longer stay in one place, it can be very economical to rent an apartment, with its own kitchen etc. For families it can mean a cheap way of accommodating the kids; for couples, individuals or groups it can be a more natural experience of the country, living as the locals do.

As with hotel accommodation, options range from the economical to the luxurious. A few recommended places are:
**Dahum**, 6 Frischmann Street, Tel Aviv, tel: (03) 5222695.
**Bet Rotman**, 17 David Remez, Nahariya, tel: (04) 9921017.
**Nitzan**, 704/14, Eilat, tel: (07) 6379037.

## Campgrounds

Israel is good for camping, with campsites providing excellent touring bases for each region. They offer full sanitary facilities, electric current, a restaurant and/or store, telephone, first-aid facilities, shaded picnic and campfire areas, and day and night watchmen. They can be reached by bus, but all are open to cars and caravans. Most have tents and cabins, as well as a wide range of equipment for hire. All sites have swimming facilities either on the site or within easy reach.

There is a reception and departure service for campers at Ben Gurion Airport. If you telephone (03) 9604524 on arrival, a camping car will come within a very short time to take participants to the reception camping site at **Mishmar Hashiva**, about 10 km (6 miles) from Ben Gurion Airport. A similar service is available from Mishmar Hashiva to the airport upon departure, if you stay the last night there.

On arrival in Israel campers can obtain assistance from the Tourist Information Office in the Arrivals Hall of the airport. At the reception camp at Mishmar Hashiva, campers are given maps and folders and are individually advised on touring the country.
**Reception Site:** Mishmar Hashiva, tel: (03) 9604524.

## Camping sites

**Beit Zait** (near Jerusalem).
Tel: (02) 5346217.
**Ein Gedi** (by Dead Sea).
Tel: (07) 6584342.
**Eilot** (near Eilat).
Tel (07) 6374362.
**Neve Yam** (near Haifa).
Tel: (04) 8844827.
**Kibbutz Ma'ayan Baruch** (Upper Galilee).
Tel: (06) 6954601.

## Youth Hostels

There are around 30 youth hostels throughout the country, operated by the Israel Youth Hostel Association (IYHA) which is affiliated to the international YHA. They offer dormitory accommodation, and most of them provide meals and self-service kitchen facilities. There is no age limit. Some hostels also provide family accommodation. Individual reservations should be made directly with the hostel. Some useful addresses are:

## The Youth Hostel Trail

The IYHA arranges package tours, called "Israel on the Youth Hostel Trail" for 14, 21 or 28 days. These include nights in any of the hostels with dinner and breakfast, unlimited bus travel, a half-day conducted tour, entrance to 31 National Parks and numerous museums, a map, and other informational materials. For further information contact: Head Office–IYHA, POB l075, 91009 Jerusalem, tel: (02) 6558430; fax: (02) 6558400.

**Head Office–IYHA,**
POB l075, 91009 Jerusalem.
Tel: (02) 6558430; fax: (02) 6558400.
**Akko,**
POB 1090, Akko.
Tel: (04) 9911982.
**Beit Bernstein,**
1 Keren ha-Yesod, 94266 Jerusalem.
Tel: (02) 6258286.
**Dead Sea.**
Tel: (07) 6584165.
**Beit Yatziv,**
POB 7, Be'er Sheva.
Tel: (07) 671490/677444.
**Carmel,**
MP Hof Ha-Karmel, Haifa.
Tel: (04) 8532516.
**Eilat,** POB 152, Eilat.
Tel: (07) 6370088.
**Ein Kerem,**
POB 17013, 91170 Jerusalem.
Tel: (02) 6416282.
**Ramot Shapira,**
POB 72l6, Beit Meir, Jerusalem.
Tel: (02) 5342691.
**Taiber,**
Poriah, POB 232, Tiberias.
Tel: (06) 6750050.
**Tel Aviv,**
32 Bnei Dan, Tel Aviv.
Tel: (03) 5441748.
**Tel Hai,**
MP Upper Galilee, Tel Hai.
Tel: (06) 6940043.
**Y.H. Taylor,**
86901 MP Dead Sea, Masada.
Tel: (07) 6584349.
**Yoram,**
MP Korazim, Kare Deshe.

Tel: (06) 6720601.
**Yoseph Mayouhas,**
POB 81, Tiberias.
Tel: (06) 6721775.

## Health Resorts

All hotels in the Dead Sea region offer medically supervised facilities. The sea's unique mineral content is beneficial for a range of ailments, including psoriasis and rheumatism. **Contact the Ministry of Tourism's Health Resorts Authority,** tel: (02) 6754811.

# Where to Eat

## What to Eat

Eating is a national pastime in Israel, one engaged in as much and as often as possible. On the street, at the beach, in every public place and in every home, day and night – you'll find Israelis tucking in to food.

The biblical residents of the Land of Canaan were nourished by the fertility and abundance of a land "flowing with milk and honey". But the milk was mainly from sheep and goats, and the honey from dates, figs and carobs. Much depended on the sun, the rains and the seasons.

## Eating Kosher

The laws of *kashrut* are extremely complex, but in practical terms they mean that many animals, most notably the pig, cannot be eaten at all. Furthermore, kosher animals such as the cow and chicken must be killed in a specific way (by having their throats cut), otherwise the meat is not considered kosher.

The blood must also be drained out of kosher meat, often making a steak, for example, somewhat desiccated and lacking in flavour.

In addition, while most fish are permissible, all seafood (prawns, lobsters, octopus, etc.) is considered unclean. Finally, meat and milk cannot be consumed together at the same meal.

This said, many secular Jews disregard dietary laws, and most restaurants in Israel, especially those outside Jerusalem, are not kosher.

Food was simple; feast predictably followed famine. Times have changed – at least in the culinary sense.

Just as Israel is a blend of cultures from all over the world, so its cuisine is a weave of flavours and textures, contrasts and similarities. There is no definitive Israeli fare, just as there is no definitive Israeli. Rather, there is a rare merging of East and West, and the results are a profusion of culinary delights.

The predominant food style reflects the country's geographical location – somewhere between the Middle East and the Mediterranean.

When dining out, don't be led astray by signs telling you that the establishment serves "oriental" food. "Oriental" refers to the Middle East, rather than the Far East. "Oriental" Jews are those of Sephardic (Spanish, Italian or Arab) heritage. Each Jewish ethnic group, whether Moroccan, Libyan, Tunisian, Yemenite, Iraqi or native born (sabra) Israeli, has its own special dish and its own holiday fare.

Their foods are similar yet quite distinct from each other. Basic herbs and spices include cumin, fresh and dried coriander, mint, garlic, onion, turmeric, black pepper, and sometimes cardamom and fresh green chilli. Dark, fruity olive oil adds further fragrance.

Arabic food is considered "oriental", and both Arabic and Jewish meals begin the same way – with a variety of savoury salads. *Hummus* – ground chickpea seasoned with *tahina* (sesame paste), lemon juice, garlic and cumin – is probably the most popular dip, spread and salad rolled into one. You'll also find the most astounding variety of aubergine salads you've ever seen; aubergine in *tahina*, fried sliced aubergine, chopped aubergine with vegetables, chopped liver-flavoured aubergine, and more. Assorted pickled vegetables are considered salads as well.

While the waiters may show some signs of disappointment, you can order a selection of these salads as a meal in themselves. Or you can follow them with kebab (grilled ground spiced meat), *shishlik* (grilled sliced lamb or beef with lamb fat), *seniya* (beef or lamb in *tahina* sauce), stuffed chicken or pigeon, chops or fish.

Don't expect pork in either a kosher or a traditional Muslim restaurant; both religions prohibit its consumption. Seafood, while forbidden by Jewish law and permissible by Muslim, is widely available. Shrimps and calamari are the predominant varieties.

Do try the fish, particularly in the seaside areas of Tiberias, Tel Aviv, Yafo and Eilat (there are no fish in the Dead Sea). Trout, grey and red mullet, sea bass and the famous St Peter's fish are generally served fried or grilled, sometimes accompanied by a piquant sauce. Authentic North African restaurants will also feature *harimeh* – hot and spicy cooked fish fragrant with an appetising blend of tomatoes, cumin and hot pepper.

And if you still have room, there's dessert. In Arabic restaurants this may mean *baklava* (filo pastry sprinkled with nuts and sweet syrup) or other rich sweets, or fruit. In typical Jewish oriental restaurants it could mean caramel crème custard, chocolate mousse or an egg-white confection laced with chocolate syrup and called (for some unknown reason) Bavarian cream. Turkish coffee or tea with fresh mint ends the meal. If you do not want sugar in your coffee, tell the waiter in advance or your coffee will be liberally sweetened.

## Snacks

Since Israelis are major-league eaters, snacks play a starring role in the day. Favourites include bagel-shaped sesame-sprinkled breads (served with *za'atar* – an oregano-based spice mixture available only in "ethnic" settings like the Old City of Jerusalem), nuts and sunflower seeds. Pizza, blintzes, waffles and burgers all come in and out of vogue.

## Yemenite Bread

In Yemeni restaurants several types of bread are served: *mallawah* (crispy fried, fattening and delicious), *lahuh* (light and like a pancake) and *jahnoon* (slow-baked strudel-like dough).

But the ultimate sabra snack has to be *felafel* (fried chickpea balls served in pitta bread with a variety of vegetables). Along the pavements of major streets you can usually find several adjoining *felafel* stands where you're free to stuff your pitta with salads for as long as the bread holds out.

Tel Aviv's Betsal'el Souk is probably the most famous of the *felafel* centres. Located near the Carmel market, it features an entire street of *felafel* vendors, with the largest salad selection this side of the Mediterranean.

### Fruit & Vegetables
A trip to the open-air Mahkane Yehuda in Jerusalem or the Carmel market in Tel Aviv will reveal a sumptuous array of fruit and vegetables: everything from apples to artichokes, kohlrabi to celeriac. Sub-tropical fruits include kiwi, mango, persimmon, loquat, passion fruit, chirimoya and papaya. Fresh dates, figs, pomegranates and the world's largest strawberries are among the seasonal treats.

### Meat & Poultry
If you like fowl and game, you will find chicken and turkey and, in more up-market restaurants, goose and mullard duck (an Israeli hybrid) excellent choices. While much beef is imported, all fowl is domestically raised.

### Dairy Products
In biblical times water was scarce and unpalatable, so milk became a major component of the diet. Goat's milk was the richest and most nourishing; next came that of sheep, then cows and finally camels. Today's Israel continues the "land of milk and honey"

tradition with a wealth of familiar cheeses (Camembert, Brie and Gouda), cottage cheese, and a wide variety of goat and sheep yogurt.

## EILAT

**La Brasserie**,
King Solomon's Palace Hotel.
Tel: (07) 6366444.
French-style brasserie which offers excellent kosher French cuisine.
**$$$**

**The Last Refuge**,
Coral Beach.
Tel: (07) 6372437.
South of the city by Coral Beach this restaurant has an excellent choice of fish and seafood. **$$$**

**El Gaucho**, 2 Ha'Arava.
Tel: (07) 6331549.
One of a well-known chain of Argentinian restaurants in Israel, this is for those who like their steaks very large. **$$**

**La Barracuda**,
Commercial Centre, Eilat.
Tel: (07) 6376222.
The right place to come if you want to know what those peculiar-looking Red Sea fish really taste like. **$$**

**Lotus Restaurant**, by the Caesar Hotel, Eilat.
Tel: (07) 6376389.
Excellent Chinese cuisine with a varied menu. **$$**

**Mamen Dagim**,
North Beach, by the Radisson Moriah Hotel.
Tel: (07) 6371958.
A good-value fish restaurant pleasantly located by the beach. **$**

**Meurav Eilat**,
127 Hatamarim Boulevard.
Tel: (07) 6371215.
Opposite the bus station, this restaurant offers wholesome Middle East fare of salads and grilled meat at reasonable prices. **$**

**Milan Café**,
the Red Shopping Mall, Eilat.
Tel: (07) 6374487.
Serves light dairy meals in a pleasant atmosphere. **$**

## HAIFA

**Villa Rose**,
8 Machanayim.
Tel: (04) 8664529.
Located in an elegant two-storey

## Prices for Eating Out

Prices are given in shekels
**$** - under NIS80 per person
**$$** - NIS80-250
**$$$** - over NIS250

villa, this tasteful restaurant specialises in Mediterranean dishes. **$$$**

**Nof Chinese Restaurant**,
Nof Hotel, 101 Hanassi Boulevard, Haifa.
Tel: (04) 8354311.
The taste buds are stimulated by an amazing view of Haifa Bay. **$$**

**Voila**,
21 Nordau, Hadar.
Tel: (04) 8664529.
Franco-Swiss restaurant with country-style decor in a garden house in mid-town Hadar, offering a wide choice of salads, meats and seafood. **$$**

**Shawarma Ahim Sabah**,
37 Allenby.
Tel: (04) 8552188.
Specialising in meat cut from the spit and eaten in pitta with a wide range of salads and relishes. **$**

## JERUSALEM

**American Colony Hotel**,
Nablus, Jerusalem.
Tel: (02) 6279777.
*A lá carte* menu and a beautiful courtyard in which to dine. **$$$**

**Cow on the Roof**, at the Jerusalem Sheraton Plaza Hotel.
Tel: (02) 6228133.
Elegant Western dining by reservation only. Located in the basement and not, as the name suggests, on the roof. Culinary emphasis, as the name implies, on beef. **$$$**

**Mishkenot Sha'ananim**,
Yemin Moshe, behind the windmill.
Tel: (02) 6251042.
Excellent French cuisine with a glorious panorama of the Old City walls. Try the filet steak. **$$$**

**Tandoori**,
Holiday Inn Crowne Plaza, Givat Ram, Jerusalem.
Tel: (02) 6588867.
One of a chain of Indian restaurants serving delicious foods including a

## Prices for Eating Out

Prices are given in shekels
**$** - under NIS80 per person
**$$** - NIS80-250
**$$$** - over NIS250

choice of vegetarian dishes. **$$$**
**Valentinos,**
Hyatt Regency Hotel, 32 Lekhi,
Jerusalem.
Tel: (02) 5331234.
Italian cuisine with excellent choice
of pasta and antipastis. **$$$**
**Mama Mia,**
38 Ha-Melekh George, Jerusalem.
Tel: (02) 6248080.
Jerusalem institution for lovers of
Italian food. But no meat served.
**$$**
**Pie House,**
5 Horkanos, Jerusalem.
Tel: (02) 6242478.
Good choice of pies and salads;
near Kikar TsiyOn (Zion Square). **$$**
**Philadelphia,**
9 E-Zahra, East Jerusalem.
Tel: (02) 6289770.
The city's most famous restaurant
for Middle East cuisine. Excellent
choice of *hors d'ouevre* salads. **$$**
**Shipudei Hagefen,**
74 Agripas, Jerusalem.
Tel: (02) 6253267.
The pick of the Middle East
restaurants; near Makhane Yehuda
market. **$$**
**Anna Ticho House,**
off Ha-Rav Kook, Jerusalem.
Tel: (02) 6244186.
Dairy food in a garden restaurant
which forms part of a museum. **$**
**Cheesecake,**
23 Yoel Salomon.
Tel: (02) 6245082.
An institution for cheesecake
lovers. Try it with blueberries. Also
serves good salads and soups. **$**
**Eucalyptus,**
7 Horkanos, Jerusalem.
Tel: (02) 6244331.
Offers an unusual choice of local
foods. Try the sorrel soup. **$**
**Rimon Cafe,**
4 Lunz, Jerusalem.
Tel: (02) 6252772.
A popular hang-out by the Ben
Yehuda Street Mall with a choice of

light meals and cakes. **$**
**Simas,**
78 Agripas, Jerusalem.
Tel: (02) 4233002.
Speedy service in the cheapest
steak house in town. **$**
**Tmol Shimshon,**
5 Shalmon, Jerusalem.
Tel: (02) 6232758.
Delightful light meals in a bookstore
café with a library. **$**

## Short and Strong

Turkish and Middle Eastern
coffee can be very small and
very strong. If you are thirsty, and
not just in need of a caffeine-
shot, order a glass of iced water
with it. Remember to tell the
waiter when you order if you
don't want your coffee sugared.

### TEL AVIV
**Golden Apple,**
40 Montefiore.
Tel: (03) 5660931.
Considered to be Israel's finest
gourmet restaurant: the tasteful
decor and cordon bleu cuisine are
designed to whet the appetites of
the most worldly connnoisseur. **$$$**
**Moul Yam,**
Tel Aviv Port.
Tel: (03) 5469920.
Offering succulent seafood, this
highly acclaimed restaurant is
located in Tel Aviv's port to the
north of the city. **$$$**
**Takamaru,**
4 Ha'Arba's, Tel Aviv.
Tel: (03) 5621629.
This is one of the very few
Japanese restaurants in Israel. Will
not disappoint. **$$$**
**Yossi Peking,**
302 Dizengoff.
Tel Aviv.
Tel: (03) 5443687.
Very good food, with all the Chinese
favourites. **$$$**
**Ba-Li,**
8 Ibn Gabirol, Tel Aviv.
Tel: (03) 6955661.
Modest Yemenite restaurant with
home-cooked food and authentic
Yemenite soups and breads. **$$**

**Elimelech,**
35 Wolfson, tel: (03) 5182478.
Excellent place for those who like
traditional Eastern European kosher
food. Located south of the business
district. **$$**
**New York New York,**
30 Ibn Gabirol Street.
Tel: (03) 6951541.
As the name implies, this
restaurant offers wholesome
New York food including deli
sandwiches, steaks and heaps
of salads. **$$**
**Taboon,**
Old Yafo Port.
Tel: (03) 811176.
In a pleasant spot in Yafo's old
port; specialises in oven-cooked
Mediterranean fish. **$$**
**Tarkari,**
68 Ha-Kishon Street, Florentin.
Tel: (03) 6834702.
An Indian vegetarian restaurant
offering exceptional value for
money. **$$**
**Zion,**
4 Peduim, Tel Aviv.
Tel: (03) 5178714.
The pick of the restaurants in the
city's famous Yemenite Quarter
(Kerem ha-Teimanim) **$$**
**David's Ful,**
22 Peduim.
Tel: (03) 5160693.
An Egyptian restaurant in the
Yemenite quarter specialising in
inexpensive savoury dishes based
on *ful* (beans). **$**
**Lev Harachav ("Wide Heart"),**
Rabbi Akiva, Carmel Market, Tel
Aviv. A no-nonsense, tasty and
cheap authentic Israeli restaurant
with excellent *hummus*. **$**
**Marsala,**
15 Yosef ha-Nasi Street, Tel Aviv,
tel: (03) 5256515.
Delicatessen and eatery serving
fresh sandwiches and salads. **$**
**Rachmo Hagadol,**
98 Petakch Tikvah.
Tel: (03) 5621022.
The pick of the *felafel* eateries near
the Central Bus Station. Excellent,
clean and astonishingly cheap. **$**
**The UP Cafe,**
56 Sheinkin, Tel Aviv.
Tel: (03) 5606071.
In the heart of Tel Aviv's bohemian

district: serves a wide range of meals. **$**

## TIBERIAS

**The House (Habayit)**, opposite Lido Beach, Tiberias, tel: (06) 6792353. Chinese cuisine. Considered to be one of the best restaurants in Israel. Located in a 19th-century landmark building. **$$$**

## Drinking Notes

### SOFT DRINKS

All the usual carbonated drinks such as colas are available. As in Britain, "soda" refers to soda water and not a flavoured carbonated drink as it does in the United States. Diet and regular soft drinks are available. The most delicious and healthiest drinks to try are the wide range of fruit juices. For a few dollars, street vendors will squeeze you an orange, carrot, grapefruit, kiwi or a dozen other fruits.

### TEA & COFFEE

Tea connoisseurs will be out of luck. Most Israeli establishments dip a feeble tea-bag into hot water. But they take their coffee seriously. Most popular are Middle Eastern coffee (*botz*), Bedouin coffee (*botz* with *hell* – a spice known as cardamom in English), Turkish coffee, Viennese coffee (*café hafuch*) and filter coffee. Instant coffee Western style is known as *Nes*. Cafés and *espresso* bars, like their counterparts in Europe, have increasingly become the centre of both social and business life.

### ALCOHOL

Israel has a wide selection of wines, both red and white. Since the 1980s many good-quality wines have been produced, but they can be expensive. There are several local beers, both bottled and draught, and a range of imported beers – but real-ale specialists will probably turn up their noses. There are both home-distilled and imported spirits and liquors. The local speciality is *arak*, very similar to Greece's *ouzo*.

Although Israel has none of the alcoholic inhibitions of its Islamic neighbours, most Israelis consume relatively small amounts of alcohol compared with Europeans and Americans. Excessive drinking is viewed with suspicion by society at large. A person who drinks, say, three pints of beer a day is likely to be branded an alcoholic.

There are plenty of bars and pubs, and all restaurants and cafés serve alcohol. Israelis will often go to a pub and spend the entire night nursing just one or two drinks. By the same token it is acceptable to sit at streetside cafés chatting for hours over just a coffee and cake.

## Bars & pubs

**Finks**, corner of Ha-Melekh George and Ha-Histadrut.
Tel: (02) 6234523. Jerusalem's oldest established watering hole. Caters to a more mature clientele. Serves good food.
**Glasnost**, 15 Haleni ha-Malkah. Tel: (02) 6256954. One of many bars in the Russian Compound, such as Sergei's, Arthur's, Cannabis and Alexander amongst others. Along this street and its arteries is where Jerusalem's nightlife begins.
**The Tavern**, 14 Rivlin. Pretty seedy, but it's a veteran Jerusalem bar and worth a visit.
**Balcony**, 5 Nakhalat Binyamin, Tel Aviv, tel: (03) 5162852. A well-appointed bar close to the Nakhalat Binyamin pedestrian precinct.
**Punch Line**, 4 Ha-Arba'a Street, Tel Aviv, tel: (03) 5610785. If you turn up early and find nobody here, remember that Tel Aviv nightlife doesn't get going til at least 11pm.
**Nachmani 22** (at the address which gives it its name), tel: (03) 5661114. A pleasant wine bar near Allenby which serves good food, too.
**The Stagecoach**, 216 Ha-Yarkan Street, tel: (03) 5241703. Near the hotel district. Live music on Thursday and Friday nights. Snacks and light meals served.
**The Godfather**, Red Shopping Mall, Eilat, tel: (07) 6373262. Offers good pub atmosphere.

# Culture

## Where to find It

Israel has a wealth of cultural and artistic entertainments. Ticket agencies in each city or town sell tickets for concerts, plays and other events. Annual festivals of all art, cultural and musical events are booked up well in advance. Calendars of Events are available at the tourist information offices.

## Music

There are several orchestras, of which the most famous is the Israel Philharmonic, playing under the baton of the great conductors of the world (Zubin Mehta since 1991) and featuring distinguished guest artists. The Jerusalem Symphony Orchestra gives a weekly concert in Jerusalem in the winter season. There are frequent performances by the Haifa Symphony Orchestra, the Rishon Le-Tsiyon Symphony Orchestra and the New Israel Opera.
**Mann Auditorium** (for Israel Symphony Orchestra), 1 Huberman, Tel Aviv, tel: (03) 5251502.
**Israel Opera** (for Israel Opera and Rishon Le-Tsiyon Symphony Orchestra), Israel Opera House, Sha'ul ha-Melekh Boulevard, tel: (03) 6927707.
**Henry Crown Hall** (for Jerusalem Symphony Orchestra), Marcus, Jerusalem, tel: (02) 5610011/5610293.

## Dance

Professional dance companies include the Israel Classical Ballet, the Batsheva Dance Company, the Bat-Dor Dance Company, Kol Hademana and the Kibbutz Dance

Company. Batsheva and Bat-Dor are both modern dance groups. All perform regularly in the three main cities, as well as in other towns and kibbutzim.
**Suzan Dalal Centre**, 6 Yekhi'el, Neve Tsedek, Tel Aviv.
Tel: (03) 5171471. For Batsheva and Inbal Dance Troupes,

## Theatre

The theatre is very popular in Israel, and there are many companies performing a wide range of classical and contemporary plays in Hebrew, including original works by Israelis. The best known are the Ha-Bima and Camari Theatres in Tel Aviv and the Haifa Municipal Theatre, which take their productions all over the country. In Jerusalem, the Centre for Performing Arts includes the Jerusalem Theatre, the Henry Crown Auditorium and the Rebecca Crown Theatre. Also Sultan's Pool Ampitheatre, located beneath the walls of the Old City, is a must for a concert. Smaller companies offer stage productions in English, Yiddish and other languages. One such theatre, Gesher (meaning bridge), founded in Tel Aviv in 1991, is the first Russian-speaking theatre in Israel.
**Jerusalem Theatre**, Marcus, Jerusalem.
Tel: (02) 5610011/5610293.
**Khan Theatre**, David Remez, Jerusalem, tel: (02) 6718281.
**Ha-Bima Theatre**, Tarsith Boulevard, Tel Aviv, tel: (03) 5266666.
**Camari Theatre**, 101 Dizengoff, Tel Aviv, tel: (03) 5233335.
**Beit Liessin Theatre**, 34 Weizmann, Tel Aviv, tel: (03) 6956222.

## Movies

There are cinemas in all the big towns; most have three showings a day, one at about 4pm and two in the evening.

For about $7 you can see the latest Hollywood offerings. You'll also find the latest movies from France, Germany, Italy, Hungary and elsewhere. These films usually have

## Film Festival

The Jerusalem Film Festival, held annually in July, has become a high-profile event. The festival kicks off with a gala at Sultan's Pool Amphitheatre, with subsequent screenings at the Jerusalem Cinemathèque.

English subtitles, but ask at the box office first.

Israel itself produces a dozen or so films a year, and these offer an insight into the local culture. These, too, have English subtitles. The local cinemathèques show golden oldies as well the more recent movies.
**Jerusalem Cinemathèque**, Derekh Hevron, tel: (02) 6724131.
**Tel Aviv Cinemathèque**, 2 Sprintzach, tel: (03) 6917181.
**Haifa Cinemathèque**, Hanassi 142, tel: (04) 8383424.

## Festivals

The Israel Festival of Music and Drama takes place in May of each year, with the participation of the country's leading talent and world-famous visiting companies and artists. The festival centres on Jerusalem.
**The Jerusalem Film Festival** – July.
**The Haifa Film Festival** – September/October.
**The Karmiel Dance Festival** – July.
**The Red Sea Jazz Film Festival** – August.
**The Akko Fringe Theatre Festival** – September/October.
In addition, the **Jerusalem International Book Fair** is held every two years in March. An International **Harp Contest** takes place every three years, drawing young musicians from all over the world. The **Zimriya**, an international choir festival, is another well-established triennial event. **Spring in Jerusalem** and **Spring in Tel Aviv**, annual festivals, include music, drama and dance, and the **Rubinstein Piano Competition** brings talented young artists from around the world to Israel.

Events in Haifa include the **International Flower Show** (Floris), when hundreds of thousands of flowers from all over the world, typical of their countries of origin, adorn the city.

## Ulpan Akiva

Ulpan Akiva is a Hebrew language school where Hebrew is taught as a living language in everyday conversation at all levels: reading, writing, speech patterns, drama and idioms. Courses are from 4–20 weeks, for families and individuals of 12 years old and upwards. The school is located at the Green Beach Hotel near Netanya, and facilities include a swimming pool, tennis and basketball courts and a lovely stretch of beach.

The programme consists of four or five hours of Hebrew study a day, lectures on the Bible, Jewish history, Hebrew literature and current affairs; and cultural activities that include folk singing and dancing, and meetings with local personalities. You can study side by side with Israelis and new immigrants, and experience the culture of Israel.

Tours can be arranged to archaeological sites and other places of interest in the area. Courses are run on a residential, full-board basis.

For further information, contact: **Ulpan Akiva**, International Hebrew Study Centre, POB 6086, 42160 Netanya, tel: (09) 8352312/3; fax: (09) 8652919.

Many kibbutzim (see page 25) also offer Ulpan courses which cost approximately $50 in return for participants' part-time work on the kibbutz. The courses last for 5½ months and are open to Jews between the ages of 17½ and 35. Students may arrive at the kibbutz a week before the course begins. Participants must be physically fit for work.

For further details, contact: **The Ulpanim's Kibbutzim Department**, The Jewish Agency, 12 Kaplan, Tel Aviv, tel: (03) 5423423.

# Nightlife

## Nightclubs

Nightlife starts late in Israel and is very vibrant. From 11pm onwards Israelis are out on the streets of Tel Aviv, and also in Jerusalem and virtually every Israeli city. Streetside cafés and restaurants are busy until well after midnight, and bars and discos have a brisk trade right through the night. Because Friday and Saturday constitute the weekend, Thursday night is a big night out.

**Tel Aviv seafront** and other hotspots are crowded right through the night. Nightclubs abound in the main cities and resort towns. Many have regular floor shows, while others offer more informal entertainment. Rock, jazz, folk and pop music are the usual fare. Jerusalem and Tel Aviv are the hot spots. Jerusalem's clubs are mostly concentrated in the Talpiyot Commercial Centre. Currently, Florentin is the area where it's all happening in Tel Aviv.

### TEL AVIV

**Allenby 58**, located at the address in Tel Aviv from which it takes its name. This nightclub has been the hottest spot in town for quite some time. A converted cinema, it has a massive sound system and a downstairs bar to cool off when the heat of the beat gets too much. Thursday and Friday nights are the best.

**The Minzar**, opposite Allenby 58. A small bar with a lively atmosphere. A perfect place to start your night if proceeding to Allenby 58.

**Ministry of Sound**, 2 Vital. A small bar with an upstairs area, this is one of many new bars that have opened up in the Florentin area, south of the centre. Others are **The Nanna Bar** and the **Laundry**, which is situated in an old laundromat equipped with the original machines.

**Porto Loco**, The Brazilian Club in Old Tel Aviv Port, Yordei ha-Sira. Tel: (03) 6836618.

In case you suddenly feel the urge during a night out, you can get your hair cut at **Vitt Rio**, on Vital Street in the Florentin district. It's a funky place that opens in the afternoon and closes at 2am.

### JERUSALEM

**Hallelujah**, Kibbutz Ramat Rachel, near Jerusalem, tel: (02) 6736828. Not as holy as it sounds.

**Canaan**, tel (02) 6735633. In the heart of Talpiyot's discoland.

## Casinos

Gambling is illegal in Israel, but two casinos are accessible on Israel's borders: in the **Taba Hilton**, just south of Eilat (and officially in Egypt), and at the **Oasis Casino** south of Jericho (technically in a Palestinian autonomous zone).

# Outdoor Activities

## Nature Reserves

There are 280 nature reserves in Israel covering 4,000 sq. km (1,544 sq. miles). Especially worth visiting are the Khai Bar Reserve in the Negev, the Carmel National Park, the Hula Reserve in the Upper Galilee and Ramon Makhtesh in the Negev.

## The Source

An archaeological dig at Khatsor ha-Glilit, in northern Israel, where an underground water system was discovered, was the inspiration for James Michener's best-selling novel *The Source*.

## Tree Planting

Visitors wishing to plant trees, for a nominal contribution, may do so on their own or as part of tours organised by the Jewish National Fund. Each planter will receive a certificate and a badge to commemorate the event.

Further details: "Plant a Tree With Your Own Hands", Meir Malca Jewish National Fund, 7 Shmu'el ha-Navi, Jerusalem. Tel: (02) 6241781.

## Nature Tours

For those visitors searching for the unusual, the **Society for the Protection of Nature in Israel** (SPNI) offers fascinating tours combining unusual learning experiences in natural settings with touring, hiking and swimming.

These Nature Trails leave the main roads and penetrate into

## Information Abroad

It is best to plan in advance if you are serious about volunteering for work on a kibbutz:

**Australia:** Ichud Habonim-Dror, pob 154, Waverley, 2024, Sydney, NSW, tel: 389-4993.
**UK:** Kibbutz Representative, 1A Accommodation Road, London NW1, tel: 0181-450 9235.
**US:** In New York direct enquiries to: The Jewish Agency, Kibbutz Aliyah Desk, 515 Park Avenue, New York, NY 10022, tel: (212) 688-4134.

relatively inaccessible areas. Experienced guides explain the natural and human history of the region and point out places of interest. All the tours include some walking. Depending on the interests and abilities of the group, this can range from a few hours per day to longer, difficult hikes for experienced trekkers. There are a number of English-guided trips to all parts of the country suitable for individuals as well as the entire family (children over 12 years old).

SPNI's shops also have a selection of publications and accessories relating to natural Israel. SPNI has a network of field schools charging about $30 per room per night.
Main offices:
**Jerusalem,**
13 Heleni ha-Malka.
Tel: (02) 6232936.
**Tel Aviv,**
4 Hashfela.
Tel: (03) 6375063.
**Haifa,**
8 Menachem.
Tel: (04) 8664136.

## National Parks

The national parks can include nature sites and sites of historical and archaeological interest. They include Khatsor, Akhziv, Nimrod Fortress, Caesarea, Ashkelon, Megiddo, Herodion, Masada, Kumran, Jericho, Tel Arad and Ein Ovdat. Visitors to sites and parks can buy a ticket for multiple entrance, permitting them to visit all of the sites or parks within a period of 14 days. In the case of groups, the ticket can be used for 21 days. It can also be purchased from the National Parks Authority.

For further information, contact:
**National Parks Authority,**
4 Makleff, Ha-Kirya, Tel Aviv 61070. Tel: (03) 6902281.

## Kibbutzim

The communal or collective settlements called kibbutzim also allow visitors to get to know the rural life of Israel. Most kibbutzim are agricultural but many also have sizeable industrial enterprises. There are over 200 kibbutzim in all parts of the country and the number of members ranges from 90 to over 2,000.

Most kibbutzim accept volunteers for varying periods. Volunteers must be between 18 and 32 years of age. Neither children nor pregnant women are accepted. For further information contact any Israel Government Tourist Office or the following organisations:
**Hakibbutz Hadati,**
Zipi Romen Volunteer Department, 7 Dubnov, Tel Aviv.
Tel: (03) 6957231.
**Ikhud Hakvutzot Vehakibbutzim** and **Hakibbutz Hemeyuhad,**
Ben Baor, 10, Dubnov, Tel Aviv.
Tel: (03) 5452622.

## Parks & Gardens

Jerusalem is famous for its parks and gardens which, as well as the city centre parks, include the Botanical Gardens beneath the Givat Ram University campus and the Sherover Walkway from Abu Tor to East Talpiyot.

Tel Aviv's Independence Gardens overlook the sea, while Yarkon Park is a pleasant expanse of greenery by the River Yarkon.

## Archaeology

Archaeology is one of Israel's best-loved national pastimes, and the opportunities for archaeological exploration here are rich and varied.

There are dozens of major archaeological sites, spanning all periods of recorded history. The most important – such as Caesarea, Ashkelon, Jericho and Masada – are national parks and open to the public on a regular basis for a modest admission fee. Often these sites include English-language signposts and have informative brochures to explain the history and design of the site.

# Children

## Activities for Children

Apart from the **zoos** (see next section), the **Israel Museum** in Jerusalem has an excellent Children's Wing, and the nearby **Bloomingfield Science Museum** has plenty of hands-on exhibits for the young and is always very popular. Children who know anything of the Christmas story are usually bowled over – at least for a while – by a visit to Bethlehem. Of course in Tel Aviv and Haifa there are wonderful golden beaches and warm, calm waters. And most children fall in love with the fish at Eilat's **Coral World Underwater Observatory**. Also bear in mind that as Israelis are so fond of children they are not frowned on in restaurants and bars.

## Zoos

The **Jerusalem Biblical Zoo**, Manhat, tel: (02) 6430111, houses animals mentioned in the Bible. Other zoos are located in Tel Aviv, Eilat and Haifa.

There is a **Safari Park**, a 100-hectare (250-acre) wildlife sanctuary in Ramat Gan near Tel Aviv, where hundreds of animals roam freely. At the Khai Bar Reserve, north of Eilat, many of the animals mentioned in the Bible can be seen. Visitors to the Safari Park and Khai Bar Reserve may tour in closed vehicles only.

# Sport

## Participant Sports

Israel is an ideal place for sports enthusiasts. Here they will find excellent facilities and an opportunity to combine interests such as skin and scuba diving, riding, tennis, golf, swimming and skiing with a general tour of the country. The Mediterranean climate guarantees most outdoor sports year round (the exception being snow skiing, which is available only in winter)

The Mediterranean shoreline and the Sea of Galilee are ideal for **water sports**: swimming, surfing, sailing and water skiing. The Tel Aviv marina offers yachting as well as sailing. All the large hotels have swimming pools, and there are municipal or private pools all over the country. Skin and aqualung diving are especially popular along the Gulf of Eilat; centres at Eilat will rent equipment and provide instruction.

**Fishing** equipment, both for angling and underwater, can be hired along the Mediterranean and the Red Sea, though the latter is now a protected area, with fishing permitted only in certain places.

**Tennis** courts are available at a number of hotels, and the Tennis Centre at Ramat Ha-Sharon, near Tel Aviv, is putting Israel on the international tennis circuit.

There is a fine 18-hole **golf** course at Caesarea. You can find **riding** clubs in Arad, Be'er Sheva, Caesarea, Eilat, Netanya, Vered ha-Galil and other places. **Bicycles** can be rented in most cities, and cycling tours of the country can be arranged. During the winter there is skiing on the slopes of Mount Hermon. Marches, races, and

swimming competitions are organised by the Ha-Po'el and Maccabi sports organisations. The highlight of the year is the annual Jerusalem March, a highly organised event, in which thousands of Israelis from all over the country, as well as overseas visitors, both individually and in groups, make a colourful and high-spirited pilgrimage to the capital. This event is held in spring, usually in April.

A programme of events is published monthly and can be obtained from the **Israeli National Sports Association**, 5 Warburger, Tel Aviv, tel: (03) 5281968.

## Sports Centres

**Caesarea Golf Club**,
POB 1010, 30660 Caesarea.
Tel: (06) 361174.
**Haifa Squash Centre**,
MP Hof, Kfar Zamir, Ha-Karmel.
Tel: (04) 8539160.
**Herzliya Squash Centre**.
Tel: (09) 8357877.
**Ramat Gan**,
Kfar Ha-Maccabiah, Sport Centre,
Ramat Chen.
Tel: (03) 6715739.
**Israel Tennis Centre**,
Ramat Ha-Sharon.
Tel: (03) 481803/485223.
**Hermon Ski Site**.
Tel: (06) 6981339.
**Moshav Neve Ativ**,
12010 MP Ramat Ha-Golan.
Tel: (06) 6981331 (for ski accommodation).
**Vered ha-Galil Ranch**,
MP Korazim.
Tel: (06) 6735785.
**Neve Ilan Ranch**,
Neve Ilan, Judean Hills (near Jerusalem).
Tel: (02) 5340535.

## Water Sports

Israel is truly a diver's paradise. Its mild climate ensures year-round diving in the crystal clear waters of both the Mediterranean and Red Seas, where hundreds of miles of easily accessible coral reefs and spectacular seascapes await the

## Diving with Dolphins

Diving with dolphins at the Dolphin Reef in Eilat is a popular activity. The dolphins appear to like it, too; they are so friendly that they are used in therapeutic programmes for children with disabilities.

diving enthusiast. A variety of diving experiences includes underwater photography, archaeological diving, grotto and cave diving. It should be noted that, unless divers have a two-star licence, they must take a special diving course, though diving without a licence can be done if you are accompanied by instructors.

### SKIN & SCUBA DIVING COURSES

The courses for beginners last about five days and cover the theory of diving, lifesaving, physiology, physics and underwater safety. The only qualifications necessary are the ability to swim, a certificate from a doctor confirming fitness to learn diving, and a chest X-ray. Beginners can also go out on individual introductory dives, lasting from one to 1½ hours, accompanied throughout by an instructor.

It is possible to rent all the necessary skin and scuba diving equipment at the following centres:

*Eilat*

**Aqua Sport,**
Red Sea Diving Centre, Coral Beach.
Tel: (07) 6334404.
**Lucky Divers,**
Moriah Hotel.
Tel: (07) 6335990.
**Dolphin Reef** (dive with the dolphins).
Tel: (07) 6375935.
**Red Sea Divers,**
Caravan Hotel.
Tel: (07) 6373145/6.

*Tel Aviv*

**Octopus Diving School,**
Tel Aviv Marina, Kikar Atarim.
Tel: (03) 5271440.

The Federation for Underwater Activities in Israel,
POB 6110, 61060 Tel Aviv.
Tel: (03) 5467968.

### WATER-SKIING AND WIND-SURFING

**Aqua Sport**, Eilat.
Tel: (07) 633440.
**Octopus Diving School**, Tel Aviv.
Tel: (03) 5271440.

### SWIMMING

Israel's mild climate allows year-round swimming on all of its coasts – the Mediterranean, the Gulf of Eilat and the Dead Sea – as well as in the Sea of Galilee. Qualified lifeguards are in attendance at all beaches and pools.

Swimming is free at most beaches. But beware: the Mediterranean currents are strong, and nearly 100 people drown every year. Most hotels have swimming pools, to which guests of the hotel are generally given free entry; many also allow use by visitors, for a fee.

## Spectator Sports

Soccer is the number one spectator sport, with several matches every week. Israeli teams participate in the major European competitions. Basketball is also very popular, and Israelis are especially proud of the Maccabi Tel Aviv basketball team, which has won the European championship twice. There are many international matches during the winter season at stadiums in the Tel Aviv area.

## Stadiums

**The Ramat Gan National Soccer Stadium**, Tel Aviv.
Tel: (03) 5799966.
**Yad Eliahu Basketball Stadium**,
Tel Aviv, tel: (03) 5272112.

# Shopping

## What to Buy

Shops in Israel offer a wide variety of merchandise and gifts. These include exclusive jewellery and diamonds; oriental carpets and antiques; fashionable ladies' wear and elegant furs; leather goods; paintings and sculptures; ceramics; silverware and copperware; embroidery and *batiks,* and religious requisites. Several hundred shops are approved by the Ministry of Tourism. These shops display a sign stating "Listed by the Ministry of Tourism" and the Ministry's emblem (two scouts carrying a bunch of grapes on a pole between them), which is the symbol of quality merchandise.

In addition, colourful oriental markets and bazaars are found in the narrow alleyways of the old cities of Jerusalem, Bethlehem, Akko, Nazareth and Hebron, and in Druze villages like Daliyat el-Karmel near Haifa. These sell handmade arts and crafts – including olive wood, mother-of-pearl, leather and bamboo items, hand-blown glass – and clothing, vegetables and fruit.

Duty-free shops are located at Ben Gurion and Eilat airports and at most of the leading hotels. Foreign-made articles such as watches, cameras, perfumes, tobaccos and liquors as well as many fine Israeli products may be purchased with foreign currency for delivery to the plane or ship prior to departure.

## Judaica

Besides these items, Israel has a unique variety of traditional crafts and Judaica for sale, ranging from religious articles like *Menorahs, mezuzot* and spice boxes to wall hangings and statuary. They range from loving reproductions to stark minimalism.

Centres for buying fine crafts include several locations in Jerusalem, among them the House of Quality, Khutsot ha-Yoster (Arts & Crafts Lane), Yochanan Migush Halav, and the Me'a She'arim area.

## Shopping Areas

In the Old City of Jerusalem and other Arab market places, bargaining is standard practice. Usually you can buy an item at 25 percent off by starting to haggle at half the quoted price. Avoid haggling if you are not really interested in buying or if an item is cheap. Brassware, carvings and fabrics are among the more popular buys.

Other popular shopping places include the weekly Bedouin market in Be'er Sheva on Thursday mornings, the Druze markets in the north, such as Daliyat el-Karmel and Nakhalat Binyamin in Tel Aviv, where artisans trade their wares on Tuesday and Friday.

## Export of Antiquities

It is forbidden to export antiquities from Israel unless a written export permit has been obtained from the Department of Antiquities and Museums of the Ministry of Education and Culture, Jerusalem. This applies also to antiquities which accompany tourists who are leaving the country. Antiquities proved to have been imported to Israel after 1900 are exempted. Antiquities are defined as objects fashioned by man before the year 1700. A 10 percent export fee is payable on the purchase price of every item approved for export.

The articles must be dispatched by post, with an accompanying cheque for the appropriate amount, or taken in person, to: **The Department of Antiquities and Museums**, Rockefeller Museum, opposite Herod's Gate, POB 586, Jerusalem. It is advisable to telephone (02) 6278627 for an appointment first.

## VAT

After your passport has been stamped by customs, apply to Bank Leumi in the exit hall. A refund of VAT (value-added tax) of 17 percent is made at the point of your departure. However, you must make sure that:

The total net sum (after the 17 percent reduction) on one invoice is not less than $50. The following items are not included in this scheme: tobacco products, electrical appliances and accessories, cameras, film and photographic equipment.

The purchased items are packed in a plastic bag with at least one transparent side.

The original invoice (white) is placed inside the bag in such a manner that the entries on it can be read.

The bag is sealed or glued shut.

The bag remains sealed during your entire stay in Israel.

When arriving at the departure hall on leaving the country, you must present the sealed bag with the purchased goods to customs for approval of refund.

After checking and placing the stamp of approval on the invoice, the customs official will direct you to the bank counter where the refund will be made in US dollars.

Note that Eilat is a VAT free zone, and these regulations do not apply to goods purchased there.

Also many hotels and stores will exempt you from VAT if you pay in foreign currency.

## How to Complain

Be persistent in arguing with shopkeepers if you have a complaint. You cannot expect a shopkeeper to respond to your problem if you do not articulate your grievance, and they are not accustomed to people accepting inferior goods or services without complaint. Be polite, but vocal. If all else fails, contact: **the Ministry of Industry & Trade's Consumer Protection Service**, 76 Maze, Tel Aviv, tel: (03) 5604611.

# Language

## Hebrew

Hebrew is the most widely spoken language in the country, and Hebrew and Arabic are the official languages. Although other languages, especially English, are also fairly widely spoken, it is a good idea to know some basic Hebrew words and phrases before coming to the country.

Here are 60 basic words which may help you find the language a little less daunting:

| | |
|---|---|
| **all-purpose greeting, (literally "peace")** | shalom |
| **good morning** | boker tov |
| **good evening** | erev tov |
| **yes** | ken |
| **no** | lo |
| **please** | bevakasha |
| **thank you** | toda |
| **very much** | raba |
| **good** | lov |
| **bad** | ra |
| **big** | gadol |
| **little** | katan |
| **more** | yoter |
| **less** | pahot |
| **I** | ani |
| **you (singular)** | m/f ata/at |
| **you (plural)** | m/f atem/aten |
| **we/us** | anahnu |
| **them** | m/f hem/hen |
| **want** | m/f rotseh/rotsa |
| **how much?** | kama? |
| **too dear** | yakar midai |
| **cheaper** | yoter zol |
| **bank** | bank |
| **restaurant** | mis'ada |
| **post office** | do'ar |
| **hotel** | malon |
| **shop** | hanut |
| **taxi** | monit |
| **train** | rakevet |
| **bus** | autoboos |

| station/bus stop | tahana |
|---|---|
| where is? | eyfo? |
| right | yemin |
| left | smol |
| when? | matai? |
| white | lavan |
| black | shahor |
| red | adom |
| blue | kahol |
| right, correct | nahon |
| wrong | lo nahon |
| straight | yashar |
| one | ehad |
| two | shtayim |
| three | shalosh |
| four | arba' |
| five | hamesh |
| six | shesh |
| seven | sheva' |
| eight | shmoney |
| nine | taysha' |
| ten | esser |
| hundred | me'a |
| thousand | elef |
| many | harbey |
| stop, wait a minute! | rega! |
| cinema | kolno'a |
| newspaper | iton' |
| water | mayim |
| food | okhel |
| bill | heshbon |

## Spelling

As of yet, there is no standardised spelling of Israeli place names. Thus one has: *"Acre"*, *"Akko"* and *"Acco"*; *"Nathanya"* *"Natanya"* and *"Netanya"*; *"Elat"*, *"Elath"* and *"Eilat"*; *"Ashqelon"* and *"Ashkelon"*; *"S'fat"*, *"Zefat"*, *"Tzfat"* and *"Safed"*, etc. As if to confuse the visitor deliberately, all such variations are used freely. This guide has attempted to standardise spellings, but do not be surprised if you come across many different versions of place names on maps and road signs.

# Further Knowledge

## Films & Videos

*Jesus Christ Superstar.* The movie is set by the Dead Sea and in the Judean Desert.
*Exodus.* Paul Newman wins independence for Israel.
*Cast a Giant Shadow.* Kirk Douglas wins independence for Israel.
*The Entebbe Raid.* Yet more Israeli heroics.
*The Little Drummer Girl.* John le Carré grapples with Middle East intrigue.

## Popular Singers

**Ahinoam Nini** (known as Noa in the West): combines Yemenite and Israeli music with western rhythms.
**Ofra Haza**: another Yemenite singer with a major following in the West.
**Rita**: also combines Eastern and Western melodies.
**Yehoram Gaon**: Israel's number one crooner.
**Dana International**: Israel's transexual Eurovision winner.

## Literature

*Altneuland* – Theodor Herzl. The Zionist visionary's dream of what a Jewish homeland might be like.
*Encyclopaedia Judaica* – offers the most comprehensive information about Judaism and Israel.
*Fathers and Sons* – Amos Eilon. Entertaining account of the Zionist founding fathers.
*My Michael* – Amos Oz, Israel's leading contemporary novelist. Oz's other novels include *To Know a Woman* and *Elsewhere Perhaps.*
*The Bible* – This is where it all happened.
*The Diary of Anne Frank* – Helps the reader understand what makes Israelis tick.
*The Source* – James Michener, basing his story on an

archaeological site Khatsor ha-Glilit in, creates fictional accounts of what might have happened in a Cannanite/Israelite/Palestinian village down the centuries.
*The Wedding Canopy* – Shai Agnon, the only Israeli winner of the Nobel Prize for literature.

## Other Insight Guides

Other books in the Insight Guides series which highlight destinations in this region include *Insight Guide*: *Jerusalem, Jordan, Egypt, Cairo* and *Yemen*.

*Insight Guide: Jordan* is the definitive guide to this alluring kingdom. From Petra to Wadi Rum, from Crusader fortresses to scuba diving.

Apa Publications also produces two other series of guidebooks:

### Insight Pocket Guides

Insight Pocket Guides provide detailed itineraries and come with a full-sized pull-out map.

### Insight Compact Guides

Insight Compact Guides are mini encyclopaedias packed with essential facts. Titles include *Israel, Jerusalem* and *Egypt*

# ART & PHOTO CREDITS

*Cartographic Editor* **Zoë Goodwin**

*Production* **Stuart A. Everitt**

*Design Consultants*
**Carlotta Junger, Graham Mitchener**

*Picture Research*
**Hilary Genin, Monica Allende**

# The World of Insight Guides

## 400 books in three complementary series cover every major destination in every continent.

### Insight Guides

Alaska
Alsace
Amazon Wildlife
American Southwest
Amsterdam
Argentina
Atlanta
Athens
Australia
Austria
Bahamas
Bali
Baltic States
Bangkok
Barbados
Barcelona
Bay of Naples
Beijing
Belgium
Belize
Berlin
Bermuda
Boston
Brazil
Brittany
Brussels
Budapest
Buenos Aires
Burgundy
Burma (Myanmar)
Cairo
Calcutta
California
Canada
Caribbean
Catalonia
Channel Islands
Chicago
Chile
China
Cologne
Continental Europe
Corsica
Costa Rica
Crete
Crossing America
Cuba
Cyprus
Czech & Slovak Republics
Delhi, Jaipur, Agra
Denmark
Dresden
Dublin
Düsseldorf
East African Wildlife
East Asia
Eastern Europe
Ecuador
Edinburgh
Egypt
Finland
Florence
Florida
France
Frankfurt
French Riviera
Gambia & Senegal
Germany
Glasgow

Gran Canaria
Great Barrier Reef
Great Britain
Greece
Greek Islands
Hamburg
Hawaii
Hong Kong
Hungary
Iceland
India
India's Western Himalaya
Indian Wildlife
Indonesia
Ireland
Israel
Istanbul
Italy
Jamaica
Japan
Java
Jerusalem
Jordan
Kathmandu
Kenya
Korea
Lisbon
Loire Valley
London
Los Angeles
Madeira
Madrid
Malaysia
Mallorca & Ibiza
Malta
Marine Life in the South
    China Sea
Melbourne
Mexico
Mexico City
Miami
Montreal
Morocco
Moscow
Munich
Namibia
Native America
Nepal
Netherlands
New England
New Orleans
New York City
New York State
New Zealand
Nile
Normandy
Northern California
Northern Spain
Norway
Oman & the UAE
Oxford
Old South
Pacific Northwest
Pakistan
Paris
Peru
Philadelphia
Philippines
Poland
Portugal
Prague

Provence
Puerto Rico
Rajasthan
Rhine
Rio de Janeiro
Rockies
Rome
Russia
St Petersburg
San Francisco
Sardinia
Scotland
Seattle
Sicily
Singapore
South Africa
South America
South Asia
South India
South Tyrol
Southeast Asia
Southeast Asia Wildlife
Southern California
Southern Spain
Spain
Sri Lanka
Sweden
Switzerland
Sydney
Taiwan
Tenerife
Texas
Thailand
Tokyo
Trinidad & Tobago
Tunisia
Turkey
Turkish Coast
Tuscany
Umbria
US National Parks East
US National Parks West
Vancouver
Venezuela
Venice
Vienna
Vietnam
Wales
Washington DC
Waterways of Europe
Wild West
Yemen

### Insight Pocket Guides

Aegean Islands★
Algarve★
Alsace
Amsterdam★
Athens★
Atlanta★
Bahamas★
Baja Peninsula★
Bali★
Bali Bird Walks
Bangkok★
Barbados★
Barcelona★
Bavaria★
Beijing★
Berlin★

Bermuda★
Bhutan★
Boston★
British Columbia★
Brittany★
Brussels★
Budapest &
    Surroundings★
Canton★
Chiang Mai★
Chicago★
Corsica★
Costa Blanca★
Costa Brava★
Costa del Sol/Marbella★
Costa Rica★
Crete★
Denmark★
Fiji★
Florence★
Florida★
Florida Keys★
French Riviera★
Gran Canaria★
Hawaii★
Hong Kong★
Hungary
Ibiza★
Ireland★
Ireland's Southwest★
Israel★
Istanbul★
Jakarta★
Jamaica★
Kathmandu Bikes &
    Hikes★
Kenya★
Kuala Lumpur★
Lisbon★
Loire Valley★
London★
Macau
Madrid★
Malacca
Maldives
Mallorca★
Malta★
Mexico City★
Miami★
Milan★
Montreal★
Morocco★
Moscow
Munich★
Nepal★
New Delhi
New Orleans★
New York City★
New Zealand★
Northern California★
Oslo/Bergen★
Paris★
Penang★
Phuket★
Prague★
Provence★
Puerto Rico★
Quebec★
Rhodes★
Rome★
Sabah★

St Petersburg★
San Francisco★
Sardinia
Scotland★
Seville★
Seychelles★
Sicily★
Sikkim
Singapore★
Southeast England
Southern California★
Southern Spain★
Sri Lanka★
Sydney★
Tenerife★
Thailand★
Tibet★
Toronto★
Tunisia★
Turkish Coast★
Tuscany★
Venice★
Vienna★
Vietnam★
Yogyakarta
Yucatan Peninsula★

★ = Insight Pocket Guides
with Pull out Maps

### Insight Compact Guides

Algarve
Amsterdam
Bahamas
Bali
Bangkok
Barbados
Barcelona
Beijing
Belgium
Berlin
Brittany
Brussels
Budapest
Burgundy
Copenhagen
Costa Brava
Costa Rica
Crete
Cyprus
Czech Republic
Denmark
Dominican Republic
Dublin
Egypt
Finland
Florence
Gran Canaria
Greece
Holland
Hong Kong
Ireland
Israel
Italian Lakes
Italian Riviera
Jamaica
Jerusalem
Lisbon
Madeira
Mallorca
Malta

Milan
Moscow
Munich
Normandy
Norway
Paris
Poland
Portugal
Prague
Provence
Rhodes
Rome
St Petersburg
Salzburg
Singapore
Switzerland
Sydney
Tenerife
Thailand
Turkey
Turkish Coast
Tuscany
UK regional titles:
    Bath & Surroundings
    Cambridge & East
        Anglia
    Cornwall
    Cotswolds
    Devon & Exmoor
    Edinburgh
    Lake District
    London
    New Forest
    North York Moors
    Northumbria
    Oxford
    Peak District
    Scotland
    Scottish Highlands
    Shakespeare Country
    Snowdonia
    South Downs
    York
    Yorkshire Dales
USA regional titles:
    Boston
    Cape Cod
    Chicago
    Florida
    Florida Keys
    Hawaii: Maui
    Hawaii: Oahu
    Las Vegas
    Los Angeles
    Martha's Vineyard &
        Nantucket
    New York
    San Francisco
    Washington D.C.
    Venice
    Vienna
    West of Ireland